Discovering Fourth Edition
THE INTERNET
COMPLETE

Discovering THE INTERNET

Fourth Edition

COMPLETE

Gary B. Shelly

Jennifer T. Campbell

COURSE TECHNOLOGY
CENGAGE Learning

SHELLY CASHMAN SERIES.

Australia • Brazil • Japan • Korea • Mexico • Singapore • Spain • United Kingdom • United States

COURSE TECHNOLOGY
CENGAGE Learning·

Discovering the Internet: Complete, Fourth Edition
Gary B. Shelly, Jennifer T. Campbell

Vice President, Publisher: Nicole Pinard

Executive Editor: Kathleen McMahon

Product Manager: Nada Jovanovic

Associate Product Manager: Caitlin Womersley

Editorial Assistant: Angela Giannopoulos

Director of Marketing: Elisa Roberts

Senior Marketing Manager: Tristen Kendall

Marketing Coordinator: Adrienne Fung

Print Buyer: Julio Esperas

Director of Production: Patty Stephan

Content Project Manager: Matt Hutchinson

Developmental Editor: Amanda Brodkin

QA Manuscript Reviewer: John Freitas

Copyeditor: Suzanne Huizenga

Proofreader: Karen Annett

Indexer: Rich Carlson

Art Director: Marissa Falco

Cover and Text Design: Joel Sadagursky

Cover Photo: Veer Incorporated

Compositor: GEX Publishing Services

Printer: RRD Menasha

For product information and technology assistance, contact us at
Cengage Learning Customer & Sales Support, 1-800-354-9706
For permission to use material from this text or product, submit all requests online at **cengage.com/permissions**
Further permissions questions can be emailed to
permissionrequest@cengage.com

Library of Congress Control Number: 2011941239

ISBN-13: 978-1-111-57767-4

ISBN-10: 1-111-57767-6

Cengage Learning International Offices

Asia
www.cengageasia.com
tel: (65) 6410 1200

Brazil
www.cengage.com.br
tel: (55) 11 3665 9900

Latin America
www.cengage.com.mx
tel: (52) 55 1500 6000

Australia/New Zealand
www.cengage.com.au
tel: (61) 3 9685 4111

India
www.cengage.co.in
tel: (91) 11 4364 1111

UK/Europe/Middle East/Africa
www.cengage.co.uk
tel: (44) 0 1264 332 424

Represented in Canada by
Nelson Education, Ltd.
tel: (416) 752 9100 / (800) 668 0671
www.nelson.com

Cengage Learning is a leading provider of customized learning solutions with office locations around the globe, including Singapore, the United Kingdom, Australia, Mexico, Brazil, and Japan. Locate your local office at: **www.cengage.com/global**

For product information: **www.cengage.com/international**
Visit your local office: **www.cengage.com/global**
Visit our corporate website: **www.cengage.com**

All screen shots are courtesy of Microsoft Corporation unless otherwise noted.

Printed in the United States of America
1 2 3 4 5 6 7 17 16 15 14 13 12 11

Chapter 6

Understanding Internet Technologies
and Security

Chapter 7

Understanding E-Business

Appendix A

Preface

The Shelly Cashman Series® offers the finest textbooks in computer education. We are proud of the fact that our textbook series has been the most widely used series in educational instruction. *Discovering the Internet: Complete, Fourth Edition* continues with the innovation, quality, and reliability that you have come to expect from the Shelly Cashman Series.

In *Discovering the Internet: Complete, Fourth Edition*, you will find an educationally sound, highly visual, and easy-to-follow pedagogy that combines Internet concepts with step-by-step projects and corresponding screens. The Internet and the World Wide Web (Web) have changed the way people find information, communicate with others, and conduct business activities. The chapters and exercises in this book are designed to help students understand how the Internet and the Web have changed today's world, understand the structure of the Internet and the Web, and understand how to use both technologies to enrich their personal and professional lives.

Objectives of This Textbook

Discovering the Internet: Complete, Fourth Edition is intended for a course that provides basic coverage of Internet and Web concepts. No experience with the Internet or the Web is assumed. The objectives of this book are:

• To teach Internet and Web history and concepts

• To demonstrate how to use a browser and online search tools

• To introduce different types of online communication tools

• To develop an exercise-oriented approach that allows learning by doing

• To encourage independent study and help those who are working alone

Organization of this Textbook

Discovering the Internet: Complete, Fourth Edition provides basic coverage of Internet and Web concepts. The material is divided into seven chapters and one appendix.

CHAPTER 1 — INTO THE INTERNET   In Chapter 1, students are introduced to basic Internet and Web terminology, learn how the Internet and Web are used, and become familiar with the history of the Internet and the Web.

CHAPTER 2 — BROWSING THE WEB   In Chapter 2, students are introduced to Web sites, Web pages, Web portals, Web servers, and Web browsers; learn to use Web browser features, such as tabbed browsing; and learn about online risks and safeguards.

CHAPTER 3 — SEARCHING THE WEB   In Chapter 3, students learn how to perform the search process and use various search tools to do basic and advanced Web searches.

CHAPTER 4 — COMMUNICATING ONLINE   In Chapter 4, students learn how to send and receive e-mail using both an e-mail client and a Web-based e-mail service. Students also learn about participating in other types of online communication, such as mailing lists, newsgroups, wikis, Web-based discussion groups, text and instant messaging. Students also are introduced to a variety of social media.

CHAPTER 5 — GETTING MORE OUT OF THE INTERNET In Chapter 5, students explore getting more out of the Internet and the Web including visiting consumer, vertical, and industry portals; getting news, weather, and sports information; experiencing streaming media; using online reference tools; exploring special interest sites; managing their personal finances; and downloading and uploading files.

CHAPTER 6 — UNDERSTANDING INTERNET TECHNOLOGIES AND SECURITY In Chapter 6, students learn about the networking technologies and communication services that make communicating over the Internet and accessing the Web possible. Students also learn more about online security risks and safeguards.

CHAPTER 7 — UNDERSTANDING E-BUSINESS In Chapter 7, students use real-world e-business examples to explore different e-business models.

APPENDIX A — EXPLORING OTHER BROWSERS Appendix A introduces students to five additional browsers: Firefox, Safari (for Windows), Opera, Google Chrome, and Flock, with each browser offering something different to users.

Online Companion

The Online Companion includes Learn It Online exercises for each chapter, as well as @Source links, @Issue links, and Steps links. To access these course materials, please visit **www.cengagebrain.com**. At the CengageBrain.com home page, search for *Discovering the Internet 4th Edition* using the search box at the top of the page. This will take you to the product page where you can click the Access Now button below the Study Tools heading.

Instructor Resources

The Instructor Resources include both teaching and testing aids and can be accessed via CD-ROM or at login.cengage.com

INSTRUCTOR'S MANUAL Includes lecture notes summarizing the chapter sections, figures and boxed elements found in every chapter, teacher tips, classroom activities, lab activities, and quick quizzes in Microsoft Word files.

SYLLABUS Easily customizable sample syllabi that cover policies, assignments, exams, and other course information.

FIGURE FILES Illustrations for every figure in the textbook in electronic form.

POWERPOINT PRESENTATIONS A multimedia lecture presentation system that provides slides for each chapter. Presentations are based on chapter objectives.

SOLUTIONS TO EXERCISES Includes solutions for all end-of-chapter and chapter reinforcement exercises.

TEST BANK & TEST ENGINE Test Banks include 112 questions for every chapter, featuring objective-based and critical thinking question types, and including page number references and figure references, when appropriate. Also included is the test engine, ExamView, the ultimate tool for your objective-based testing needs.

DATA FILES FOR STUDENTS   Includes all the files that are required by students to complete the exercises.

ADDITIONAL ACTIVITIES FOR STUDENTS   Consists of Chapter Reinforcement Exercises, which are true/false, multiple-choice, and short answer questions that help students gain confidence in the material learned.

SAM: Skills Assessment Manager

SAM 2010 is designed to help bring students from the classroom to the real world. It allows students to train on and test important computer skills in an active, hands-on environment.

SAM's easy-to-use system includes powerful interactive exams, training, and projects on the most commonly used Microsoft Office applications. SAM simulates the Microsoft Office 2010 application environment, allowing students to demonstrate their knowledge and think through the skills by performing real-world tasks such as bolding word text or setting up slide transitions. Add in live-in-the-application projects, and students are on their way to truly learning and applying skills to business-centric documents.

Designed to be used with the Shelly Cashman Series, SAM includes handy page references so that students can print helpful study guides that match the Shelly Cashman textbooks used in class. For instructors, SAM also includes robust scheduling and reporting features.

Content for Online Learning

Course Technology has partnered with the leading distance learning solution providers and class-management platforms today. To access this material, instructors will visit our password-protected instructor resources available at login.cengage.com. Instructor resources include the following: additional case projects, sample syllabi, PowerPoint presentations per chapter, and more. For additional information or for an instructor user name and password, please contact your sales representative. For students to access this material, they must have purchased a WebTutor PIN-code specific to this title and your campus platform. The resources for students may include (based on instructor preferences), but are not limited to: topic review, review questions, and practice tests.

CourseNotes

course|notes™
quick reference guide

Course Technology's CourseNotes are six-panel quick reference cards that reinforce the most important and widely used features of a software application in a visual and user-friendly format. CourseNotes serve as a great reference tool for students, both during and after the course. CourseNotes are available for software applications such as Microsoft Office 2010, Word 2010, Excel 2010, Access 2010, PowerPoint 2010, and Windows 7. Topic-based CourseNotes are available for Best Practices in Social Networking, Hot Topics in Technology, Web 2.0: Recharged, and many more. Visit www.cengagebrain.com to learn more!

A Guided Tour

Add excitement and interactivity to your classroom with "*A Guided Tour*" product line. Play one of the brief mini-movies to spice up your lecture and spark classroom discussion. Or, assign a movie for homework and ask students to complete the correlated assignment that accompanies each topic. "*A Guided Tour*" product line takes the prep work out of providing your students with information about new technologies and applications and helps keep students engaged with content relevant to their lives; all in under an hour!

About Our Covers

The Shelly Cashman Series is continually updating our approach and content to reflect the way today's students learn and experience new technology. This focus on student success is reflected on our covers, which feature real students from Naugatuck Valley Community College using the Shelly Cashman Series in their courses, and reflect the varied ages and backgrounds of the students learning with our books. When you use the Shelly Cashman Series, you can be assured that you are learning computer skills using the most effective courseware available.

Textbook Walk-Through

Figure 2-4 An IP address is the numeric equivalent of a URL.

FACTS @HAND IP addresses are actually stored as binary numbers, meaning they are stored in bits and bytes. IP addresses, such as the Cengage Learning address mentioned previously, are stored in a 32-bit format, consisting of four numbers ranging from 0 to 255, separated by dots. This format, known as IPv4, limits the number of unique IP addresses to about 4.3 billion. Since the mid-2000s, IPv6, which uses 128-bit IP addresses, has been in widespread use, allowing for many more individual IP addresses at once.

Domain Names

Because complex, numeric IP addresses Web servers typically are referenced by a dor alias for one or more IP addresses. The doma responds to the IP address, 69.32.133.79 . W is entered into the browser, the browser mus requesting the IP address from a name serve databases with domain names and the numer The DNS name server translates or "resolve address, and returns the IP address to the br then can be sent to the Web server where th part of the **Domain Name System (DNS)**.

FACTS @HAND You can find the numeric IP address tha by using the nslookup command. To use Start button, and type nslookup in the s search results list to open the nslookup domain name after the > prompt and p addresses associated with the domain n

Because domain names must be uniqu trademarks. The organization that oversees r

Facts@Hand
Each chapter contains multiple Facts@Hand tips that provide industry statistics or usage Information relevant to the Internet and Web concepts discussed in the chapter.

E-mailing a Web Page

When you find a Web page that you think might interest someone else, you can share it by sending it to him or her by e-mail. You can send a Web page by e-mail by clicking the Page button on the Command bar and clicking the 'Send page by e-mail' command. The recipient receives an e-mail with the Web page in the body of the message. You also can send a link to a Web page by clicking the Page button and clicking 'Send link by e-mail.' Finally, you can copy a link and paste it into an e-mail message. When the message recipient clicks the link, his or her browser starts and opens the Web page. You will learn more about sending and receiving e-mail in Chapter 4.

Saving a Web Page Image

While browsing the Web, you might find an image that you want to save. Be careful when saving and using Web page images! Most Web page images are the property of their owners and are protected by U.S. copyright law. You cannot use copyright-protected images without permission from the owner or source. Some images, such as many images found at U.S. government Web sites, are in the public domain. Images in the public domain may be used freely; however, you are generally required to provide information about the source of public domain images. Many Web sites that offer public domain images also provide the wording for an image credit line.

You can save a public domain image, such as the one shown in Figure 2-71, by right-clicking the image and then clicking the 'Save picture as' command on the shortcut menu. The shortcut menu also includes commands for printing the image and saving the image as the Windows desktop background wallpaper.

@SOURCE
Copyright
For more information on U.S. copyright laws, visit the Book Companion Site Web page at **www.cengagebrain.com**. Under the Chapter 2 @Source links, click the link for Copyright.

Figure 2-71 You can use a shortcut menu to save, print, or e-mail an image.

Changing Browser Options

The browser window and some browser features can be customized in various ways. For example, you can customize the browser window to show or hide the menu bar, the Favorites bar, and other plug-in toolbars. You also can customize the Command bar. As

@Source
Each chapter includes multiple @Source tips that direct students to the *Discovering the Internet, Fourth Edition* Online Companion, where they will find links to useful information.

Step-By-Step Instruction

Step-by-step hands-on instructions now provide a context beyond the point-and-click. Each step provides information on why students are performing each task, or what will occur as a result.

To Open and Close Multiple Web Page Tabs

The following steps open multiple Web pages in separate tabs using the Address bar and Web page links, view and close Web pages, reopen several Web pages, and then close Internet Explorer. Next, the browser and the Web pages that were opened during the last work session are reopened.

1
- Click the Internet Explorer Browser icon on the Start menu to open Internet Explorer.
- Click the New Tab button on the tab row to open a New Tab page (Figure 2-25).

Q&A Why is my New Tab page empty or different?
The New Tab page reflects the browsing history on your computer. Yours will show different Web sites, or it may be empty if you are new to Internet Explorer or working on a lab computer.

Figure 2-25

2
- Type **espn.com** in the Address box.
- Press the ENTER key to open the ESPN home page in the new tab (Figure 2-26).

58   Chapter 2   Browsing the Web

Q&A

Q&A boxes identify questions students may have when working through the steps and provide additional information about what they are doing, right where they need it.

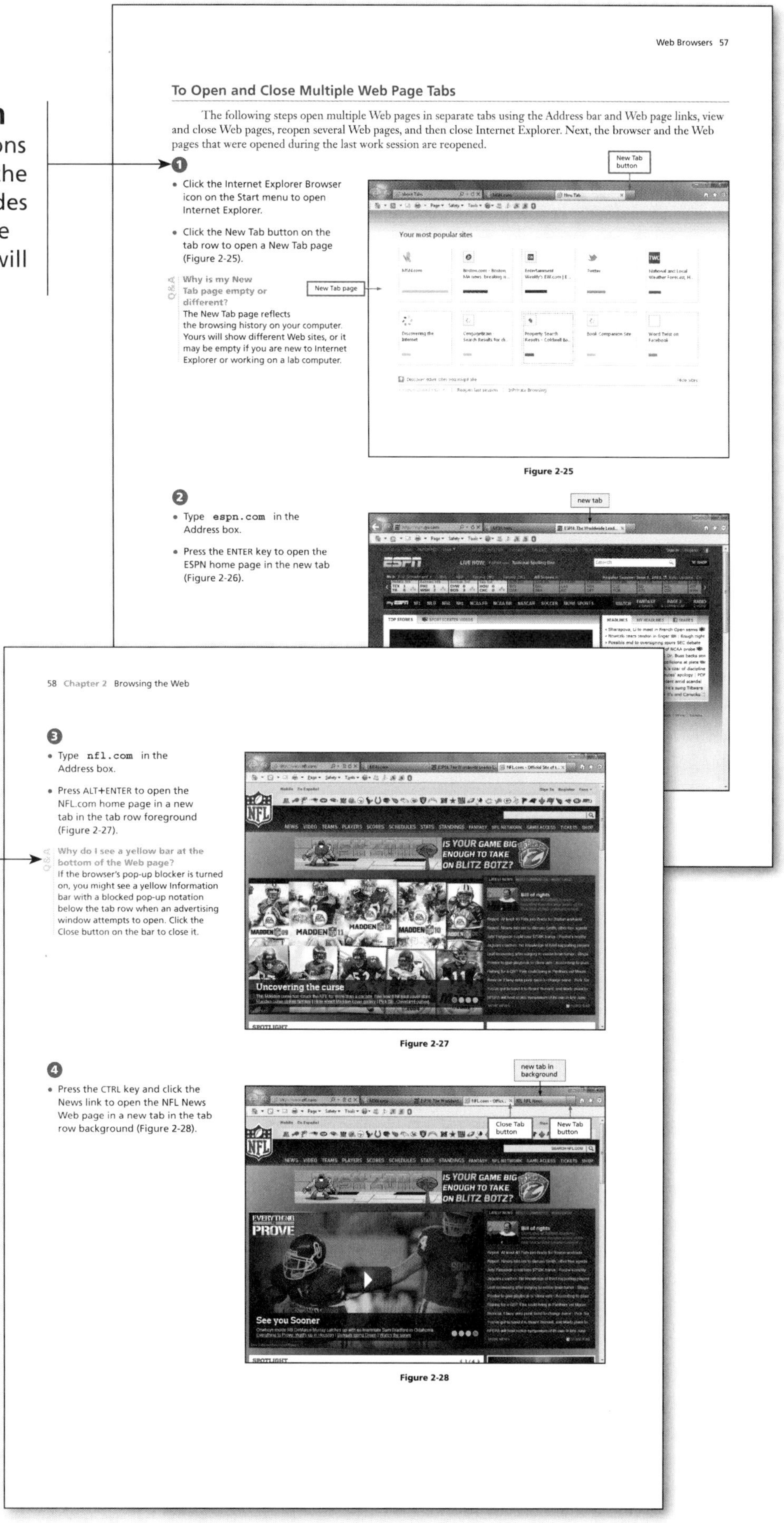

3
- Type **nfl.com** in the Address box.
- Press ALT+ENTER to open the NFL.com home page in a new tab in the tab row foreground (Figure 2-27).

Q&A Why do I see a yellow bar at the bottom of the Web page?
If the browser's pop-up blocker is turned on, you might see a yellow Information bar with a blocked pop-up notation below the tab row when an advertising window attempts to open. Click the Close button on the bar to close it.

Figure 2-27

4
- Press the CTRL key and click the News link to open the NFL News Web page in a new tab in the tab row background (Figure 2-28).

Figure 2-28

100 Chapter 2 Browsing the Web

@ISSUE Opting Out

Although Web site owners have a responsibility to post and adhere to privacy policies, consumers can take actions to protect their own privacy. For example, consumers can take time to review the privacy policy statements posted at their favorite Web sites. To protect against third-party or other undesirable cookies on their computers, consumers can delete all unwanted cookies and set options to restrict cookie acceptance. Then they can check for opt-out instructions at Web sites and submit forms to opt out of receiving cookies, data collection, and advertising. Taking these actions can help protect and maintain privacy when browsing the Web. For more information on opting out, visit the Book Companion Site Web page at **www.cengagebrain.com**. Under the Chapter 2 @Issue links, click the links for Opting Out.

INPRIVATE BROWSING   As you learned earlier in this chapter, information about the Web sites you visit is recorded in your browsing history. In some circumstances, you might not want to record your browsing history during a specific browsing session (for example, when you share a computer and do not want others to see your browsing history). To browse privately, you can open a new tab and click the InPrivate Browsing link on the New Tab page, or click the Safety button on the Command bar and then click InPrivate Browsing to open a new browser window. An InPrivate browsing indicator appears to the left of the Address bar when InPrivate Browsing is turned on. Note that InPrivate Browsing does not protect your personally identifiable information from being gathered at Web sites while you browse; it only keeps information about the browsing session from being stored on your computer. To close InPrivate Browsing, simply close the browser window. For more information on InPrivate Browsing, see Internet Explorer Help.

INPRIVATE FILTERING   Earlier in this section, you learned about Web beacons or bugs. As you browse the Web, you view many Web pages that contain content, such as advertising, provided by others, sometimes called content providers. When you visit a Web site containing content provided by third parties, the content providers might be capturing information about your browsing habits using Web bugs. For example, content providers could display specific advertisements that might be of interest to you based on the types of Web sites you visit. To protect against this[...] on the Internet Explorer InPrivate Filtering featur[...] Command bar and clicking InPrivate Filtering. Wh[...] turned on, each Web page you visit is analyzed for[...] found, you will have the option of blocking the sus[...] an option to have the InPrivate Filtering feature au[...] tent. For more information on browsing with the I[...] Explorer Help.

@Issue

Each chapter includes one or more @Issue sections that provide additional discussion of important Internet and Web issues.

---

❸

- Open the Favorites Center.
- Click the Feeds tab, if necessary, to view the Feeds list.
- Right-click the CNN.com – Technology feed in the Feeds list to open the shortcut menu (Figure 2-60).

Figure 2-60

❹

- Click Delete to display the confirmation dialog box (Figure 2-61).
- Click the Yes button in the confirmation dialog box to confirm the deletion.
- Close Internet Explorer.

Figure 2-61

Other Ways
1. Click Tools button on Command bar, point to Explorer bars, click Feeds
2. CTRL+SHIFT+G
3. CTRL+G

Other Ways

Other Ways boxes that follow many of the step sequences explain the other ways to complete the task presented.

Chapter Review
A review of the Internet and Web concepts discussed in the chapter.

Chapter Review

Web pages are designed to attract and hold the attention of visitors, and typically include some or all of the following: a logo or name, images, links, advertisements, a search tool, a copyright statement, and a link to a privacy policy statement.

An IP address is the unique numerical address of a computer on a network and is used to address and send data over a network, such as the Internet. A domain name is an easy-to-remember text alias for one or more IP addresses. A URL, also called a Web address, is the unique address of a Web page; it consists of the http:// protocol, the server name, and the domain name, and can include the path and file name.

You can load Web pages by typing each Web page's URL in the Address box on the Address bar and clicking the Go button or pressing the ENTER key. You also can load a Web page by clicking a Web page link. You can navigate among recently loaded Web pages during the current browser session, load a fresh copy of the current Web page, stop loading a Web page, and load the browser's home page by clicking the Back, Forward, Refresh, Stop, and Home buttons.

You can use several browser shortcuts to visit Web pages including Favorites, History, Web Slices, Accelerators, RSS feeds, the New Tab page, the Address bar drop-down list, and the Suggested Sites Web Slice. You can view a Print Preview and print a copy of the current Web page to reference its contents later. You also can save a Web page in a variety of formats that include or exclude its related files, such as graphics. You can send a snapshot of or a link to a Web page to someone by e-mail. Individual Web page images can be saved for private use in a variety of different formats.

You can change browser options, such as displaying and hiding toolbars and changing the home page to a new home page or a group of home pages that open in separate tabs, using the keyboard, a shortcut menu, and the Internet Options dialog box. You also can use Internet Explorer features, such as SmartScreen Filter, Tracking Protection, and ActiveX Filter, to browse the Web more securely. Using the InPrivate Browsing feature can help you restrict the information shared about your browsing habits.

Terms To Know
A listing of the keywords emphasized in the chapter, including a page number reference for each keyword.

TERMS TO KNOW

After reading this chapter, you should know each of these Key Terms.

Accelerators (71)
adware (99)
AutoComplete (78)
client (41)
client/server computing (41)
Compatibility View (89)
cookie (98)
country-code top-level domain (ccTLD) (43)
display area (44)
domain name (42)
Domain Name System (DNS) (42)
dynamic IP address (41)
FAQs (frequently asked questions) (39)
favicon (79)
favorite (63)
hacker (91)
History list (68)
home page (38)
information privacy (96)
Internet Corporation for Assigned Names and Numbers (ICANN) (43)
Internet filters (95)

IP address (Internet Protocol address) (41)
malicious Web site (96)
name server (42)
offline (82)
personally identifiable information (PII) (98)
portal (39)
privacy statement (97)
secure connection (94)
Secure Sockets Layer (SSL) (94)
spyware (99)
static IP address (41)
tabbed browsing (56)
top-level domain (TLD) (43)
Tracking Protection Lists (TPLs) (94)
Uniform Resource Locator (URL) (43)
virus (92)
Web address (43)
Web bug (99)
Web content filters (95)
Web portal (39)
Web Slices (71)

Test Your Knowledge
Ten true/false and 10 multiple-choice questions, including a page number reference for each question.

TEST YOUR KNOWLEDGE

Complete the Test Your Knowledge exercises to solidify what you have learned in the chapter.

True or False

Mark T for True and F for False. (Answers are found on page numbers in parentheses.)

___ 1. A server is an application that runs on a computer, such as a personal computer, and requests resources or services from another computer. (41)

___ 2. Advertisements with attention-grabbing sounds and animation are called rich media ads. (50)

___ 3. The protocol (http://) and the domain name in a URL are not case sensitive, but the path and file name can be. (44)

___ 4. An IP address consists of three groups of numbers, each separated by periods, or dots. (41)

___ 5. To access a recently viewed Web page, you can click a URL in the Address box drop-down list. (78)

___ 6. A computer hacker is a small, potentially damaging computer program that can infect a computer and then be passed to other computers. (91)

___ 7. A printed Web page often has a header and footer containing the name of the Web page, the page numbers, the Web page's URL, and the date printed. (81)

___ 8. A filter is a security system that uses hardware and/or software to prevent unauthorized access to a computer on a network. (95)

Learn It Online

Five online exercises that reinforce the Internet and Web concepts discussed in the chapter: Chapter Reinforcement, Flash Cards, Practice Test, Who Wants To Be a Computer Genius, and Crossword Puzzle Challenge.

Exercises

Ten in-depth exercises that require students to use the Internet and the Web to research issues or solve problems.

Inset page 1 (104 Chapter 2 Browsing the Web):

104 Chapter 2 Browsing the Web

7. A Web server with a permanent Internet connection needs a(n) _____ IP address. (41)

   a. dynamic

   b. private

   c. static

   d. assigned

8. PII stands for _____ (98)

   a. private Internet information

   b. personally identifiable information

   c. portal for Internet information

   d. personal InPrivate portal

9. The Internet Explorer browser feature that helps protect you against malicious Web sites as you browse the Web is _____. (100)

   a. Cookies

   b. SmartScreen Filter

   c. Tracking Protection

   d. InPrivate Browsing

10. _____ is a general name for any technology that accesses your computer system without your knowledge or approval to gather information. (99)

    a. Adware

    b. Gatherware

    c. Spyware

    d. Privacyware

LEARN IT ONLINE

Test your knowledge of chapter content and key terms.

Instructions: To complete the following exercises, please visit **www.cengagebrain.com**. On the CengageBrain home page, enter the book title *Discovering the Internet* and then click the Find button. On the product Web page for this book, click the Access Now button below the Study Tools heading. On the Book Companion Site Web page, click the drop-down menu, select Chapter 2, and then click the link for the desired exercise.

Chapter Reinforcement TF,

Practice Test

A series of multiple-choice questions that test your knowledge of chapter content and key terms.

Who Wants To Be a Computer Genius?

An interactive game that challenges your knowledge of chapter content in the style of a television quiz show.

Inset page 2 (Chapter Review 105):

Chapter Review 105

Wheel of Terms

An interactive game that challenges your knowledge of chapter key terms in the style of the television show, *Wheel of Fortune*.

Crossword Puzzle Challenge

A crossword puzzle that challenges your knowledge of the key terms presented in the chapter.

EXERCISES

Use the Exercises to gain hands-on experience working with the Internet and the Web.

1 | Visit Portals and Change the Browser Home Page

1. Start Internet Explorer, if necessary. Visit the Book Companion Site Web page for this book, and click a link below Chapter 2, Exercise 1 to view links to several Web portals. Open each Web portal in a new tab.

2. Use the Back and Forward buttons and the New Tab page to view and then revisit each portal.

3. Add the portal page of your choice as an additional home page using the Home button on the Command bar. Close Internet Explorer. Reopen Internet Explorer to verify the additional home page.

4. Remove the new portal home page from your home page group. Close and reopen Internet Explorer to verify that your original home page or pages open.

5. Close Internet Explorer.

2 | Identify Characteristics of a Web Page

1. Start Internet Explorer, if necessary. Visit the Book Companion Site Web page for this book, and click the links below Chapter 2, Exercise 2 to open in separate tabs the home page for two local news Web sites. Use the Web page tabs to navigate between the two Web pages; then click the Print button on the Command bar to print one of the Web pages. Save one of the Web pages to a flash drive or to a folder on your hard drive. Use Windows Explorer to delete the saved Web page.

2. In Internet Explorer, examine the Web page you printed to locate the following items. On the printout, label the following items that might appear on the Web page:

   a. Logo or name of the Web site

   b. Image as a link

   c. Text as a link

   d. Advertisement for another company's product or service

   e. Copyright statement or link

   f. Privacy policy link

   g. Other elements such as connectivity tools (Facebook, etc.) and slide shows or carousels

3. Click various links on the Web site's home page to browse its other Web pages. Use the Back and Forward buttons to revisit the recently viewed Web pages.

4. Use the Address box drop-down list to revisit recently viewed Web pages.

1 | Into the Internet

Introduction

Internet. E-mail. Web. Twitter. RSS. Google. Facebook. Cloud computing. You have most likely heard these terms regardless of your level of Internet experience. New Internet terminology constantly enters our vocabulary as new technologies evolve to change the way people communicate and collaborate with others, access information, and purchase products and services.

In this chapter, you will learn the meaning of these and several other Internet-related terms and discover the many ways the Internet is used. You also will review the history of the Internet and learn how the Internet is managed. Finally, you will learn how individuals and businesses connect to the Internet.

Objectives

After completing this chapter, you will be able to:

1. Define the Internet

2. Describe how the Internet is used

3. Discuss the history of the Internet and the World Wide Web

4. Describe how individuals and businesses connect to the Internet

Defining the Internet

The **Internet** is a global network of computers that allows individual and business computer users around the world to share information and other resources and to conduct business transactions. More specifically, the Internet is an interconnected network of networks, where each **host** — a computer directly connected to the Internet — has a number of other computers connected to it (Figure 1-1). When a user connects to the Internet to access information and services, he or she is considered to be **online**.

Figure 1-1　The Internet is a global network of computers that allows individual and business users around the world to share information and other resources and to conduct business transactions.

All computers and mobile devices, including smartphones, home and business personal computers, and supercomputers used by government and researchers, share a common method of communicating known as a protocol. A **protocol** is a standard or set of rules that computer network devices follow when transmitting and receiving data. Every computer connected to the Internet uses the **Transmission Control Protocol/Internet Protocol (TCP/IP)**. TCP/IP makes it possible for different types of computers using a variety of operating systems to communicate. Wireless devices, such as smartphones or laptop computers enabled with wireless access, use wireless protocols that work in conjunction with TCP/IP. You will learn more about TCP/IP and other Internet technologies in later chapters.

Internet communications are transmitted across high-speed fiber-optic networks that connect other networks around the world. These high-speed networks, which provide the Internet framework, are operated by a number of communication carriers, including AT&T, Verizon, XO Communications, and Qwest in the United States; Global TeleSystems and British Telecommunications (BT) in Europe; and Telstra and CERNET in Asia.

Although these communication carriers play an important role, they do not control the Internet. In fact, no single organization owns or controls the Internet. Several groups, such as the Internet Corporation for Assigned Names and Numbers (ICANN), the Internet Assigned Numbers Authority (IANA), and the Internet Society (ISOC), oversee and standardize the development of Internet technologies and manage some Internet processes.

Using the Internet

Without a doubt, the Internet has profoundly changed nearly every aspect of life (Figure 1-2). For example, the Internet has revolutionized the way people access information for personal or business use; the way individual shoppers or commercial buyers purchase products and services; the way people enjoy entertainment offerings; the way students do their schoolwork; and the way people communicate with friends, family, colleagues, and others. Additionally, the Internet also overwhelmingly has changed the way businesses interact with their customers, vendors, and business partners.

Figure 1-2   People use the Internet for many different purposes.

Who Uses the Internet?

The Internet is used by people in all occupations and stages of life: students and teachers, businesspeople and professionals, homemakers, children, and retirees. For example, students often rush home from school to play online games or interact with their friends at social networking Web sites. Colleges and universities use the Internet to host online classes or to provide methods for students to submit assignments or take online tests; instructors use the Internet to find scholarly articles and data for their research, make instructional material available outside of the classroom, post grades, and publish class announcements electronically.

Individuals of all ages use the Internet to search for information on almost any topic — entertainment, sports, politics, science, art, history, and so forth. For example, medical professionals use the Internet to research new drugs, current treatments, and trends in medical practice. Students use the Internet to find information on assigned topics. Potential homebuyers search for houses or condominiums in a certain geographic location and price range.

> **FACTS @HAND**
>
> Data gathered by Nielsen//NetRatings and reported at Internetworldstats.com indicates there are more than 266 million U.S. Internet users and almost 2 billion Internet users worldwide.

Adults with similar interests or hobbies interact and exchange information by participating in online discussions. Consumers shop online, pay bills, reconcile bank statements, and even complete and submit their taxes online. Senior citizens use the Internet to keep in contact with family and friends.

People also use the Internet to publish online diaries, known as a **blog** (short for **weblog**). Blogs can cover any topic, such as humor or news, or allow users to publish a résumé or travel photos. Some members of the U.S. Congress and Senate keep their constituents updated by **microblogging**, sending brief text messages throughout the day to interested subscribers. Another way people interact on the Internet is by posting comments on blogs published by others or to articles posted by news organizations.

Businesspeople and professionals use the Internet to communicate with clients and colleagues whether at home or on the road using e-mail, chat, or video conferencing; work on office computers from their laptops while traveling; view up-to-the-minute business news; and check stock prices. New uses of the Internet are evolving continually, making the Internet increasingly valuable to individuals and businesses.

For more information about blogging and microblogging, visit **www.cengagebrain.com**. On the CengageBrain.com home page, enter the book title, *Discovering the Internet, Fourth Edition,* and then click the Find button. On the product page for this book, click the Access Now button below the Study Tools heading. On the Book Companion Site Web page, click the drop-down menu, select chapter 1, and then click the @Source link. Click the links under Blogging and Microblogging.

Internet Activities

The Internet supports a wide range of activities, including the following:

- Browsing and searching for information on the World Wide Web
- Communicating with others through e-mail, text or video chat, social networking, instant messaging, Web-based discussion groups, newsgroups, mailing lists, blogs and microblogs, and other media
- Downloading and uploading files
- Accessing remote computers or servers
- Conducting business activities
- Online shopping

The following sections define and describe each of these activities.

THE WORLD WIDE WEB   The **World Wide Web**, commonly called the **Web**, is a subset of the Internet that includes a vast collection of documents that feature text with pictures, sound, animation, and video. These documents, called **Web pages**, are grouped in Web sites all over the world. A **Web site**, or **site**, is a collection of related Web pages managed by an individual or organization. Web site examples (Figure 1-3) include college and university Web sites; corporate Web sites; Web sites for companies that sell products or services, such as Avon; Web sites for nonprofit organizations, such as the United Way; and personal Web sites.

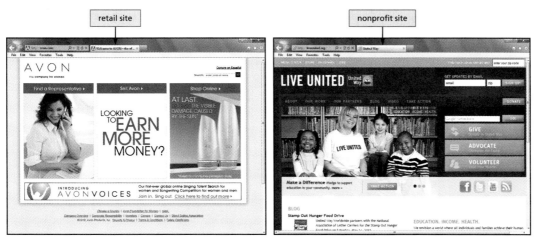

Figure 1-3   Web site examples include college and university, corporate, retail, nonprofit, and personal Web sites.

Web pages are created using codes or tags that define the layout and/or content of the pages; the codes or tags are often specified using **Hypertext Markup Language (HTML)** or **Extensible Hypertext Markup Language (XHTML)**. A Web page can be created by typing HTML or XHTML tags and other related information in a simple text editor program, such as Notepad. Today, however, most Web pages are created with **Web authoring software**, such as Adobe Dreamweaver or Microsoft Expression Web, which automatically generate the appropriate HTML or XHTML tags as the user creates the Web page using a familiar user interface containing menus, panels, and buttons. After a Web page is created, it must be uploaded, or **published**, to a Web server so that other users may access it. A **Web server** is a computer on which Web pages are stored.

You can access and view Web pages using a software program called a **Web browser**, or **browser**. Popular browsers include Internet Explorer®, Mozilla Firefox®, Opera™, Avant, Google Chrome™, and Safari®. The illustrations in this book use the Windows® Internet Explorer® 9 browser. You can learn more about other browsers in Appendix A.

A Web page is connected to other Web pages by hyperlinks. A **hyperlink**, or **link**, is text or a picture on a Web page that you click with the mouse pointer to view a different location on the same Web page, another Web page at the same Web site, a Web page at a different Web site, or to an e-mail address or PDF document (Figure 1-4).

Figure 1-4 A hyperlink is text or a picture that you click to view a different location on the same Web page, another Web page at the same Web site, a Web page at a different Web site, or to an e-mail address or PDF document.

Exploring the Web by clicking links from one Web page to another sometimes is called **browsing** or **surfing** the Web. For example, when planning a trip, you might first visit an airline Web page and book a flight; then click a link on the airline Web page to visit a hotel Web page and book your accommodations; and, finally, click a link on the hotel Web page to view a Web page containing yet more links to restaurants and entertainment venues near the hotel. When reading an article on a Web page, you can often find background information or articles on related topics by clicking links within the text of the article, or in a sidebar or list beside or below the article. In Chapter 2, "Browsing the Web," you will learn how to use a Web browser to access Web pages and how to click hyperlinks to view other Web pages.

FACTS @HAND The first published use of the phrase, surfing the Internet, was in a 1992 article written by Jean Armour Polly, who publishes the kid-friendly Net-mom® Web site that offers Internet safety tips for families.

A **search tool** is a Web-based resource that helps you find specific information on the Web. One type of search tool is a search engine, such as Google, which is used to search for Web pages that contain specific keywords or phrases. Another type of search tool is a directory, such as the Open Directory Project, which maintains a searchable index by category. Figure 1-5 illustrates a Google search results Web page and a DMOZ directory Web page. You will learn how to use Google, the DMOZ Open Directory Project, and other search tools in Chapter 3, Searching the Web.

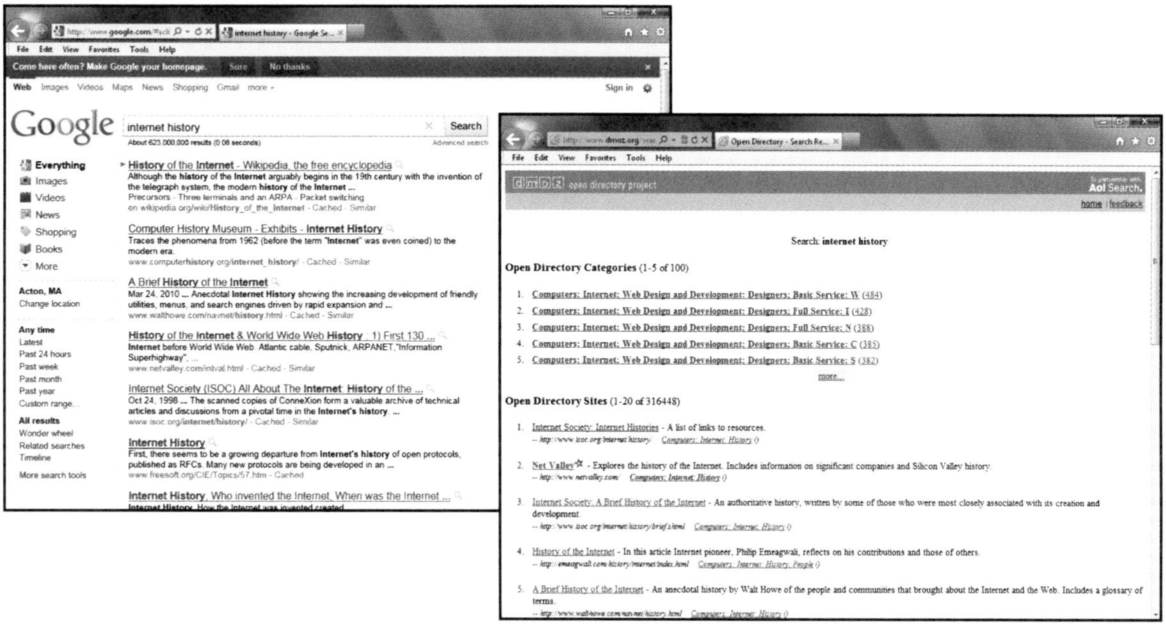

Figure 1-5 Search tools help users find information on the Web.

Just as no single entity controls the Internet, no single entity controls the Web. However, some organizations, such as the **World Wide Web Consortium (W3C)**, support the Web by developing and promoting Web technologies and standards.

E-MAIL AND OTHER COMMUNICATIONS TOOLS **E-mail**, short for **electronic mail**, allows Internet users to send and receive messages and files over a local computer network or the Internet. One of the most popular and frequently used Internet activities, e-mail offers several advantages over other means of communication, such as sending letters or faxes, or making telephone calls. Sending an e-mail message is less expensive and faster than regular mail or express delivery services, such as UPS and FedEx. E-mail also can be more convenient than making a telephone call, especially to others in different time zones around the world. You can send e-mail when it is convenient for you, and the recipient can read it and respond when it is convenient for him or her. You use an **e-mail program**, such as Microsoft Outlook® or Mozilla Thunderbird®, or Web-based e-mail, such as Gmail™ or Yahoo!® Mail, to create, send, receive, and manage e-mail.

In addition to e-mail, the Internet offers several other ways for individuals and groups to communicate (Figure 1-6), including instant messaging (IM), Internet Relay Chat (IRC), newsgroups and mailing lists, and social networking. These communications tools allow Internet users to connect with others online to converse about a topic or an activity of interest, share information, conduct business, and play. You will learn more about e-mail and other online communications tools, including various online tools categorized as social media, in Chapter 4, Communicating Online.

Perhaps the first person to send an e-mail message who was not a computer scientist was Queen Elizabeth II, who sent an e-mail message on March 26, 1976 from an Army base.

Internet Communication Methods

Online Communication	Description	Must Users Be Online at the Same Time?
E-mail	Users send and receive text with or without attached files	No
Instant messaging (IM)	Two or more users take turns exchanging brief messages	Yes
Internet Relay Chat (IRC) or chatting	Users type text into a chat window; all users can see what other users type	Yes
Newsgroups and mailing lists	Users subscribe to a newsgroup discussion or mailing list on a certain topic and receive messages about that topic	No
Social networking	Users share status updates, microblogs, photos and videos, links, and personal commentary using a variety of online tools	No

Figure 1-6 The Internet offers several ways for people to communicate.

DOWNLOADING AND UPLOADING FILES One of the most useful Internet activities is downloading files from a server or uploading files to a server. A **server** is a computer on a network used to store files. As you learned earlier, a Web server stores Web pages. Other server examples are a mail server that stores e-mail messages and a file server that stores electronic files. To **download** is to copy or transfer files from a server to your computer; to **upload** is to copy, post, or transfer files from your computer to a server (Figure 1-7). The Internet standard or protocol that allows you to download files from or upload files to a server connected to the Internet is the **File Transfer Protocol (FTP)**. Music, software, word processing, picture, and other files can be downloaded or uploaded using FTP.

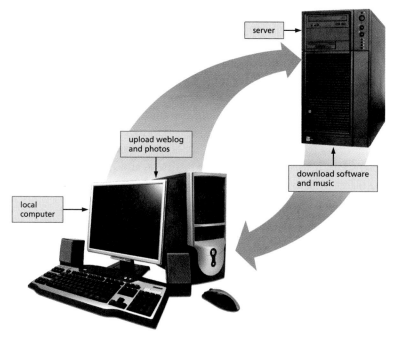

Figure 1-7 FTP is used to download and upload files.

Peer-to-peer media file sharing was made popular in the late 1990s by Web sites such as Napster that allowed individual users to upload music files and share them with others, without permission from, or reimbursement for, the copyright holder. Companies such as Rhapsody and Pandora were created in response to the popularity of peer-to-peer Web sites to offer subscription-based radio and downloadable music files that are licensed by the copyright holders and available to individual users.

FACTS @HAND

REMOTE COMPUTING   Developments in remote data access, storage, and collaboration technologies have led to what is now known as **cloud computing**. Cloud computing users access computer services, such as data storage and productivity software, using remote servers. Users of cloud computing are said to be working "in the cloud," meaning that users can access a variety of software and storage methods by using a computer with Internet access and browser software. Google Docs™ is an example of cloud computing. Google Docs is a group of software products available online, including word processing (Figure 1-8), spreadsheet, and presentation software. When logged on to Google Docs, a user can use the software to create a document, such as a spreadsheet, save and store the document online, and share the document with others to collaborate on changes — all without owning or running the original software application.

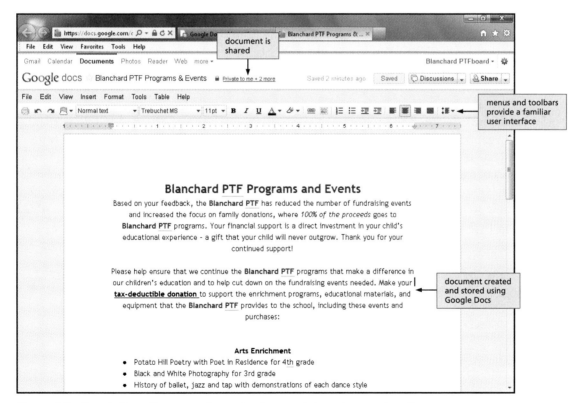

Figure 1-8   Google Docs allows users to create, store, and share documents online.

Businesses can take advantage of many remote computing technologies to keep employees productive while they travel, work from home, or interact with colleagues located around the world. One technology is a **virtual private network (VPN)**. A VPN provides a secure, encrypted connection between a remote user and a local area network.

Web conferencing allows remote employees to participate in meetings, training sessions, and more. Web conferencing is a broad term that can include using the Web to view slide show presentations, use live or streaming video, participate in surveys and polls, communicate using text chat, or view the presenter's screen using screen sharing.

Telnet is a standard or protocol that allows users to log in and to access a remote computer, usually one with significantly higher processing power. While the public typically does not use Telnet, it still has many valuable uses. Computer system administrators, for example, can use Telnet to log in to a remote computer to troubleshoot problems, and researchers use Telnet to employ the computing power of supercomputers at distant institutions. It is also used by some for Internet gaming.

CONDUCTING BUSINESS ACTIVITIES   Businesses and organizations that use the Internet to generate a profit, promote their goods and services, or maintain goodwill with their partners, members, or customers are engaged in **e-business**. E-business is a broad term that includes electronically transmitted financial transactions, such as placing orders, sending invoices, or paying by credit card online. E-business also includes the functions of supporting and enhancing business relationships by sharing information with customers, suppliers, and employees. Although the terms e-business and e-commerce are often used interchangeably, e-business can refer to any use of the Internet to conduct a company's business, whereas e-commerce refers to Internet use for the purpose of generating sales of goods or services, or creating and maintaining customer relations.

E-business can take a variety of forms or models (Figure 1-9). **Business-to-consumer (B2C)** is when a consumer uses the Internet to interact with an online business. Customers checking airfares on the Southwest Airlines Web site or tracking packages on the UPS Web site are examples of B2C e-business in action. One business using the Internet to purchase goods and services or complete other transactions with another business is an example of **business-to-business (B2B)**. An example of a B2B activity is when a company's purchasing manager goes online to buy materials using a vendor's Web site. B2B transactions make up the majority of e-business dollars spent. An organization might also use the Internet for **business-to-employee (B2E)** functions, such as connecting its employees to its Human Resources system. Finally, when a consumer uses the Internet to conduct business with another consumer, the e-business model being followed is **consumer-to-consumer (C2C)**. A collector purchasing a collectible item from another individual through an auction Web site is an example of C2C e-business activity.

E-Business Models

Model	Description
B2C	Consumers interacting with an online business
B2B	Businesses using the Internet to purchase goods and services or complete transactions with other businesses
B2E	Companies connecting with and providing services for their employees
C2C	Consumers conducting business with other consumers

Figure 1-9   E-business models can be classified by the parties involved in the transaction.

The Dark Side of the Internet

In addition to its many valuable uses, the Internet also has a dark side. The qualities that make the Internet and the Web so powerful also make them vulnerable to misuse. Because anyone can publish Web pages and make his or her page content appear credible, even ideas that may be illegitimate, biased, or unfounded can garner a huge audience.

The vast informational resources of the Web also include adult-oriented Web sites and hate Web sites. Adults and children may stumble across them or other Web pages with objectionable material. The ease of communicating over the Internet also makes it easy for destructive computer programs to spread quickly and widely. The anonymity provided by the Internet makes it possible for criminals to steal credit card numbers, break into computers, engage in identity theft, or frighten others by **cyberstalking**, which is threatening or harassing people over the Internet.

For more information on the dark side of the Internet, visit the Book Companion Web site at **www.cengagebrain.com**. Under the Chapter 1 @Issue links, click the links for The Dark Side of the Internet.

History of the Internet

Although the Internet and the Web are based on continually evolving technologies, millions of people now consider both to be indispensable, and their influences permeate almost every aspect of society. In this section, you will learn about the origins of the Internet and the Web and the factors that spurred their growth.

Origins in ARPANET

The Internet traces its origins to the early 1960s, when several seemingly unrelated circumstances led to the development of the world's first computer network. The development of this network resulted from a collaboration among academia, industry, and government.

In the early 1960s, computers had been used for only a few years, and not by the general public. Roughly 10,000 computers existed, many of which were mainframes used by the U.S. government to perform specific, mission-critical work for the Census Bureau, the Pentagon, and other government agencies.

The Soviet Union's 1958 success in launching Sputnik, the first space satellite, fueled concerns that the United States was falling behind its Cold War competitors in the realm of science and technology. Furthermore, the U.S. government was concerned that existing computer systems were vulnerable to nuclear attack. The government decided that, for the sake of national security, it was important to connect computers so they could distribute computing power and data to more than one location, rather than having them centralized and thus vulnerable to attack.

The U.S. government initiated a push for scientific advances and charged the Department of Defense (DoD) with creating the **Advanced Research Projects Agency (ARPA)**. In 1962, J.C.R. Licklider, formerly of the Massachusetts Institute of Technology (MIT), was appointed to head ARPA's computer and information processing research efforts. Licklider wrote a series of memos outlining his vision of a Galactic Network of interconnected computers, wherein users could share data and resources from around the world. His memos were the first published references to the idea of the Internet as it is now known.

In the early 1960s, the telephone system's vast network of cabling covered all parts of the United States. Telephone systems work by using a technology known as circuit switching. **Circuit switching** allows a caller to dial a number to establish and maintain a private circuit across the wires from the time the receiver is lifted until one of the parties hangs up. At the time, circuit switching seemed to be the only method to connect two or more remote computers and exchange data.

In 1961, Leonard Kleinrock (Figure 1-10), a scholar at the University of California, Los Angeles (UCLA), wrote his doctoral dissertation and outlined the idea of data networking and packet switching, in contrast to circuit switching. Instead of sending data in a continuous stream over a dedicated circuit like a telephone company does, **packet switching** involves separating data from a sending computer into small units known as **packets**, sending each packet independently over cables, and then reassembling the packets on the receiving computer. Each packet can even follow different routes to its destination. According to Kleinrock, packet switching would make the network more robust and less vulnerable to attack because the data would move in individual packets over different routes, rather than over a single dedicated connection.

Figure 1-10 Leonard Kleinrock, shown here with the first ARPANET node, helped to develop packet-switching technology.

@SOURCE

For more information about Leonard Kleinrock and Douglas Engelbart, visit the Book Companion Site Web page at **www. cengagebrain.com**. Under the Chapter 1 @Source links, click a link for Kleinrock and Engelbart.

A brief experiment in 1965 connected a computer in Massachusetts to a computer in California. The experiment demonstrated two things: (1) It was possible to run programs and share data on a remote computer, and (2) telephone circuits were too slow and unreliable to support data and resource sharing. Kleinrock convinced ARPA to use packet switching instead, and, in 1966, the effort to create the new network of computers, based on a plan developed by Lawrence G. Roberts at ARPA, was launched. The new network was named **ARPANET**.

With government funding, the ARPANET team began work in earnest. Because of Kleinrock's research, the team chose the computer at UCLA to be the first computer on ARPANET. The team then selected the computer at the Stanford Research Institute (SRI) in Menlo Park, California, headed by Douglas Engelbart, as the second. Next, the government awarded a contract to Bolt Beranek and Newman (BBN), a company in Cambridge, Massachusetts, to create the programming, design, and hardware for the refrigerator-sized switches called IMPs (Interface Message Processors) that would be used to send the packets of data.

On September 2, 1969, representatives from BBN delivered the first IMP to the UCLA lab. Too large to fit into the elevator, the IMP had to be hoisted through a window to the third-floor computer room. About 20 people from the government, the telephone company, and the university watched as a gray cable connected the mainframe to the IMP, and the packets flowed perfectly. Kleinrock said later, "We didn't think of this as a key event in any historical sense. We didn't even have a camera."

On October 29 of the same year, the second IMP was delivered to SRI and the connection was initiated over telephone lines. At UCLA, a student named Charley Kline began to log on, as Kleinrock watched. Kline typed the letters, L-O-G — and then the new network crashed. After a quick fix, the first packets were flowing from computer to computer.

By December 1969, the University of California Santa Barbara and the University of Utah joined the ARPANET network, making these four university connections the foundation of the global network known today as the Internet.

Growth and Development of ARPANET

As quickly as BBN could create the necessary hardware, more computers, or hosts, were connected to ARPANET. Thirteen research centers had joined ARPANET by the end of 1970. It grew steadily during the next 15 years, roughly doubling in size every year. The first international connections were made to England and Norway in 1973, and other nations came online in the late 1980s and early 1990s.

During those early years, programmers had to make constant changes to programs and hosts on the new network because no common communications protocol was in use. In 1972, Robert Kahn and Vinton Cerf (Figure 1-11) developed two new protocols for ARPANET, TCP and IP, which solved these and other problems. **Transmission Control Protocol (TCP)** provided flow control over the network and error checking for lost packets; **Internet Protocol (IP)** addressed and sent the packets. In 1983, DARPA (Defense Advanced Research Projects Agency) mandated the use of this suite of communications protocols, referred to as TCP/IP. Since then, every computer and device connected to the Internet has been required to use TCP/IP to communicate.

Figure 1-11 Internet pioneers (from left) Vinton Cerf, Lawrence Roberts, Robert Kahn, and Tim Berners-Lee.

Originally, researchers used ARPANET to log in to and use the computing power of remote computers and to share files. It was not long, however, before the network was used more often for interpersonal communication. In 1971, the first live computer-to-computer chat took place between Stanford University in California and BBN in Massachusetts. Late in 1971, Ray Tomlinson, a scientist at BBN, developed the first e-mail program that could send and receive messages to and from remote computers (Figure 1-12). He is also credited with the use of the @ symbol in e-mail addresses. E-mail instantly became popular among researchers because it allowed them to collaborate on the continual development of ARPANET. By 1973, e-mail constituted 75 percent of the data traffic over ARPANET.

Figure 1-12   The two computers between which the first e-mails were sent.

@SOURCE

To learn more about the first network e-mail message, visit the Book Companion Site Web page at **www. cengagebrain.com**. Under the Chapter 1 @Source links, click the links for First Network E-Mail Message.

@SOURCE

To learn more about the history of the Internet, visit the Book Companion Site Web page at **www. cengagebrain.com**. Under the Chapter 1 @Source links, click the links for History of the Internet.

In 1975, the first mailing list, titled SF-Lovers, for science fiction fans, was created. A **mailing list** allows participants to send a single message to the list, which then automatically routes the message to every other participant.

Beyond Research, to the Public

Several factors led to the burgeoning growth of the new network. The academic community established networks, such as Usenet (1979) and BITNET (1981), which were open to all members of the academic community and were not restricted to the computer science researchers involved in the Internet. Furthermore, with the introduction of the Apple II, Macintosh, and IBM PC computers, many more members of the general public began to use computers daily, mostly for business use, although home personal computers were becoming more popular. Most people had no access to the Internet until 1979, when CompuServe first offered a subscription service for sending electronic mail (as it then was called). The following year, CompuServe also made real-time chat available to subscribers.

In 1985, the National Science Foundation (NSF) established a new network called NSFNET. NSFNET connected five regional supercomputer centers at Princeton University; University of Pittsburgh; University of California, San Diego; University of Illinois; and Cornell University using high-speed connections. In 1987, then-Senator

Al Gore called for a national computer network for research, and sponsored a bill to fund research that would enhance the speed of the Internet **backbone**, the main long-distance lines and the hardware that connect computers to the Internet. By 1990, NSFNET super-seded ARPANET as the main network linking universities and research facilities, and the military portion became a separate network called MILNET. When NSFNET was opened to the entire academic community, the number of universities, K–12 schools, and community colleges connected to the Internet increased significantly.

Commercial activity on NSFNET was prohibited by law until 1992, when the U.S. Congress changed the law to allow commercial activity over the network. From that point, commercial activity over the network exploded. In 1995, the NSF moved the connections from the original NSFNET backbone to a commercial Internet backbone supported by commercial network providers, such as MCI and AT&T. In the mid-1990s, the Internet became easier for people to use when the long series of numbers originally used to identify computer hosts were replaced with English-language names, such as www.cengagebrain.com.

The Beginnings and Rise of the Web

Two additional events that occurred in the early 1990s were pivotal in the commercial explosion of the Internet. Paul Lindner and Mark McCahill, graduate students at the University of Minnesota, invented a new protocol to form a hierarchical directory-based system to deliver information across the Internet. They named the system **Gopher** after the university's mascot. For the first time, users could navigate easily through online text resources by clicking directory links to open folders and access files stored in those folders (Figure 1-13). Many universities quickly followed suit and created Gopher systems to catalog their online resources. Because Gopher created an index of the documents on the server, it was easy to extend Gopher's capabilities to enable searching using an early search engine.

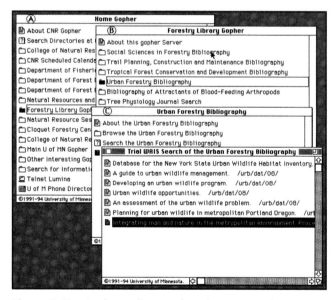

Figure 1-13   Gopher, a directory-based system, made it easier to find documents on servers connected to the Internet.

During that same period, Tim Berners-Lee, who was working at CERN in Switzerland, envisioned the use of hyperlinks to make connections between related ideas in separate documents. **Hypertext**, which is a system of hyperlinks that allows users to click on a word to jump to another location within the same file, was already in use. Hypertext also allowed users to link to different files in the same location, but only when an index of the links was kept in a central database. Frustrated with these limitations, Berners-Lee visualized a system in which all of the various projects at CERN could cross-reference each other easily. He wrote a proposal outlining his vision, suggesting that hyperlinked resources should not be restricted to text, but could include graphics, video, or other document elements.

With the help of his CERN colleague Robert Cailliau, Berners-Lee created three technologies to make his ideas about hyperlinked documents a reality. First, he created Hypertext Markup Language (HTML), which is a markup language that is used to create a document whose layout and content — text, graphics, and links — can be read by a special software program. Berners-Lee then created a special software program, the first browser known as WorldWideWeb (spelled with no spaces), to provide a way to view HTML documents. Finally, because document links had to refer to a specific server where the linked documents were stored, Berners-Lee devised a Web addressing system and **Hypertext Transfer Protocol (HTTP)**, a protocol that defines how HTML documents are transmitted to a browser. Figure 1-14 shows an early version of Berners-Lee's WorldWideWeb browser and HTML documents.

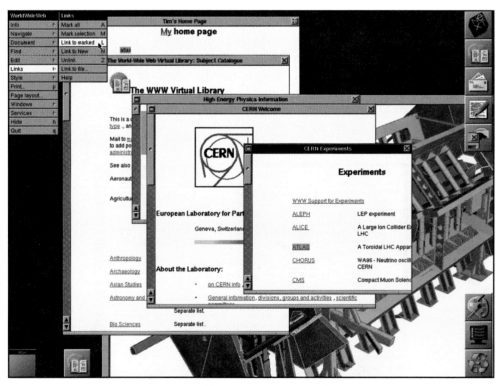

Figure 1-14 Berners-Lee's original WorldWideWeb browser and HTML documents.

@SOURCE To learn more about Tim Berners-Lee and the early development of the Web, visit the Book Companion Site Web page at **www. cengagebrain.com**. Under the Chapter 1 @Source links, click a link for Tim Berners-Lee and Early Web Development.

Programmers began developing other browsers, but the one most widely used at universities and colleges was Mosaic™. The Mosaic browser was created in March 1993 by Marc Andreessen and Eric Bina, two University of Illinois graduate students employed at the university's National Center for Supercomputing Applications (NCSA). Mosaic was easy to install and use, and free to university faculty and students, so it instantly became popular.

The next year, with businesses clamoring for a browser to use, Andreessen broke ties with the University of Illinois, which claimed ownership of the Mosaic browser. He joined with Silicon Valley entrepreneur Jim Clark to found a new company, Netscape

Communications. During the summer of 1994, the company created the first commercial browser, called Netscape Navigator.

By 1994, the Internet was growing exponentially. The growth largely was fueled by increased usage of the new World Wide Web. Commercial and individual Web sites proliferated, radio stations began broadcasting over the Internet, and companies posted the first banner ads and sent the first bulk advertising by e-mail, now called **spam**. By the end of 1994, the Web had approximately 10 million users. Today, there are almost 2 billion worldwide Internet users with access to the Web.

As commercial use of the Internet continued to grow, universities wanted to regain a high-speed network reserved specifically for research and education, much like the original Internet. In 1996, a new initiative called **Internet2 (I2)** was born. I2 is a collaboration among universities, government, and industry to develop advanced network technologies and new uses for the Internet. I2 and its Canadian counterpart, **CANARIE** (Figure 1-15), now have enlisted more than 200 universities to join with industry organizations and government agencies to collaborate on developing several new technologies: an ultra high-speed network, new streaming video technologies, an infrastructure for distributing the storage of Web resources closer to the user, and standardized software to enhance security and operation of the I2 network. Although I2 is not available for general use, the results of its research eventually will affect the general population of Internet users.

@SOURCE To learn more about Marc Andreessen and his role in the early development of commercial Web browsers, visit the Book Companion Site Web page at **www.cengagebrain.com**. Under the Chapter 1 @Source links, click a link for Marc Andreessen and Web Browser Development.

@SOURCE To learn more about Internet2 and CANARIE, visit the Book Companion Site Web page at **www.cengagebrain.com**. Under the Chapter 1 @Source links, click a link for Internet2 and CANARIE.

Figure 1-15 Internet2 (I2) and its Canadian counterpart, CANARIE, are collaborations by universities, government, and industry to develop high-speed networking technologies.

Connecting to the Internet

To enjoy all the benefits that the Internet and the Web have to offer, individuals and businesses must first connect their computers to the Internet. Some individuals rely on organizations, such as libraries, schools, and businesses, to provide access to the Internet, either through Internet-connected computers available for use, or by supplying a wireless network to which individuals can connect using their own computers. For example, most public libraries have Internet-connected computers that anyone can use and a free, non-password-protected wireless connection. College and university students generally have access to the Internet through campus networks, computer labs, and wireless capabilities. Businesses provide their employees with connected computers so that they can accomplish the tasks that have become essential to their jobs, including e-mail and file sharing.

Libraries, schools, businesses, and other organizations typically connect their computers into a **local area network (LAN)**. A LAN connects computers using cables or wireless capabilities within a building or campus so users can share data and resources, such as printers. When an organization connects its local area network directly to the Internet, all the computers on the local area network have access to the Internet. Increasingly, users can connect to the wireless Internet connections provided at airports, train stations, hotels, coffee shops, bookstores, and other businesses.

Internet Service Providers (ISPs)

A company that provides Internet access for homes and businesses is called an **Internet service provider (ISP)**. Thousands of local, regional, and national ISPs (Figure 1-16) offer a wide variety of services. An individual or a business must weigh several considerations when choosing an ISP, including the following:

- The speed or bandwidth of the connection
- The type of connection and cost of service
- The availability of customer service and technical support

 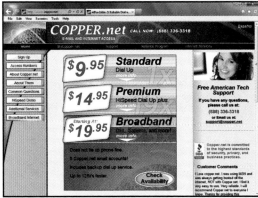

Figure 1-16   Thousands of local, regional, and national ISPs offer a variety of services.

@SOURCE

To review various ISPs , visit the Book Companion Site Web page at **www. cengagebrain.com**. Under the Chapter 1 @Source links, click a link under Internet Connections.

The speed of an Internet connection depends on **bandwidth**, which is the capacity of the communications channel. Just as the speed of travel depends on the capacity of a road — for example, whether the road is a multilane freeway or is unpaved — the bandwidth of an Internet connection defines the amount of data that can be transmitted in a fixed amount of time.

The bandwidth of an Internet connection is measured in **bits per second (bps)**. A **bit**, short for binary digit, is the smallest unit of electronic data. A bit is represented as the digit one (1) or zero (0), which is why computer processes are described using the term, digital. Thousands of bits flow each second, even over the slowest connection. Connection speeds can range from a thousand bits per second, called **kilobits per second (Kbps)**, to a million bits per second, called **megabits per second (Mbps)**, to a billion bits per second, called **gigabits per second (Gbps)**.

As noted previously, the speed of the transmission is just one factor to consider when choosing an ISP. You also need to consider how you will physically connect your computer to the Internet, whether through wireless, DSL, cable, or dial-up connections. Each of these Internet connection methods has advantages and disadvantages related to speed, cost, features, and convenience.

Many ISPs offer premium services, including a custom interface, exclusive content, e-mail, instant messaging, and space to store Web pages or photographs online. By contrast, a free ISP offers free Internet access with basic features, but requires users to view on-screen advertisements as they use the service. Between these two extremes are many other ISPs that offer simple packages with e-mail and Web page hosting services for a monthly fee.

Customer service and technical support offered by an ISP are always important factors and should be available 24 hours a day, seven days a week.

Connection Methods

Generally, local area networks are connected to an ISP through high-speed telephone lines or cable. A home computer is generally connected to an ISP using a telephone line or cable connection. Other connection methods include satellite, microwave, and wireless connections. In the following sections, you will learn about different ways to connect to the Internet.

DIAL-UP   The method for connecting to an ISP using a regular telephone line is known as **dial-up access**. Formerly the primary way home users connected to the Internet, dial-up has been surpassed by other methods, such as cable, which are faster and do not either tie up the phone line or require a second phone line dedicated to the Internet. Dial-up access is the slowest connection option, with a maximum speed of 56.6 Kbps. Dial-up access works just like a standard phone connection, except that the call connects computer devices rather than people. To use a dial-up connection, a computer must have a **modem**, which is a card or device that converts a computer's digital data to an analog signal that can be sent over telephone lines. The U.S. telephone system supports digital data, except for the short distance between the switching station and a customer's home, which often is called the last mile. Because the last mile is analog, a modem, which connects using a phone jack (Figure 1-17), still is required for dial-up access. A dial-up connection is considered a temporary connection because you must reconnect to the ISP each time you access the Internet.

Figure 1-17   Notebook phone jack.

DIGITAL SUBSCRIBER LINE (DSL)   A high-speed alternative to dial-up access is a **digital subscriber line (DSL)**. DSL condenses digital data and then sends it at high speeds over standard telephone wires. Just like dial-up, DSL uses existing telephone lines but requires a special type of modem, called a DSL modem. DSL comes in several variations; however, the DSL type used in most homes is ADSL, or asymmetric DSL. This DSL type is called asymmetric because it allows for faster data downloading than uploading.

The main advantage of ADSL is its fast speed, which is significantly faster than that of a dial-up connection. Web pages appear quickly using ADSL at download speeds ranging from 768 Kbps to 8 Mbps, and downloading music, software, and video is much faster than with a dial-up connection. ADSL uses **broadband** transmission, which means it divides the telephone wire into separate channels for sending data, receiving data, and transmitting voice calls. Because it is broadband, you can talk on the telephone while the computer is online. In contrast, **baseband** transmission, like dial-up access, allows only one channel to function at a time.

Another advantage to using ADSL is its dedicated connection. With a **dedicated connection**, the computer is always connected to the ISP and the Internet. Unlike dial-up access, there is no waiting while the computer dials up and there is no risk of getting a busy signal. A dedicated connection, however, also makes a computer more vulnerable to online intruders. For this reason, many ADSL services include a **firewall**, which is a security system that uses hardware and/or software to protect the computer from online intruders.

One disadvantage of ADSL is its lack of availability in some areas. ADSL is available only in areas close to the telephone company's local exchange, called the central office (CO). ADSL also is more costly than dial-up.

CABLE   Another high-speed Internet connection option is cable, which connects to the Internet using the same cable connection used by a cable television service. Cable access is a popular Internet connection option with many consumers who already have cable television service in their homes. Cable access, like ADSL, provides a dedicated connection to achieve maximum speeds of about 5 Mbps.

Cable Internet connections require a coaxial cable, a **line splitter** that divides the television signals from the data signals, a cable modem, and a network expansion card inside the computer (Figure 1-18). A **cable modem** is a particular type of modem used for high-speed cable connections.

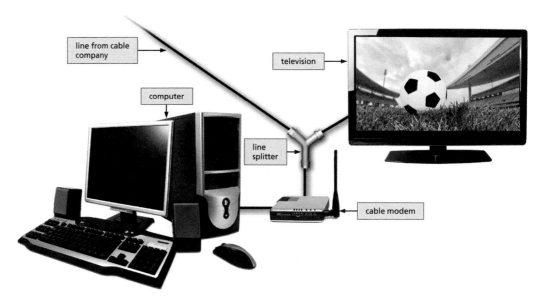

Figure 1-18   Cable Internet access requires a line splitter and cable modem.

FACTS @HAND   According to research by the Pew Internet & American Life Project, 66 percent of all U.S. adults have broadband Internet access at home.

Like ADSL, cable is asymmetric, meaning that it offers faster download speed than upload speed. Unlike ADSL, however, the Internet connection is made over a cable shared with others in the neighborhood. As more people get online, the shared connection has less bandwidth available and becomes slower for everyone. Two major companies providing cable Internet service are Time Warner and Comcast, although other local cable TV providers also might provide cable Internet service. Home service costs between $10 and $75 per month, depending on the number of Mbps you require.

FIXED WIRELESS People who live in a rural area where neither ADSL nor cable service is offered must use a wireless connection to get high-speed Internet access. Wireless Internet access offers the additional benefit of having access to bandwidth that might not be limited by the capacity of the wires or cabling.

In a home or an office, wireless Internet access is probably a **fixed wireless connection**; that is, a connection from a permanent, stationary location. Fixed wireless connections use microwaves to transmit data and require specialized outside equipment: an antenna and a small dish or receiver. Transceivers called **repeaters** relay data from the user to the service provider, called a **wireless Internet service provider (WISP)**. Microwave access depends on a rotating frequency of radio waves, and its speed ranges from 128 Kbps to 2 Mbps, depending on the traffic. Although it is available in rural areas, microwave access is limited because the user's location must be within 35 miles of the microwave tower. Furthermore, the

Figure 1-19 Microwave Internet access must be within line of sight to prevent signal interference.

Internet user's location must have a clear line of sight to the microwave tower because mountains or tall buildings will interfere with the microwave signal (Figure 1-19).

Satellite Internet access comes in two varieties: one-way and two-way (Figure 1-20). One-way satellite access uses the satellite for downloading data, and uses a slow, regular telephone line and modem for uploading data. A better alternative is two-way satellite access, which uses the faster satellite connection for both uploading and downloading data. The speed for a two-way satellite transmission is around 1 Mbps. Satellite Internet

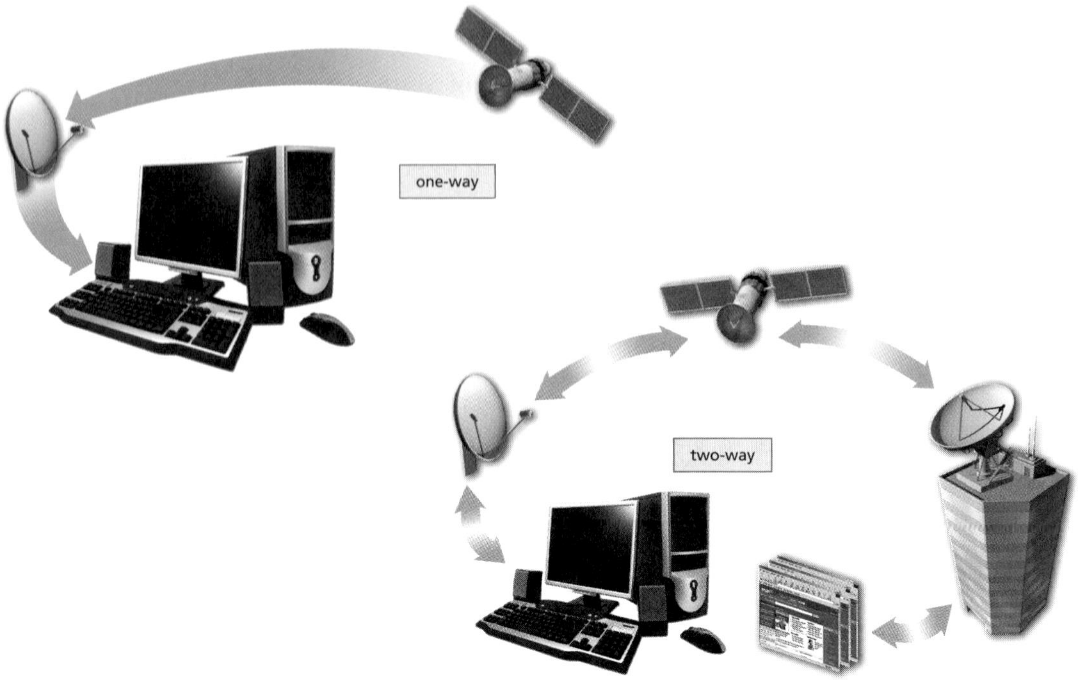

Figure 1-20 Satellite Internet access can be one-way or two-way.

access can be expensive both in monthly access fees and equipment costs, but satellite access may be the only alternative in rural areas.

Like other types of Internet connections, digital satellite has some disadvantages. Snow, rain, wind, or even clouds may affect the clarity of the signal. Furthermore, the lengthy distance to the orbiting satellites can create a significant lag in the response time. The lag is not noticeable while browsing Web pages; but for communications such as instant messaging or chat, which take place simultaneously, or in **real time**, the lag may be noticeable.

MOBILE WIRELESS As you have learned, individuals access the Internet in other places besides at home or in the office. Public libraries often make Internet-connected computers available for the public to use. Travelers can gain access to the Internet by using Wi-Fi Internet connections at airports and other public places around the world. Although Wi-Fi usage incurred a charge in the past, now it is usually free. Today, many people access the Internet using mobile broadband connections and laptop computers or handheld devices, such as smartphones and tablet computers.

FACTS @HAND According to the Pew Internet & American Life Project, nearly half of the adults in the United States get some or all of their news from their cell phone or tablet.

@SOURCE

To find more Internet statistics, demographics, and articles from the Pew Internet & American Life Project, visit the Book Companion Site Web page at **www. cengagebrain.com**. Under the Chapter 1 @Source links, click a link for Internet Statistics.

One way to connect a notebook computer to the Internet when you are away from your home or business is to rely on one of the wireless networks that use Wi-Fi technologies. **Wi-Fi** is a family of wireless networking standards that uses radio waves to allow a computer to communicate with other computers on a local area network or the Internet.

A **hotspot** is a specific geographic location in which a wireless access point provides public Internet access. Hotspots can be found in hotels, airports, restaurants, coffee shops, convention centers, and other venues where people with notebook computers or handheld wireless devices are likely to need Internet access. A hotspot typically covers a 100-foot range from the wireless access point, although some may provide a greater range. A **wireless access point** is a hardware device with an antenna that is connected to a wired network and is used to send and receive radio waves to and from notebook computers or other wireless devices.

To connect to a wireless access point in a hotspot, a notebook computer must have a Wi-Fi card or other wireless connectivity technology, such as a USB adapter, installed (Figure 1-21). After the computer is turned on, the software searches for a hotspot, and, if it finds one, connects to the Internet at speeds from 1 to 54 Mbps or higher. Wi-Fi connections can suffer interference from nearby microwave ovens or other devices using the same radio frequency.

USB wireless adapter

notebook computer with built-in wireless mobile technology

Wireless

wireless USB network adapter

Figure 1-21 A notebook computer with a Wi-Fi card or other wireless connectivity technology can connect to a wireless access point at a hotspot.

Cellular wireless providers, such as AT&T, Verizon, and Sprint, also offer **mobile broadband** Internet access. Users of mobile broadband can use a laptop equipped with a mobile data card or modem (Figure 1-22), a cell phone, a smartphone, or a personal digital assistant (PDA) (Figure 1-23) to connect to the Internet and browse the Web. The primary advantage of mobile broadband Internet access is mobility: You can access the Internet anywhere in the cellular broadband wireless provider's access area. The disadvantages of mobile broadband include the risk of poor or no reception in some areas, some restrictions on bandwidth usage, and a slightly higher cost when compared with other access methods.

@SOURCE To learn more about wireless broadband and wireless hotspots for Internet access, visit the Book Companion Site Web page at **www. cengagebrain.com**. Under the Chapter 1 @Source links, click a link for Wireless Internet.

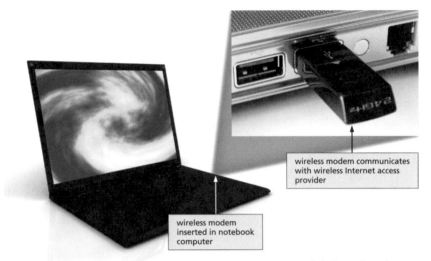

wireless modem communicates with wireless Internet access provider

wireless modem inserted in notebook computer

Figure 1-22   Computers can access the Internet using mobile broadband services offered by cellular wireless providers, such as AT&T, Verizon, and Sprint.

stylus

Figure 1-23   PDAs and smartphones can connect to the Internet using a wireless connection.

HIGH-SPEED BUSINESS CONNECTIONS   As more people use a single connection, more bandwidth is required. For this reason, businesses — even small businesses — generally need higher-speed connections than individuals and thus typically choose a high-speed Internet connection, such as DSL or cable. Business DSL or cable connections usually offer higher-speed connections than those for individuals and are more expensive. Figure 1-24 summarizes ISP and Internet connections, including advantages, disadvantages, typical connection speeds, and typical costs per month.

Internet Access Method Comparison

Method	Advantages	Disadvantages	Approximate Transmission Speeds	Approximate Cost per Month
Dial-up	• Least expensive • Available wherever there is a telephone connection	• Slowest • Cannot make telephone calls while connected • Might encounter busy signals • Might be disconnected after set amount of time	Up to 56.6 Kbps	$10–$25
High-speed dial-up	• Inexpensive • Available wherever there is a telephone connection	• See dial-up	Advertised at five to seven times faster than standard dial-up; uses faster authentication process and other techniques to improve performance over standard dial-up	$10–$25
ADSL	• High speed • Dedicated connection, so no busy signals • Always connected • No need for extra line for voice telephone calls	• Available only near telephone company central office	768 Kbps–8 Mbps downstream, 64 Kbps–1 Mbps upstream	$20–$80, plus activation fee
Cable	• High speed • Dedicated connection, so no busy signals • Always connected	• Available only where cable TV is offered • Slows down when too many neighbors are online	5 Mbps downstream, 256 Kbps upstream	$45, plus installation
Satellite	• High speed • Available everywhere	• Expensive equipment needed • Weather can interfere with signal • Potential lag time	1–1.5 Mbps downstream, 256 Kbps–1 Mbps upstream	$60–$350, plus equipment and installation
Microwave	• High speed	• Line of sight to tower required • Only available locally • Range must be within 35 miles of tower	128 Kbps to 2 Mbps downstream, 128 Kbps upstream	$50–$100, plus equipment
Wi-Fi	• High speed • Wireless • Mobility	• Limited availability • Must remain within 300 feet of receiver • Might experience interference from cordless phone or microwave oven • Requires Wi-Fi card	11 Mbps–60 Mbps	$10–$80
Mobile wireless	• High speed • Mobility	• Risk of poor or no connectivity in some areas • Bandwidth usage restrictions • Cost	600 Kbps–1.5 Mbps downstream, 500–800 Kbps upstream	$40–$60, plus additional charges per KB of data; data limits vary

Figure 1-24 Comparison of major Internet connection methods.

As businesses grow and their demand for bandwidth increases, their technology requirements also increase. Typical medium to large businesses might lease or install a fiber-optic loop directly into their building. A **fiber-optic loop** is a dedicated, high-speed telephone line that uses fiber-optic cable with T-1 or other fiber-optic technology. A leased **T-1 line** is a type of fiber-optic line that supports data transfer rates of 1.5 Mbps for hundreds of users simultaneously and costs in the range of $350 to $1,200 per month. A faster option is a T-3 line, which offers about 45 Mbps in the range of $3,000 to $12,000 per month. The largest firms requiring the highest capacity and speed use high-speed fiber-optic networks that cost many thousands of dollars a month.

Chapter Review

The Internet is a worldwide network of networks that individuals, institutions, and businesses use to communicate, share information, and conduct business transactions. People of all ages and stations in life find that using the Internet enriches their lives by allowing them to acquire useful information; send and receive e-mail; exchange instant messages; participate in online chats; exchange thoughts, photos, files, and links with others; and subscribe to mailing lists and newsgroups. Businesses conduct business transactions with their customers, vendors, and employees over the Internet.

The Web is a subset of the Internet that supports Web pages, which can include text, graphics, animation, sound, or video. A Web site is a collection of related Web pages. Web pages are interconnected by hyperlinks, which enable a user to move from one Web page to another, on the same or another Web site. A browser, such as Internet Explorer or Firefox, allows users to access and view Web pages, while a search tool allows users to find specific Web-based resources.

The Internet has its roots in ARPANET, a research and defense initiative of the U.S. government in collaboration with technology firms and universities. In 1990, NSFNET superseded ARPANET as the main government network linking universities and research facilities. The U.S. Congress opened the Internet to commercial use in 1992. Tim Berners-Lee's development of the Web in 1991 caused Internet usage to explode. Berners-Lee developed the use of hyperlinks between different files, HTML to create Web documents, the addressing scheme, and the WorldWideWeb browser. In 1994, the first commercial Web browser allowed businesses and individuals to discover the possibilities available online, and the use of the Internet expanded rapidly.

Individuals and businesses use telephone lines, cable broadband, or wireless connections to access the Internet through a wide array of methods with varying speeds and costs.

After reading this chapter, you should know each of these key terms.

Advanced Research Projects Agency (ARPA) (11)
ARPANET (12)
backbone (15)
bandwidth (18)
baseband (20)
bit (18)
bits per second (bps) (18)
blog (4)
broadband (19)
browser (5)
browsing (6)
business-to-business (B2B) (10)
business-to-consumer (B2C) (10)
business-to-employee (B2E) (10)
cable modem (20)
CANARIE (17)
circuit switching (12)
cloud computing (9)
consumer-to-consumer (C2C) (10)
cyberstalking (11)
dedicated connection (20)
dial-up access (19)
digital subscriber line (DSL) (19)
download (8)
e-business (10)
electronic mail (7)
e-mail (7)
e-mail program (7)
Extensible Hypertext Markup Language (XHTML) (5)
fiber-optic loop (26)
File Transfer Protocol (FTP) (8)
firewall (20)
fixed wireless connection (21)
gigabits per second (Gbps) (18)
Gopher (15)
host (2)
hotspot (22)
hyperlink (5)
hypertext (15)
Hypertext Markup Language (HTML) (5)
Hypertext Transfer Protocol (HTTP) (16)
Internet (2)

Internet Protocol (IP) (13)
Internet service provider (ISP) (18)
Internet2 (I2) (17)
kilobits per second (Kbps) (18)
line splitter (20)
link (5)
local area network (LAN) (17)
mailing list (14)
megabits per second (Mbps) (18)
microblogging (4)
mobile broadband (23)
modem (19)
online (2)
packet switching (12)
packets (12)
protocol (2)
published (5)
real time (22)
repeaters (21)
search tool (6)
server (8)
site (5)
spam (17)
surfing (6)
T-1 line (26)
Telnet (10)
Transmission Control Protocol (TCP) (13)
Transmission Control Protocol/Internet Protocol (TCP/IP) (2)
upload (8)
virtual private network (VPN) (9)
Web (5)
Web authoring software (5)
Web browser (5)
Web conferencing (10)
Web pages (5)
Web server (5)
Web site (5)
weblog (4)
Wi-Fi (22)
wireless access point (23)
wireless Internet service provider (WISP) (21)
World Wide Web (5)
World Wide Web Consortium (W3C) (7)

TEST YOUR KNOWLEDGE

Complete the Test Your Knowledge exercises to solidify what you have learned in the chapter.

True or False

Mark T for True and F for False. (Answers are found on page numbers in parentheses.)

____ 1. The Internet is an interconnected network of computers. (2)

____ 2. Every computer connected to the Internet uses the Transmission Control Protocol/Internet Protocol (TCP/IP). (2)

____ 3. ADSL Internet connections allow downloading and uploading of data at the same speeds. (19)

____ 4. A hotspot is a hardware device with an antenna that is connected to a wired network and is used to send and receive radio waves to and from notebook computers or other wireless devices. (22)

____ 5. Telnet is used to log in to remote computers. (10)

____ 6. The term, e-business, specifically refers to buying and selling goods over the Internet. (10)

____ 7. The person who first outlined the idea of packet switching was Leonard Kleinrock. (12)

____ 8. Telecommunications firms own the Internet. (2)

____ 9. The bandwidth of an Internet connection typically is measured in bits per second. (18)

____ 10. The Mosaic browser was created in March 1993 by Vincent Cerf. (16)

Multiple Choice

Select the best answer. (Answers are found on page numbers in parentheses.)

1. Which of the following is true about cloud computing? (9)

   a. Google Docs includes software products available for online use.

   b. Storing and sharing files online is an example of cloud computing.

   c. Cloud computing users only need a browser and an Internet connection on their computers.

   d. all of the above

2. A(n) _____ is a standard or set of rules that computer network devices follow when transmitting and receiving data. (2)

   a. FTP

   b. network

   c. WAN

   d. protocol

3. A(n) _____ is a software program used to view Web pages. (5)

   a. browser

   b. FTP client

   c. search engine

   d. Web authoring package

4. FTP is used for _____. (8)

   a. e-mail

   b. chatting and instant messaging

   c. uploading and downloading files

   d. Web conferencing

5. Web pages can be created using _____ codes or tags. (5)

   a. backbone

   b. HTTP

   c. HTML

   d. Wi-Fi

6. The B2C e-business model is when _____. (10)

   a. customers interact with an online business

   b. firms conduct business online with other firms and businesses

   c. businesses stay in contact with consultants

   d. businesses connect with their employees

7. _____ was a network linking four major universities that created the foundation for the Internet as we know it today. (12)

   a. Mosaic

   b. Gopher

   c. CANARIE

   d. ARPANET

8. The person who is credited with inventing hypertext is _____. (16)

   a. Tim Berners-Lee

   b. Marc Andreessen

   c. Vinton Cerf

   d. Leonard Kleinrock

9. A telephone Internet connection that provides a high-speed, dedicated, and always-on connection to the Internet is _____. (19)

   a. cable

   b. regular dial-up

   c. ADSL

   d. high-speed dial-up

10. _____ refers to the capacity of a communications channel. (18)

 a. bps

 b. bandwidth

 c. broadband

 d. baseband

Test your knowledge of chapter content and key terms.

Instructions: To complete the following exercises, please visit **www.cengagebrain.com**. On the CengageBrain home page, enter the book title *Discovering the Internet, Fourth Edition*, and then click the Find button. On the product page for this book, click the Access Now button below the Study Tools heading. On the Book Companion Site Web page, click the drop-down menu, select Chapter 1, and then click the link for the desired exercise.

Chapter Reinforcement TF, MC, and SA

A series of true/false, multiple-choice, and short-answer questions that test your knowledge of the chapter content.

Flash Cards

An interactive learning environment where you identify chapter key terms associated with displayed definitions.

Practice Test

A series of multiple-choice questions that test your knowledge of chapter content and key terms.

Who Wants To Be a Computer Genius?

An interactive game that challenges your knowledge of chapter content in the style of a television quiz show.

Wheel of Terms

An interactive game that challenges your knowledge of chapter key terms in the style of the television show, *Wheel of Fortune.*

Crossword Puzzle Challenge

A crossword puzzle that challenges your knowledge of the key terms presented in the chapter.

Use the Exercises to gain hands-on experience working with the Internet and the Web.

1 | Survey of Internet Usage by Students

1. According to a study by the Pew Internet & American Life Project, many students rely on the Internet to help them in their academic work. Survey five students to find out how they use the Internet for their studies. When they answer, listen to see if they mention items a through f, as outlined in Step 2.

2. Tabulate how many of the five students use the Internet for each of the following purposes:

   a. To look up information, to act as a reference library, or to get sources for reports, presentations, and projects

   b. To access podcasts, lecture notes, or other instructor-provided resources

   c. To collaborate with classmates on projects, or to study or share class notes with classmates

   d. To keep track of class schedules, assignments, and syllabi

   e. To communicate with their instructors and to submit assignments and receive feedback

   f. To participate in a class that is completely virtual, with all interactions between student and instructor, including lectures, occurring only online

3. Ask the students whether they have access to the Internet during class time under teacher direction, or only outside of class or during lab time. As a follow-up question, ask how effective they think that approach is.

4. Find out how students primarily access the Internet to do their schoolwork: school computer lab, personal computer at home or dorm, library computers, iPad or other tablet computer, or smartphone.

5. Summarize the importance of the Internet to students, according to the results of your survey.

2 | Survey of Social Networking Usage by Students

1. Survey five students who have accounts with at least one social networking Web site (Facebook, Twitter, LinkedIn, or other Web sites).

2. Ask them to list the social networking Web sites they use.

3. Ask them the frequency with which they interact with each Web site: daily, weekly, or multiple times per day.

4. Ask them to list the purposes for which they use each Web site:

   a. To keep in touch with friends and family who are far away

   b. To post pictures, videos, and links

   c. To send e-mail

   d. To chat or send instant messages

   e. To play games

   f. To post information about their thoughts, locations, or activities

5. Ask them what concerns they have about privacy, and what measures they take to protect themselves.

6. Ask them how they access the Web sites: smartphone, iPad or other tablet computer, personal laptop, or school or library computers. Are there restrictions in their school or library computer lab regarding access to these Web sites?

7. Ask them whether their overall experiences have been positive or negative. If their experiences have been negative, what specific issues have come out of their social networking activities?

3 | ISP Survey

1. Survey five people who use various ISPs, asking the following questions to determine their level of satisfaction.:

   a. How satisfied are you with the speed of your connection?

   b. Was the connection easy to set up?

   c. Have you ever had to contact technical support or billing services? Did you contact them by telephone or e-mail? Was your problem answered promptly and solved to your satisfaction?

   d. Have you had any billing troubles? How much effort did it take to resolve them?

   e. With what aspects of your ISP are you most satisfied? Least satisfied?

2. Compare the results. Determine where ISP users seem to have the most problems and where they have the best experiences.

3. Summarize whether these users are satisfied with their ISPs overall or would prefer to change to another ISP.

4. Write a paragraph analyzing which ISP seems to give the best customer service and satisfaction based on your survey.

4 | Internet History Research

1. Use written resources to learn more about the Internet's history. If you prefer, you can use links to online resources located on this book's companion Web site by visiting **www.cengagebrain.com** and entering the book title, *Discovering the Internet, Fourth Edition*, and then clicking the Find button. On the product Web page for this book, click the Access Now button below the Study Tools heading, and then click a link below Chapter 1, Exercise 4.

2. Find the names and accomplishments of two individuals not mentioned in this chapter who played key roles in the development of the Internet and the Web.

3. Write a paragraph on the origin or development of one of the following elements of the Internet:

   a. Usenet

   b. LISTSERV or mailing lists

   c. BITNET

   d. IRC

   e. hypertext

   f. any computer hardware or device used to access the Internet

5 | Internet Terminology

To perform the following exercise, you must be connected to the Internet and know how to browse and search the Web.

1. Open your browser, and go to Google or another search engine to find definitions of the following terms. If you are unfamiliar with Internet search engines, visit the Book Companion site Web page, and then click a link below Chapter 1, Exercise 5 to find definitions for the following terms:

   a. Internet

   b. Web

   c. cloud

   d. HTTP

   e. Wi-Fi

   f. blog

2. Write down each term and its definition, and note the Web source for that definition. Then write a paragraph to evaluate how effective the Web sites you used are as a resource for learning about the Internet.

6 | Internet and Web Usage Statistics

To perform the following exercise, you must be connected to the Internet and know how to browse and search the Web.

1. Visit the Book Companion site Web page, and then click the Google link below Chapter 1, Exercise 6.

   a. Using Google or another search engine, search for current Web usage articles and read at least three articles. If you are unfamiliar with Internet search engines, visit the Book Companion site Web page, and then click the Internet World Stats link below Chapter 1, Exercise 6.

   b. Write down the total Internet usage and the percentage of Internet usage growth since 2000. Identify three factors that have contributed to the growth in Internet usage.

   c. Summarize what you learned about Web usage in a brief report.

7 | ISP Research

To perform the following exercise, you must be connected to the Internet and know how to browse and search the Web.

1. Visit **the Book Companion site Web page**, and then click the link for The List: ISP Directory below Chapter 1, Exercise 7 to access the Web site for an Internet services buyer's guide.

2. Click the link to display a list of ISPs by Location/Area Code. List four ISPs for your area that offer dedicated or high-speed connections. List one specializing in being a low-cost provider. For each provider, list which services they offer: phone, Internet, cable, and cell phone. Identify which one has the best costs and most services.

3. Click the link to display a list of nationwide U.S. ISPs. List four ISPs for your area that offer dedicated or high-speed connections. For each provider, list which services they offer: phone, Internet, cable, and cell phone. Identify which one has the best costs and most services.

4. Click the link to display a list of ISPs by Country Code. Select a small country and examine the ISPs. Write down how many ISPs exist in that country, and describe what types of connections are available.

8 | Connection Speed Test

To perform the following exercise, you must be connected to the Internet and know how to browse and search the Web.

1. Visit **the Book Companion site Web page**, and then click the links below Chapter 1, Exercise 8 to view connection speed tests.

2. Try the bandwidth tests and record the results.

3. Summarize the results of the tests and explain whether the connection speeds are considered slow, average, or fast, according to the bandwidth speed test Web sites.

4. At the direction of your instructor, repeat the tests at different times of the day over several days. Write a brief paragraph explaining any variation in connection speeds among the different days and times of day.

9 | Survey of Smartphone Usage

To perform the following exercise, you must be connected to the Internet and know how to browse and search the Web.

1. Visit **the Book Companion site Web**, and then click the Bing link below Exercise 9. Search for information you can use to:

   a. Identify the demographics for the typical smartphone user.

   b. Find a list of the top five most popular smartphone applications.

   c. Find and print at least one business article published in the previous week about smartphones.

2. Develop a brief report that summarizes your findings and submit it to your instructor.

10 | Mobile Broadband Research

This activity requires outside research at the store of a cellular mobile broadband provider or at a consumer electronics store.

1. At the direction of your instructor, visit a cellular mobile broadband provider or consumer electronics store for a demonstration of how you can connect a laptop to a mobile broadband provider's broadband service.

2. Write a paragraph summarizing your visit and describing how easy or difficult it is to connect to the Internet using mobile broadband. Describe any additional hardware or software needed.

2 Browsing the Web

Introduction

Internet users rely on the World Wide Web, commonly called the Web, for access to a wealth of information, entertainment, and other resources. In Chapter 1, you were introduced to the basics of the Web: Web sites, Web pages, Web servers, and Web browsers. In this chapter, you will learn more about Web sites and the characteristics of Web pages. You are introduced to the role that IP addresses, domain names, and URLs play in locating Web pages stored on Web servers around the world. You also will learn how to use a Web browser and how to change Web browser options. Finally, you will discover the risks of browsing the Web and safeguards you can employ to protect against those risks.

Objectives

After completing this chapter, you will be able to:

1. Describe a Web site, common Web page characteristics, and Web servers

2. Explain the role IP addresses, domain names, and URLs play in locating Web pages

3. Start a Web browser and view Web pages

4. Visit Web pages using browser shortcuts

5. Save online information for later use

6. Change Web browser options

7. Discuss the risks and safeguards related to using the Web

Web Sites, Web Pages, and Web Servers

Internet Statistics
To see the latest statistics on Internet usage, visit **www. cengagebrain.com**. On the CengageBrain home page, enter the book title *Discovering the Internet* and then click the Find button. On the product Web page for this book, click the Access Now button below the Study Tools heading. On the Book Companion Site Web page, click the drop-down menu, select Chapter 2, and then click the @Source link. Click a link below Internet Stats.

@SOURCE

The Web consists of millions of Web sites and billions of Web pages. Estimating the number of Web sites and Web pages is virtually impossible because of the dynamic nature of the Web: New pages are continually being added to existing Web sites, old Web pages are being removed, and new Web sites are being published at an astounding pace. In this section, you will learn about the types of Web pages, the general characteristics of a Web page, and the role Web servers play in making these sites and pages available to people around the world.

Web Sites

The number of Web pages at a Web site varies based on the site's purpose as well as the type of content and services it provides. Web sites can consist of a single Web page or thousands of pages. Businesses use Web sites to market and sell their products and services; to promote their standing in a specific industry; and to communicate with customers, business partners, and other stakeholders. Organizations of all types, from local youth sports programs to international charities, use Web sites to inform interested parties of ongoing activities, promote their programs, and solicit contributions. Personal Web sites might include content that highlights individual or family activities, such as holiday trips, hobbies, or genealogy research.

A **home page** is the primary Web page at a Web site. A personal Web site, for example, might consist of a single home page containing relevant information about an individual or a family. Alternatively, the Web site might also include additional Web pages containing photos, a résumé, a portfolio of school projects, a list of hobbies, or other content. All of the Web pages are then linked together so visitors can move quickly among them.

The home page of a news Web site, such as www.cnn.com, offers constantly evolving content based on the latest developments around the world. To provide a variety of updated content, a news home page uses features such as tabs so users can find information on more specific topics, and slide shows or carousels, which change content every few seconds (Figure 2-1).

Figure 2-1 A news Web site uses tabs and slide shows to make it easy for users to find the content they are looking for.

Typically, the Web site for an e-business or other organization includes multiple Web pages: a home page with general, introductory information and links to a variety of related Web pages containing information about products and services, employment opportunities, the organization's history, contact information, and so forth (Figure 2-2). Many organizations also include one or more Web pages listing **FAQs (frequently asked questions)**. FAQ Web pages provide answers to questions commonly asked by the Web site's visitors.

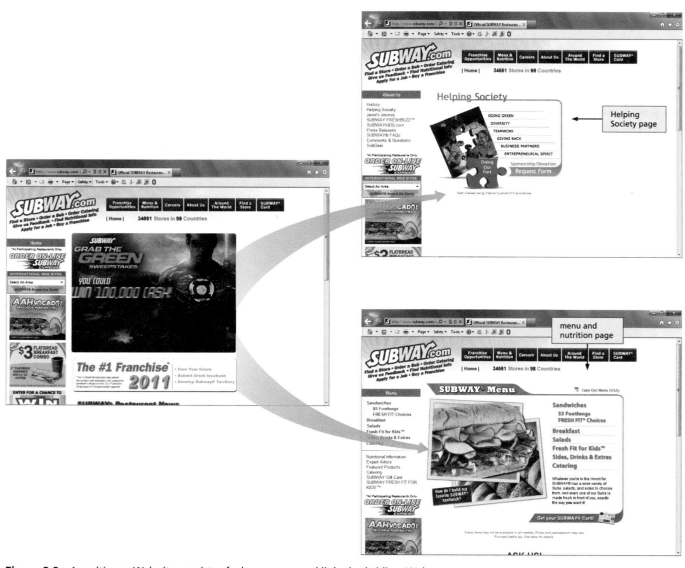

Figure 2-2 A multipage Web site consists of a home page and linked subsidiary Web pages.

A **Web portal**, or simply a **portal**, is a special type of Web site that offers a doorway to a vast range of content and services. Some Web portals are created specifically to serve as an all-encompassing starting point for visitors when they open their browsers. These types of portals generally offer local, national, and international news; weather and sports scores; access to reference tools, such as online white or yellow pages; market information and stock tickers; maps and driving instructions; links to other general-purpose Web sites; and a search tool. Web sites such as Yahoo!, AOL, and MSN are general-interest portals. Other portals, such as Golf.com or the Creativity Portal, focus on a more narrow range of information and services, and appeal to visitors with specific interests, such as golf or the creative arts.

@SOURCE

Slide Shows and Carousels
For more information about slide shows and carousels, visit the Book Companion Site Web page at **www.cengagebrain.com**. Under the Chapter 2 @Source links, click a link below Slide Shows and Carousels.

Web Pages

A Web designer's goal is to design Web pages that will attract and hold a visitor's attention so that he or she will spend time viewing and interacting with the home page or other pages on the Web site. A well-designed Web page draws a visitor to items of potential interest and includes links that lead the visitor to investigate other Web pages. Most commercial Web pages (and many noncommercial Web pages also) share some or all of the following characteristics that make them attractive, easily identifiable, and easy to use:

- A logo and/or the e-business's name, generally appearing at or near the upper-left corner of a Web page to help visitors identify the Web site
- Various images, including photographs, graphics, and animations, which make a Web site more interesting and attractive
- Links to related Web pages, often displayed as a navigation bar or group of tabs, to make accessing the Web site's other Web pages more convenient
- Advertisements, which can be text or images, to generate revenue for the Web site (Advertisements might be for the company's own products and services or from other companies that pay a fee to use the Web page space. Advertisement text or images are often links to other Web pages at the Web site, or to other Web sites.
- A search tool that allows visitors to locate specific information at the Web site
- Connectivity links or icons, which enable a user to use social networking sites to share content or access information about the company or organization
- A copyright statement notifying visitors that all the content at the Web site is protected by copyright law
- A link to a privacy and security policy statement informing visitors about the type of information collected from them at the Web site and how it is used, which is commonly found at the bottom of a commercial Web page

Figure 2-3 illustrates these common features.

Figure 2-3 Most commercial Web pages share common characteristics, such as logos, images, links, search tools, advertisements, a copyright statement, connectivity tools, and a link to a privacy and security statement.

As you have learned, Web sites and individual Web pages are dynamic, meaning they can change content, layout, and design frequently. Because of the dynamic nature of the Web, the Web pages you see on your screen as you work through the projects in this text might not look exactly like the corresponding Web page illustrations.

Web Servers

Before a Web browser can display a Web page, it must first send a request for a copy of the page to the Web server where the page is stored. The Web server responds to the request by sending a copy of the Web page to the browser. This process is an example of **client/server computing**, in which a client, the Web browser, requests services from another computer, the Web server.

Typically, a **client** is an application that runs on a computer, such as a personal computer, and requests resources or services from another computer. A server is a computer that "serves up," or provides, the requested resources or services. A server might be located in the same building, in a nearby building, or, in the case of a Web server, anywhere in the world.

A single Web server can store or host many small Web sites. For example, hundreds of students at a college or university can create personal Web sites and store them on the university's Web server. Larger Web sites, such as those created by e-businesses or other organizations, may be stored across multiple Web servers.

IP Addresses, Domain Names, and URLs

For a Web browser to request a Web page, it must use the domain name and URL to find the IP address where the Web page is stored. In this section, you will learn how an IP address is structured, how the Domain Name System (DNS) and domain names are used, and the components of a Uniform Resource Locator (URL).

IP Addresses

An **IP address (Internet Protocol address)** is a number that uniquely identifies each computer or device connected to the Internet. Just as a postal service relies on mailing addresses to ensure that mail is delivered to the correct recipient, the Internet relies on a computer's unique IP address to ensure that data is sent to the correct computer or device. An IP address consists of four groups of numbers, each separated by periods, or dots. For example, the IP address, 69.32.133.79, is the IP address of a Cengage Learning Web server. Cengage Learning is the parent company of Course Technology, the publisher of the Shelly Cashman Series books. If a user types 69.32.133.79 into the Address bar of his or her browser, the user will reach www.cengage.com (Figure 2-4 on the next page).

Computers that are always connected to the Internet, such as Web servers or personal computers with a broadband connection, may have a permanent or **static IP address** that seldom changes. A personal computer at home or at the office must have an IP address when it is connected to the Internet. Computers that connect to the Internet through a temporary connection, such as dial-up, are generally assigned a temporary or **dynamic IP address** for the duration of the connection.

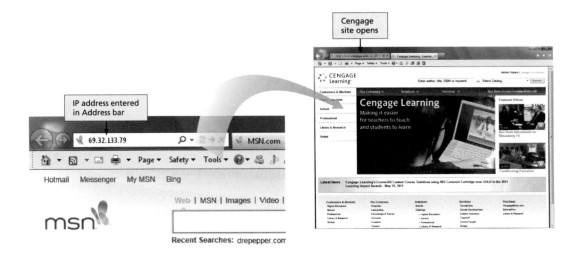

Figure 2-4 An IP address is the numeric equivalent of a URL.

IP addresses are actually stored as binary numbers, meaning they are stored in bits and bytes. IP addresses, such as the Cengage Learning address mentioned previously, are stored in a 32-bit format, consisting of four numbers ranging from 0 to 255, separated by dots. This format, known as IPv4, limits the number of unique IP addresses to about 4.3 billion. Since the mid-2000s, IPv6, which uses 128-bit IP addresses, has been in widespread use, allowing for many more individual IP addresses at once.

Domain Names

Because complex, numeric IP addresses are difficult for people to remember, Web servers typically are referenced by a domain name. A **domain name** is a text alias for one or more IP addresses. The domain name cengage.com, for example, corresponds to the IP address, 69.32.133.79 . When a domain name such as cengage.com, is entered into the browser, the browser must look up the corresponding IP address by requesting the IP address from a name server. A **name server** is a server that contains databases with domain names and the numeric IP addresses to which they correspond. The DNS name server translates or "resolves" the domain name to its numeric IP address, and returns the IP address to the browser so that the request for a Web page then can be sent to the Web server where the Web page is stored. Name servers are part of the **Domain Name System (DNS)**.

You can find the numeric IP address that corresponds to a domain name by using the nslookup command. To use the nslookup command, click the Start button, and type nslookup in the search box. Click nslookup in the search results list to open the nslookup command prompt dialog box. Type a domain name after the > prompt and press the ENTER key. The IP address or addresses associated with the domain name will appear.

Because domain names must be unique, domain names are registered, much like trademarks. The organization that oversees naming and numbering functions in the

DNS and controls the domain name registration system is the **Internet Corporation for Assigned Names and Numbers (ICANN)**. ICANN is a nonprofit organization that currently operates under the auspices of the U.S. Department of Commerce.

Domain names are grouped by **top-level domain (TLD)**, which is an abbreviation that identifies the type of organization associated with the domain. Originally, only seven generic top-level domains, including .com, .edu, and .org, were created. Today, there are many more top-level domains, as shown in Figure 2-5. Each nation of the world also has its own **country-code top-level domain (ccTLD)**, such as .us for the United States, .ca for Canada, and .uk for the United Kingdom.

@SOURCE

ICANN
To learn more about ICANN, visit the Book Companion Site Web page at **www. cengagebrain.com**. Under the Chapter 2 @Source links, click the link for ICANN.

Top-Level Domains

TLD Abbreviation	Type of Domain	TLD Abbreviation	Type of Domain
.com	Commercial firms	.aero	Aviation industry
.edu	Educational institutions	.biz	Businesses
.gov	Government entities	.coop	Cooperatives
.mil	U.S. military	.info	All uses
.net	Major networking centers	.museum	Museums
.org	Nonprofit organizations	.name	Individuals
.int	International organizations	.pro	Credentialed professionals
.mobi	Mobile products and services	.jobs	Human resources professionals
.travel	Travel industry	.asia	Pan-Asian and Asia Pacific community
.tel	Business and individual contact information	.cat	Catalan linguistic community

Figure 2-5 Domains in the DNS are grouped by type of organization or sponsoring group.

Uniform Resource Locators (URLs)

Each Web page also has its own unique address. A **Uniform Resource Locator (URL)** is a unique address, sometimes called a **Web address**, that identifies an individual Web page or other Web-based resource. A URL has several components, as shown in Figure 2-6.

Figure 2-6 A URL includes a protocol and a domain name. Some URLs also include the path and file name.

The first part of the URL is http://, the protocol or set of rules used to transmit a Web page from a Web server to a Web browser. The second part of the URL is the name of the server hosting the Web page and generally consists of the www Web server designation and the server's domain name, such as website.com. A URL also can contain the path to and the file name of a specific Web page. For example, in Figure 2-6, the path is /path/ and the file name is webpage.htm. When a user types a URL in a browser, the http:// protocol and the www designation are optional. For example, entering either http://www.cengage.com or cengage.com in a browser loads the Cengage Learning home page in a browser. When a user types a URL without a specific path and file name, the Web page returned to the browser is generally the Web site's home page.

Domain names are not case sensitive, meaning they can be entered in a browser in either uppercase or lowercase characters. For example, entering any of these three domain names — cengage.com, Cengage.Com, or CENGAGE.COM — in a browser accesses the same Cengage Learning home page. On some Web servers, however, the path and file name might be case sensitive, which means a Web page will not be located if the path and file name are entered in the browser incorrectly.

Web Browsers

As you learned in Chapter 1, a Web browser is a software program used to access and view Web pages. The most widely used browser for personal computers in home and business settings is Microsoft's Windows Internet Explorer. Appendix A provides an overview of other popular browsers, such as Mozilla Firefox®, Opera™, Google Chrome™, and Safari®. The browser illustrations in this text use Internet Explorer version 9. Figure 2-7 illustrates the Windows® Internet Explorer® 9 (IE 9) browser window.

The features within Internet Explorer 9 that help users browse the Web include the:

- Home page, which is a single Web page or group of tabbed Web pages that load when the browser starts
- **Display area**, which contains the Web page requested from a Web server
- Back and Forward buttons, which are used to revisit recently viewed Web pages
- Address bar, which contains a text box in which a URL or search keywords are typed; the Search button, which initiates a search based on what the user enters in the Address text box; the Show Address bar Autocomplete button, which provides a drop-down menu of previously viewed and favorite Web sites; the Refresh button, which requests a fresh copy of the current Web page from the Web server; the Compatibility View button, which appears only if there are compatibility issues and is used to fix issues in Web pages designed for previous browser versions; and the Stop button, which halts the download of a requested Web page

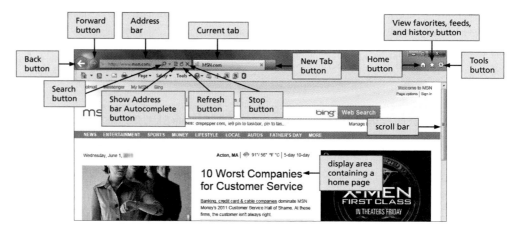

Figure 2-7 The Internet Explorer 9 (IE 9) Web browser contains features for convenient Web browsing.

- Home button, which reopens the home page(s) or changes the home page setting
- 'View favorites, feeds, and history' button, which opens the Favorites Center pane, containing lists of frequently viewed Web pages and a History list
- Tools button, which allows you to print, zoom, specify safety options, and set other browser settings
- Tabs for each open Web page
- New Tab button, which is used to open an additional Web page in a new tab
- Scroll bar, which appears whenever a Web page is too long or wide to fit in the display area

The Command bar (Figure 2-8) is an optional, customizable toolbar that contains the:

- Home button, which reopens the home page(s)
- Home button arrow, which changes the home page settings
- Add Web Slices or Feeds buttons, which is used to subscribe to Web-based content
- Read mail button, which opens your e-mail client software
- Print button and Print button arrow, which is used to preview or print a Web page
- Page button, which is used to set preferences for viewing Web pages
- Safety button, which is used to set privacy and security preferences
- Tools button, which is used to access other Web browser options
- Help button, which opens the Internet Explorer Help window
- Connectivity tools, which allow you to add a Web page to your blog, send an instant message, or use OneNote (These tools might not appear on your Command bar).

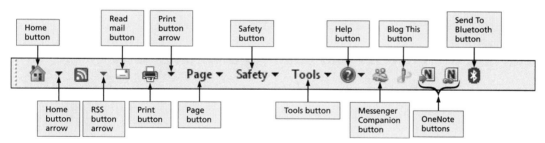

Figure 2-8 The Command bar is an optional toolbar.

You will learn more about how to use the Command bar buttons and other Internet Explorer browser features as you work through this and the remaining chapters in this text.

Internet Explorer v. 9.0 has several new features that make browsing, searching, and using tabs even easier (Figure 2-9 on the next page).

Internet Explorer 9 features

Feature	Description
Pinning sites to the taskbar	Enables you to create an icon on the taskbar that you can click to open a site in Internet Explorer.
Searching in the Address bar	In addition to entering URLs, you can also enter search keywords. When you press the ENTER key, the search results are displayed.
Using the Download Manager	Provides a list of files you download, and their level of security, location, and download status.
Tracking Protection	Keeps your information private by not allowing sites on a certain list to track any information or search criteria you enter.
ActiveX Filtering	Enables you to block ActiveX scripts from running on certain sites.
Notification bar	Provides information in a bar at the bottom of the screen, such as download status, enabling you to continue browsing.

Figure 2-9 List of Internet Explorer 9 new features.

Q&A

Why are some elements in my browser window different from the illustrations in this text?
The Internet Explorer browser has a number of features that might be visible or hidden, such as the menu bar, the Favorites bar, and the Favorites Center pane. You will learn how to work with these features later in the chapter. For now, you can press the ALT key to hide or display the menu bar, right-click the title bar, and then click an option such as the Command bar shortcut menu to show or hide toolbars.

Internet Explorer has other features that might appear in the browser window, such as a menu bar, the Information bar, and the customizable Favorites bar. The menu bar contains menus of commands you can use to open, close, and print Web pages; cut, copy, and paste Web page content; create and manage favorites; and get Help. The Information bar appears at the bottom of the screen when necessary to provide security information, such as a Web site's attempt to download and install a file on your computer or to indicate a blocked pop-up window. The Favorites bar contains various types of Web page shortcuts. Therefore, as you work through the projects in this text, your browser window might not look exactly like Figure 2-7 or other browser illustrations.

Starting the Browser and Loading a Web Page

To open your Web browser, double-click the browser icon on the Windows desktop or click the browser's program icon or name on the Start menu. The browser opens with its starting or home page. The home or starting page can be any Web page. For example, many colleges, universities, and businesses use their organization's Web site home page as their home page. Many individuals use a portal Web site for their home page. The MSN portal Web page is the home page for illustrations in this text. You will learn more about changing the home page later in this chapter.

After the browser opens, you can type the URL of the Web page you want to visit in the Address box on the Address bar and press the ENTER key. Depending on the speed of your Internet connection and the contents of the Web page, it might load very quickly or it might take several seconds to load. For example, a Web page with numerous graphics might take longer to load than a Web page with few or no graphics. The status bar at the bottom of the browser window displays information about the loading process: the URL of the Web page being loaded and a progress bar showing the duration of the loading process.

To Open Your Browser and Load a Web Page

The following steps open the Web browser, type a URL in the Address box, and press the ENTER key to load a Web page in the browser window. These steps use the Internet Explorer v. 9.0 browser. If you are using a different browser, your instructor will modify the steps.

- Click the Start button on the Windows taskbar (Figure 2-10).

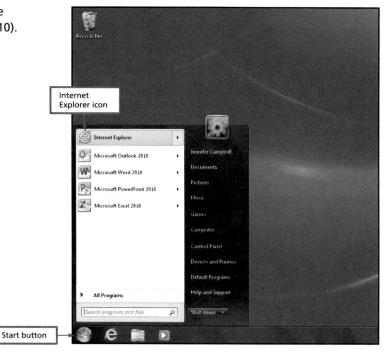

Figure 2-10

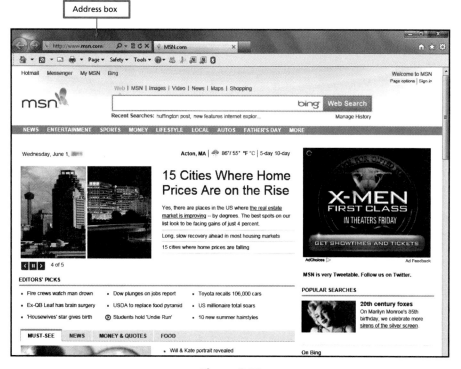

- Click the Internet Explorer icon on the Start menu, or click All Programs, and then click the Internet Explorer icon if it is not pinned to the Start menu to open Internet Explorer (Figure 2-11).

Why is my home page different?
A default home page is specified when a browser is installed. Users typically replace this home page with one or more other Web pages to suit their needs. You will learn more about changing the home page settings later in this chapter. Even if you have MSN as your home page, the content of this page will differ.

Figure 2-11

- Click in the Address box on the Address bar.

- Type **www.cengage.com** as the URL (Figure 2-12).

Q&A

Why do I see a list below the Address bar as I type the URL?

Internet Explorer remembers URLs you have previously typed and also provides Web page suggestions based on the URL you are currently typing, both of which appear in the Address bar drop-down list. You will learn more about using the Address bar drop-down list later in this chapter. Your Address bar drop-down list might look different.

Figure 2-12

④

- Press the ENTER key to open the Cengage home page (Figure 2-13).

Figure 2-13

5

- Click the Buy, Rent, Access CengageBrain.com link to open the CengageBrain Web site in your browser (Figure 2-14).

Figure 2-14

Other Ways

1. Double-click Internet Explorer icon on desktop or taskbar
2. Click Internet Explorer icon in All Programs list on Start menu

Using a Web Page Search Feature and Clicking Links

Many Web sites include a keyword search feature to allow you to find a specific Web page within a Web site. You can type keywords in the search feature's text box and then click a Search button to find Web pages at the Web site that contain those keywords. You will learn more about keyword searches in Chapter 3. Some Web sites, such as The Weather Channel's, have special search tools designed to find information organized by common categories, such as ZIP code, city, or state. Others, such as CengageBrain, allow you to type general information, such as a topic or author name, or narrow your results to be more specific, such as by typing an ISBN.

@ISSUE Pop-Up Blocker

As you browse the Web, you may notice a barrage of advertisements. Web advertisements can appear in pop-up windows in front of the Web page currently displayed or in pop-under windows that appear behind the browser window. Some advertisements with attention-grabbing sounds and animation, called rich media ads, even appear right in the middle of or floating across the Web page you are viewing. Most visitors consider these approaches to Web advertising increasingly invasive, distracting, and bothersome.

Blocking or filtering ads is particularly important when children are browsing the Web. According to research by Dr. Jakob Nielsen, a Web usability pioneer, children are less able than adults to distinguish between Web ads and content. When a child sees a cartoon character in an ad, for example, he or she likely will click the ad expecting to see more cartoons. Using an ad filter or blocker can help reduce the likelihood that children will click ads and navigate to Web pages selling products and services.

Most current Web browsers include a feature that blocks pop-up ads; however, other kinds of ads, including rich media ads, may still appear. To turn on the Pop-up Blocker feature in Internet Explorer, click the Tools button, and then click Internet options. In the Internet Options dialog box, click the Privacy tab, and then click the Turn on Pop-up Blocker check box if necessary.

To Use a Search Box to Find Information

The following step uses a Web site search feature to find the Book Companion Site Web page for this book. The Book Companion site Web page links to the Student Online Companion, which includes links for chapter exercises, @Source boxes, and end-of-chapter exercises. You will need to access this Web page frequently while using this text.

- Type **Discovering the Internet** in the Find your Textbook or Materials text box.

- Press the ENTER key to search for the Book Companion Site Web page for this text (Figure 2-15).

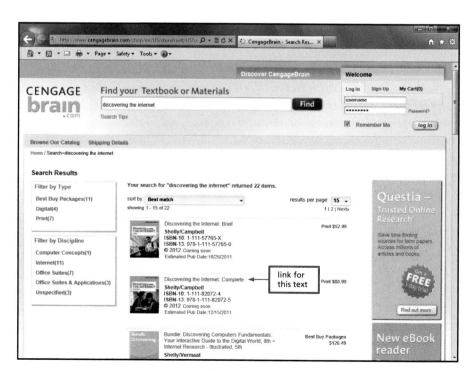

Figure 2-15

- Click the link for this text to open a new page (Figure 2-16).

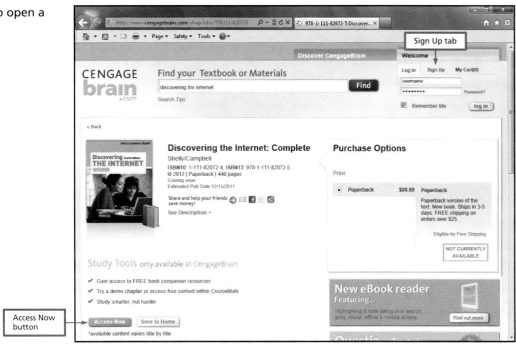

Figure 2-16

- Click the Access Now button to open the Book Companion Site Web page (Figure 2-17).

Q&A

How can I easily find the Book Companion Site Web page again?
If necessary, click the Sign Up tab in the upper-right corner of the CengageBrain home page and complete the required information, such as your name, e-mail address, and school. Follow any other instructions. Then search for the book again and click its link. Click the Save to Home button. Now when you log on to **www.cengagebrain.com**, you will have access to the Book Companion site Web page by clicking the Open button next to Free Study Tools.

Q&A

Why does an advertising window open?
If an advertising window opens with a Web page, your browser's pop-up blocker might be turned off. Alternatively, if the browser's pop-up blocker is turned on, you might see a yellow Information bar with a blocked pop-up notation at the bottom of the screen when an advertising window attempts to open. For the remainder of this chapter and in the hands-on activities in the remaining chapters in this book, you should close any pop-up, pop-under, or rich media advertising windows or, with your instructor's permission, turn on your browser's pop-up blocker feature.

Figure 2-17

A simple way to load another Web page in the browser window is to click a link on the current Web page. Web page links can be text, a graphic button, or an image. Text links generally appear underlined in a different color from other text on the Web page. It may be difficult to determine whether a graphic button or image is a link. To determine whether any Web page element — text, graphic button, or image — is a link, point to the element with the mouse pointer. If the mouse pointer changes to a pointing hand pointer and a URL appears in the status bar, the element is a link.

After a Web page loads in the browser, you then can click various links to locate additional information or use other features presented on the Web page. For example, the Book Companion Site Web page for this text has links to files and to the Student Online Companion.

To View a Web Page by Clicking a Link

The following steps display the Student Online Companion for this text and open a new window. You then use the vertical scroll bar to view the new information.

- Click the Select a chapter list arrow, and then click 2. Browsing the Web to open the resources for Chapter 2 (Figure 2-18).

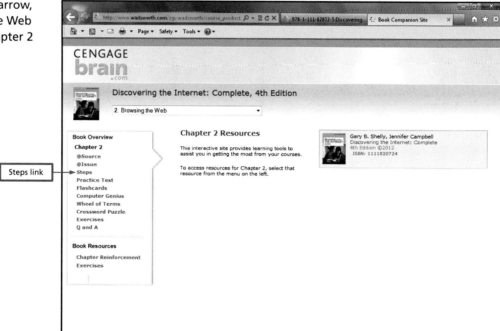

Figure 2-18

2

- Click the Steps text link to view the links for the text (Figure 2-19).

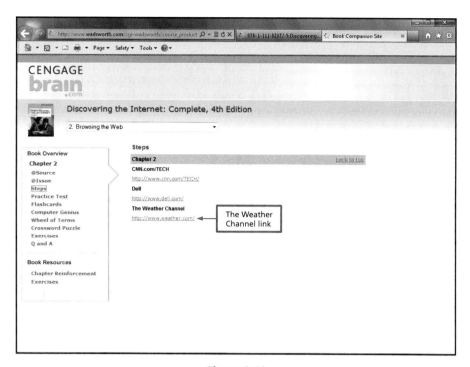

Figure 2-19

3

- Right-click the The Weather Channel link, and then click 'Open in new window' to open www.weather.com in a new browser window. Maximize the window if necessary.

- Drag the scroll box on the vertical scroll bar down to view the content at the bottom of the Web page, and then drag the scroll box on the vertical scroll bar up to view the top of the Web page (Figure 2-20).

Q&A

Can I maximize the new browser window?

Sometimes when a link opens a Web page in a new browser window, the window is minimized, meaning that it is smaller than your screen size. To maximize the window so that it fills the screen, click the Maximize button in the upper-right corner of the browser window (next to the red X Close button).

Figure 2-20

Navigating Recently Viewed Web Pages

You can use buttons in the Internet Explorer browser window to move back and forth between recently viewed Web pages, reopen the default browser home page, reopen the current Web page, and stop the process of opening a Web page. In this section, you will learn about navigating recently viewed Web pages using the Back and Forward, Refresh buttons to the left of the Address bar, the Stop and Refresh buttons in the Address bar, and the Home button on the Command bar. Later in this chapter and in Chapters 3 and 4, you will learn how to use other Internet Explorer browser features.

BACK AND FORWARD BUTTONS Clicking the Back button once returns you to the Web page you viewed immediately before the current Web page. Clicking the Forward button once returns you to the Web page you viewed before you clicked the Back button. The Back button is dimmed until you have browsed to a second Web site or Web page. The Forward button is dimmed until you have used the Back button.

STOP AND REFRESH BUTTONS The Stop button allows you to stop opening a Web page. For example, if you change your mind about viewing the Web page that is currently loading in the browser, you can click the Stop button to stop the process.

The Refresh button opens an updated or current copy of the current Web page. The Refresh button is useful when you want to reopen a Web page for which you stopped the transfer or when you need to refresh Web pages with content that changes every few minutes, such as stock quotes, weather, and news.

HOME BUTTON The Home button on the Command bar opens or refreshes the home page. You can click the Home button to view the home page at any time while you are browsing the Web. The Home button also provides a list of options you can use to reset the browser's default home page. You will learn more about resetting the browser's home page options later in this chapter.

To Navigate Through Recently Viewed Pages

The following steps use the Back, Forward, Refresh, and Home buttons in the Internet Explorer browser window.

- Verify that Internet Explorer is open with The Weather Channel home page open.

- Click any link on The Weather Channel home page to open a new Web page in the same browser window and tab.

- Click the Back button to return to The Weather Channel home page (Figure 2-21).

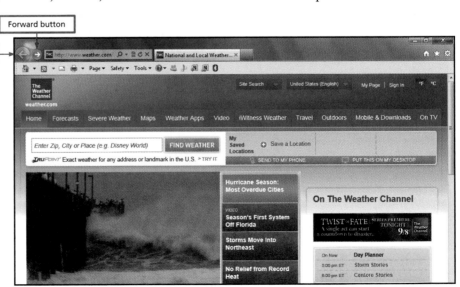

Figure 2-21

2

- Click the Forward button to return to the Web page you were viewing before you clicked the Back button (Figure 2-22).

- Click the Refresh button to open a fresh copy of the Web page to view any updated temperature or other new information on the Web page.

Figure 2-22

3

- Click the Home button to open the browser's default home page (Figure 2-23).

- Click the browser Close button to close Internet Explorer; close all tabs, if asked.

- If necessary, close any other open Internet Explorer windows.

Other Ways

1. Press ALT+LEFT ARROW to return to previously viewed Web page
2. Press ALT+RIGHT ARROW to return to Web page you were viewing before you pressed ALT+LEFT ARROW or clicked Back button
3. Press ALT+HOME to open home page
4. Press F5 to refresh Web page
5. Right-click tab and click Refresh

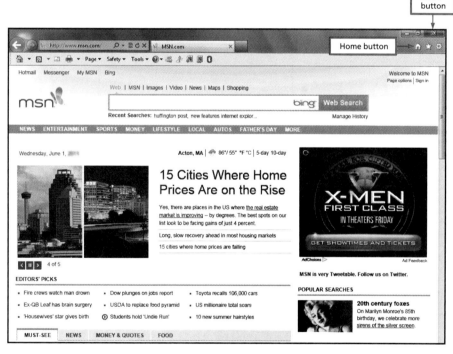

Figure 2-23

Using Tabbed Browsing

Tabbed browsing allows you to open multiple Web pages in a single browser window, as shown in Figure 2-24. Each Web page you open appears in its own tab on the tab row. The active tab appears in the foreground on the tab row and the remaining tabs appear on the tab row background. You can bring a background Web page tab to the foreground for viewing by clicking the tab. Pointing to a tab displays a ScreenTip containing the open Web page's title and URL.

The tabbed browsing feature is turned on by default. If the tabbed browsing feature is turned off, each additional Web page you open will open in a separate browser window. You will learn more about turning on or off browser features, such as tabbed browsing, later in this chapter.

Figure 2-24   Tabbed browsing allows you to open multiple Web pages in a single browser window.

You can click the New Tab button on the tab row to display a blank tab and then type a URL in the Address box to open a Web page in the new tab. You can also press the ALT+ENTER keys after you type a URL to open the Web page in a new tab. Either method places the new tab on the tab row foreground.

To open a linked Web page in a new tab, press the CTRL key as you click the link to open the tab on the tab row background, or press the CTRL+SHIFT keys as you click the link to open the tab in the foreground. To close a tab, click the Close Tab button that appears on the right side of the tab. When you close Internet Explorer, you can close all the open Web page tabs at one time.

When you click the New Tab button to create a new tab, you see a New Tab page that contains browsing options. You can show or hide a list of tabs that you closed during the current browsing session and reopen all the tabs that were open the last time you closed Internet Explorer by clicking links on the New Tab page. The New Tab page also gives you access to InPrivate Browsing. You will learn more about this feature later in this chapter.

To Open and Close Multiple Web Page Tabs

The following steps open multiple Web pages in separate tabs using the Address bar and Web page links, view and close Web pages, reopen several Web pages, and then close Internet Explorer. Next, the browser and the Web pages that were opened during the last work session are reopened.

1

- Click the Internet Explorer Browser icon on the Start menu to open Internet Explorer.

- Click the New Tab button on the tab row to open a New Tab page (Figure 2-25).

 Why is my New Tab page empty or different?
The New Tab page reflects the browsing history on your computer. Yours will show different Web sites, or it may be empty if you are new to Internet Explorer or working on a lab computer.

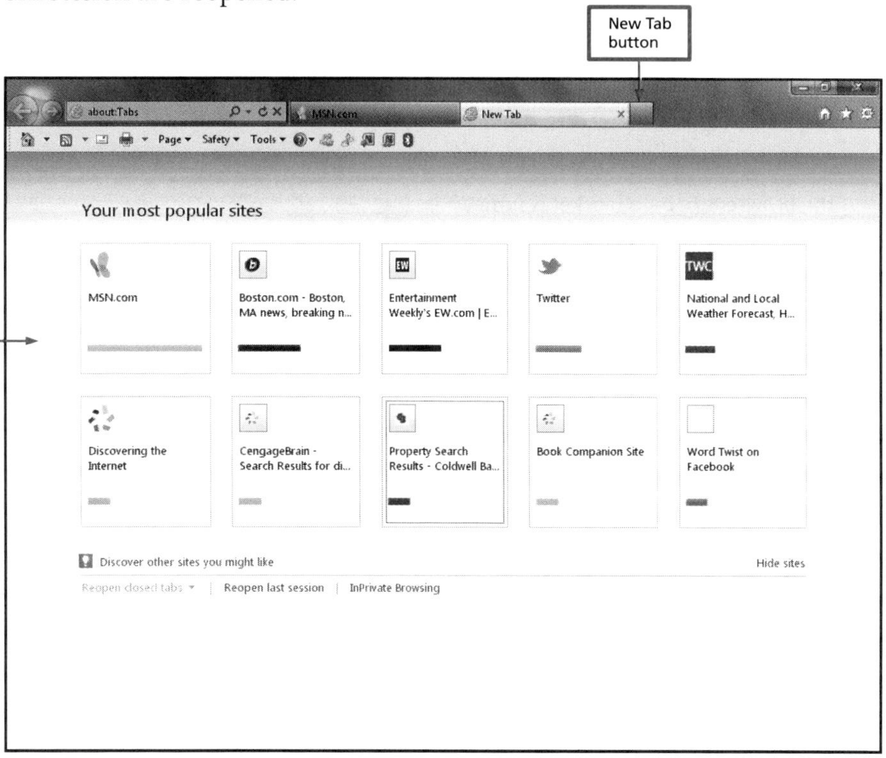

Figure 2-25

2

- Type **espn.com** in the Address box.

- Press the ENTER key to open the ESPN home page in the new tab (Figure 2-26).

Figure 2-26

- Type `nfl.com` in the Address box.

- Press ALT+ENTER to open the NFL.com home page in a new tab in the tab row foreground (Figure 2-27).

Why do I see a yellow bar at the bottom of the Web page?
If the browser's pop-up blocker is turned on, you might see a yellow Information bar with a blocked pop-up notation below the tab row when an advertising window attempts to open. Click the Close button on the bar to close it.

Figure 2-27

- Press the CTRL key and click the News link to open the NFL News Web page in a new tab in the tab row background (Figure 2-28).

new tab in background

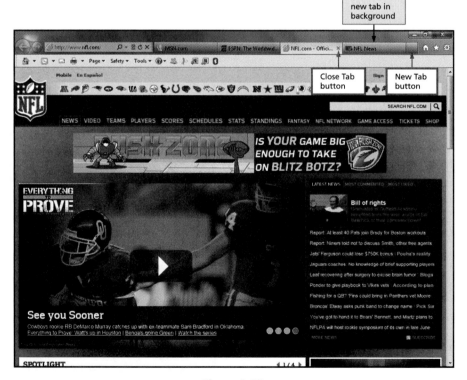

Close Tab button

New Tab button

Figure 2-28

5

- Click the NFL News tab to display the tab in the foreground (Figure 2-29).

Figure 2-29

6

- Click the Close Tab button (Figure 2-28) on the NFL News Web page tab to close the Web page.

- Click the New Tab button on the tab row to open a New Tab page.

- Click the 'Reopen closed tabs' link on the New Tab page, if necessary, to see a list of closed tabs (Figure 2-30).

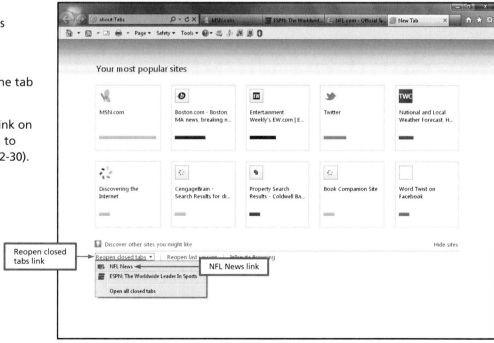

Figure 2-30

- Click the NFL News link to reopen the Web page in a new tab (Figure 2-31).

Figure 2-31

8

- Close Internet Explorer and close all tabs, if asked.

- Click the Internet Explorer Browser icon on the Start menu to start Internet Explorer.

- Click the New Tab button on the tab row to open a New Tab page (Figure 2-32).

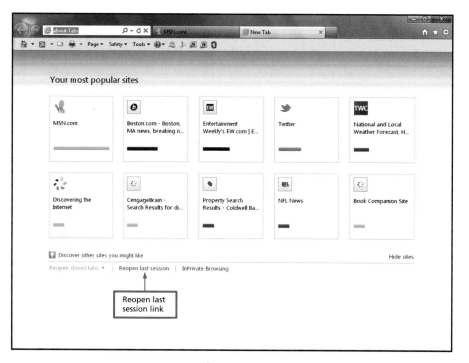

Figure 2-32

9

- Click the 'Reopen last session' link to reopen the tabs that were open when you closed Internet Explorer (Figure 2-33).

Q&A Why do I have two home page tabs? When you started your browser, you opened the browser's home page. Reopening the last browsing session opens all Web pages you were viewing when the browser was closed, including the home page.

restored tabs

Figure 2-33

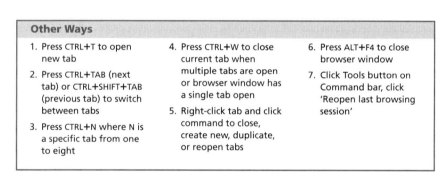

Other Ways

1. Press CTRL+T to open new tab

2. Press CTRL+TAB (next tab) or CTRL+SHIFT+TAB (previous tab) to switch between tabs

3. Press CTRL+N where N is a specific tab from one to eight

4. Press CTRL+W to close current tab when multiple tabs are open or browser window has a single tab open

5. Right-click tab and click command to close, create new, duplicate, or reopen tabs

6. Press ALT+F4 to close browser window

7. Click Tools button on Command bar, click 'Reopen last browsing session'

The tab row can display up to eight open Web page tabs; additional open Web page tabs are hidden. When Web page tabs are hidden, left and right tab scrolling buttons (small buttons with left- or right-pointing arrows) appear on the tab row. You can click a tab scrolling button to scroll to view hidden Web page tabs. Using the New Tab page, you can link to previously or frequently viewed Web pages.

To View Open Web Pages Using the New Tab Page

The following steps use the New Tab page to open a Web page.

- Click the New Tab button to open the New Tab page (Figure 2-34).

Q&A

Why does the NFL News button not appear?

If your version of Internet Explorer has been used frequently, it might not appear. Type **www.nfl.com/news** in the Address bar, and then press the ENTER key.

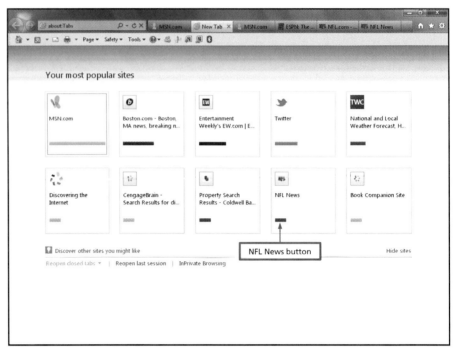

Figure 2-34

- Click the NFL News button to open the NFL News Web page (Figure 2-35).

- Close Internet Explorer and all tabs.

Figure 2-35

Using Browser Shortcuts to Visit Web Pages

As you become more familiar with Web pages and their content, you likely will want to quickly find useful Web page content, often by revisiting specific Web pages. The Internet Explorer browser provides several shortcuts for accessing Web page content and revisiting Web pages, including:

- Favorites
- History
- Accelerators
- RSS feeds and Web Slices
- Address bar drop-down list
- Suggested Sites

Favorites

A **favorite** (or bookmark) is a browser shortcut to a frequently viewed Web page. You can create a favorite, which includes the Web page's title and URL, for the current Web page by clicking the Favorites button to the right of the tab row to open the Favorites Center. Then click the Add to Favorites button.

When you want to revisit the Web page, you simply open the Favorites Center, click the Favorites tab to view your favorites, and click the desired favorite. Favorites are stored, by default, in a Favorites folder. However, you can create subfolders within the Favorites folder to better organize your favorites. For example, you could create a folder with your favorite recipes, which includes subfolders for main dishes, soups, salads, and desserts. As you create a favorite, you can replace the Web page title with a more meaningful name. When you no longer need a favorite or a favorite subfolder, you can delete it.

To Create a Favorite Subfolder and Add a Favorite

The Favorites Center pane contains the Favorites, Feeds, and History tabs. Internet Explorer also refers to these tabs as Explorer Bars. The Favorites tab provides a list of individual favorites and subfolders used to organize favorites; the History tab provides a list of visited Web pages; and the Feeds tab provides a list of RSS feeds and Web Slices to which you have subscribed. The following steps create a favorite for the Dell home page (www.dell.com) and save it in a new subfolder inside the Favorites folder. Your Favorites list will look different from the Favorites list in the figures.

• Start Internet Explorer and open the Student Online Companion Web page at **www.cengagebrain.com** by following the same set of steps as you did earlier in the chapter.

• Click the Select a chapter list arrow, and then click 2. Browsing the Web to open the resources for Chapter 2.

• Click the Steps link in the left navigation bar to open the Steps Web page.

• Click Dell to open the Dell home page in the current tab (Figure 2-36).

Figure 2-36

• Click the Favorites button to open the Favorites Center pane (Figure 2-37).

• Click the Favorites tab, if necessary, to view your list of favorites and subfolders.

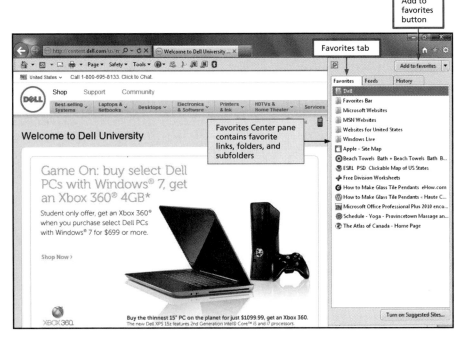

Figure 2-37

- Click the 'Add to favorites' button to display the Add a Favorite dialog box.

- Type **Dell** in the Name text box (Figure 2-38).

Figure 2-38

- Click the New folder button to display the Create a Folder dialog box.

- Type **Technology Sites** in the Folder Name text box (Figure 2-39).

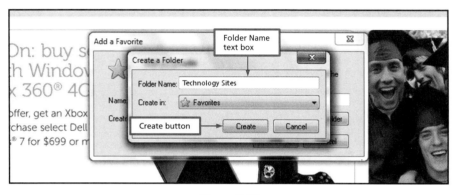

Figure 2-39

- Click the Create button to create the new Technology Sites subfolder inside the Favorites folder.

- Click the Add button in the Add a Favorite dialog box to add the Dell favorite to the new Technology Sites folder.

- Click the New Tab button to display the New Tab page.

- Click the Favorites button to open the Favorites Center.

- Click the Technology Sites folder to view its contents (Figure 2-40).

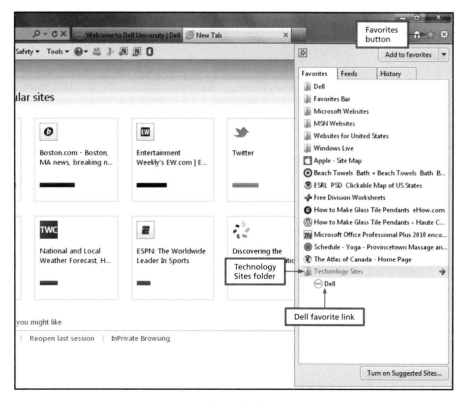

Figure 2-40

- Click the Dell favorite link to open the Dell home page in the current tab (Figure 2-41).

Other Ways

1. Click Tools button on Command bar, point to Explorer Bars, click Favorites

2. Press ALT+C to open Favorites Center, view Favorites list

3. Press ALT+Z to display Add to favorites menu, click Add to favorites

4. On menu bar, click Favorites, click Add to favorites

5. Right-click favorite in Favorites list, click Open in new tab

6. On menu bar, click Favorites, point to subfolder, if necessary, click favorite

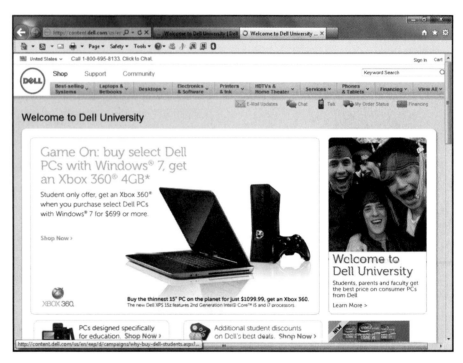

Figure 2-41

To Delete a Favorites Subfolder and Its Contents

When you no longer need a Favorites subfolder or an individual favorite, you can delete it. The following steps open the Favorites Center and delete the Technology Sites subfolder and its contents.

1

- Click the Favorites button to open the Favorites Center.

- Click the Favorites tab, if necessary, to display your list of favorites and subfolders.

- Right-click the Technology Sites subfolder to display the shortcut menu (Figure 2-42).

Figure 2-42

- Click Delete to display the Delete Folder confirmation dialog box (Figure 2-43).

- Click the Yes button to confirm the deletion.

- Close Internet Explorer.

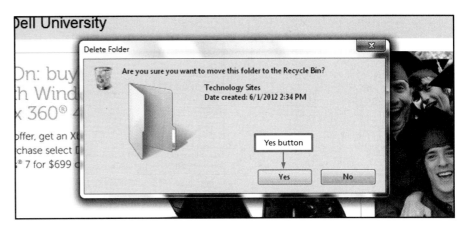

Figure 2-43

SAVING A GROUP OF TABBED FAVORITES   You can save a group of Web pages as a single favorite. First, open the Web pages in individual tabs. Then click the 'Add to favorites' button arrow in the Favorites Center pane to display the Add to Favorites menu and click 'Add current tabs to favorites.' In the Add Tabs to Favorites dialog box (Figure 2-44), type a name for the tab group's subfolder in the Folder Name text box, and then click Add.

Figure 2-44   You can add a group of open Web pages to a favorites subfolder.

ORGANIZING FAVORITES   You can manage your favorites by adding, renaming, and deleting favorites and subfolders, or by moving a favorite to another folder using options in the Organize Favorites dialog box (Figure 2-45). To open the Organize Favorites dialog box, click the 'Add to favorites' button arrow in the Favorites Center pane and click Organize favorites on the Add to favorites menu.

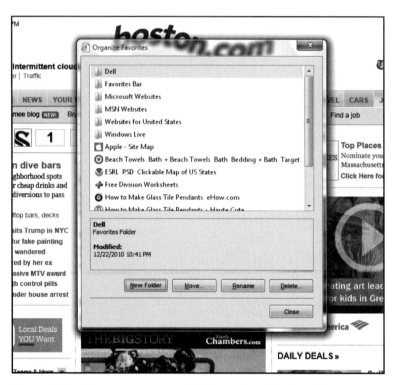

Figure 2-45 You can manage your Web page favorites by adding, renaming, and deleting favorites and subfolders, or by moving a favorite to a new folder.

FAVORITES BAR The Favorites bar is a customizable toolbar that offers a one-click method to add a favorite link to frequently visited Web pages. You also can add RSS feeds and Web Slices to your Favorites bar. You will learn more about Web Slices and RSS feeds later in this section. You can display or hide the Favorites bar by right-clicking the Command bar and clicking Favorites bar on the Toolbars shortcut menu.

SHARING FAVORITES You can share your favorites by exporting them to an HTML file, and then using the HTML file to import the favorites into another browser on the same computer or into a browser on a different computer. You also can import favorites into Internet Explorer that were created in a different browser or on a different computer. To import or export favorites, you use the Import/Export Settings Wizard, which is a series of step-by-step dialog boxes that take you through the import or export process. To start the Import/Export Settings Wizard, click the 'Add to favorites' button arrow in the Favorites Center and click 'Import and export' on the Add to Favorites menu. Then follow the wizard steps.

History

Another easy way to revisit a Web page is to use a history of the Web sites and Web pages you have visited during a specific number of days. You can display a list of these sites and pages by opening the Favorites Center and clicking the History tab.

The **History list** in the History tab displays browsing data for the number of days specified in the Internet Options dialog box; therefore, the History list might contain icons for Web sites visited several weeks ago, last week, and every day of the current week, including today. When you click one of these icons, a list of Web page folders appears — each folder represents a Web site visited during that time period. You can expand each Web site folder to view links to the individual Web pages viewed at the Web site.

You also can reorganize your view of the History list by clicking the View By Date button at the top of the list and selecting a different viewing order: By Site, By Most Visited, or By Order Visited Today. Additionally, you can search for previously viewed Web pages by clicking the View by Date button and clicking Search History.

To Revisit a Web Page Using the History List

The following steps use a link in the History list to revisit a Web page. Additionally, these steps assume all the previous hands-on projects in this chapter have been completed on the same day. If that is not the case, your instructor might modify the following instructions.

- Start Internet Explorer.

- Click the Favorites button to open the Favorites Center.

- Click the History tab to view the History list (Figure 2-46).

Q&A

Why do I have multiple collapsed and expanded week and day icons and Web site folders?
You can clear the History list and set options for the number of days to retain the browsing history in the Internet Options dialog box. Additionally, you or other users might have visited different Web sites besides those used in this text. For these reasons, your History list will likely be different from the History list illustrations in this section.

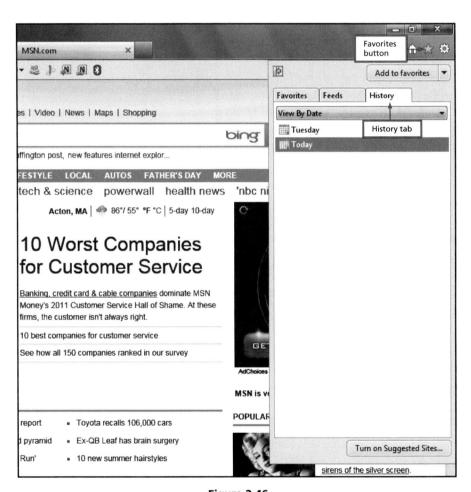

Figure 2-46

- Click the Today icon, if necessary, to expand the list of Web pages visited today (Figure 2-47).

Figure 2-47

3

- Click the nfl (www.nfl.com) folder link in the History list to view links to individual Web pages visited at the NFL Web site (Figure 2-48).

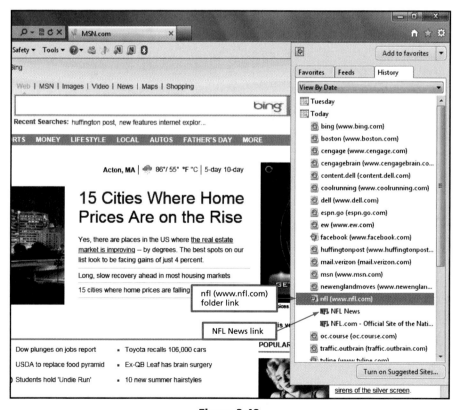

Figure 2-48

4

- Click the NFL News link to close the Favorites Center and open the NFL News Web page in the current tab (Figure 2-49).

- Close Internet Explorer.

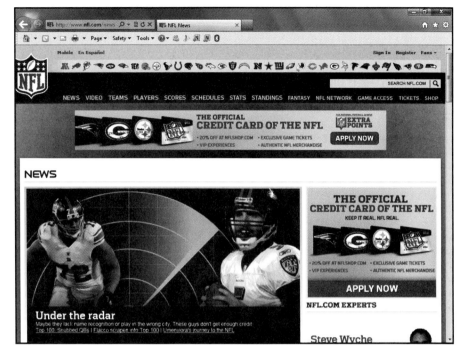

Figure 2-49

Other Ways

1. Click Tools button on Command bar, point to Explorer bars, click History
2. CTRL+SHIFT+H

Web Slices

The **Web Slices** feature allows you to quickly preview frequently updated Web page content, such as weather reports or sports scores. When you create a Web Slice, you are subscribing to an automatic feed of information from a Web site to your computer. If Web Slices are available at a Web page, a green Add Web Slices button appears on the Command bar when you open the Web page in Internet Explorer. By clicking the Add Web Slices button, you subscribe to content from the Web page, which adds a related Web Slices button to the Favorites bar.

When Web Slice content is updated, the Web Slice button on the Favorites bar is highlighted. You then can click the Web Slice button to preview the updated information and, if desired, view the updated content.

Accelerators

Accelerators are add-ons to Internet Explorer that allow you to access Web content or take some action based on selected Web page text. For example, you can select Web page text and then open an online dictionary to see a definition of the word or translate the word into another language, or use it as a search keyword — all by using an Accelerator add-on.

When you select text on a Web page, an Accelerator button appears below and to the right of the selected text. Clicking the Accelerator button displays a menu of available Accelerators (Figure 2-50). Pointing to an Accelerator on the menu might display content provided by the Accelerator, such as a word definition or a map.

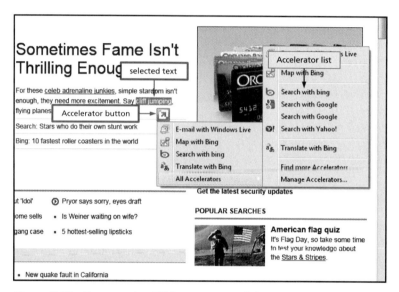

Figure 2-50 You can select Web page text and then use an Accelerator to access Web content or take some action based on the selected text.

Some Accelerators can be added on when you install Internet Explorer. You also can add Accelerators by opening the Internet Explorer 9 Add-ons Gallery: Accelerators page (Figure 2-51). To open the Gallery, click the Page button on the Command bar, point to All Accelerators, and click Find more Accelerators in the submenu. You also can add, remove, or disable Accelerators with options in the Manage Add-ons dialog box. To open the dialog box, click Manage Accelerators in the All Accelerators submenu or click the Tools button on the Command bar and click Manage add-ons.

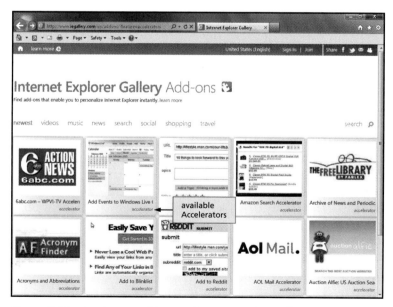

Figure 2-51 Accelerator add-ons to Internet Explorer allow you to access Web content or take some action based on selected Web page text.

RSS Feeds

A popular tool for keeping up with news headlines and other dynamic Web content is an RSS reader. An RSS reader is software that has features you can use to subscribe to and read syndicated Web site content, including blogs. RSS (Really Simple Syndication or Rich Site Summary) is an Extensible Markup Language (XML) technology that syndicates (distributes) news headlines, links to Web site content, and blog postings to subscribers.

Sometimes called a news aggregator, an RSS reader can be an e-mail client or Web browser plug-in. Popular browsers, such as Internet Explorer and Firefox, have a built-in RSS reader. You also can download stand-alone RSS readers, such as NewzCrawler, or subscribe to online RSS services, such as Bloglines. Whatever your RSS reader choice, current headlines, other Web site content, or new blog postings to which you have subscribed — generally for free — can be automatically distributed to you through your RSS reader.

The Internet Explorer browser checks each Web site you visit for available RSS feeds to which you can subscribe. When an RSS feed is found at a Web site, the Feeds button on the Command bar becomes active. You can click the Feeds button arrow to see the list of feeds available at the Web site. Clicking a feed in the list opens a Web page in Feed view that provides details about the feed's content and a link you can click to subscribe to the feed. Clicking the Feeds button opens a Web page for the first feed in the list. As you subscribe to the feed, you can also add a button for the feed to the Favorites bar.

After you subscribe to a feed, you can open the feed Web page at any time for viewing content, updating content, or setting feed preferences. Click the Feeds tab in the Favorites Center to view a list of feeds to which you have subscribed and then click the feed. To refresh the feed with the most current content, point to the feed in the Feeds list and click the Refresh button to the right of the feed's name. You can change feed properties, such as how often the feed should be automatically updated, by clicking the 'View feed properties' link on the feed Web page. To quickly unsubscribe to a feed, right-click the feed in the Feeds list and click Delete on the shortcut menu.

To Subscribe to an RSS Feed

The following steps open the technology news Web page at a news-oriented Web site and subscribe to a news feed from the Web site.

- Start Internet Explorer and open the Book Companion Site Web page at **www.cengagebrain.com** by following the same set of steps as you did earlier in the chapter.

- Click the Select a chapter list arrow, and then click 2. Browsing the Web to open the resources for Chapter 2.

- Click the Steps link in the left navigation bar to open the Steps Web page (Figure 2-52).

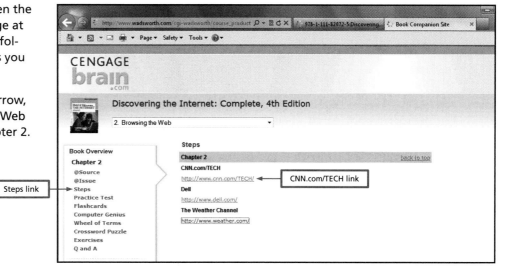

Figure 2-52

- Click CNN.com/TECH to open the CNN.com/technology Web page in the current tab (Figure 2-53).

Figure 2-53

- Click the Feeds button arrow to view the available feeds at the CNN Web site (Figure 2-54).

Figure 2-54

- Click 'CNN – Technology [RSS] (new)' (or a different feed of your choice) to open the feed Web page in the same tab in Feed view (Figure 2-55).

- Scroll the Web page to view the news stories available through this feed.

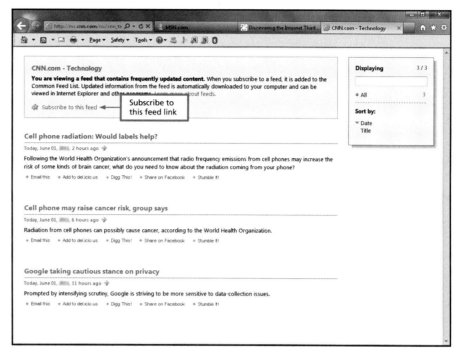

Figure 2-55

- Click the 'Subscribe to this feed' link near the top of the Web page to display the Subscribe to this Feed dialog box (Figure 2-56).

Figure 2-56

- Click the Subscribe button to display the confirmation Web page indicating that you have successfully subscribed to a CNN.com RSS feed (Figure 2-57).

- Click the Close Tab button to close the confirmation Web page.

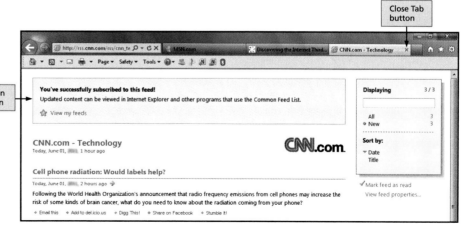

Figure 2-57

To View and Delete an RSS Feed

You can view your RSS feeds by clicking the Feeds tab in the Favorites Center to display the list of RSS feeds to which you subscribe. Then click a specific feed in the list to view its feed Web page in the current tab in your browser. When you no longer want to subscribe to an RSS feed, you can quickly unsubscribe by deleting the feed from the Feeds list using a shortcut menu. The following steps display and then delete the feed from CNN.com.

- Open the Favorites Center.

- Click the Feeds tab to view the list of RSS feeds to which you have subscribed (Figure 2-58).

Why does my Feeds list look different?
The RSS feed subscriptions on your browser might be different from those in the illustrations in this section.

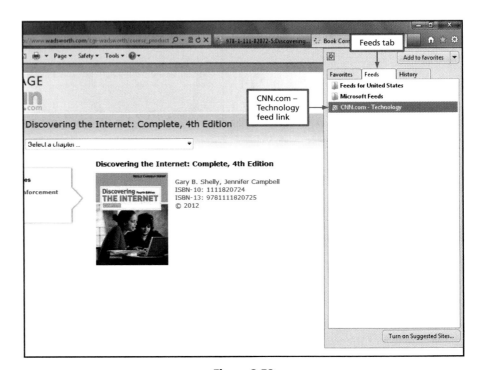

Figure 2-58

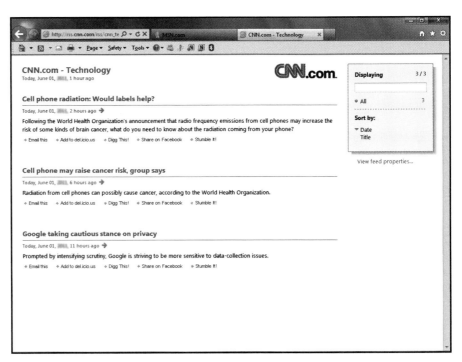

- Click CNN.com – Technology in the Feeds list to open the feed Web page in the current tab (Figure 2-59).

Figure 2-59

- Open the Favorites Center.

- Click the Feeds tab, if necessary, to view the Feeds list.

- Right-click the CNN.com – Technology feed in the Feeds list to open the shortcut menu (Figure 2-60).

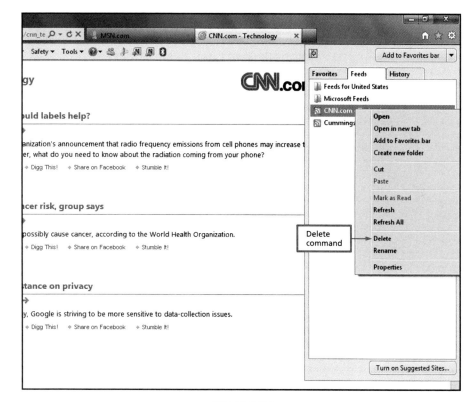

Figure 2-60

- Click Delete to display the confirmation dialog box (Figure 2-61).

- Click the Yes button in the confirmation dialog box to confirm the deletion.

- Close Internet Explorer.

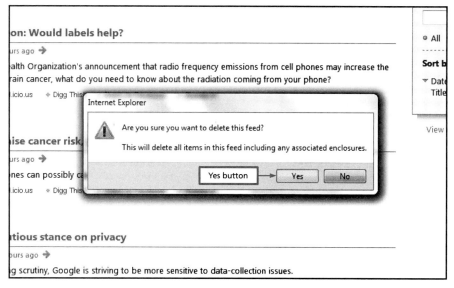

Figure 2-61

Other Ways

1. Click Tools button on Command bar, point to Explorer bars, click Feeds

2. CTRL+SHIFT+G

3. CTRL+G

You can set preferences for how RSS feeds and Web Slices are handled by Internet Explorer in the Content tab in the Internet Options dialog box. For example, you can change the frequency of feed updates, or turn notifications for updates on or off. To open the dialog box, click the Tools button on the Command bar and click Internet options. You will learn more about setting preferences in the Internet Options dialog box later in this chapter.

Address Bar Drop-Down List

You can revisit a Web page by clicking a URL in the Address bar drop-down list. The Address bar drop-down list displays a list of previously viewed Web pages based on a match between what you type and information about the previously visited Web pages. The list also includes suggested keywords for common and previously used searches.

The **AutoComplete** feature, which stores the URLs you type in the Address box, looks at the first few characters you type in the Address box, and then suggests Web sites and search keywords based on stored URLs and displays them in the Address bar drop-down list. Internet Explorer also looks at Web page information stored in Favorites and History to suggest possible matches for the URL you are typing in the Address bar.

The Address bar drop-down list organizes its suggestions by:

- AutoComplete suggestions
- History
- Favorites

You can navigate the Address bar drop-down list (Figure 2-62) by pressing the up arrow and down arrow keys to move between individual items. To quickly open the first Web page in the AutoComplete Suggestion section, press SHIFT+ENTER. To remove a Web page from the Address bar drop-down list, point to the Web page and click the Delete button that appears to the right of it. You can expand the Address bar drop-down list to view additional keyboard shortcuts by clicking the Expansion arrow at the bottom of the list.

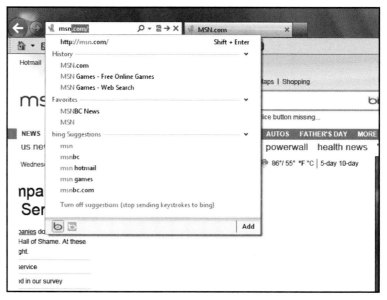

Figure 2-62 The Address bar drop-down list displays a list of previously viewed Web pages based on a match between what you type and stored information from previously visited Web pages.

Suggested Sites

The Suggested Sites feature allows Internet Explorer to use your Web browsing habits to present suggestions for additional browsing. You can turn on the Suggested Sites feature when originally installing Internet Explorer or by clicking a link in the Favorites Center. You also can turn the feature on or off by clicking the Tools button on the Command bar and then clicking Suggested Sites.

When the Suggested Sites feature is turned on, information about Web sites you visit is captured and stored by an online service hosted by Microsoft. Internet Explorer then uses this stored information to suggest additional Web sites of interest based on your browsing history. You can view a Web page of suggested Web sites (Figure 2-63) — based on the Web page you are viewing and your browsing habits — by clicking the See Suggested Sites button that appears at the bottom of the Favorites Center pane when the feature is on. You also can click the Suggested Sites Web Slice button on the Favorites bar, if one has been added, to view a list of suggested Web sites.

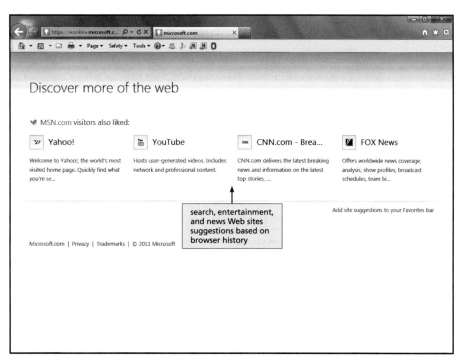

Figure 2-63 You can turn on the Suggested Sites feature to allow Internet Explorer to suggest other Web sites of interest.

Pinning a Web Site to the Taskbar

Pinning a Web site to the taskbar, a new feature of Internet Explorer 9, creates an icon that you can click to open a Web site or Web page in Internet Explorer. The icon next to the URL in the Address text box is called a **favicon**, short for favorite icon.

To Pin a Web Site to the Taskbar

The following steps pin a Web site to the taskbar, and then unpin it.

- Open Internet Explorer and navigate to www.msn.com if it is not your home page.

- Click the favicon (Figure 2-64).

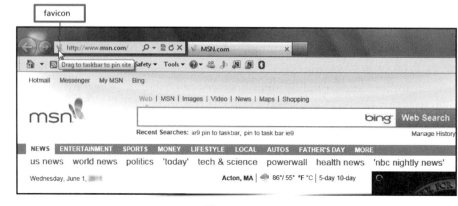

Figure 2-64

- Drag the favicon to the taskbar to pin it (Figure 2-65).

- Close the browser.

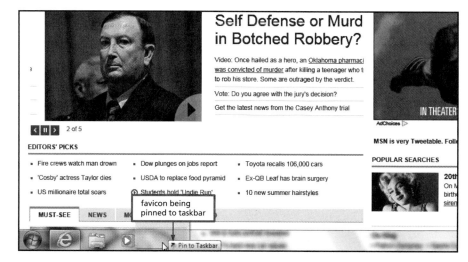

Figure 2-65

- Click the icon on the taskbar to open the Web site.

- Right-click the icon on the taskbar to open a shortcut menu (Figure 2-66).

- Click 'Unpin this program from taskbar' to remove the taskbar icon.

Figure 2-66

Saving Online Information

As you browse the Web, you may want to print a hard copy of a Web page in order to reference its contents later. Web pages also can be saved in a variety of formats. For example, you can save a snapshot of the Web page or the complete HTML page with all of its associated files. You also can save just a Web page image. You can send the entire Web page or a link to the Web page to someone using e-mail. You also can copy selected Web page content, including images, and then paste the selection into another document, such as a word processing document or the body of an e-mail message.

Printing a Web Page

You can print a Web page by clicking the Print button on the Command bar to send the entire Web page to the default printer. Clicking the Print button arrow allows you to use Print Preview to view the Web page; open the Page Setup dialog box and change the paper size, page margins, and print orientation; and change other setup options, such as header and footer content.

By default, the hard copy printout of a Web page includes a header on each page showing the Web page title and page number. A footer on each page shows the URL and the date on which the Web page was printed. To print part of a Web page — for example, a single picture or a selected portion of the text — use one of the following methods:

- Select the information to be printed by dragging across it with the mouse pointer, right-clicking the selection, and clicking Print to open the Print dialog box. In the Print dialog box, click the Selection option button and click Print.
- Right-click the picture and then click Print picture. Click Print in the Print dialog box.

You also can preview Web pages to see how they will look when printed by clicking Print preview on the Print button menu. You can use buttons on the Print Preview toolbar to view specific Web pages, zoom the view in or out, or open the Print dialog box and print the Web pages. Figure 2-67 illustrates a Web page in Print Preview.

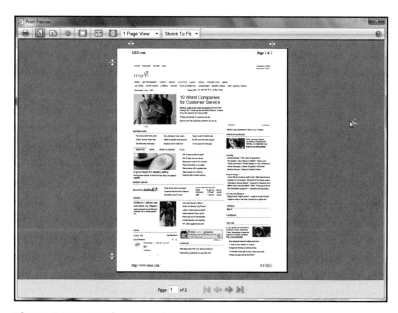

Figure 2-67 A Web page in Print Preview.

Saving a Web Page

You can save a Web page by clicking the Page button on the Command bar and clicking Save as to open the Save Webpage dialog box. The 'Save as type' list in the Save Webpage dialog box offers four options for saving a Web page:

- Webpage, complete (*.htm, *.html) saves not only the HTML Web page, but also all of the other files needed to display the complete Web page, such as graphics.
- Web Archive, single file (*.mht) saves the Web page and its contents, including graphics, in one file.
- Webpage, HTML only (*.htm, *.html) saves the HTML Web page, but does not save other related files, such as the Web page's graphics. When you view this Web page later, the links will work, but an icon might appear in place of an image.
- Text File (*.txt) saves the text on the Web page in plain text format. The links, graphics, and other formatting are not saved.

If you use either of the first two options, you can view the entire Web page, including graphics, while you are working offline. Working **offline** means that you are viewing previously loaded or saved Web pages in the browser, but you are not connected to the Internet.

Another way to save a Web page is to save it directly from a link. If you see a link to a Web page that you want to save, right-click the link and then click 'Save target as' on the shortcut menu.

To Save a Web Page

The following steps save a snapshot of your browser's home page to a folder specified by your instructor.

- If necessary, start Internet Explorer.

- Click the Page button on the Command bar to view the Page button menu (Figure 2-68).

Q&A
Why is the Command bar not displayed?
If the Command bar is not displayed, right-click the title bar, and then click Command bar on the shortcut menu.

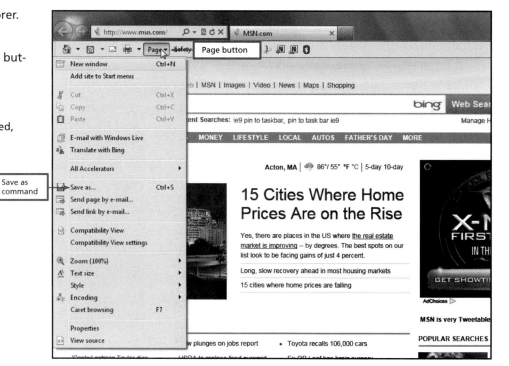

Figure 2-68

- Click Save as to display the Save Webpage dialog box.

- Navigate to the folder specified by your instructor.

- Click the 'Save as type' box arrow to view the available file types (Figure 2-69).

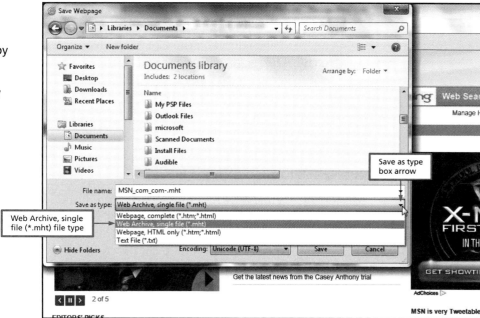

Figure 2-69

3

- Click Web Archive, single file (*.mht), if necessary, to select the desired file type (Figure 2-70).

- Click the Save button.

- Close Internet Explorer.

Q&A

How do I know that the Web page was successfully saved?
To verify that the Web page was saved, use Windows Explorer to open the folder to which you saved it, and double-click the folder and files for the saved Web page.

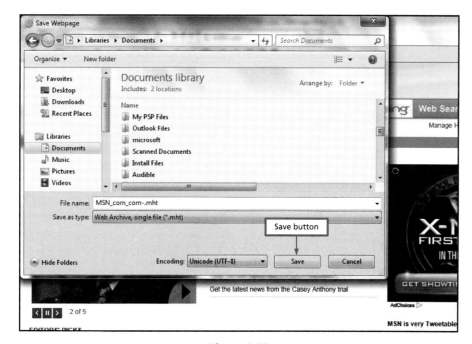

Figure 2-70

E-mailing a Web Page

When you find a Web page that you think might interest someone else, you can share it by sending it to him or her by e-mail. You can send a Web page by e-mail by clicking the Page button on the Command bar and clicking the 'Send page by e-mail' command. The recipient receives an e-mail with the Web page in the body of the message. You also can send a link to a Web page by clicking the Page button and clicking 'Send link by e-mail.' Finally, you can copy a link and paste it into an e-mail message. When the message recipient clicks the link, his or her browser starts and opens the Web page. You will learn more about sending and receiving e-mail in Chapter 4.

Saving a Web Page Image

While browsing the Web, you might find an image that you want to save. Be careful when saving and using Web page images! Most Web page images are the property of their owners and are protected by U.S. copyright law. You cannot use copyright-protected images without permission from the owner or source. Some images, such as many images found at U.S. government Web sites, are in the public domain. Images in the public domain may be used freely; however, you are generally required to provide information about the source of public domain images. Many Web sites that offer public domain images also provide the wording for an image credit line.

You can save a public domain image, such as the one shown in Figure 2-71, by right-clicking the image and then clicking the 'Save picture as' command on the shortcut menu. The shortcut menu also includes commands for printing the image and saving the image as the Windows desktop background wallpaper.

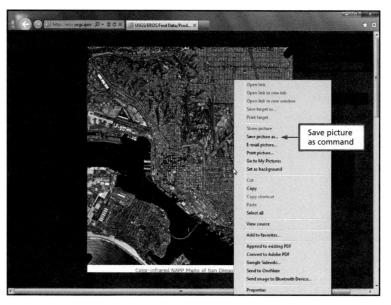

Figure 2-71 You can use a shortcut menu to save, print, or e-mail an image.

Changing Browser Options

The browser window and some browser features can be customized in various ways. For example, you can customize the browser window to show or hide the menu bar, the Favorites bar, and other plug-in toolbars. You also can customize the Command bar. As you have learned, the browser's home page can be changed, and the History list can be changed to show a different number of days of history, or it can be cleared completely. You can use the keyboard, Command bar buttons, shortcut menus, and Internet Options dialog box to change browser options.

Showing and Hiding the Menu Bar and Toolbars

The menu bar, which contains menus and commands you can use to perform specific tasks in the browser, is hidden by default. This is because many of the commonly used commands, such as saving or printing a Web page, also are available by clicking Command bar buttons. Although it is easy to use the Command bar buttons, you may prefer to use menu commands to perform browser tasks. For this reason, you easily can toggle on or off the menu bar by pressing the ALT key.

As you learned earlier, the Favorites bar is a customizable toolbar to which you can add favorites and other shortcuts. You can customize the Favorites bar by adding and removing favorites, and adding or removing Web Slices. You can reorganize shortcuts on the Favorites bar by dragging them to a new location on the bar.

When the Favorites bar is displayed, the Favorites bar buttons appears to the left of the Command bar buttons. You can reposition the Favorites button from the Favorites bar row by clicking the 'Lock the toolbars' command on the Toolbars shortcut menu to unlock the toolbars. Then drag the Favorites button separator (a vertical dashed line) to the new location.

You can turn on or off the view of the Favorites bar, the menu bar, and plug-in toolbars by clicking the Tools button, pointing to Toolbars, and clicking the desired toolbar name in the submenu. You also can right-click any toolbar to view the Toolbar shortcut menu and then click a toolbar name to show or hide the toolbar.

You can drag a Web page icon from the Address bar to the Favorites bar to create a shortcut on the Favorites bar. Web Slices are automatically added to the Favorites bar. You can choose to add a feeds shortcut or the Suggested Sites Web Slice to the Favorites bar.

FACTS @HAND

To Show and Hide the Menu Bar and the Favorites Bar

The following steps display and hide the menu bar using the keyboard. Then you display and hide the Favorites bar using the Tools button on the Command bar and a shortcut menu.

- Start Internet Explorer.

- Press the ALT key to display the menu bar below the Address bar (Figure 2-72).

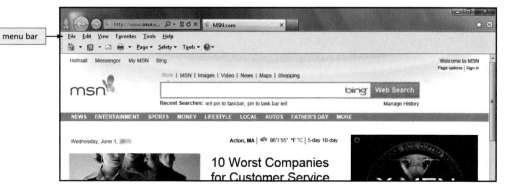

Figure 2-72

2

- Press the ALT key to hide the menu bar.

- Click the Tools button on the Command bar.

- Point to Toolbars to display the Toolbars submenu (Figure 2-73).

 Why do I have different toolbars listed in my Toolbars submenu? Additional toolbars for browser plug-ins or software installed on your computer might appear in your Toolbars submenu.

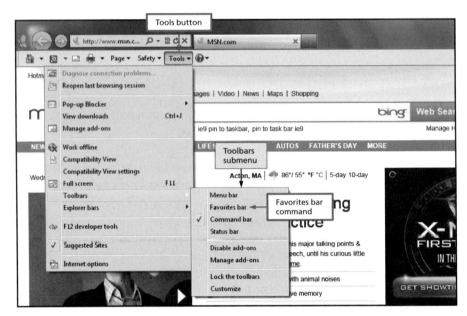

Figure 2-73

3

- Click Favorites bar on the Toolbars submenu to display the Favorites bar below the Address bar (Figure 2-74).

 Why does my Favorites bar look different? The favorites, Web Slices, and RSS feeds and Web Slices shortcuts added to your Favorites bar might be different. Additionally, you might not have the Suggested Sites feature turned on; or if it is on, the Web Slice might not be added to your Favorites bar.

Figure 2-74

4

- Right-click a blank area at the end of the Favorites bar to display the Toolbars shortcut menu (Figure 2-75).

- Click Favorites bar on the shortcut menu to hide the Favorites bar.

- Close Internet Explorer.

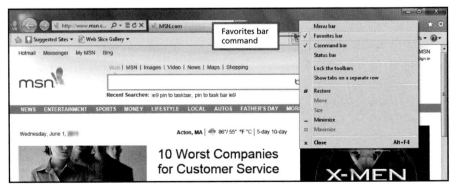

Figure 2-75

Customizing the Command Bar

By default, the Command bar contains the Home, Add Web Slices or Feeds, Read Mail, Print, Page, Safety, Tools, Help, and Research buttons. The Research button is visible when you click the toolbar Expansion arrow to the right of the Help button on the Command bar. You can customize the Command bar by changing the display of the text labels for Command bar buttons by removing the text labels to show only icons or adding text labels to all buttons, or by adding or removing buttons. To customize the Command bar, click Tools on the menu bar, point to Toolbars, and then click Customize to open the Customize Toolbar dialog box, as shown in Figure 2-76.

You also can resize the Command bar to show or hide buttons. Click the 'Lock the toolbars' command on the Toolbars shortcut menu to unlock the toolbars and then drag the Command bar separator (a vertical dashed line) to the left or right. When the toolbars are unlocked, you can reposition the Command bar by dragging it up to the Favorites bar and then back down to the tab row. To learn more about using Command bar buttons not discussed in this chapter and customizing the Command bar, see Internet Explorer Help.

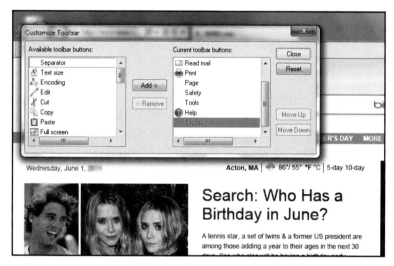

Figure 2-76 You can customize the Command bar by changing the text labels or adding or removing buttons.

Changing the Browser's Home Page

As you have learned, you can have a single home page or multiple home pages open in tabs when the browser starts or when you click the Home button on the Command bar.

In the Add or Change Home Page dialog box, you can specify the current Web page as your only home page, or add it to a group of home pages that open in multiple tabs when you start the browser.

FACTS @HAND

To Add a Browser Home Page

The following steps change the browser's home page settings to add The Weather Channel home page to your current browser home page. Then you remove the second home page to return to your original browser home page. Note that these steps assume your browser currently has only one browser home page. If your browser already has a group of browser home pages specified, your instructor might modify these steps.

- Start Internet Explorer.

- Type **weather.com** in the Address bar and press the ENTER key.

- Click the Home button arrow on the Command bar to display the Home button menu (Figure 2-77).

Figure 2-77

- Click 'Add or change home page' to display the Add or Change Home Page dialog box.

- Click the 'Add this webpage to your home page tabs' option button to add the current Web page as a home page tab (Figure 2-78).

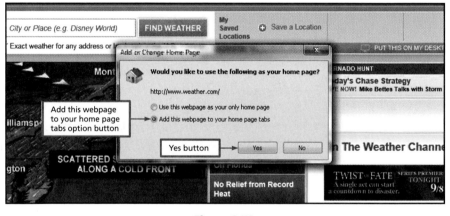

Figure 2-78

- Click the Yes button to add the Web page to your home page tabs.

- Close Internet Explorer.

- Start Internet Explorer to view two home page tabs (Figure 2-79).

Figure 2-79

4

- Click the Home button arrow on the Command bar to view the menu.

- Point to the Remove command to view the submenu (Figure 2-80).

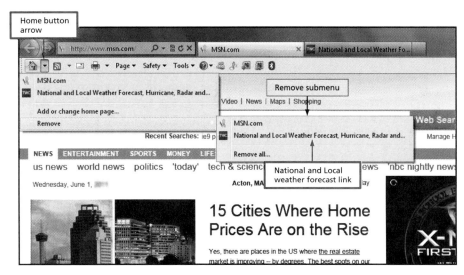

Figure 2-80

5

- Click National and Local Weather Forecast... to open the Delete Home Page dialog box (Figure 2-81).

- Click the Yes button in the Delete Home Page dialog box to confirm the removal of the second home page.

- Close Internet Explorer.

- Start Internet Explorer to confirm that The Weather Channel's home page is no longer one of the home page tabs.

- Close Internet Explorer.

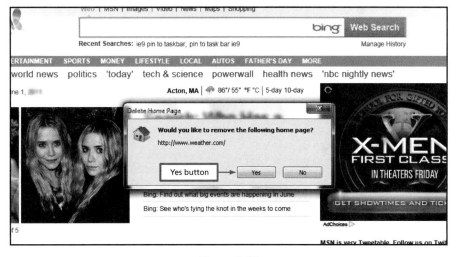

Figure 2-81

Viewing a Web Page in Compatibility View

Some Web pages created for earlier versions of Internet Explorer might not appear correctly in Internet Explorer 9. If a Web page you open is not displayed correctly (for example, if it appears with images or text boxes that are not correctly aligned), click the Tools button on the Command bar and click Compatibility View to turn on the feature and try to improve how the Web page looks. Each time you revisit the Web site, its Web pages will appear in **Compatibility View** until they are updated to display correctly in Internet Explorer 9.

Zooming a Web Page

You can change the view of the entire current Web page by enlarging or reducing it in a process often called "zooming." To zoom a Web page up or down, click the 'Change zoom level' button arrow on the right side of the status bar and click the desired zoom percentage on the menu. If the zoom percentage you want is not available on the menu, click Custom to open the Custom Zoom dialog box. Then set the zoom percentage you want to use and click OK. Zooming a Web page up to enlarge it can be especially helpful for people with vision problems (Figure 2-82).

Figure 2-82   Web site viewed at 150% zoom.

Setting Other Browser Options

The Internet Options dialog box is used to set a variety of browser options. For example, you also can change the browser's home page or pages with options on the General tab in the Internet Options dialog box (Figure 2-83): Add or delete a home page URL, change the home page back to the home page that was specified when you installed the browser, or use a blank Web page as your home page. To open the Internet Options dialog box, click the Tools button on the Command bar and click Internet options.

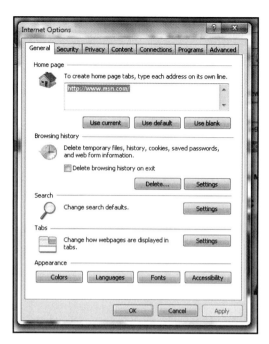

Figure 2-83 You can set a variety of browser options in the Internet Options dialog box.

On the General tab in the Internet Options dialog box, you also can manage your browsing history, change how Web page tabs are displayed, modify the settings for temporary Internet files (such as cookies), delete temporary Internet files, and change settings that affect the browser's overall appearance. You will learn more about cookies and the Security and Privacy options available in the Internet Options dialog box in the next section. You will learn about the browser's search features in Chapter 3.

Using the Web: Risks and Safeguards

As you browse the Web, you access information stored on servers located all over the world. Even as you use the Web from the privacy of your home or office, you are venturing into a very public arena that connects millions of computers and people from around the globe. Although this global connectivity has many positive aspects, it also creates the possibility that you might be exposed to unethical people, objectionable material, or attacks from hackers. In the next few sections, you will learn about the risks of using the Web and safeguards that can protect you from these risks.

Protecting Your Computer from Hackers

Anyone connected to the Internet should take precautions to protect his or her computer from hackers. A **hacker** is an individual who uses his or her computer skills to access a network and the computers on that network without authorization. A criminal or unethical hacker sometimes is called a "cracker" or a "black hat hacker." A hacker typically accesses a computer by connecting to it and then logging on as a legitimate user. Once logged on to a computer, the hacker can access data and programs, save files, or hijack its computing power, all without the owner's knowledge or permission. Users with a dial-up connection have a somewhat limited exposure to hackers because of the temporary nature of the connection; however, the level of exposure is significantly greater for users with an always-on DSL or cable Internet connection.

@SOURCE

Virus Protection Software
To learn more about virus protection software, visit the Book Companion Site Web page at **www. cengagebrain.com**. Under the Chapter 2 @Source links, click a link below Virus Protection Software.

A firewall (Figure 2-84) protects a computer or a network from unauthorized access by hackers. A firewall, which can be hardware or software, can examine network communications and then directly block or warn the user about those communications that do not meet a set of predetermined rules. For example, a firewall on a home computer connected to the Internet might be set to block certain outgoing communications from a specific software application or operating system utility, or it could prevent incoming communications from an unknown source.

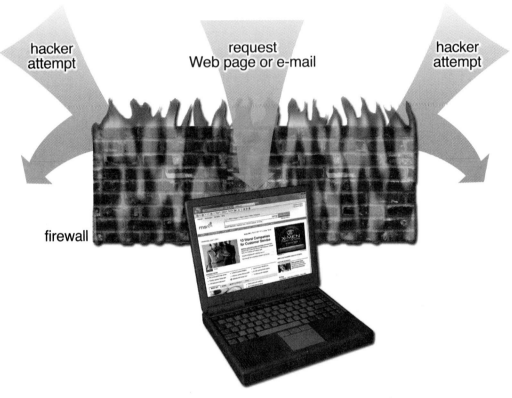

Figure 2-84 A firewall helps to protect your computer against hackers and crackers.

The Windows 7 operating system provides a personal firewall, Windows® Firewall, which is useful for protecting home computers with Internet connections. Other popular personal firewall products can be purchased from vendors, such as ZoneAlarm® and PC Tools™. Businesses use a variety of sophisticated firewalls for their local area networks.

Protecting Your Computer from Viruses

A computer **virus** is a small, potentially damaging computer program that can infect a computer and then be passed to other computers. Browsing the Web typically does not expose a computer to damaging viruses. More often, a computer is infected with a virus by an e-mail message or attachment when software and utility programs are downloaded or when infected word processing or spreadsheet files are exchanged with other users. One way to guard against viruses is to never open an e-mail attachment unless you trust the source and you are expecting the attachment. You will learn more about the risks of and safeguards for using e-mail in Chapter 4. Another way to guard against viruses is to install virus protection software, such as Norton™ AntiVirus or McAfee® VirusScan software, and keep the virus definitions updated regularly.

Shopping Safely Online

Shopping online is convenient because consumers can read quickly about product features, view pictures, and compare prices. In most circumstances, shopping online is a safe activity; however, there are some risks. The risks of online shopping include not knowing with whom you are doing business and making payments online. By following a few guidelines, you can enjoy safe and successful shopping online.

Before making a purchase from an online vendor, determine whether the business is reputable. For example, by purchasing products or services from well-known companies, such as Dell, Barnes & Noble, or Delta Air Lines, consumers can feel more confident about the purchase. Shoppers should read the company's security assurances on their Web site to confirm that the company will not use their customer information or payment information illegally. On the other hand, purchasing a collectible doll from an anonymous seller at an online auction Web site is inherently more risky because the seller may not have a well-known public reputation. The OnGuard Online U.S. government Web site (Figure 2-85) is a great resource for learning about shopping online safely and other computer and online safety issues.

Figure 2-85 The OnGuard Online Web site offers a wealth of information about shopping safely online.

In addition to choosing an online vendor carefully, consumers should be cautious when making payments over the Internet. Most online vendors accept credit cards, currently the most popular online payment method, which limits the consumer's liability. Other payment methods include electronic checks and third-party payment services, such as PayPal (Figure 2-86 on the next page) and Western Union, which allow consumers to send money to anyone by e-mail or money order. Third-party payment services are a popular means of paying for consumer-to-consumer (C2C) transactions.

@SOURCE
Shopping Safely Online
To learn more about shopping safely online, visit the Book Companion Site Web page at **www.cengagebrain.com**. Under the Chapter 2 @Source links, click a link below Online Shopping Safety.

Figure 2-86 Third-party payment services are a popular way to send money using a secure Internet connection.

When paying for an online purchase using a credit card, be sure the Web site is accessed with a secure connection. A **secure connection** uses https:// rather than http:// as its connection protocol, and a locked padlock icon appears on the Security Status bar in the right side of the Address bar. The secure https:// protocol and the locked padlock icon signify that the information is being encrypted and sent over a secure connection using Secure Sockets Layer. **Secure Sockets Layer (SSL)** is a commonly used protocol for managing the security of message transmissions on the Internet. Using a secure connection, such as the PayPal connection shown in Figure 2-86, ensures the verifiable identity of the Web site based on information provided to an organization, called a certificate authority. You can click the padlock to view Web site verification information. You also can click a link below the verification information to view the Internet Explorer Help topic on trusted Web sites.

Finally, never send a credit card number or other personal or sensitive information by e-mail. An e-mail message could be intercepted en route and it is easily forwarded without your knowledge. Following these simple guidelines can help you shop online more safely and confidently.

Filtering Web Content

Web users may mistakenly access objectionable material, such as offensive language, sexually explicit or violent material, or hate propaganda, while browsing the Web. One of the Web's greatest strengths is that it is unregulated and open to all; however, that also means that the Web is an unprotected environment that contains material some may find objectionable. The prevalence of objectionable content can be particularly problematic for children using the Internet and browsing the Web.

Tracking Protection Lists (TPLs) are used to control Web sites that can track your content on the Internet. Every time you visit a Web site, it can potentially track your searches, clicks, and other activity, and share that information with other Web sites; those

Web sites then use the information to personalize or target the ads and content you see. A TPL operates like a telephone Do Not Call list, and consists of a list of Web addresses that a browser will interact with only if the user clicks a link to the Web site or enters the address in the Address bar, limiting the amount of information a Web site can track. By default, a user's TPL is empty; a user must choose to create or enable a TPL. When using TPLs, keep in mind that some Web sites rely on tracking, cookies, and other methods to fully function; and by limiting their ability, you may be limiting the functionality of the Web site.

To change your TPL settings, click the Safety button on the Command bar, and then click Tracking Protection. The Manage Add-ons dialog box opens. Click the Get a Tracking Protection List online link to open a browser window with a list of user- and business-created TPLs; or click a list in the dialog box, and then click the Settings button to open the Personalized Tracking Protection List dialog box (Figure 2-87). Click Web sites in the list, and then click the Allow or Block button to change a Web site's tracking status.

@SOURCE

Web Content Filtering
To learn more about Web content filtering, visit the Book Companion Site Web page at **www.cengagebrain.com**. Under the Chapter 2 @Source links, click a link below Web Content Filtering.

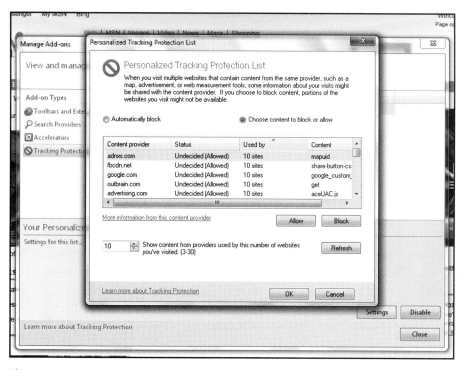

Figure 2-87 Personalized Tracking Protection List dialog box.

Web content filters, also called **Internet filters**, are hardware and/or software that filters the display of Web content based on user settings. For example, parents can use a Web content filter to protect their children from objectionable material. Employers can use a Web content filter to prevent their employees from viewing objectionable material at work.

Some Web content filters, such as iPrism® (for businesses), McAfee® SmartFilter (for schools), and Net Nanny® parental controls (for home use), might use specific filters that block certain Web pages based on keywords or a predefined database of objectionable Web sites. In addition, browsers have built-in content filter features that can help block objectionable material. Internet Explorer provides content filtering options in the Content tab in the Internet Options dialog box (Figure 2-88).

@SOURCE

Online Safety for Kids
To learn more about keeping children safe online, visit the Book Companion Site Web page at **www.cengagebrain.com**. Under the Chapter 2 @Source links, click a link below Online Safety for Kids.

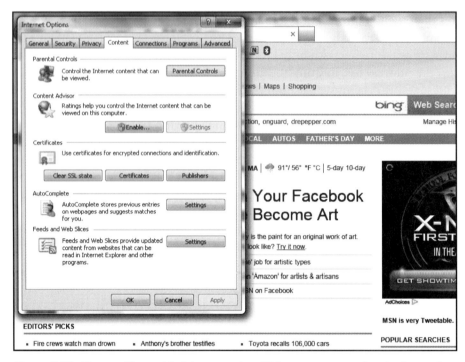

Figure 2-88   You can filter or block inappropriate Web page content using the Parental Controls and Content Advisor options in the Content tab in the Internet Options dialog box.

Protecting Against Malicious Web Sites

A **malicious Web site** is a Web site that is designed to look like a legitimate Web site, such as a Web site for downloading online games, but actually is owned by hackers or online thieves who use its content to capture your sensitive personal information, such as your name and password, or to distribute malicious software, such as a keystroke logger that records all your keystrokes.

Internet Explorer has a built-in filter for detecting malicious Web sites, called the SmartScreen Filter. As you browse the Web, the SmartScreen Filter works in the background, analyzing the Web pages you visit and looking for suspicious attributes that might indicate threats. If the SmartScreen Filter suspects you are visiting a malicious Web site, a warning message appears. The SmartScreen Filter automatically blocks any Web sites previously identified as malicious. You can turn the SmartScreen Filter feature off or on and manually check the current Web page by clicking the Safety button on the Command bar and pointing to SmartScreen Filter to view the submenu.

Keeping Your Personal Information Private

Information privacy refers to the right of individuals and companies to deny or restrict the collection and use of personal information. Today, personal information entered in Web page forms is tracked by Web sites and stored in company databases. Although this information should be accessible only to authorized users, some people question whether this data really is private. Some companies and individuals collect and use your personal information and record your online activities without your authorization. Entities such as your employer, your Internet service provider (ISP), government agencies, the Web sites you visit, and third-party advertisers all might be tracking your online activities.

Some people are less concerned about protecting their personal information and enjoy the benefits of targeted marketing, personalized e-mail messages, and direct mail, such as catalogs, as a result of information gathered about them while they browse the Web. But many people are very concerned that their private information is not protected from entities such as third-party advertisers. The following sections discuss the entities that might be collecting and using your private information and the laws that protect your information privacy.

EMPLOYERS   An employer can legally monitor employee use of its computer equipment and time spent on the Web at the workplace. Employers often publish policies explaining that they have the legal right to monitor employees' computer usage and require that their employees acknowledge that right before accepting employment. Most employers, however, do not abuse their right to monitor employees; employers only want to protect themselves from any illegal or harmful use of their network and computer systems.

INTERNET SERVICE PROVIDERS   An ISP is capable of tracking online usage because all of its customers' Web traffic goes through the ISP's network. Unlike an employer, however, an ISP has no legitimate reason to track online behavior. Most ISP customers respond negatively to news that an ISP is gathering their private information. Although an ISP has the ability to record online activities, many ISPs publish a privacy statement; a statement of their privacy policy specifically describing what information they collect, how they use it, and whether they share this information with third parties. The terms of such a privacy policy then are made available to their customers in the form of a privacy statement, usually posted at the ISP's Web site.

GOVERNMENT AGENCIES   The concern about privacy has led to the passage of federal and state laws regarding the storage and disclosure of personal data. Several of these laws protect certain kinds of information, such as medical records and financial data, from being revealed to anyone without the individual's permission. Other laws limit the U.S. government's right to track online activities to specific circumstances, such as to investigate crime or in cases of national defense.

PRIVACY ADVOCATES   Maintaining privacy is an important issue for Web users. Organizations, such as the Electronic Privacy Information Center (EPIC), are dedicated to informing government agencies and consumers about privacy issues and maintaining information about privacy issues at their Web sites.

E-BUSINESS WEB SITES   E-business Web sites can collect personal information, such as names, addresses, telephone numbers, or credit card information, from shoppers or visitors and then store that information in a database. Consumers visiting Web sites should be aware of what information is collected, how it is used, and how it is protected. Consumers can learn how a company handles personal information collected at its Web site by reading the Web site's privacy statement.

Like ISPs, most e-businesses publish their privacy policies in an easily accessible **privacy statement** posted at their Web sites. You typically can find a link to a privacy statement at the bottom of an e-business's home page. Many companies demonstrate a commitment to privacy by becoming a member of the TRUSTe program. The TRUSTe program is a voluntary program in which a company's Web site and business practices are reviewed by TRUSTe to ensure that the Web site adheres to established privacy principles and complies with ongoing TRUSTe review and consumer resolution procedures. TRUSTe members can display the TRUSTe trustmark at their Web sites. Figure 2-89 on the next page illustrates the privacy statement and TRUSTe trustmark at the Microsoft Web site.

@SOURCE

Electronic Privacy
To learn more about electronic privacy issues, visit the Book Companion Site Web page at **www.cengagebrain.com**. Under the Chapter 2 @Source links, click the link for Electronic Privacy.

@SOURCE

TRUSTe
To learn more about the TRUSTe program, visit the Book Companion Site Web page at **www.cengagebrain.com**. Under the Chapter 2 @Source links, click the link for TRUSTe.

@SOURCE

COPPA
To learn more about the Children's Online Privacy Protection Act, visit the Book Companion Site Web page at **www.cengagebrain.com**. Under the Chapter 2 @Source links, click the link for COPPA.

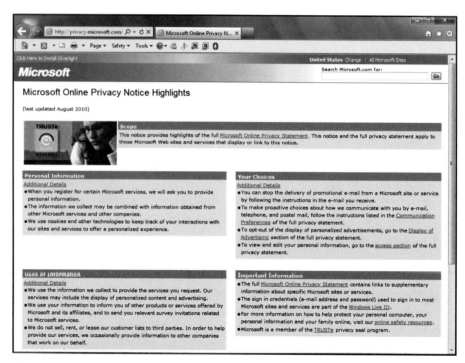

Figure 2-89 A privacy statement explains a company's privacy policy.

To be an informed consumer and Web user, you should make a habit of viewing the privacy statement at frequently visited Web sites to see exactly what information is collected and how it is used. The privacy statement should indicate how the company handles **personally identifiable information (PII)**, such as e-mail addresses, names and addresses, or even more sensitive personal information, such as health, financial, political, or religious information.

Web sites are prohibited from collecting personal information from children under the age of 13. The Children's Online Privacy Protection Act (COPPA) requires that Web sites get explicit permission from parents before marketing to or collecting personal data from children.

@SOURCE

Cookies and Spyware
To learn more about cookies, spyware, and adware, visit the Book Companion Site Web page at **www. cengagebrain.com**. Under the Chapter 2 @Source links, click a link below Cookies and Spyware.

COOKIES E-businesses and other Web sites often rely on cookies to identify users and customize Web pages. A **cookie** is a small text file stored on a computer's hard drive that can contain data, such as a username, password, shipping address, or viewing preferences. E-businesses then can use the information stored in cookies to customize Web pages, to remember a username and password, or to present targeted advertisements on a Web page. E-businesses also use cookies to track which Web site pages users visit most often and other Web site visitor statistics. Cookies can provide a positive visitor experience by speeding up the checkout or login process and by displaying recommended articles or sale items. Cookies still can be a cause for concern because the information is collected without the visitor's express consent and can be used by the Web site or sold to other Web sites without consent.

The Internet Explorer browser allows you to set options for cookie handling in the Advanced Privacy Settings dialog box (Figure 2-90). To open the dialog box, click the Advanced button in the Privacy tab in the Internet Options dialog box. When modifying browser privacy settings, you might not want to refuse all cookies. Some Web sites require the use of cookies; if you block all cookies, you may not be able to purchase merchandise, airline tickets, or services or benefit from customized content at such Web sites.

Figure 2-90 You can set options for accepting or blocking cookies on the Privacy tab in the Internet Options dialog box.

Cookies can be deleted from a hard drive; however, deleting all cookies also deletes those that are useful, such as cookies that store personal profiles and preferences for frequently visited Web sites. Deleting cookies one at a time is preferable because it allows you to specify which ones to delete. For more information on deleting cookies, see Internet Explorer Help.

SPYWARE AND ADWARE   **Spyware** is a general term usually applied to any technology that accesses your computer system to gather information without your knowledge and approval. **Adware** is a form of spyware that gathers information and then uses that information to deliver targeted Web advertising. Visitors sometimes unknowingly download adware when downloading other software. Another type of spyware is a Web bug, also called a Web beacon. A **Web bug** is a tiny hidden graphic embedded in a Web page. Third-party advertisers sometimes use Web bugs to collect information about Web site visitors. Web bugs gather information, such as a computer's IP address, the type of browser used to retrieve the bug, the Web address of the Web page from which the user came, and the time and date the Web page was viewed. Unlike cookies, which can be located on a hard drive and deleted, Web bugs are invisible. Although Web bugs are commonly used to customize a user's experience or to gather statistics on the Web site, the invisible nature of Web bugs fuels privacy debates. To protect yourself from spyware, you can install spyware and adware protection software. Additionally, some virus protection software also checks for and removes spyware. Be sure to research any company before you download its software; some programs that claim to check for spyware are actually malicious programs.

@ISSUE ## Opting Out

Although Web site owners have a responsibility to post and adhere to privacy policies, consumers can take actions to protect their own privacy. For example, consumers can take time to review the privacy policy statements posted at their favorite Web sites. To protect against third-party or other undesirable cookies on their computers, consumers can delete all unwanted cookies and set options to restrict cookie acceptance. Then they can check for opt-out instructions at Web sites and submit forms to opt out of receiving cookies, data collection, and advertising. Taking these actions can help protect and maintain privacy when browsing the Web. For more information on opting out, visit the Book Companion Site Web page at **www.cengagebrain.com**. Under the Chapter 2 @Issue links, click the links for Opting Out.

INPRIVATE BROWSING   As you learned earlier in this chapter, information about the Web sites you visit is recorded in your browsing history. In some circumstances, you might not want to record your browsing history during a specific browsing session (for example, when you share a computer and do not want others to see your browsing history). To browse privately, you can open a new tab and click the InPrivate Browsing link on the New Tab page, or click the Safety button on the Command bar and then click InPrivate Browsing to open a new browser window. An InPrivate browsing indicator appears to the left of the Address bar when InPrivate Browsing is turned on. Note that InPrivate Browsing does not protect your personally identifiable information from being gathered at Web sites while you browse; it only keeps information about the browsing session from being stored on your computer. To close InPrivate Browsing, simply close the browser window. For more information on InPrivate Browsing, see Internet Explorer Help.

INPRIVATE FILTERING   Earlier in this section, you learned about Web beacons or bugs. As you browse the Web, you view many Web pages that contain content, such as advertising, provided by others, sometimes called content providers. When you visit a Web site containing content provided by third parties, the content providers might be capturing information about your browsing habits using Web bugs. For example, content providers could display specific advertisements that might be of interest to you based on the types of Web sites you visit. To protect against this type of data gathering, you can turn on the Internet Explorer InPrivate Filtering feature by clicking the Safety button on the Command bar and clicking InPrivate Filtering. When the InPrivate Filtering feature is turned on, each Web page you visit is analyzed for suspicious third-party content; if any is found, you will have the option of blocking the suspicious content. If desired, you can set an option to have the InPrivate Filtering feature automatically block any third-party content. For more information on browsing with the InPrivate Filtering feature, see Internet Explorer Help.

Chapter Review

Web pages are designed to attract and hold the attention of visitors, and typically include some or all of the following: a logo or name, images, links, advertisements, a search tool, a copyright statement, and a link to a privacy policy statement.

An IP address is the unique numerical address of a computer on a network and is used to address and send data over a network, such as the Internet. A domain name is an easy-to-remember text alias for one or more IP addresses. A URL, also called a Web address, is the unique address of a Web page; it consists of the http:// protocol, the server name, and the domain name, and can include the path and file name.

You can load Web pages by typing each Web page's URL in the Address box on the Address bar and clicking the Go button or pressing the ENTER key. You also can load a Web page by clicking a Web page link. You can navigate among recently loaded Web pages during the current browser session, load a fresh copy of the current Web page, stop loading a Web page, and load the browser's home page by clicking the Back, Forward, Refresh, Stop, and Home buttons.

You can use several browser shortcuts to visit Web pages including Favorites, History, Web Slices, Accelerators, RSS feeds, the New Tab page, the Address bar drop-down list, and the Suggested Sites Web Slice. You can view a Print Preview and print a copy of the current Web page to reference its contents later. You also can save a Web page in a variety of formats that include or exclude its related files, such as graphics. You can send a snapshot of or a link to a Web page to someone by e-mail. Individual Web page images can be saved for private use in a variety of different formats.

You can change browser options, such as displaying and hiding toolbars and changing the home page to a new home page or a group of home pages that open in separate tabs, using the keyboard, a shortcut menu, and the Internet Options dialog box. You also can use Internet Explorer features, such as SmartScreen Filter, Tracking Protection, and ActiveX Filter, to browse the Web more securely. Using the InPrivate Browsing feature can help you restrict the information shared about your browsing habits.

TERMS TO KNOW

After reading this chapter, you should know each of these Key Terms.

Accelerators (71)
adware (99)
AutoComplete (78)
client (41)
client/server computing (41)
Compatibility View (89)
cookie (98)
country-code top-level domain (ccTLD) (43)
display area (44)
domain name (42)
Domain Name System (DNS) (42)
dynamic IP address (41)
FAQs (frequently asked questions) (39)
favicon (79)
favorite (63)
hacker (91)
History list (68)
home page (38)
information privacy (96)
Internet Corporation for Assigned Names and Numbers (ICANN) (43)
Internet filters (95)

IP address (Internet Protocol address) (41)
malicious Web site (96)
name server (42)
offline (82)
personally identifiable information (PII) (98)
portal (39)
privacy statement (97)
secure connection (94)
Secure Sockets Layer (SSL) (94)
spyware (99)
static IP address (41)
tabbed browsing (56)
top-level domain (TLD) (43)
Tracking Protection Lists (TPLs) (94)
Uniform Resource Locator (URL) (43)
virus (92)
Web address (43)
Web bug (99)
Web content filters (95)
Web portal (39)
Web Slices (71)

TEST YOUR KNOWLEDGE

Complete the Test Your Knowledge exercises to solidify what you have learned in the chapter.

True or False

Mark T for True and F for False. (Answers are found on page numbers in parentheses.)

____ 1. A server is an application that runs on a computer, such as a personal computer, and requests resources or services from another computer. (41)

____ 2. Advertisements with attention-grabbing sounds and animation are called rich media ads. (50)

____ 3. The protocol (http://) and the domain name in a URL are not case sensitive, but the path and file name can be. (44)

____ 4. An IP address consists of three groups of numbers, each separated by periods, or dots. (41)

____ 5. To access a recently viewed Web page, you can click a URL in the Address box drop-down list. (78)

____ 6. A computer hacker is a small, potentially damaging computer program that can infect a computer and then be passed to other computers. (91)

____ 7. A printed Web page often has a header and footer containing the name of the Web page, the page numbers, the Web page's URL, and the date printed. (81)

____ 8. A filter is a security system that uses hardware and/or software to prevent unauthorized access to a computer on a network. (95)

___ 9. The secure https:// protocol and a padlock icon signify that your information is being sent over a secure connection. (94)

___10. InPrivate Browsing protects you from data gathering as you browse the Web. (100)

Multiple Choice

Select the best answer. (Answers are found on page numbers in parentheses.)

1. An online dictionary that you can use to define terms on a Web page is an example of a(n) _____. (71)

   a. RSS feed

   b. Accelerator

   c. Internet filter

   d. favorite

2. Top-level domains include _____. (43)

   a. .com for commercial firms

   b. .gvt for government

   c. .net for nonprofit institutions

   d. all of the above

3. A Web site that offers links to a wide range of content and services and is often used as a default starting Web page is called a(n) _____. (39)

   a. home page

   b. server

   c. Web portal

   d. FAQ

4. To revisit a Web page without having to type the entire URL, you can _____. (63–71)

   a. click the URL in the Address bar drop-down list

   b. click a link in the History list

   c. click a favorite in the Favorites list

   d. all of the above

5. To pin a Web page to the taskbar, drag its _____ to the taskbar. (80)

   a. favicon

   b. cookie

   c. URL

   d. FAQ

6. When you add a favorite to the Favorites list, you can _____. (63)

   a. change the name of the favorite

   b. specify an existing folder in which to store it

   c. create a new folder in which to store it

   d. all of the above

7. A Web server with a permanent Internet connection needs a(n) _____ IP address. (41)

   a. dynamic

   b. private

   c. static

   d. assigned

8. PII stands for _____. (98)

   a. private Internet information

   b. personally identifiable information

   c. portal for Internet information

   d. personal InPrivate portal

9. The Internet Explorer browser feature that helps protect you against malicious Web sites as you browse the Web is _____. (100)

   a. Cookies

   b. SmartScreen Filter

   c. Tracking Protection

   d. InPrivate Browsing

10. _____ is a general name for any technology that accesses your computer system without your knowledge or approval to gather information. (99)

   a. Adware

   b. Gatherware

   c. Spyware

   d. Privacyware

LEARN IT ONLINE

Test your knowledge of chapter content and key terms.

Instructions: To complete the following exercises, please visit **www.cengagebrain.com**. On the CengageBrain home page, enter the book title *Discovering the Internet* and then click the Find button. On the product Web page for this book, click the Access Now button below the Study Tools heading. On the Book Companion Site Web page, click the drop-down menu, select Chapter 2, and then click the link for the desired exercise.

Chapter Reinforcement TF, MC, and SA

A series of true/false, multiple-choice, and short-answer questions that test your knowledge of the chapter content.

Flash Cards

An interactive learning environment where you identify chapter key terms associated with displayed definitions.

Practice Test

A series of multiple-choice questions that test your knowledge of chapter content and key terms.

Who Wants To Be a Computer Genius?

An interactive game that challenges your knowledge of chapter content in the style of a television quiz show.

Wheel of Terms

An interactive game that challenges your knowledge of chapter key terms in the style of the television show, *Wheel of Fortune*.

Crossword Puzzle Challenge

A crossword puzzle that challenges your knowledge of the key terms presented in the chapter.

Use the Exercises to gain hands-on experience working with the Internet and the Web.

1 | Visit Portals and Change the Browser Home Page

1. Start Internet Explorer, if necessary. Visit the Book Companion Site Web page for this book, and click a link below Chapter 2, Exercise 1 to view links to several Web portals. Open each Web portal in a new tab.

2. Use the Back and Forward buttons and the New Tab page to view and then revisit each portal.

3. Add the portal page of your choice as an additional home page using the Home button on the Command bar. Close Internet Explorer. Reopen Internet Explorer to verify the additional home page.

4. Remove the new portal home page from your home page group. Close and reopen Internet Explorer to verify that your original home page or pages open.

5. Close Internet Explorer.

2 | Identify Characteristics of a Web Page

1. Start Internet Explorer, if necessary. Visit the Book Companion Site Web page for this book, and click the links below Chapter 2, Exercise 2 to open in separate tabs the home page for two local news Web sites. Use the Web page tabs to navigate between the two Web pages; then click the Print button on the Command bar to print one of the Web pages. Save one of the Web pages to a flash drive or to a folder on your hard drive. Use Windows Explorer to delete the saved Web page.

2. In Internet Explorer, examine the Web page you printed to locate the following items. On the printout, label the following items that might appear on the Web page:

    a. Logo or name of the Web site

    b. Image as a link

    c. Text as a link

    d. Advertisement for another company's product or service

    e. Copyright statement or link

    f. Privacy policy link

    g. Other elements such as connectivity tools (Facebook, etc.) and slide shows or carousels

3. Click various links on the Web site's home page to browse its other Web pages. Use the Back and Forward buttons to revisit the recently viewed Web pages.

4. Use the Address box drop-down list to revisit recently viewed Web pages.

5. Close Internet Explorer and all tabs. Reopen Internet Explorer and reopen all the tabs in the last browsing session.

6. Close Internet Explorer.

3 | Pin a Web Page to the Taskbar

1. Start Internet Explorer, if necessary.

2. Search for the Web page of your choice by entering search terms in the Address bar, and then pressing the ENTER key.

3. Click the Web page in the search results to open it.

4. Position the pointer over the favicon for the Web page, and then click and drag the favicon to the taskbar.

5. Close Internet Explorer.

6. Click the icon on the taskbar to open the Web site.

7. Close Internet Explorer.

8. Right-click the icon on the taskbar, and then click 'Unpin this program from taskbar.'

4 | Use the History List

1. Start Internet Explorer, if necessary. Click the Favorites button to open the Favorites Center and click the History tab to view the History list.

2. Click the Today icon or text link in the History list, if necessary, to view a list of folders for Web sites visited by anyone using the computer today.

3. Click a folder in the Today list to expand it, if necessary, and view the links to individual Web pages visited at that Web site today. Click a link to any Web page to revisit it.

4. Open the Favorites Center and view the History list. Click the same folder expanded in Step 3 to collapse it so that only the folder icon is visible, and not its contents.

5. Click the Last Week icon or text link, if available, to view the folders for Web sites visited last week. Open a folder, revisit a Web site, open the Favorites Center again, and close the folder.

6. Click the icons or text links to collapse the lists of Web site folders.

7. Close the Favorites Center.

8. Close Internet Explorer.

5 | Add a Favorite to the Favorites Bar and Sign Up for an RSS Feed

1. Start Internet Explorer, if necessary. Click the New Tab button on the tab row to open a new blank tab. If available, click the Book Companion Site Web page link on the New Tab page. Otherwise, use the steps you learned earlier in the chapter to open the Web page.

   a. Right-click anywhere on the Command bar and click Favorites bar to display the Favorites bar, if necessary.

   b. Move the mouse pointer to the Book Companion Site Web page icon in the Address box. Drag the icon to a blank area on the Favorites bar to add the Book Companion Site Web page favorite to the Favorites bar.

   c. Click the home page tab to bring the tab into the foreground. Click the @Source page favorite on the Favorites bar to open the Book Companion Site Web page in the current tab.

   d. Click the Home button to reopen the home page in the current tab.

2. Open the Book Companion Site Web page, if necessary, and then open the Web page for Exercises. Click Boston.com under the Chapter 2, Exercise 5 links.

   a. Click the Add Web Slices button arrow.

   b. Click Top Stories RSS feed from the menu.

   c. Click the 'Subscribe to this feed' link.

   d. In the Subscribe to this Feed dialog box, click the Subscribe button.

   e. Click the 'View my feeds' link.

   f. Right-click the Boston.com Top Stories feed, and then click Delete.

   g. Click the Yes button in the dialog box to confirm the deletion.

3. Right-click the Book Companion Site Web page favorite on the Favorites bar, click Delete, and then click Yes to remove the shortcut if necessary.

4. Right-click a blank area of the Favorites bar, and then click Favorites Bar to hide the toolbar.

5. Close Internet Explorer.

6 | Send a Web Page by E-Mail and Save a Web Page

This exercise requires you to send a Web page by e-mail and save a Web page to your computer's hard drive. Check with your instructor for the recipient's e-mail address, and the name and location of the folder in which to save the Web page.

1. Start Internet Explorer, if necessary. In the Address bar, type search criteria for an Internet topic that interests you. Find and read a current news article on an Internet topic that you think your instructor might be interested in reading.

2. Click the Page button on the Command bar, and then click 'Send page by e-mail' or 'Send link by e-mail' to open your e-mail client software. Enter the recipient's e-mail address provided by your instructor and click Send. If necessary, close the e-mail application window.

3. Click the Page button on the Command bar and click Save as to open the Save Webpage dialog box. Switch to the folder specified by your instructor, change the Save as type to Webpage, complete (*.htm; *.html), if necessary, and then click Save.

4. Close Internet Explorer.

7 | Review Tips for Staying Safe Online

1. Start Internet Explorer, if necessary. Visit the Book Companion Site Web page for this book, and then open US-CERT Shopping Safely Online below Chapter 2, Exercise 7 in a new tab.

   a. Review the US-CERT Cyber Security Tip Web page on Shopping Safely Online.

   b. Create an outline you can use to present these tips to a group of classmates.

2. Visit the Book Companion Site Web page for this book, and then open TRUSTe below Chapter 2, Exercise 7 in a new tab.

   a. Click the Consumers Privacy link on the home page to review information targeted to consumers.

   b. Locate and print tips on online safety. Be prepared to discuss the tips with your classmates.

3. Visit the Book Companion Site Web page for this book, and then open Child Safety Online below Chapter 2, Exercise 7 in a new tab.

   a. Review information about online child safety.

   b. Write a report that describes the risks to children using the Internet and the Web, and suggestions for ways to protect children from those risks.

4. Visit the Book Companion Site Web page for this book, and then open OnGuard Online below Chapter 2, Exercise 7 in a new tab.

   a. Review the top tips for computer security.

   b. Take the interactive quizzes.

   c. Report back to your class on what you learned at the Web site.

5. Close Internet Explorer.

8 | Browse a Web Site

1. Start Internet Explorer, if necessary. Visit the Book Companion Site Web page for this book, and then open USA Today or FOXNews below Chapter 2, Exercise 8 in a new tab on the tab row foreground.

   a. Follow at least 10 links of interest from the news Web site home page to browse its other Web pages or pages at other sites. Use the Back button to return to the news Web site if following a link takes you to a Web page outside the news site.

   b. Write a brief summary describing your browsing experience. How many links took you to Web pages within the news Web site? How many links took you to Web pages outside the news Web site? How easy or difficult was it to identify the content of the Web page you would visit before you clicked a link? What did you enjoy most about browsing the news Web site?

9 | Research Privacy Policies

1. Start Internet Explorer, if necessary. Open the following e-commerce Web sites in tabbed Web pages. Locate and click the link to each company's privacy policy statement.

   a. Amazon (www.amazon.com)

   b. Target (www.target.com)

   c. Hewlett-Packard (www.hp.com)

2. Answer the following privacy issue questions for each Web site:

   a. What information is collected from users? Is personally identifiable information collected?

   b. Why is the information collected?

   c. Does the company share the collected information with its business partners?

   d. How long is the information retained?

   e. Can a user opt out of the information collection; and if so, how?

    f. Does the Web site post any privacy guarantees, such as TRUSTe?

    g. Does the Web site use cookies or Web bugs; and if so, why?

3. Close Internet Explorer.

10 | Research Internet and Web Threats

1. Start Internet Explorer, if necessary. Visit the Book Companion Site Web page for this book, and then open the links below Chapter 2, Exercise 10 in new tabs. Click each tab in turn to research the following Internet and Web threats.

    a. criminal or unethical hackers

    b. viruses

    c. adware

    d. spyware

2. Using your research, write at least four paragraphs describing each threat and how to protect against it using Internet Explorer tools and good judgment.

3. Close Internet Explorer.

3 Searching the Web

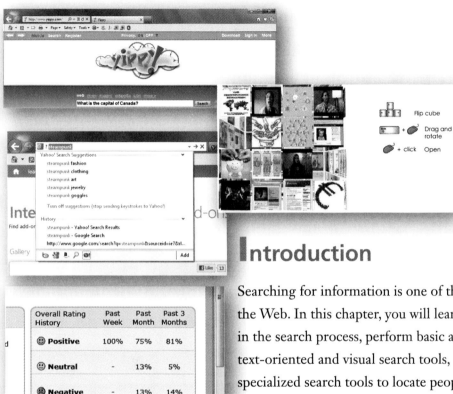

Introduction

Searching for information is one of the most powerful and useful features of the Web. In this chapter, you will learn how to describe and follow the steps in the search process, perform basic and advanced searches using general text-oriented and visual search tools, use browser search features, and use specialized search tools to locate people, businesses, current news stories, geographic information, video, social media, and products and services. You also will learn about online research alternatives to search tools.

Objectives

After completing this chapter, you will be able to:

1. Describe the search process

2. Use different types of search tools and compare search results

3. Apply search tool shortcuts and advanced features, including Boolean operators

4. Perform searches using browser search features

5. Identify and use specialized search tools

6. Identify online research alternatives to standard search tools

The Search Process

Many people rely on the Web to find specific information quickly. As you learned in Chapter 2, when you know the URL for a Web page, you can enter the URL in your browser's Address box or click a favorite to open the page. In this way, you can get the latest scores or team standings for your favorite sports teams, keep up with current news and trends, and purchase products or services from your preferred online stores.

At other times, you might need specific information but not know the Web page's URL, or you might require specific information but not know where to find it. For example, suppose you want to learn more about The White House by visiting Web pages that provide that information. One way you could do so is to guess an appropriate URL — something like www.whitehouse.gov — and enter that guess in the browser's Address box. New to Internet Explorer 9, the Address box will return search results based on what you enter. So if you guess an incorrect URL or decide to just enter keywords, such as *The White House*, Internet Explorer will search for appropriate URLs and provide you with a suggested list. Figure 3-1 illustrates a specific process you can follow when searching the Web. In the next sections, you will learn more about this process.

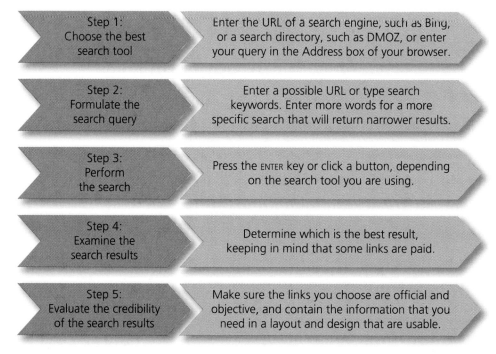

Step 1: Choose the best search tool	Enter the URL of a search engine, such as Bing, or a search directory, such as DMOZ, or enter your query in the Address box of your browser.
Step 2: Formulate the search query	Enter a possible URL or type search keywords. Enter more words for a more specific search that will return narrower results.
Step 3: Perform the search	Press the ENTER key or click a button, depending on the search tool you are using.
Step 4: Examine the search results	Determine which is the best result, keeping in mind that some links are paid.
Step 5: Evaluate the credibility of the search results	Make sure the links you choose are official and objective, and contain the information that you need in a layout and design that are usable.

Figure 3-1　The Web search process.

Choosing the Best Search Tool

Searching the Web effectively starts with selecting the best search tool to use for a particular search. Many different types of search tools, such as Google, StumbleUpon, Bing, and blinkx (Figure 3-2), are prevalent on the Web. You will learn more about these and other search tools and how to use them later in the chapter. It is important to realize that search tool features and performance vary from tool to tool and change over time, and that new search tools are continually being developed. Also, a user's search needs might vary from one search to another, making one tool more appropriate for that type of search. The best approach is to become familiar with and use multiple search tools, which allows you to evaluate search tools and then choose the tool best suited for a particular search. In general, when evaluating search tools, look for tools that:

- Are easy to use
- Return search results quickly
- Provide access to frequently updated large indexes of Web pages and other Web-based files
- Present the most relevant search results for a keyword search
- Clearly indicate paid or sponsored links in their search results list

Figure 3-2 A variety of search tools, such as Google and blinkx, are available on the Web.

As more and more people use mobile or smartphones to search the Internet, search engines that specifically search for mobile versions of Web sites have been developed. Mobile versions of Google, Ask.com, and Bing are available.

According to the Pew Internet & American Life Project, 58 percent of Americans have researched a product or service online, and 57 percent of American adult Internet users have used a search engine to search for their own name.

Formulating the Search Query

The next step in the process of searching the Web is to formulate a search query. A **search query** is a question that defines the information you seek. A query should include at least one **keyword**, a specific word that describes that information. To get the best results, choose keywords carefully and use specific rather than general keywords whenever appropriate. For example, suppose you recently visited an animal shelter and are considering adopting one of two dogs you saw at the shelter. But before you adopt your new pet, you want to use the Web to learn more about the nature, characteristics, and care requirements of your two adoption possibilities: a sheltie and a golden retriever. Using the search keywords, *sheltie* or *golden retriever*, generates more relevant results than using the search keyword, *dog*.

Search keywords are entered in a search tool's **search text box**, or with Internet Explorer 9, in the Address box. A search tool then uses the keywords to identify relevant Web pages and return a **search results list** containing the URL, title, and description of and links to Web pages that are determined by the search tool as being the most relevant to the keywords. Each Web page item listed in a search results list is called a **hit**. Figure 3-3 illustrates a search using the keyword, *sheltie*, and the resulting hits.

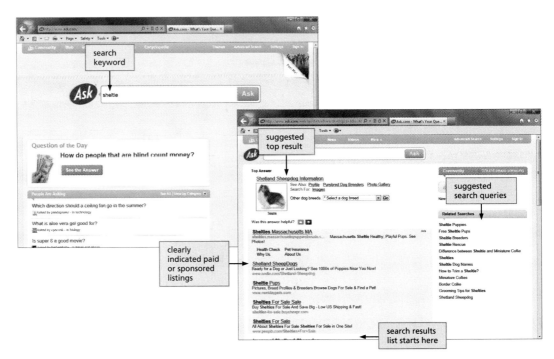

Figure 3-3 Search keywords entered in a search tool's search text box are used to return a search results list containing relevant Web page hits.

When you use multiple keywords, such as *golden retriever*, most search tools automatically assume the word, and, exists between keywords, meaning the Web pages returned in the list of hits will contain *golden* and *retriever*. But assuming the word, and, exists between keywords does not guarantee that the keywords will appear close together on the Web pages. Most search tools allow you to surround keywords with quotation marks when the keywords must appear together as a phrase. For example, a keyword search for *congressional bill* might return Web pages containing the word, congressional, and the first name, Bill. Using quotation marks around the phrase, "*congressional bill*", narrows the results to hits that contain that exact phrase.

The more keywords you include in a query, the more focused the results will be. For example, assume you are planning a vacation and want to find information about a specific national park. Searching for Web pages using the keyword, *park*, will return a list of millions of pages, far more than you can or want to review and most of which are irrelevant to the information you seek. Using the phrase, "*Grand Canyon National Park*", returns more relevant hits because the search process returns Web pages that contain all of those keywords together and places the pages at or near the top of the list of hits. Omitting the quotation marks will likely produce slightly different search results — but Web pages containing information about the Grand Canyon National Park still should be positioned at or near the top of the search results list.

Although it is always better to spell search keywords correctly, some search tools either might list search results for correctly spelled keywords or suggest the correct spelling. For example, searching for information about a musical instrument using the keyword, *accordian*, might return a list of Web pages based on the correct spelling *accordion*, depending on which search tool is used.

Your research might seek a specific answer, such as the amount of rain that falls annually in the Amazon rainforest, or you might want more general information without a specific fact in mind. The number of hits returned in a search results list depends on a query's structure and keywords. For example, a **targeted search** seeks specific information using keyword combinations such as *"average rainfall" Amazon rainforest*. This type of targeted search might require you to examine only a few Web pages to find useful information. An **open-ended search** seeks information on a broader scale using a simple keyword such as *rainforest*. An open-ended search like this typically generates thousands of hits and requires you to review multiple Web pages to gather appropriate information. Scholarly research often involves open-ended searches.

Some search tools allow you to put the query in the form of a statement or question, such as, *What is the capital of Canada*? A search that uses complete sentences is sometimes called a **natural language search** (as in the Yippy search tool, Figure 3-4). Small, unimportant words in a natural language search query, called **stop words**, are ignored and only the more important words are used. Examples of stop words include what, where, is, the, of, in, and how.

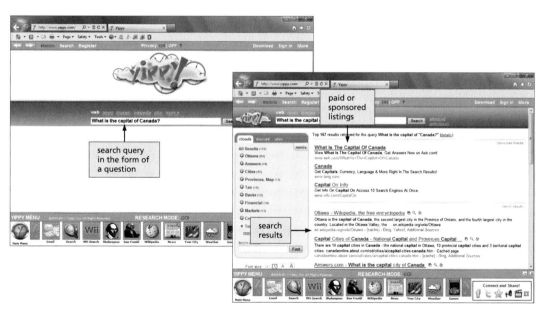

Figure 3-4   The Yippy search tool with a complete question as the search query.

Because each search tool has its own method for evaluating keywords and determining what Web pages are relevant to the keywords, it is a good idea to review a search tool's FAQ pages or Help section for information about the best way to formulate queries for that search tool.

Examining the Search Results

Because different search tools perform a search and display hits in the search results list in various ways, you should become familiar with and use a variety of search tools. As you have learned, the hits in a search results list are presented in a certain order, usually with more relevant hits at or near the top of the list. Some search tools place hits for recommended Web sites at the top of a search results list because a human editor has determined that the sites are the most relevant to the keywords. Other search tools might place hits for paid placement or sponsored listings near or at the top of a search results list because these Web sites pay the search tools to do so. Although listed at or near the top, paid placement site hits might or might not provide the best information for a query. For this reason, it is important to know how to identify any paid or sponsored hits that appear among the search results and, if necessary, scroll further down a search results list to review other, possibly more relevant, hits.

FACTS @HAND A wiki is a Web site that allows users to edit, update, and add content. Popular television shows, such as *Glee*, have large wikis with Web pages on characters and episodes. Wikipedia is a comprehensive online encyclopedia that is written and edited by users. When using Wikipedia or any other open-content wiki, keep in mind that some articles could be edited or written by biased or unauthorized writers, and that you should verify information you learn from a wiki with an outside source.

Because a Web search can return thousands or millions of hits, most people typically look only at the first 10 or 20 hits in a search results list. If no relevant Web pages are found, they then reformulate the search query and search again using the same search tool or a different search tool. When a search results list with potentially relevant Web pages is returned, the next step is to click links associated with relevant hits and review each Web page to find the desired information.

Evaluating the Credibility of Search Results

A key step in the search process is to evaluate the credibility of the Web pages you open from a search results list. A search results list can contain an assortment of Web pages; and although all pages might contain information related to the query, there is no guarantee that all will contain accurate or useful information. Because anyone can publish information to the Internet, it is important to carefully assess the credibility of the Web page content by looking at the authority of the source, the objectivity of the text, the scope and quality of the content, and the Web site's design and functionality.

AUTHORITY The first step in determining the quality of the information on a Web page is to examine its authority. To do this, determine who owns or sponsors the page's Web site and, if possible, who authored the page content. Try to determine if the content's author and/or the Web site's sponsor has the appropriate expertise to present the information authoritatively. To do this, look for and read any background information posted about a Web page's author or the site's sponsoring organization.

Some search tools give extra weight to governmental and educational Web pages, listing these hits at or near the top of a search results list. However, you should look past the top-level domain to the country-code top-level domain when evaluating the authority of these Web sites. For example, information presented by agencies of a totalitarian government that limits free speech or free access to the Internet and the Web might not be unbiased or completely accurate. Web sites with the .edu top-level domain represent educational institutions, but a Web page at an educational site might be the work of a student rather than a scholar. The highest quality and more authoritative results come from primary sources. A **primary source** is any document, item, or other data that provides first-hand information about a particular topic. For example, when searching for the history of the Web, an authoritative primary source would be a Web page with an account written by Tim Berners-Lee, who participated in the development of the Web firsthand.

OBJECTIVITY   When examining a Web site's objectivity, determine whether the Web page information is fair, whether the content contains any subtle or clear biases, or whether the information is skewed toward commercial or political interests. For example, when looking for information about vitamins or nutritional supplements, determine whether a Web page bases its recommendations on facts reported by other sources, or whether it is part of a commercial Web site that profits by promoting the sale of its particular formulas. One way to assess objectivity is to look on the Web page for links with recognizable, reputable domain names that link to other related Web sites.

SCOPE AND QUALITY   Evaluating the scope of Web page content — the depth of coverage and the amount of detail provided — can help determine its value. The intended audience — whether children or adults, professionals or enthusiasts — often determines the scope of a Web site. Additionally, high-quality Web page content should be accurate and up to date.

One technique for determining scope and quality is to compare several Web page sources that discuss the same topic. Different Web pages might offer different information on the same topic. For example, in searching for the origin of pizza, the name, Queen Margherita, appears in a number of documents. If several Web pages refer to her, but one page spells her name incorrectly or omits a reference to her entirely, you might consider that page to be a less valuable source of information. Some Web page authors publish information gathered from others without careful research. Web page content that has been carefully researched typically offers more details and depth, as well as contains citations or references to other sources, either as links or in a list at the end of the article or page. Therefore, comparing Web page coverage of the same topic can be helpful in evaluating the scope and quality of information on different pages. In addition, look for dates on Web pages indicating when the information was published or last updated, especially when researching trends or a developing story. Depending on the currency of the topic, an article published a year ago might be considered to be updated; for breaking news, currency is measured in hours or even minutes.

DESIGN AND FUNCTIONALITY   Your first impression of the Web site also offers insight to its credibility. Web pages with grammar or spelling errors, poor organization, missing images, or broken links — links that no longer work — at best indicate poor attention to detail and at worst might indicate the page is a poor-quality source. Be aware, however, that having an attractive and professional looking Web page does not guarantee high-quality, credible content.

Figure 3-5 lists several key questions to ask as you evaluate the credibility of Web page content. Using these questions and the guidelines outlined above can help you identify valuable information resources from among the many hits listed in a search results list.

Evaluating Web Pages
For more information about evaluating Web pages, visit **www. cengagebrain.com**. On the CengageBrain. com home page, enter the book title, *Discovering the Internet*, and then click the Find button. On the product page for this book, click the Access Now button below the Study Tools heading. On the Book Companion Site Web page, click the drop down menu, select Chapter 3, and then click the @Source link. Click the links below Evaluating Web Pages.

Evaluating the Credibility of Web Pages

Area	Questions
Authority	• Is this a primary source document? • Is the Web page's sponsoring organization or author a noted authority? • Are the Web pages up to date?
Objectivity	• Is the Web page objective? • Is any bias clearly stated?
Scope	• What is the intended audience for this Web site? • How does the information on the Web page compare with others on the same topic?
Design and functionality	• Does the Web page have a professional appearance? • Do all parts of the Web page work correctly?

Figure 3-5   Questions to ask when evaluating the credibility of Web pages.

Search Tools

Web-based search tools help users around the world locate all types of information, including informational Web pages, businesses, people, multimedia files, document databases, and more. Search tools used to find Web-based information can be broadly classified as directories, search engines, and metasearch engines. In the following sections, you will learn how to identify directories, search engines, and metasearch engines; their characteristics; and how to use them to perform basic searches.

Directories

A human-compiled, hierarchical list of Web pages organized by category is called a **directory**. One of the first directories was created by Jerry Yang and David Filo (Figure 3-6), two doctoral students at Stanford University, who began to keep a list of interesting Web pages for their personal use. Their Stanford classmates and friends soon began asking to share the list, originally called Jerry's Guide to the World Wide Web. Soon the list became long and unwieldy, so Filo and Yang divided the list into categories and then later, as the number of Web pages continued to grow, into subcategories. In 1995, the Jerry's Guide directory was renamed Yahoo!. The original Yahoo! directory has evolved to become the Yahoo! network of online tools and services including Yahoo! Search, Yahoo! Directory, Yahoo! Mail, Yahoo! Shopping, and more.

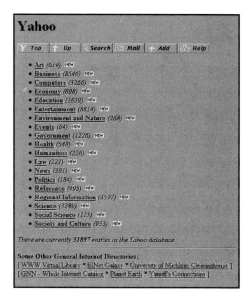

Figure 3-6   An early version of Yahoo!, the first widely popular Web directory.

Directories, which are compiled and indexed by a staff of human editors, are useful search tools that present links to Web sites organized into easy-to-understand categories. Directories offer a way to locate Web-based information by browsing from a general category to an ever more specific category until the desired information is located. For example, using the DMOZ Open Directory Project directory to locate a Web site that offers a trip planner and maps can involve clicking a number of links to move from a general category, such as Reference, through additional subcategories, to a useful Web page link and, finally, to the Web site (Figure 3-7). This process is sometimes called **drilling down** the directory categories.

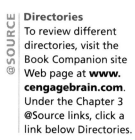

@SOURCE

Directories
To review different directories, visit the Book Companion site Web page at **www. cengagebrain.com**. Under the Chapter 3 @Source links, click a link below Directories.

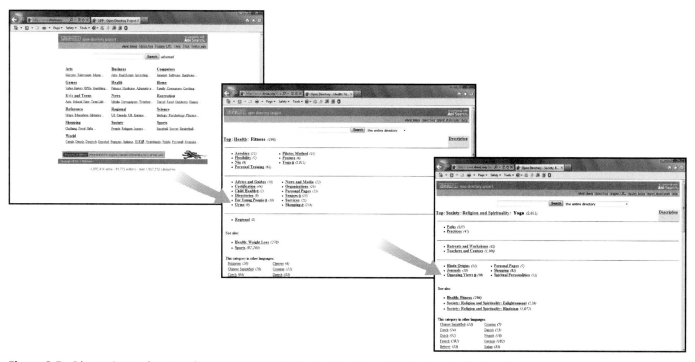

Figure 3-7   Directories use human editors to organize Web sites into hierarchical categories that can be browsed, or drilled down, by clicking links.

At the top of the Web page, some directories show a horizontal list of links to categories and subcategories through which you have drilled down to reach the current page. This list of category and subcategory links is called a breadcrumb trail. A **breadcrumb trail** shows the hierarchical arrangement of categories and subcategories through which you have clicked. You can click any link in the breadcrumb trail to move back and forth between categories and subcategories and return to the home page.

Using human editors to compile a directory's index of Web resources is both a strength and a weakness. Human editors can organize lists of Web resources in a logical way, making browsing or drilling down through a directory's categories an organized process. Using human editors also is a weakness, however, because of the time it takes for human editors to review new Web pages and add them to a directory's index. Additionally, human editors determine what pages are accepted for the index and what pages are not accepted. Using a directory, therefore, might not provide links to a number of appropriate and useful Web pages on any particular topic simply because the pages have not yet been indexed or were rejected for inclusion by the editors. In addition to the DMOZ Open Directory Project, other directories include Yahoo! Directory and Business.com.

To Use a Directory

The following steps drill down through DMOZ category links to find Web pages that contain information about Grace Hopper, a computer programming pioneer. Then they return you to the DMOZ home page using the breadcrumb trail.

- Start Internet Explorer.

- Visit the Book Companion Site Web page for this text (Figure 3-8).

- Click the Select a chapter list arrow, click the option for Chapter 3, and then click the Steps link in the left side of the page.

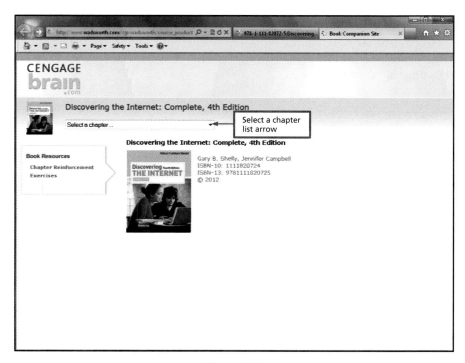

Figure 3-8

- Right-click the DMOZ Open Directory Project link, and then click 'Open in new window' to open the DMOZ home page in a new window (Figure 3-9).

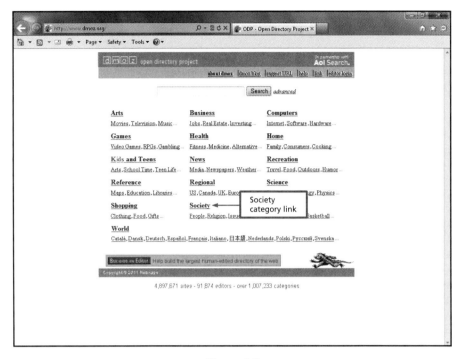

Figure 3-9

- Click the Society category link to view the Society subcategories page in the same tab (Figure 3-10).

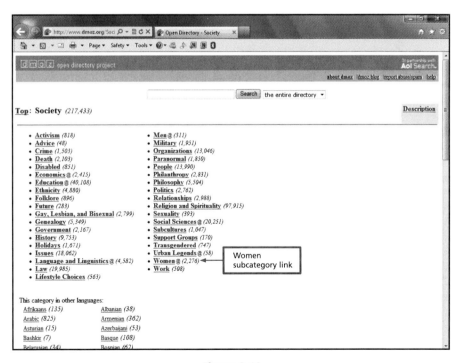

Figure 3-10

4

- Click the Women subcategory link to view the subcategory page (Figure 3-11).

Why do I see a list of horizontal links above the category links?
You can see the path of the links you have clicked to reach the current Web page in the breadcrumb trail at the top of the page (Top: Society: People: Women). You can move back to a previously viewed Web page by clicking that page's link in the breadcrumb trail.

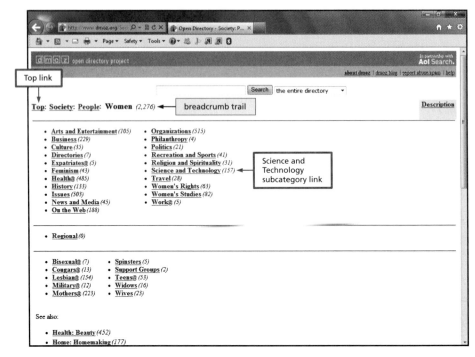

Figure 3-11

5

- Click the Science and Technology subcategory link to view the subcategory page.

- Click the Computers and Internet subcategory link to view the subcategory page.

- Click the Hopper, Grace Murray link to view the subcategory page.

- Click a Grace Murray Hopper link or another link of interest to view a Web page containing information about Grace Hopper (Figure 3-12).

- Click the Back button to view the previous DMOZ page.

- Click the Top link in the breadcrumb trail to return to the DMOZ home page (see Figure 3-11).

- Close the browser.

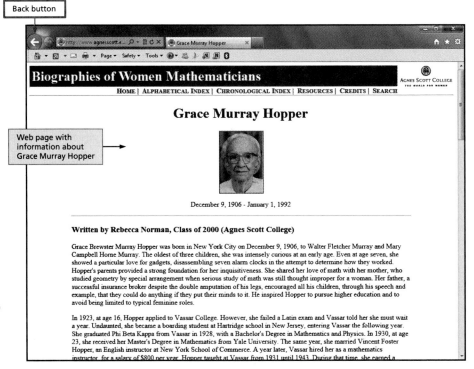

Figure 3-12

Most directories have strategic partnerships with powerful search tools, called search engines, to enable users to search the directory's index by keywords instead of drilling down through categories and subcategories, or search the partner search engine's index of Web pages. You will learn more about search engines in the next section.

Search Engines

Search engines include general-purpose search tools, such as Google, Ask.com, Bing, AltaVista, and Gigablast (Figure 3-13). Additionally, specialty search tools, such as Bizrate (shopping), Technorati (blogs), and Fact Monster (kid-friendly searches), abound (Figure 3-14). Some search engines, such as Google, provide search technologies or Web page indexes for other search engines. For example, AOL Search results are "enhanced" by Google. AltaVista is owned by Yahoo!, which provides its indexes.

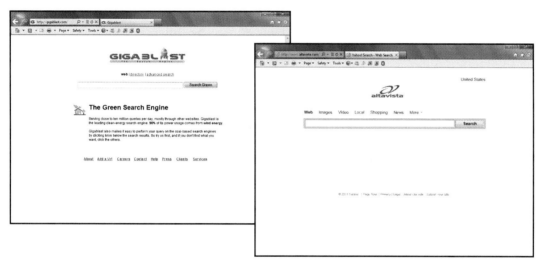

Figure 3-13 Search engines include general-purpose search tools, such as Gigablast and AltaVista.

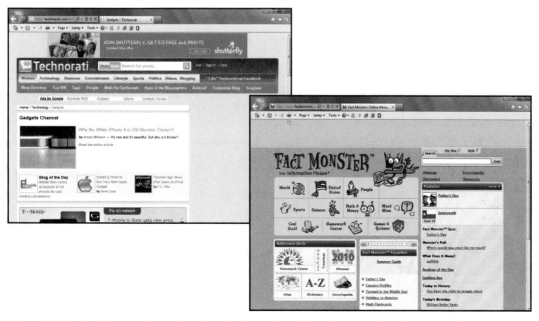

Figure 3-14 Specialty search tools, such as Technorati and Fact Monster, abound on the Web.

In contrast to directories, which are compiled by humans, a **search engine** uses software called a **spider**, **bot** (short for robot), or **Web crawler** that browses the Web, automatically adding the URLs and other information about Web pages to a searchable index. Yahoo! Slurp, Googlebot, and Bingbot are all examples of Web crawlers.

Different search engines collect different kinds of information about each Web page, but Web crawlers typically scan for some or all of the following information to create their indexes:

- Page title — coded title that appears on the browser title bar when the Web page is opened
- URL — specifically, the domain name (for example, cheaptickets.com)
- **Meta tag keywords** — descriptive keywords coded into the Web page's HTML that are readable by the Web crawler but invisible to the user
- Occurrence of keywords — both the frequency of use and where they appear on a Web page
- All of the words on the Web page, which is known as **full-text searching**
- Internal links within the Web page to other pages on the Web site (for example, site maps)
- Number and relevancy of other Web pages that link to the page

The Web page information retrieved by a Web crawler is stored in a database on one or more servers, creating an **index** similar to the index at the back of a book. Web crawlers continually browse the Web to update their indexes with modified Web page content or new, previously unknown Web pages. When a user interacts with a search engine, it accesses the results of the Web crawler's searches, but doesn't interact with the Web crawler directly.

When a user enters keywords into a search engine's search text box, the search engine compares the keywords with its index, compiles a list of Web pages for which the keywords are relevant, and arranges the list in a specific order. Each search engine uses its own unique software and formula or algorithm to determine the relevance of a Web page to specific keywords, and the order in which to rank or list the pages in the search results.

Most search engines attempt to present the most useful and relevant results or hits at or near the top of a search results list to make their search engine more useful and to attract more users. As discussed earlier in this chapter, however, some search engines also accept payment from advertisers to prominently feature their Web pages based on certain search keywords. These paid listings are generally labeled and/or highlighted and positioned in a prominent place on a search results Web page, often at the top of the page or on the right side of the page.

Finally, many search tools today have become hybrids — basing their results on indexes created both by Web crawlers and by human editors. For the remainder of this text, the term, search engine, will be used to refer to various types of search tools.

@SOURCE

Search Engines
To review different search engines, visit the Book Companion Site Web page at **www. cengagebrain.com**. Under the Chapter 3 @Source links, click a link below Search Engines.

To Use Search Engines

The following steps use four different search engines (Google, Ask.com, Yahoo! Search, and Bing) to find Web pages that contain information about community-supported agriculture. As you use each search engine, carefully review each search results page to note the differences in the first 10 hits, the position of paid placement or sponsored listings, and any other features offered by the search engine.

You will open each search engine page in a new window using a shortcut menu. Remember that, because of the dynamic nature of Web pages, the content you see on your screen might vary from that in the figures in this chapter.

- Start Internet Explorer.

- Visit the Book Companion Site Web page for this text, click the Select a chapter list arrow, select the link for Chapter 3, and then click the Steps link to open the Steps page.

- Right-click the Google link, and then click 'Open in new window' to open the Google search page in a new window.

- Type **community-supp** in the search text box to display a list of options in the Search text box drop-down list, and to display search results in the Google window (Figure 3-15).

Q&A

Why do I see a drop-down list below the search text box?
Some search engines suggest search queries based on the characters you type in the search text box. You can click a suggested search query to use it, or close the list by pressing the ESC key or clicking a Close button or link.

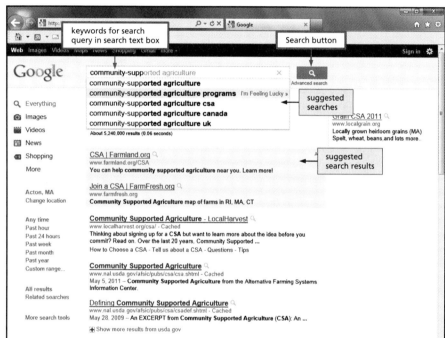

Figure 3-15

- Type `orted agriculture` in the search text box to finish the keywords, and then click the Search button to view the search results page (Figure 3-16).

- Scroll the search results page to view the sponsored links and the top hits.

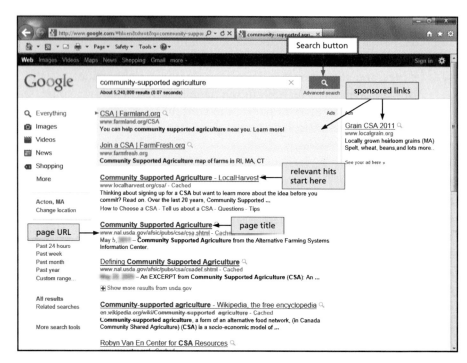

Figure 3-16

- Click the browser window Close button and return to the Discovering the Internet, Chapter 3 Steps page.

- Right-click the Ask.com link, and then click 'Open in new window' to open the Ask.com search page in a new window.

- Type `community-supported agriculture` in the Ask search text box, and then click the Ask button.

- Scroll the search results page to view suggested additional search options, the sponsored results, Related Searches, and the top hits (Figure 3-17).

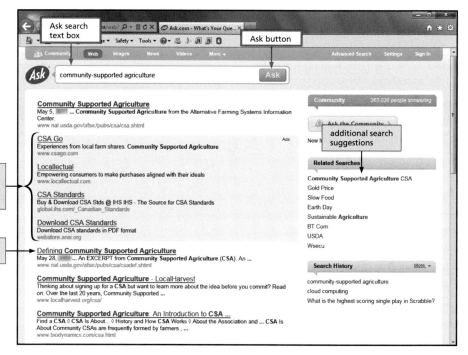

Figure 3-17

4

- Click the browser window Close button, and then return to the Discovering the Internet, Chapter 3 Steps page.

- Right-click the Yahoo! Search link, and then click 'Open in new window' to open the Yahoo! Search search page in a new window.

- Type **community-supported agriculture** in the search text box, and then click the Search button.

- Scroll the search results page to view more search options, Sponsored Results, and the top hits (Figure 3-18).

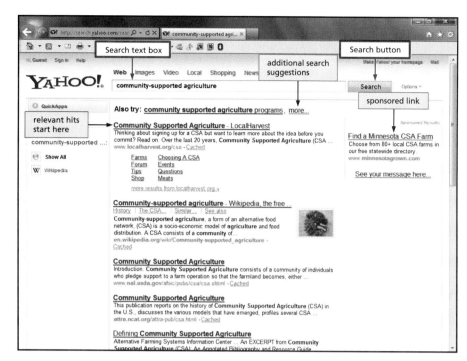

Figure 3-18

5

- Click the browser window Close button and return to the Discovering the Internet, Fourth Edition Steps page.

- Right-click the Bing link, and then click 'Open in new window' to open the Bing search page in a new window.

- Type **community-supported agriculture** in the search text box.

- Click the Search button at the end of the text box.

- Scroll the search results page to view more search options, Ads, and Related Searches links (Figure 3-19).

- Close all browser windows and tabs.

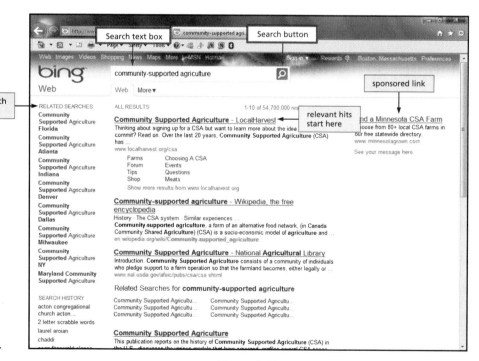

Figure 3-19

Why do I see pop-up text?

Bing search results also include a Quick Preview pop-up that provides a brief synopsis of the related Web page. You can view search results Quick Previews by dragging the mouse pointer down the right edge of the search results.

A review of the search results returned by each search engine shows that a search results list based on the same search query likely will not be identical — either in Web pages listed or in the ranking of those pages — when using different search engines. Also, other features such as sponsored listings might be different, and each search engine might offer special features.

Some search providers, such as Google, Yahoo!, and Microsoft, allow users to download toolbars as free browser plug-ins for Internet Explorer. These toolbars are designed to make searching with a search provider's specific search engine easier and to provide access to some of the provider's other tools. You can learn more about downloading, installing, and using these toolbars by visiting the providers' Web sites. You can turn on or off the installed Google, Yahoo!, and Bing toolbars (Figure 3-20) by clicking the Tools button on the Command bar, and then the toolbar's name on the Toolbars submenu.

Figure 3-20 A search provider's toolbar can make it easier to search using the provider's search engine or to access the provider's other tools.

Most general search engines provide their search results in a traditional list format. However, because of the increasing popularity and availability of broadband Internet connections, some newer search engine startups, such as search-cube (Figure 3-21) and Middlespot, present **visual search results**, such as a carousel of Web pages, pop-up windows, or animated linking relationships.

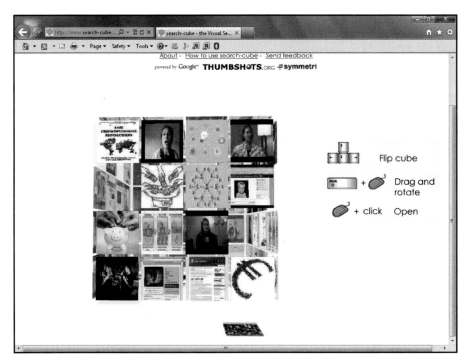

Figure 3-21 Unlike traditional text-based search results lists, some new search engine startups, such as search-cube, present visual search results.

Finally, paid or sponsored listings might not be as clearly indicated on some search results pages as others. For these reasons, it is important to become familiar with and comfortable using more than one search engine. Reviewing a search engine's Help feature can provide insight for using the search engine and its special features more effectively.

According to a recent report by the Hitwise and Nielsen Online marketing companies, Google, with more than 60 percent market share, is the most popular search engine in the United States followed by Yahoo! Search, Bing, AOL Search, and Ask.com.

FACTS @HAND

Kid-Friendly Searches

@ISSUE

Using the Web to help a child research a school project seems like a great idea: Kids are computer-savvy, and it saves you a trip to the library. However, allowing children to use a general search engine might result in some hits that link to objectionable content. A seemingly innocuous search query can result in hits that link to Web pages that include offensive language, sexually explicit or violent material, or hate propaganda.

For this reason, many search engines include a feature to block objectionable content. For example, Google, Yahoo! Search, and Bing provide a SafeSearch feature. Parents and teachers should check these filtering options and make certain they are turned on before children use a general search engine.

A number of other search engines are designed specifically for children. These search engines return search results that include only Web sites that are appropriate for children and young teens, and they specifically exclude from the results any sites that feature sexually explicit text or images, violence, hate speech, and gambling. Search engines for kids also might serve the needs of children and young teens better by offering search results focused on their level of reading and understanding. Some return only Web sites selected by an editorial staff that reviews the content of each site.

Some of the more widely used children's search engines include:
- Ask Kids
- Google SafeSearch for Kids
- Yahoo! Kids
- CyberSleuth Kids
- Awesome Library
- Fact Monster
- Yippy

To view kid-friendly search engines, visit the Book Companion Site Web page at **www. cengagebrain.com**. Under the Chapter 3 @Issue links, click a link below Kid-Friendly Searches.

Metasearch Engines

Performing the same search multiple times using different search engines to get the best search results can be cumbersome. A **metasearch engine** is a special type of search tool that compiles the search results from multiple search engines into a single search results list, effectively performing multiple different searches at once. Metasearch engines include MetaCrawler, Dogpile, KartOO, Mamma.com, and Ixquick. The KartOO metasearch engine (Figure 3-22) returns visual search results with animated links to related pages.

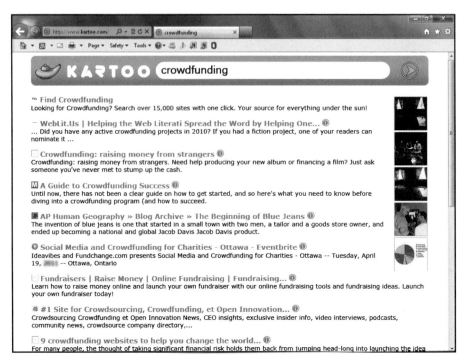

Figure 3-22 Metasearch engines submit a search query to multiple search engines and compile the hits in one search results list. The KartOO metasearch engine returns visual search results with animated links.

@SOURCE

Metasearch Engines
To learn more about metasearch engines, visit the Book Companion Site Web page at **www.cengagebrain.com**. Under the Chapter 3 @Source links, click a link below Metasearch Engines.

When you enter search query keywords in a metasearch engine's search text box, the metasearch engine submits the search query to a number of search engines at one time and then compiles the results from all of them into a single list of hits. A good metasearch engine should eliminate duplicate entries, categorize the hits based on topic, order the hits by relevance, and indicate which search engines provided the search results. Metasearch engines typically rely heavily on sponsored listings, and some metasearch engines mix non-paid and sponsored hits together in the same search results list; therefore, it is important that you carefully review the source of each hit returned by a metasearch engine to eliminate sponsored listings that might not be the most relevant to your search query.

To Use Metasearch Engines

The following steps use three metasearch engines to search for Web pages containing information about crowdfunding. As you complete each step, pay careful attention to each metasearch engine's features and the search engine indexes it uses to create the search results list. You will open each metasearch engine in a new window using a shortcut menu.

- Start Internet Explorer.

- Visit the Book Companion Site Web page for this text, click the Select a chapter list arrow, click the link for Chapter 3, and then click the Steps link to open the Steps page.

- Right-click the Mamma link, and then click 'Open in new window' to open the Mamma metasearch page in a new window.

- Type **crowdfunding** in the search text box, and then click the Search button.

- Scroll the search results page to view the results (Figure 3-23).

- Identify non-paid and sponsored hits in the list.

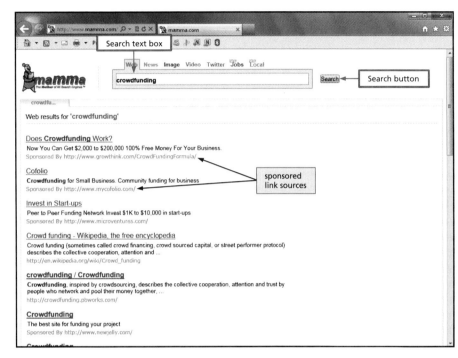

Figure 3-23

- Click the browser window Close button and return to the Discovering the Internet Chapter 3 Steps page.

- Right-click the Dogpile link, and then click 'Open in new window' to open the Dogpile metasearch page in a new window.

- Type **crowdfunding** in the search text box, and then click the Go Fetch! button.

- Scroll the search results in the list (Figure 3-24).

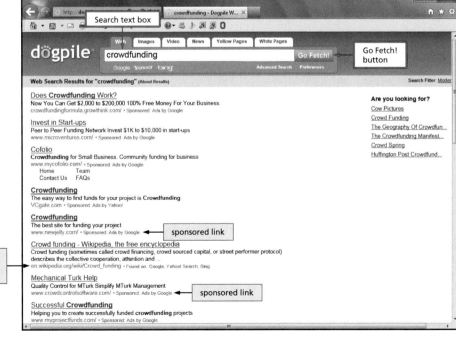

Figure 3-24

3

- Click the browser window Close button and return to the Discovering the Internet, Chapter 3 Steps page.

- Right-click the Ixquick link, and then click 'Open in new window' to open the Ixquick metasearch page in a new window.

- Type **crowdfunding** in the search text box, and then click the Search button.

- Scroll the search results page to identify non-paid and sponsored hits in the list (Figure 3-25).

- Close all browser windows and tabs.

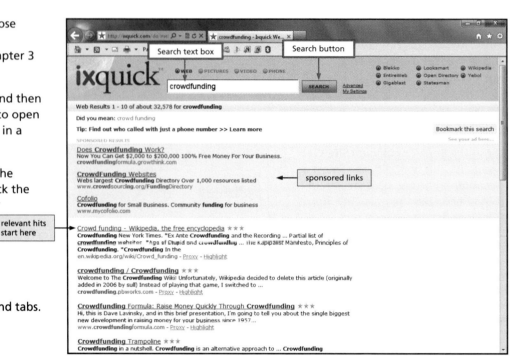

Figure 3-25

Advanced Search Techniques

Simple searches, such as the ones demonstrated so far in this chapter, offer a basic approach to finding information on the Web. More complex searches require additional consideration in formulating the query, as well as understanding advanced search techniques. You might have already used some of these advanced search techniques, such as Boolean operators, without realizing it.

For example, suppose you are researching an answer to the following question: How many college students play sports and why? After selecting a search engine to use, the next task is to formulate the search query by selecting the keywords that will perform the search most efficiently — *college* and *students* and *sports*. There is no need to include stop words, such as *how*, *and*, and *why* because a search engine likely will ignore them. There is also no need to include the word *why* in the search query because the question of causes is implied.

Performing the search using the three keywords *college*, *students*, and *sports* in the query will get good results, but refining the search will achieve more targeted results. For example, grouping *college* and *students* together in a single phrase surrounded by quotation marks indicates that Web pages in the search results must contain the phrase, *college students*. Adding more related keywords to the query, such as *intramural*, however, might further narrow the scope of the search, potentially eliminating good resources. Search engines offer a variety of search tips and shortcuts for formulating a complex search query.

Search Engine Tips and Shortcuts

A **Boolean operator** is a conjunction used in a logical expression. When given multiple keywords in a query, a search engine uses the AND, OR, and NOT (typed in all capital letters) Boolean operators to specify which keywords should be included or excluded from the search results. Figure 3-26 lists several typical methods for using Boolean operators to formulate a search query; however, be aware that not all search engines handle Boolean operators in the same way. You can review a search engine's Help pages for tips on using Boolean operators in search queries.

Boolean Operators

Task	Procedure
Search for all the words in any order.	Type AND between keywords. Example: Canada AND nickel AND mines
Search for at least one of the words.	Type OR between keywords. Example: ocean OR sea
Search for a phrase in the given order.	Surround the phrase with quotation marks. Example: "Catalina yachts"
Exclude a concept from the search results.	Type NOT before the excluded word. Examples: orange NOT Florida or sometimes: kayak AND NOT inflatable

Figure 3-26 Typical methods for formulating a search query using Boolean operators.

The AND operator indicates a keyword must be found in a search results hit. As you learned earlier in this chapter, most search engines assume that a list of several keywords entered into the search text box are connected by the AND operator; thus a search engine returns a search results list in which the hits include all of the words in the query. Some search engines permit the inclusion of multiple keywords in a query by preceding them with a plus sign instead of the AND operator.

Suppose you want the search results in the previous research example to include Web pages that refer to students from either a university or a college. To find Web pages that include either a university or a college, you must use an OR operator. To specify an either-or condition, you must specifically enter OR between the keywords to indicate that hits should include either of the keywords rather than both of the words.

To exclude a keyword from a search, some search engines require you to use the NOT operator before the excluded term (for example, diamonds NOT baseball). Other search engines might require a minus sign before the excluded term (for example, diamonds-baseball).

In addition to Boolean operators, major search engines also offer a number of searching shortcuts, such as the examples shown in Figure 3-27.

You should check out a search engine's Help pages for more information about searching tips and shortcuts.

Sample Search Engine Shortcuts

Search Engine	To Do This:	Type This Search Query:
Yahoo! Search	Use the Yahoo! Maps feature to find a city map and have the map appear on your search results page	map! Boston
	Find a specific keyword as part of a Web page title	intitle:New York (no space following the colon)
Bing	Convert a specific number of dollars to euros or another currency	150 dollars in euros (or Canadian dollars, Mexican pesos, and so forth)
	Find a local business by location and type of business	Austin coffee shop (or other location and business)
Google	Get local weather information	weather: 78218 or weather: Chicago (or other ZIP code or location with or without the space after the colon)
	Perform an addition (+), subtraction (-), multiplication (*), or division (/) calculation	2598+1587 34687-25812 156798*7 2879/3
	Convert measurements	20 inches in cm (centimeters) 5,000 meters in miles

Figure 3-27   Major search engines also offer a number of searching shortcuts.

FACTS @HAND   Major search providers continue to update their search engines with new features in order to profitably compete with other search providers. For example, Google has incorporated a number of new features, such as more options for refining search results and an option for adding more detail to each hit in a search results list. Additionally, search engines based on new or improved search technologies continue to appear. For example, Microsoft Live Search was replaced by Bing. For these reasons, it is a good idea to periodically survey available search engines to see what is new in online search.

Advanced Search Forms

A search engine generally provides an advanced search form you can use to structure a complex search query. An advanced search form typically prompts you to specify Boolean operators and other criteria, such as filtering the results by language, file type, or domain (such as .gov or .edu).

Creating a complex search in an advanced search form is a great way to learn more about how to use specific search engine shortcuts and Boolean operators. As you fill in the form, the search engine creates the search query based on the form's content, and then displays the completed search query at the top of the form and/or at the top of the search results page. You can review a completed search query to learn how to create similar searches by typing shortcuts and Boolean operators directly in the search engine's search text box.

To Use an Advanced Search Form

The following steps use the Bing advanced search form to structure a search query that finds Web pages with information about the use of social media in political elections in the United Kingdom. Next, you use the Google advanced search form to find PDF files published at educational institutions that contain information about jobs or careers in economics. Finally, you use the Yahoo! Search advanced search form to find Web pages that have been updated in the last six months and contain either the word, galaxies, or the word, planets, in the page title.

- Start Internet Explorer.

- Visit the Book Companion Site Web page for this text, click the Select a chapter list arrow, click the link for Chapter 3, and then click the Steps link to open the Steps page.

- Right-click the Bing link, and then click 'Open in new window' to open the Bing search page in a new window.

- Type **social media political elections** in the search text box (Figure 3-28).

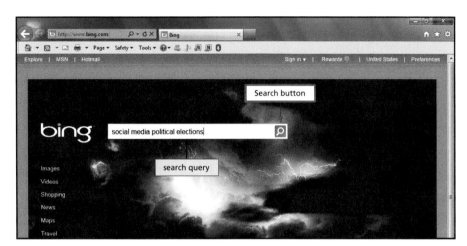

Figure 3-28

- Click the Search button to view the search results page, which shows the initial search query, social media political elections, in the Bing text box at the top of the page (Figure 3-29).

- Scroll the page to view the search results list. The search results list might contain Web pages from around the world. You want to refine the search to show only Web pages from the United Kingdom.

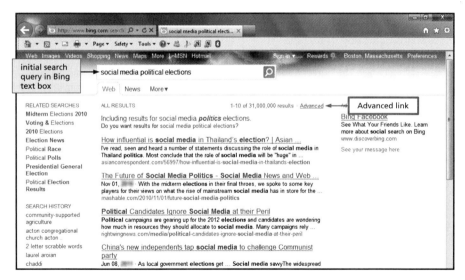

Figure 3-29

- Drag down the right edge of the hit list to view each hit's Quick Preview, a brief synopsis of the Web page's content (Figure 3-30).

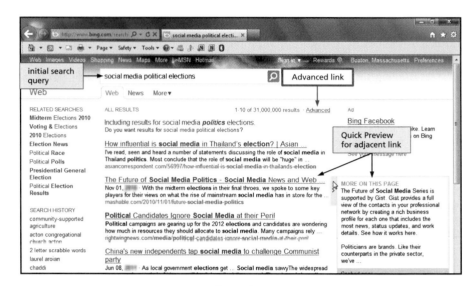

Figure 3-30

❹

- Click the Advanced link to open the Advanced search box at the top of the search results list.

- Click the Site/Domain link to instruct the search engine to search only in specific domains. You can specify domains to include or exclude in this form, and then click 'Add to search' to refine the current search results list.

- Click the 'Look for results only in the following site or domain.' option button, if necessary.

- Type **.uk** in the 'Look for results only in the following site or domain.' text box (Figure 3-31).

Figure 3-31

5

- Click the 'Add to search' button to filter the search results for Web sites from the United Kingdom.

- View the search query, social media political elections site:.uk, in the Bing search text box at the top of the page.

- Scroll the search results page. The search results list is filtered to only show results from Web sites in the .uk domain.

- Drag down the right edge of the hit list to view each hit's Quick Preview (Figure 3-32).

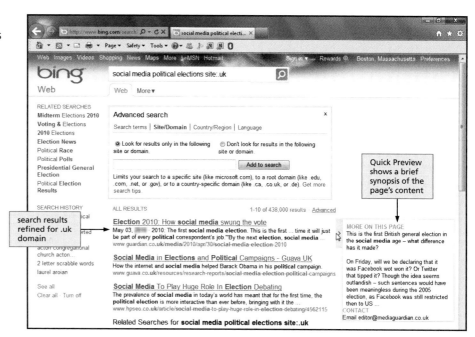

Figure 3-32

6

- Click the browser window Close button and return to the Discovering the Internet, Chapter 3 Steps page.

- Right-click the Google link, and then click 'Open in new window' to open the Google search page in a new window.

- Type **economics** in the Search text box to start the search (Figure 3-33).

Figure 3-33

7

- Click the Advanced search link to view the Advanced Search form.

- Delete economics from the 'Find web pages that have all these words' text box if necessary.

- Type **economics** in the 'Find web pages that have this exact wording or phrase' text box to enter the first search term.

- Type **jobs** in the first 'Find web pages that have one or more of these words:' text box.

- Type **careers** in the second 'Find web pages that have one or more of these words:' text box.

- Click the File type arrow, and then click Adobe Acrobat PDF (.pdf) in the list to specify that the search results must be PDF files.

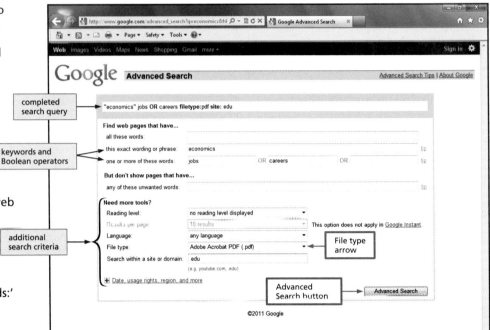

Figure 3-34

- Type **.edu** in the 'Search within a site or domain:' text box.

- Observe the completed search query, "economics" jobs OR careers filetype:pdf site:.edu, in the Google search text box at the top of the form (Figure 3-34).

8

- Click the Advanced Search button to start the search.

- Scroll the search results page to view the list of relevant PDF files published at educational institutions (Figure 3-35).

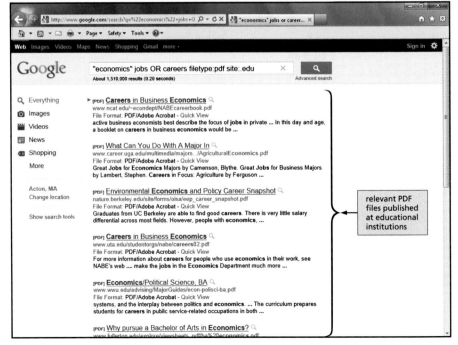

Figure 3-35

- Click the browser window Close button and return to the Discovering the Internet, Chapter 3 Steps page.

- Right-click the Yahoo! Search link, and then click 'Open in new window' to open the Yahoo! Search search page in a new window.

- Click the More link to display its list (Figure 3-36).

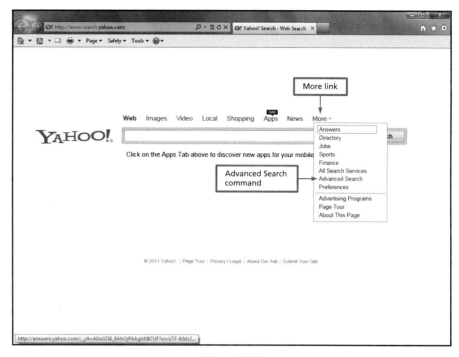

Figure 3-36

10

- Click Advanced Search to open the Advanced Web Search form.

- Type **galaxies planets** in the 'Show results with any of these words' text box.

- Click the 'Show results with any of these words' list arrow and click 'in the title of the page'.

- Click the Updated list arrow and click 'within the past 6 months'.

- Click the 'File Format: Only find results that are:' list arrow.

- Click HTML (.htm, .html) in the list to limit the results to HTML pages (Figure 3-37).

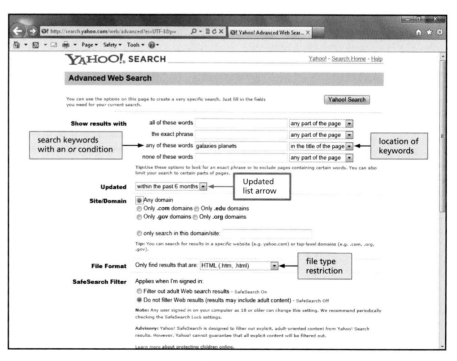

Figure 3-37

- Scroll to view the bottom of the Advanced Search Form page.

- Click the Yahoo! Search button to perform the search and open the search results page. The search query criteria appear at the top of the search results page (Figure 3-38).

- Scroll the search results list to verify that the Web pages returned meet the search criteria.

- Close all open browser windows and tabs.

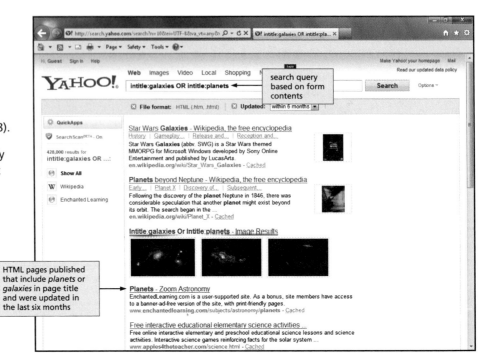

Figure 3-38

Browser Searches

In Chapter 2, you learned how to add Accelerators, including search engine Accelerators, to your browser. The Internet Explorer browser also provides search capabilities through the Address bar, the Search box, the Find Bar, and the Research Explorer Bar.

In the following sections, you will learn how to enter a search query in the Address box on the Address bar, how to change the default search engine used by the Address bar, how to add and remove search engines on the Search box's QuickPick menu, how to perform a keyword search on a page using the Find Bar, and how to search online reference sources offered by Microsoft using the Research Explorer Bar.

Address Bar Searches

You can search the Web by entering a search query in the Address box on the Address bar. After you enter the search query, you can press the ENTER key or click the Search button to open the search results page in the current tab. Pressing the ALT+ENTER keys opens the search results page in a new window.

Internet Explorer uses a designated default search engine for both Address bar searches. In the figures in this section, Bing is the default search engine; your default search engine might be different.

To Search Using the Address Box on the Address Bar

The following steps enter a search query in the Address box to search for Android ringtones using the default search engine. Next, a slightly more complex search query using the Address box and the default search engine is created: a search for Web pages containing information about the U.S. Department of Agriculture MyPlate suggested food serving icon; the search is limited to U.S. government Web sites. Each search results page is opened in a new tab.

- Start Internet Explorer.

- Type **Android ringtones** in the Address box, and then press ALT+ENTER to open the default search engine's search results page in a new window (Figure 3-39).

- Scroll the page to review the search results list.

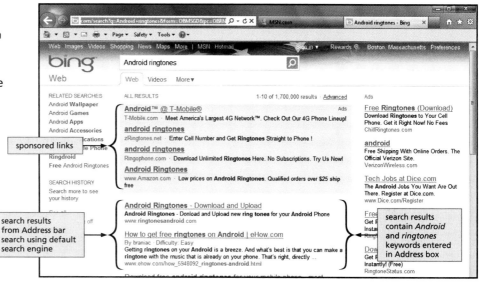

Figure 3-39

- Type **"MyPlate" usda .gov** in the Address box (be sure to type the space between usda and .gov), and then press ALT+ENTER to open the default search engine's search results page in a new window (Figure 3-40).

- Scroll the page to confirm that the search results page lists Web pages at U.S. government Web sites that contain information about the U.S. Department of Agriculture MyPlate food icon.

- Close the browser.

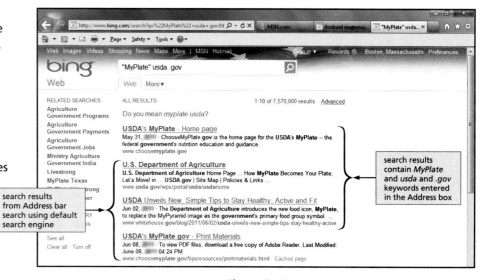

Figure 3-40

Other Ways

1. ALT+D to select Address box contents, then type search keywords

QuickPick Menu Searches

You can use the QuickPick menu and the current search query to search the Web using a different search engine. When you click in the Address box to position the insertion point, the QuickPick menu appears below the Search box. The QuickPick menu contains icons for additional search engines.

As you begin typing keywords in the Search box, a list of textual and/or visual search suggestions appears. The search suggestions list contains suggested searches based on AutoComplete suggestions from previous searches, suggestions from the default search engine, and suggestions from your browsing history, so yours will be different based on past usage. You can click a search suggestion, if desired, to complete your search using the suggestion instead of your original search query.

To Search Using the QuickPick Menu

The following steps search for Web pages containing information about the steampunk culture. You will select different search engines from the QuickPick menu and view each search engine's suggested search queries. The default search engine used in these steps is Bing. Your default search engine and the search engines available on the QuickPick menu in your browser might be different. Your instructor will modify these steps, as necessary, for any differences.

- Start Internet Explorer.

- Type **steampunk** in the Address box (Figure 3-41).

Figure 3-41

● Click the Google icon and view
the search suggestions, if available
(Figure 3-42).

Q&A

What if I do not see the Google icon?
You can click a different icon to view
the search results offered by another
search engine. In the next section, you
will learn how to add an icon from the
Internet Explorer Add-ons Gallery: Search
Providers page to the QuickPick menu.

search results
from Google

Figure 3-42

● Type **steampunk** in the
Address box.

● Click the Yahoo! Search icon to view
the search suggestions (Figure 3-43).

● Leave the browser open for the next
section.

search results
from Yahoo!

Figure 3-43

Other Ways

1. CTRL+E to move
insertion point into
Search box or select
Search box contents

You can add-on additional search engines to the QuickPick menu by selecting a search engine provider in the Internet Explorer Add-ons Gallery: Search Providers page. Open the gallery by clicking the 'Add search providers' button next to the QuickPick menu, and then clicking the Search link to open a scrollable and searchable list of search engine providers.

To Add a New Search Engine to the QuickPick Menu

The following steps open the Internet Explorer Add-ons Gallery: Search Providers page and add the Amazon.com Web site search feature to the QuickPick menu. The search query suggestions from the Amazon.com site are viewed, and a Web page at the Amazon.com site is opened from the suggestions.

- Click the Show Address bar Autocomplete button to view the Autocomplete menu (Figure 3-44).

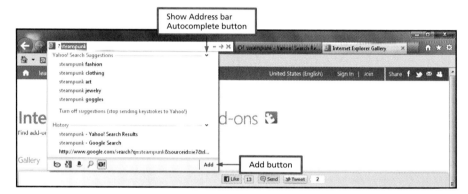

Figure 3-44

- Click Add to open the Internet Explorer Add-ons Gallery (Figure 3-45).

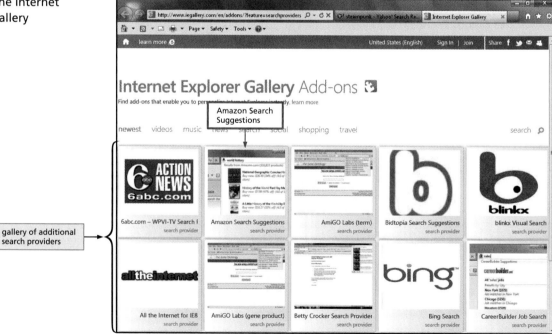

Figure 3-45

- Click the Amazon Search Suggestions icon to open its page (Figure 3-46).

Figure 3-46

- Click the 'Click to install' link to open the Add Search Provider dialog box (Figure 3-47).

Q&A **Can I change my default search engine?**
You can specify that the search provider you are adding will become your browser's default search engine, and specify search suggestions in this dialog box.

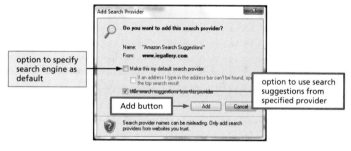

Figure 3-47

- Click the 'Use search suggestions from this provider' check box, if necessary, to select it.

- Click the Add button to add the Amazon.com site search engine to your search providers.

- Click the Show Address bar Autocomplete button to display the QuickPick menu (Figure 3-48).

Figure 3-48

6

- Type **steampunk** in the Address box.

- Click the Amazon Search Suggestions icon to view the visual search query suggestions, which are based on a search of the Amazon.com site (Figure 3-49).

- Leave the browser open for the next section.

Q&A

What should I do if my list does not contain any search suggestions?
Click the 'Turn on suggestions' link to view the search suggestions.

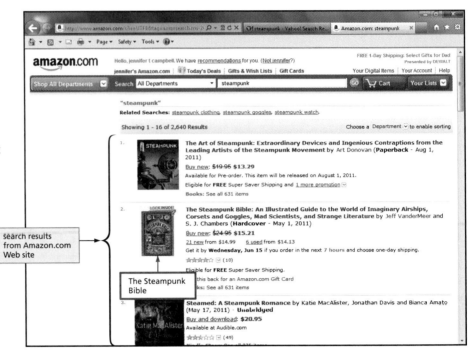

search results from Amazon.com Web site

The Steampunk Bible

Figure 3-49

Other Ways

1. Click Search box; CTRL+DOWN ARROW to open search provider menu

To Remove Amazon Search Suggestions from the QuickPick Menu

You can remove a search engine from the QuickPick menu by opening the Manage Add-ons dialog box, selecting the search engine, and clicking the Remove button. You can open the Manage Add-ons dialog box by clicking Manage add-ons on the Tools menu. The following steps open a page on the Amazon.com Web site, open the Manage Add-ons dialog box, and remove the Amazon Search Suggestions search provider.

1

- Verify that you are viewing the Amazon.com search results.

- Click *The Steampunk Bible* or another visual search suggestion to open the linked page at Amazon.com.

- Click the Tools button to view the Tools menu (Figure 3-50).

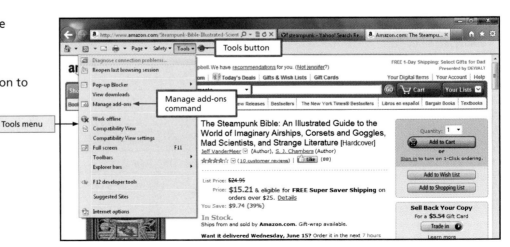

Tools button

Manage add-ons command

Tools menu

Figure 3-50

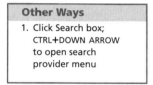

②

- Click Manage add-ons to display the Manage Add-ons dialog box.

- Click Search Providers in the left pane to display the installed search engines (Figure 3-51).

- Click the Amazon Search Suggestions button to select it.

- Click the Remove button to remove the Amazon Search Suggestions from the list of available search providers.

- Click the Close button to close the dialog box.

- Close the browser.

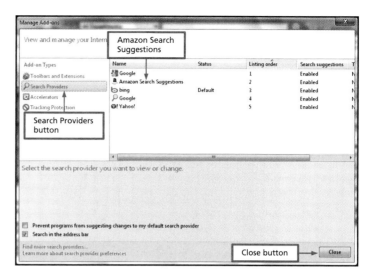

Figure 3-51

Other Ways

1. Click Search box; CTRL+DOWN ARROW to open search provider menu

Find Bar Page Searches

Sometimes it is difficult to locate specific information on a Web page, especially when a page's content is complex. Visually scanning the page can take some time and you might overlook the specific information you need. To more quickly locate needed information, you can perform a keyword search on a page using the Find Bar. To quickly display the Internet Explorer Find Bar, press the CTRL+F keys.

The Find Bar (Figure 3-52) contains:

- The Close the Find bar icon
- The Find text box, in which you can enter or edit keywords
- The Previous and Next buttons, which you can click to move to the previous or next instance of the keyword on the page
- The Highlight all matches button, which allows you to turn on or off highlighting of all instances of the keyword on the page
- The Options button, which allows you to specify a match for whole words only and case
- A search status notation

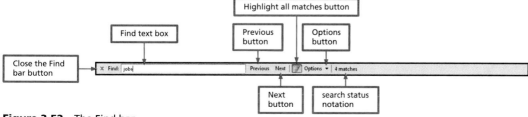

Figure 3-52 The Find bar.

To Search a Web Page Using the Find Bar

The following steps open a Web page in the browser, display the Find Bar, and search the contents of the current page.

- Start Internet Explorer.

- Visit the Book Companion site Web page for this text, click the Select a chapter list arrow, click the link for Chapter 3, and then click the Steps link to open the Steps page.

- Right-click the USA.gov link, and then click 'Open in new window' to open the USA.gov Web page in a new window.

- Press CTRL+F to open the Find Bar below the Command bar (Figure 3-53).

Figure 3-53

- Type **jobs** in the Find text box. The Find Bar search status notation indicates four matches on the Web page (Figure 3-54).

Q&A | **How do I view all the matches?**
You can continue to click the Next button to move from match to match. When no more matches are available, a search status notation indicating no more matches appears on the Find Bar.

Q&A | **Why do I only see one match?**
Your number or matches may differ. If you only get one match, skip the first two bullets of Step 3.

Figure 3-54

3

- Click the Next button to select the next match.

- Continue clicking the Next button until the message, You have reached the last match on the page., appears on the Find bar (Figure 3-55).

- Click the Close the Find bar button.

- Close all open browser windows and tabs.

Figure 3-55

Other Ways

1. alt to display menu bar, click Edit, click Find on this page

2. ENTER to select next match

3. SHIFT+ENTER to select previous match

Search Engine Privacy

@ISSUE

Search engines often use cookies to record search behavior. Although the search information typically does not correspond to personal information, such as name or address, it does correspond to the IP address of your computer. Because broadband users generally have a static IP address that seldom changes, this is tantamount to collecting personal identification.

To learn more about search engine privacy issues, visit the Book Companion Site Web page at **www.cengagebrain.com**. Under the Chapter 3 @Issue links, click a link below Search Engine Privacy.

Specialized Searches

Searching for people, news, magazine or journal articles, video, blogs and other social media, products, or services can be made easier when you use specialized search engines. The following section suggests a variety of search engines you can use to perform specialized searches. Additionally, online sources you can use to find other types of information, such as company financial data, are introduced.

People and Business Search

Web users often search for information about an individual or a business for either professional or personal reasons. One way to find Web pages containing information about an individual or a business is to use the individual's name or the company name as search keywords. Looking for other information, such as an e-mail address or telephone number, is more efficient when you use a specialized directory, such as an online **white pages directory** or **yellow pages directory**. Named for their similarity to telephone directories, white pages and yellow pages directories include Yahoo! People Search, Lycos Whowhere, WhitePages (Figure 3-56), and Superpages.com. Some white pages and yellow pages directories offer additional services such as reverse lookup, which is useful when you know a telephone number and want to discover the name associated with it.

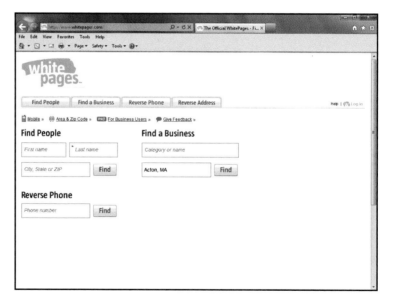

Figure 3-56   Online white pages and yellow pages directories are used to locate individuals and businesses.

News and Current Events Search

Online news sources are diverse. For example, headlines often appear on the home pages of portal sites such as MSN and Yahoo!. Current news is available on the Web sites for broadcast television and radio stations, and you can read the online version of various newspapers. Because most news is distributed through one of the major news wire services, such as the Associated Press (AP), United Press International (UPI), or Reuters, headlines tend to be repeated at various Web sites.

As you observed earlier in this chapter, some search engines provide keyword-related news headlines as part of their search results list. Additionally, major search engines offer alternative news sites, such as Google News, Yahoo! News, and Bing News (Figure 3-57), which focus on providing up-to-the-minute news stories and information on current events as well as news-oriented search tools.

@SOURCE

News and Current Events Search
To review Web sites that focus on news and current events and provide news-oriented search, visit the Book Companion Site Web page at **www. cengagebrain.com**. Under the Chapter 3 @Source links, click a link below News and Current Events.

Figure 3-57 News Web sites such as Bing News provide up-to-the-minute news stories, information on current events, and news-oriented search.

Video Search

A growing number of search engines, such as Google Video, ClipBlast (Figure 3-58), and Yahoo! Video, specialize in indexing Web sites that offer video clips.

Figure 3-58 Specialized search engines are available for locating videos.

Social Media Search

Another area of interest to Internet users is social media, which includes online tools used to communicate ideas, share links, contribute personal commentary, and interact online with other Web users in various ways. (You will learn more about social media in Chapter 4.) Specialized search engines, sometimes called **social media aggregators**, such as Technorati, Google Blog Search, Digg (Figure 3-59), and Newsvine, are used to locate social media resources.

Figure 3-59   You can use specialized search engines such as Digg to locate social media resources.

Shopping Search

Many thousands of products and services are for sale on the Web. Shopping search engines, such as DealTime (Figure 3-60), Nextag, Yahoo! Shopping, and Bing Shopping, are sometimes called **shopping bots** or **shopping aggregators**. Shopping search engines aggregate information about consumer products or services, and help online shoppers compare models, prices, shipping costs, and other variables from various sellers before they buy.

According to Forrester Research, U.S. online retail sales will grow to $229 billion by 2013.

Figure 3-60 Shopping search engines can help online shoppers compare models, prices, shipping costs, and other variables before they buy.

To Shop for a Webcam

The following steps use a shopping search engine to comparison shop online for a Web camera, or webcam, which can be used for online video chats or video conferencing. A highly rated webcam is selected and then prices at different online stores are compared. You also compare customer ratings and reviews for each store.

 1

- Start Internet Explorer.

- Visit the Book Companion Site Web page for this text, click the Select a chapter list arrow, click the link for Chapter 3, and then click the Steps link to open the Steps page.

- Right-click the Shopzilla link, and then click 'Open in new window' to open the Shopzilla home page in a new window.

- Type **Canon webcam** in the 'I'm shopping for' text box (Figure 3-61).

Q&A

Why do I see a message that a pop-up has been blocked?
If your Pop-Up Blocker is turned on, turn it off for this step-by-step activity by clicking the Tools button on the Command bar, pointing to Pop-up Blocker, clicking Turn off Pop-up Blocker on the submenu, and clicking Yes if necessary.

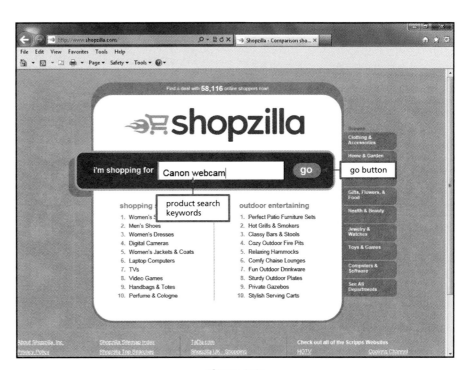

Figure 3-61

- Click the go button to view a list of Canon webcams sorted by the most popular models (Figure 3-62).

Figure 3-62

- Click the Sort arrow and click Price High-Low to sort the list by the highest- to lowest-priced Canon webcam (Figure 3-63).

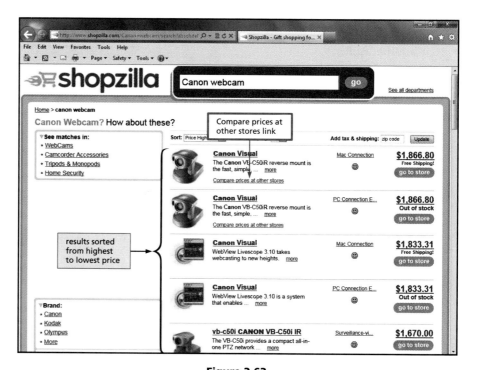

Figure 3-63

4

- Click the 'Compare prices at other stores' link for the first camera in the list to open its comparison page in a new window.

- Maximize the window, if necessary, to view the list of stores that sell the selected camera.

- Click the Sort by arrow and click Price to sort the list by camera price in ascending order.

- Point to the first green smiley face in the store list to see the overall customer rating ScreenTip for the related store (Figure 3-64).

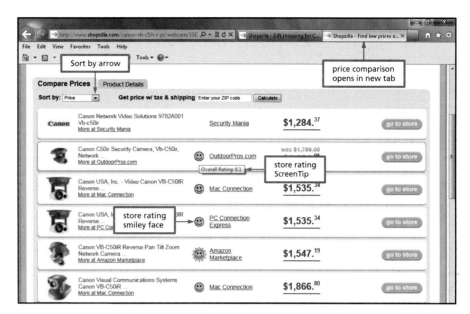

Figure 3-64

5

- Click the green smiley face to review the store's rating details (Figure 3-65).

- Scroll the Web page to read several user reviews for the store.

- Turn on the Pop-Up Blocker, if desired.

- Close all browser windows and tabs.

Figure 3-65

Many online retailers, such as Amazon.com, integrate social media connectivity tools, such as Facebook, allowing you to post a purchase or review of a product to your Facebook wall or Twitter feed.

Other specialized search engines might provide links to sources for military records, alumni databases, criminal information, property transactions, and other types of data. To protect privacy, many of these records are open only to authorized people. For example, Memory Lane and other alumni databases require you to register and include yourself in the list, after which you are given access to the names of others who also have voluntarily made their information available. Several Web sites, such as Docusearch (Figure 3-66) and US Search, charge users a fee to access compiled information. Prices vary by type and length of report. For example, an instant, simple search of a person's address history might cost about $2, while a more thorough background search might cost $50 or more.

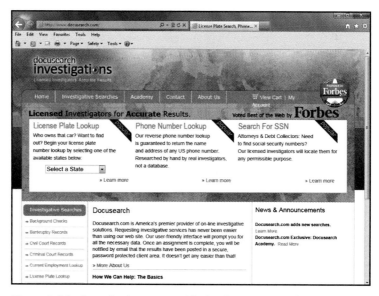

Figure 3-66 Some businesses provide database searches for individuals and businesses for a fee.

Research Alternatives to Search Engines

Research Tools
To review online tools that are useful for specific types of research, visit the Book Companion Site Web page at **www.cengagebrain.com**. Under the Chapter 3 @Source links, click a link below Research.

Search engines produce search results with links to vast resources; but depending on the keywords you enter for the search, it might take a while to sift through the results to find the specific information you seek. For in-depth or scholarly research, a more effective strategy is to access specialized collections of electronic resources. Although many such collections offer online access to information, finding them is not always so easy.

In this section, you will learn about a few of the more powerful and well-known services, such as LexisNexis (Figure 3-67), ingentaconnect, FindLaw, Dun & Bradstreet, Hoover's, and Dialog, which offer access to specialized information collections. These services are usually available only through paid subscriptions because of the specialized and proprietary information they contain and/or the efforts that go into compiling, obtaining, and updating the information they include. Many higher educational institutions subscribe to these services; therefore, students and faculty might have free access. If a school is not a subscriber, individuals still might use these services through a public library that subscribes, by paying for an individual subscription, or with a pay-as-you-go fee.

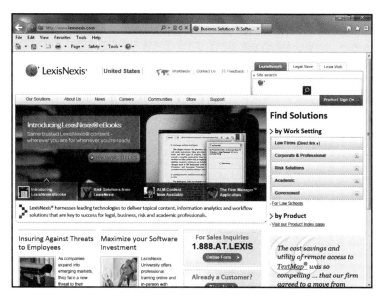

Figure 3-67 Several companies offer fee-based online access to specialized collections.

The LexisNexis service offers a Web-based interface to find abstracts and articles on business, news, government, medical, and legal topics from a vast database of information. LexisNexis provides access to U.S. congressional and state government documents, statistics produced by governmental agencies and organizations, and primary and secondary sources of historical documents. It offers many sources of information on current issues and events, including organizational newsletters and governmental briefings not published commercially. Ideal for both academic scholars and students, LexisNexis is the first stop for many researchers.

The ingentaconnect service provides more than 10,000 online articles from more than 30,000 academic and professional publications. Any researcher can search and view summaries of articles. A subscription or fee is required to obtain the full article online.

Hoover's and Dun & Bradstreet are two widely used resources for finding information on small and large businesses. Hoover's, a Dun & Bradstreet company, offers profiles on both public and private businesses, as well as extensive financial statements and analyses, management team information, and lists of competitors and market information. Dun & Bradstreet offers similar types of business and market information. It offers information that businesses of all size can use to find prospective customers, research suppliers, and check the credit risk of a potential partner or customer.

FindLaw is a portal for legal resources. It offers separate Web sites for the public and legal professionals. FindLaw is useful for finding information about laws and court cases, as well as for locating an attorney in your area or an attorney with a specific area of expertise. Whether you are dealing with a property complaint, a traffic ticket, criminal law, or a personal injury, this Web site offers an abundance of legal information.

Dialog provides information services to the business, science, engineering, finance, and law communities over the Internet or an internal intranet. It offers in-depth information on news, business, chemistry, engineering, the environment, government, intellectual property, medicine, and pharmaceuticals. The depth of information comes from source materials, such as journals, books, newspapers, magazines, trade journals, newsletters, and citation bibliographies, as well as market research reports.

@SOURCE

Government Resources
To access government resources, visit the Book Companion site Web page at **www. cengagebrain.com**. Under the Chapter 3 @Source links, click a link below Government Resources.

Government resources also can serve as excellent sources of information. For example, consumers can profit from information supplied by the Federal Citizen Information Center, while taxpayers can download forms and publications from the Internal Revenue Service Web site. The U.S. Census Bureau Web site supplies census statistics, the U.S. Bureau of Labor Statistics Web site offers government information on employment and labor economics, and the Library of Congress's Web site (named THOMAS, after Thomas Jefferson) provides searchable databases of legislative information. The U.S. Small Business Administration Web site has many resources for entrepreneurs and small business owners, and the U.S. National Park Service Web site contains excellent travel advice. An easy-to-use portal for the U.S. federal government is the USA.gov Web site, which you searched earlier in this chapter.

@ISSUE — Citing Web Sources

In a research paper, scholars and students often quote another's writing and ideas. This practice is acceptable as long as certain rules are followed. The quotation must be set apart, either with quotation marks (if the quotation is short) or by indentation (if it is long). Furthermore, you must cite the author and source of the quote, using an appropriate citation. Using more than a few lines of a person's writing or not crediting the source constitutes plagiarism and is wrong.

This holds true not only for printed materials, such as books and magazines, but also for Internet sources, such as Web pages or online books. The only exception is if you use information based on common knowledge or facts that are documented in a number of sources; in this case, you do not need to cite the specific source from which you got the information.

Colleges and universities have differing requirements for citing sources, typically adhering to one of the following: *MLA Handbook for Writers of Research Papers* (MLA style), *Publication Manual of the American Psychological Association* (APA style), *The Chicago Manual of Style* (Chicago style), and *Scientific Style and Format: The CSE Manual for Authors, Editors, and Publishers* (CSE style).

To learn more about citing electronic resources, visit the Book Companion Site Web page at **www.cengagebrain.com**. Under the Chapter 3 @Issue links, click a link below Citing Electronic Sources.

FACTS @HAND

Search engines typically index only the core of the Web, leaving a huge number of Web-based resources untapped or invisible to the typical Web user. These resources are called the **Invisible Web** or sometimes the **Deep Web**. These resources typically are not indexed because they are dynamically generated by a search query, unlinked to other Web pages, or private or password-protected. Elements of the Invisible Web are electronic books, product catalogs, library catalogs, government records, and other databases that typically must be accessed directly from a specialized search engine within the resource. Researchers continue to work on search technologies that will enable access to information currently hidden on the Invisible Web.

Plagiarism

With a deadline approaching, many students turn to the Web not only to do research on the topic, but also to take a shortcut right to the completed research paper. Some Web sites — referred to as paper mills — offer completed papers and assignments on a vast number of topics and from a variety of viewpoints. Some are free, some require an exchange (post a paper to take a paper), and some charge a fee based on the length of the paper.

Just as quoting a few lines without citing the source is plagiarism, so is turning in a paper from a paper mill. The consequences for plagiarism might be grave. Instructors often can detect if a student turns in a paper from an online paper mill. Instructors know what to look for when evaluating student papers for plagiarism. When students cannot answer questions about sections of their papers, the evidence is stronger. At some schools, screening software also is used to detect plagiarism.

Students can use search engines to assist in the research process, but they should resist the temptation to avoid the work of writing the research paper altogether. Not only are the consequences grave when cheating is caught, but turning in one's own work is a matter of honor.

For more information on plagiarism, visit the Book Companion Site Web page at **www.cengagebrain.com**. Under the Chapter 3 @Issue links, click a link below Plagiarism.

Chapter Review

During the search process, you must choose the best search tool for the job, formulate the search query, examine the search results, and evaluate the credibility of the Web pages listed in the search results list.

Search tools are generally classified as directories, search engines, and metasearch engines. A directory is a human-compiled index of Web pages organized into hierarchical categories and subcategories. In contrast, a search engine uses a software program called a Web crawler to browse the Web and compile a searchable index without human intervention. Today, most search tools are hybrids, offering both directory categorization and the ability to search their index of Web pages using a search query.

A search query can be one or more keywords, a phrase, or a complete sentence or question and is entered in a search engine's Address box or search text box. The search engine then returns a search results list of relevant Web pages or hits from its index of pages.

Many search engines provide shortcuts to quickly retrieve information, and advanced search forms that make creating complex search queries easier. An advanced search form might allow the user to restrict search results not only by what keywords are included or excluded, but also by date, language, geographic region, domain, file types, and so forth. You can access various search engines at their respective Web sites or through the Search box in the browser.

Specialized search engines are useful for finding people, businesses, news, video, social media, and shopping Web sites. To find more scholarly or in-depth information, you can use specialized electronic databases and collections.

TERMS TO KNOW

After reading this chapter, you should know each of these Key Terms.

Boolean operator (133)
bot (124)
breadcrumb trail (120)
Deep Web (158)
directory (118)
drilling down (119)
full-text searching (124)
hit (114)
index (124)
Invisible Web (158)
keyword (113)
meta tag keywords (124)
metasearch engine (129)
natural language search (115)
open-ended search (115)

primary source (117)
search engine (124)
search query (113)
search results list (114)
search text box (114)
shopping aggregators (152)
shopping bots (152)
social media aggregators (152)
spider (124)
stop words (115)
targeted search (115)
visual search results (128)
Web crawler (124)
white pages directory (150)
yellow pages directory (150)

TEST YOUR KNOWLEDGE

Complete the Test Your Knowledge exercises to solidify what you have learned in the chapter.

True or False

Mark T for True and F for False. (Answers are found on page numbers in parentheses.)

___ 1. Using multiple keywords in a search query narrows the scope of the query. (114)

___ 2. The first hit in the list of search results is always the Web page most relevant to the search query. (116)

___ 3. If you misspell a keyword, the search results return an error. (115)

___ 4. Where, what, the, and is are examples of stop words. (115)

___ 5. Breadcrumb trails are only used in search directories. (120)

___ 6. A metasearch engine uses human editors to compile an index of Web pages. (129)

___ 7. The Boolean operators AND, NOT, or OR are used in advanced search techniques to include or exclude keywords. (133)

___ 8. Internet Explorer uses a designated default search engine for Address bar and Search box searches. (140)

___ 9. You can change the search engine by clicking a search icon on the QuickPreview menu. (142)

___10. The Invisible Web is the portion of the Web that is typically accessed directly from a search engine within the resource. (158)

Multiple Choice

Select the best answer. (Answers are found on page numbers in parentheses.)

1. For the most effective search results, choose keywords that are _____. (113)

    a. Boolean

    b. specific

    c. general

    d. stop words

2. To search for a Web page that contains a specific phrase, _____. (114)

    a. no special action is required

    b. surround the phrase with brackets

    c. insert the word, AND, between every word

    d. surround the phrase with quotation marks

3. A list of hits typically contains _____. (116)

    a. a link to each Web site

    b. a description of the Web page or a sample of text from the page

    c. Web sites that are sponsored or have paid to have their pages placed at the top of the list

    d. all of the above

4. The most popular search engine in the United States is _____. (129)

    a. Google

    b. Bing

    c. Yahoo!

    d. Internet Explorer

5. A shopping _____ collects information about consumer products or services, and helps online shoppers compare models, prices, shipping costs, and other variables from various sellers. (152)

    a. consolidator

    b. search engine

    c. aggregator

    d. crawler

6. Googlebot is an example of a(n) _____. (124)

    a. metasearch engine

    b. Web crawler

    c. search directory

    d. aggregator

7. _____ is an example of a metasearch engine. (129)

   a. Dogpile

   b. Googlebot

   c. StumbleUpon

   d. Shopzilla

8. To search the contents of the Web page you are currently viewing, press _____ to display the Find Bar. (147)

   a. ALT+F

   b. ALT+ENTER

   c. TAB+F

   d. CTRL+F

9. For academic research, specialized information collections, such as LexisNexis or Dialog, are good resources because they _____. (156)

   a. are free

   b. are available only to librarians

   c. can provide information on business, news, government, medical, and legal topics

   d. require a subscription

10. Which of the following Google search engine queries will return PDF files containing one of the following words — horses or burros — in a Web site published in the educational domain? (135)

   a. "horses or burros" .com

   b. horses OR burros filetype:pdf site:.edu

   c. horses.pdf NOT burros.pdf site:.com

   d. horses AND burros filetype:pdf site:.edu

LEARN IT ONLINE

Test your knowledge of chapter content and key terms.

Instructions: To complete the following exercises, please visit **www.cengagebrain.com**. On the CengageBrain home page, enter the book title *Discovering the Internet* and then click the Find button. On the product page for this book, click the Access Now button below the Study Tools heading. On the Book Companion Site Web page, click the drop-down menu, select Chapter 3, and then click the link for the desired exercise.

Chapter Reinforcement TF, MC, and SA

A series of true/false, multiple-choice, and short-answer questions that test your knowledge of the chapter content.

Flash Cards

An interactive learning environment where you identify chapter key terms associated with displayed definitions.

Practice Test

A series of multiple-choice questions that test your knowledge of chapter content and key terms.

Who Wants To Be a Computer Genius?

An interactive game that challenges your knowledge of chapter content in the style of a television quiz show.

Wheel of Terms

An interactive game that challenges your knowledge of chapter key terms in the style of the television show, *Wheel of Fortune*.

Crossword Puzzle Challenge

A crossword puzzle that challenges your knowledge of the key terms presented in the chapter.

EXERCISES

Use the Exercises to gain hands-on experience working with the Internet and the Web.

1 | Online Scavenger Hunt

Find solutions to three of the following scenarios using online resources. Even if you already know the answer or can ask someone who knows, search the Web to find the answer. For each scenario, complete the following steps:

1. Visit the Book Companion Site Web page for this text, click the Select a chapter list arrow, click the link for Chapter 3, and then click the Exercises link. Click a link below Directories, Search Engines, or Metasearch Engines, to choose a search engine.

2. Determine the keywords you will use in the search query.

3. Time how long it takes you to find the information you are seeking.

4. Record the search engines and keywords you used. Note whether you found the desired information using your original keywords and search engine choice, or had to search again using different keywords or a different search engine. Judge the value and authenticity of the result pages the search engine returns.

Scenario 1: Your cousin Ted recently moved to a new condominium in Houston, Texas. You want to send Ted a gift certificate to a hardware store as a housewarming gift. Locate the name and telephone number of three local Houston hardware stores. Write down the URLs and note whether you can order the gift certificate from the hardware stores' Web sites.

Scenario 2: Your professor assigned an autobiography as some independent reading for a business class. The professor could not remember the title or author of the book, but told you that a female former CEO of Hewlett-Packard wrote it. Find the title and author of the book and find out how much it costs at an online bookstore. If possible, see whether the book is available in your school's library or the local library, or obtain the library telephone number so you can call to ask about availability.

Scenario 3: Your sister tells you that her coworker is expecting a baby, and she wants you to see if you can find a searchable list or dictionary of names. Find one that allows you to search by gender, origin, and at least two other criteria, such as starting letter or number of syllables. Perform a search of names using search criteria of your choice and write down the top three recommended names for each gender.

Scenario 4: Your boss is a die-hard Boston Red Sox fan, and you would like to impress him with your knowledge of the team. Find the first and last time the team won the World Series, and list the names of a few notable players who have been inducted into the Baseball Hall of Fame. Also, find the name of the current manager.

Scenario 5: You decide to go to the movies. Find out what film is the current number one box-office hit. Read a critic's review of the movie. See whether it is playing at a local theater and the times of the showings.

Scenario 6: A friend wants to go on a white-water rafting trip through the Grand Canyon and wants you to go along. Find out what time of year is best, what experience is necessary, what river rafting companies are available, how much such a trip costs, and how far in advance you have to make a reservation for the trip.

Scenario 7: You and your fiancé or fiancée decide to have your wedding in Hawaii. Price the airfare and determine a range of prices for wedding packages for up to 25 guests. List the requirements for a marriage license. Find the name of a person to officiate the ceremony in Hawaii.

Scenario 8: You and your friends have been discussing roller coasters, and now you want to know more about them. Find the origins of roller coasters; the oldest one in the United States, Canada, and Europe; as well as the highest and fastest ones.

2 | Searching for Health Information

1. Choose a fitness or diet plan to research.

2. Determine the keywords you will use in the search query.

3. Time how long it takes you to find the information you are seeking using multiple search engines and the Internet Explorer Search box and QuickPick menu.

4. Evaluate how well you perform the search:

   a. Record how many Web sites you visit.

   b. For each site you visit, evaluate the quality of information and credibility of the site. List the qualities that make the site more or less credible.

   c. For the fitness or diet plan that you choose, find out the recommendations for exercise and any major food restrictions.

   d. Write down what further steps you should take to evaluate the quality of the information.

3 | Job Search

1. Visit the Book Companion Site Web page for this text, click the Select a chapter list arrow, click the link for Chapter 3, and then click the Exercises link. Click a link below Directories, Search Engines, or Metasearch Engines, to choose a search engine and then search for a job in your chosen field.

2. Determine the keywords you will use in the search query.

3. Time how long it takes you to find the information you are seeking.

4. Evaluate how well you performed the search.

   a. Choose at least three occupations in your chosen field.

   b. Research average salaries for each occupation.

   c. Find out whether your chosen field is a fast-growing one.

   d. Select a city to which you would like to relocate. Determine the climate by researching the average temperatures, rainfall, and snowfall.

   e. Research school districts in the area and find out which one seems the best.

   f. Find the prices of a two-bedroom apartment and a four-bedroom home in that community.

   g. Find the difference in the cost of living between your current location and the destination.

   h. Get an estimate of how much it would cost to move the contents of a two-bedroom apartment from your current location to the destination.

4 | Internet Archive

1. Visit the Book Companion Site Web page for this text, click the Select a chapter list arrow, click the link for Chapter 3, and then click the Exercises link. Click Internet Archive below Exercise 4.

   a. Review the Web site and its features.

   b. Use the Wayback Machine to search for earlier versions of frequently used Web pages of your choice.

   c. Write a brief summary that describes the Internet Archive. What is its purpose? How valuable is the Internet Archive as a resource? Would you use the Internet Archive as a source? If yes, why? If no, why not?

5 | Visual Search

1. Visit the Book Companion site Web page for this text, click the Select a chapter list arrow, click the link for Chapter 3, and then click the Exercises link. Click a link below Exercise 5 to review search engines that present visual search results.

   a. Open the home page for each of the listed search engines and explore the features offered by each using the search query of your choice.

   b. Write a brief paragraph describing each search engine and the presentation of its search results list. Indicate how useful you find visual search results compared with traditional text-based search results. Which reviewed search engine do you prefer? Why?

   c. Use your preferred search engine to search for Web pages containing information about the slow food movement. Review several pages and then write a short paragraph describing the slow food movement.

6 | Video and Shopping Search

1. Visit the Book Companion Site Web page for this text, click the Select a chapter list arrow, click the link for Chapter 3, and then click the Exercises link. Click a link below Exercise 6 Video Search, to select search engines that index video clips.

   a. Open the home page for each of the listed search engines and explore its features.

   b. Write a brief paragraph describing each search engine and its features. Based on the descriptions, which reviewed search engine do you prefer? Why?

   c. Use your preferred search engine to search for video clips on a topic of your choice. Write a brief paragraph describing the relevancy of the search results list of videos to your keywords. How many videos were listed in the search results list? How relevant were the top 10 videos in the list?

2. Visit the Book Companion Site Web page for this text, click the Select a chapter list arrow, click the link for Chapter 3, and then click the Exercises link. Click a link below Exercise 6 Shopping Search, to review three shopping search engines: DealTime, Bizrate, and Nextag.

   a. Use the three shopping search engines to search for the same consumer electronic product of your choice.

   b. Review the top-rated product and the ratings of the stores that offer the product presented by each shopping search engine.

   c. Write a brief summary of your shopping experience using each shopping search engine.

7 | People and Business Search

1. Visit the Book Companion Site Web page for this text, click the Select a chapter list arrow, click the link for Chapter 3, and then click the Exercises link. Click each of the links below Exercise 7, to answer the following questions:

    a. Is your name or the name of a relative listed in an online white pages directory?

    b. Which white pages directories list information for you or your family members?

    c. Which white pages directories list your information correctly with the most current street address and telephone number, and which ones list outdated information? Do any require you to sign up before viewing the information?

    d. Write down your feelings about having your name, street address, and e-mail address listed in the white pages directories. Do any directories offer methods to remove your name?

2. Visit the Book Companion Site Web page for this text, and then click the Exercises link. Click Superpages.com below Chapter 3, Exercise 7.

    a. Review and list the resources offered at the Superpages.com site.

    b. Compare Superpages.com with other white pages directories you have used.

    c. Use a reverse lookup to find the owner of a telephone number, using the telephone number of your choice.

8 | News and Social Media Search

1. Visit the Book Companion Site Web page for this text, click the Select a chapter list arrow, click the link for Chapter 3, and then click the Exercises link. Click the News links below Exercise 8 to review Web sites that offer news and current events information and news-oriented search.

    a. Perform a search at each Web site to search for the same news or current event topic of your choice. Compare the results from each news search engine. How are the results alike? How are they different?

    b. Write a brief paragraph describing your search experiences at each Web site.

2. Visit the Book Companion Site Web page for this text, click the Select a chapter list arrow, click the link for Chapter 3, and then click the Exercises link. Click the Social Media links below Exercise 8 to review three social media search engines: Digg, Newsvine, and Technorati.

    a. Look for information on a topic of your choice using each of the social media search engines.

    b. Write a brief paragraph describing the focus of each search engine and your search experience using each search engine.

9 | Using Search Engine Shortcuts and Advanced Search Forms

1. Visit the Book Companion Site Web page for this text, click the Select a chapter list arrow, click the link for Chapter 3, and then click the Exercises link. Click a link below Directories, Search Engines, or Metasearch Engines to create a complex search using search engine shortcuts or an advanced search form to find:

    a. jobs in the .edu TLD

    b. the product of 340986*3

    c. the current weather for your city

d. the conversion of 150 U.S. dollars to Mexican pesos

e. a map of Ballwin, Missouri

f. a pharmacy in your city

g. Web pages with page titles containing the word, football

h. PDF files published by businesses in the .com TLD containing information about Bluetooth technologies

i. 10,500 meters converted to miles

10 | Library Collections and Electronic Resources

To complete all parts of this exercise, you must have both electronic and physical access to a school and public library.

1. Visit your school's Web site and examine the resources available at the school's online library page.

   a. List the main electronic collections and the topics each collection covers.

   b. List the resources that are restricted to faculty, staff, and students at your institution.

   c. List items that are available through the Internet versus the ones that must be accessed within the library.

2. Visit the Web site for your local public library. List the main electronic collections and the topics each collection covers. List items that are available through the Internet versus those that must be accessed within the library.

3. Schedule an interview with a school or public librarian, if possible, to discuss the online research capabilities offered through the library that go beyond those available to any user on the Web.

4. Visit your school or local public library and use FirstSearch, ingentaconnect, InfoTrac, or another electronic resource to search for articles on search engines.

   a. Write or print a list of available articles.

   b. Print the abstract from one of the articles.

4 | Communicating Online

Introduction

Internet users around the world use online tools — such as e-mail, social networking, microblogging, instant messaging, IRC or Web chat, mailing lists, newsgroups and Web-based discussion groups, wikis, blogs, and more — to communicate and collaborate with friends, family members, coworkers, classmates, and others. For example, individual, professional, and business Internet users utilize online tools to do the following:

- Share information, exchange files, and arrange appointments using e-mail, instant messaging, chat, and microblogging.
- Broadcast messages using microblogging or video sharing.
- Participate in Web-based discussion groups or newsgroups.
- Communicate with customers, business partners, the public, and other interested parties through blogs.
- Collaborate on ongoing projects using wikis.
- Solicit political and charitable contributions using e-mail and Web sites.
- Build networks at social networking Web sites.
- Share content with others at social bookmarking or content-sharing Web sites.
- Share reviews of product or service providers at social opinion Web sites.

In this chapter, you will learn how widespread broadband Internet access and innovative Web technologies have revolutionized the way we communicate and collaborate with others.

Objectives

After completing this chapter, you will be able to:

1. Describe the components of e-mail systems and e-mail messages

2. Discuss and apply e-mail etiquette

3. Use the Windows® Live Mail™ 2011 e-mail client to send, receive, and organize e-mail messages and contacts, and discuss e-mail viruses

4. Set up a Web-based e-mail account and use Web-based e-mail services

5. Describe various online social media tools and discuss how they are used

E-Mail Systems

E-mail is one of the most popular online communication tools. E-mail communications now are indispensable for businesses and other organizations. As recently as the late 1990s, businesses used the telephone as their primary means of communicating with customers, business partners, and vendors. Today, businesses of all sizes rely heavily on e-mail for communications among coworkers and to communicate with vendors, customers, investors, and others. People use e-mail for nonbusiness communications with their school, organizations, family, and friends.

FACTS @HAND According to the Pew Internet & American Life Project, more than 94 percent of Internet-connected American adults use e-mail.

The volume of personal and business e-mail messages sent daily is staggering, exceeding the number of pieces of paper mail handled by major national postal systems. Some e-mail messages are spam, the unsolicited junk e-mail you learned about in Chapter 1. You will learn more about spam later in this chapter.

FACTS @HAND The estimated percentage of unsolicited e-mail (spam) of all e-mail ranges from 70 percent to 95 percent, depending on the source. However, you never see most spam e-mail because it is blocked by your e-mail client, which recognizes messages as spam based on content, domain, and other criteria.

Using e-mail has several distinct benefits, including speed of delivery, low cost, accessibility, convenience, and ease of management:

- Speed of delivery — E-mail messages can be composed by the sender, sent, and received by the recipient in seconds. The recipient can send a reply just as quickly, thus providing rapid feedback, or reply at his or her own convenience.
- Low cost — E-mail is a cost-effective way to communicate with others and to share documents quickly. For example, sending an e-mail message is free, compared with the costs of the paper, envelope, and stamp required for writing and sending a letter. Sending an electronic file attached to an e-mail message is also free and can save you the cost and time of sending a printed document using a courier service.
- Accessibility — E-mail messages can be accessed from any computer or device with Internet access. For example, a user can read all of the mail sent to his or her e-mail account from any Internet-connected computer, or from a smartphone, tablet computer, or other portable device.

- Convenience — E-mail messages can be sent when it is convenient for the sender and read when it is convenient for the recipient. Using e-mail can promote increased collaboration among coworkers or the members of a social group.
- Ease of management — Users can manage their e-mail messages by storing them in folders on their computers or mail servers where the messages can be arranged and viewed by date, sender, or other criteria, or deleted.

In the next sections, you will learn about the components of an e-mail system: addresses, clients, servers, and protocols.

E-Mail Considerations @ISSUE

Although e-mail messages may seem less formal than paper-based communications, they can be used as official communication or notification. Companies can use e-mail to communicate important information about your account or billing. Employers can use e-mail to distribute important information about your healthcare plan or other company business. In addition, information sent in an e-mail can be used in court as evidence.

Keep in mind that any personal e-mail you send using your work e-mail address is the property of the company you work for, and you must comply with company rules regarding the use of e-mail. For example, if you forward an offensive e-mail to colleagues, you can be disciplined, or even fired, for contributing to a hostile work environment.

Remember that everything sent in an e-mail can be forwarded on to other recipients without your knowledge or permission.

E-Mail Addresses

To be delivered to the correct destination, an e-mail message must have a unique delivery address consisting of a user ID and a host name, as well as a top-level domain, as shown in Figure 4-1.

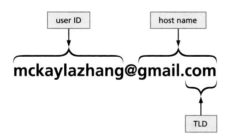

Figure 4-1 Components of an e-mail address.

The **user ID** is a unique identifier for the recipient, and the **host name** identifies the server where the recipient's e-mail account or mailbox resides. In Figure 4-1, the host name is gmail.com. The host name includes a top-level domain (TLD), such as .com or .net. The user ID and host name are separated by the @ symbol. An e-mail address is entered in a message window provided by an e-mail client.

E-Mail Clients, Servers, and Protocols

The steps in the transmission of an e-mail message from origin to destination address, using servers instead of post offices, parallel those followed in the delivery of a letter by a traditional postal service. An e-mail message has a unique delivery address, is routed from server to server over the Internet until it reaches its destination, and then is delivered to its recipient's mailbox.

E-MAIL CLIENTS   An **e-mail client** is any program used to create, send, and receive e-mail messages. Microsoft® Outlook®, Microsoft Windows Live Mail, Opera Mail, and Mozilla® Thunderbird® are all examples of e-mail clients that you install on your computer and instruct to manage your incoming e-mail from a server or a Web-based e-mail service. Microsoft Outlook is available with the Microsoft Office suite; Windows Live Mail can be downloaded from the Windows Live Web site; Opera Mail is a built-in feature of the Opera browser; and Mozilla Thunderbird is available from the Mozilla Web site. Other e-mail clients, such as the open source program Eudora, which was developed by Qualcomm and others, are available as stand-alone programs that users can download from vendor/sponsor Web sites. When you install an e-mail client, you must set it up to sync and download e-mail from your e-mail address. If you are a student or an employee, often this is done for you by your school or company. If you are using a system such as Windows Live Mail, you will be prompted to provide your e-mail address and password in order for the e-mail client to access your e-mail. Web-based e-mail services, such as Gmail or Yahoo! Mail, provide a user with an e-mail address (such as mckaylazhang@gmail.com) as well as access using a Web browser. They can also be managed using an e-mail client. You will learn more about managing Web-based e-mail with an e-mail client in this chapter.

FACTS @HAND   Many colleges and universities provide e-mail services for their students, and these services often require a particular e-mail client. For example, Alpine is an e-mail client developed at the University of Washington. It was based on the original Pine e-mail client developed to provide e-mail services to large numbers of University of Washington students while requiring only modest resources.

@SOURCE

E-Mail Clients
For more information about popular e-mail clients, visit **www. cengagebrain.com**. On the CengageBrain home page, enter the book title *Discovering the Internet* and then click the Find button. On the product Web page for this book, click the Access Now button below the Study Tools heading. On the Book Companion Site Web page, click the drop-down menu, select Chapter 4, and then click the @Source link. Click a link under E-Mail Clients.

E-mail clients typically offer tools to:

- Create and send outgoing e-mail messages
- Read, save, and print incoming e-mail messages and their attachments
- Sort, archive, and delete messages
- Create folders in which to organize messages

Web-based e-mail services are widely used by individuals at home, at school, and at work. Web-based e-mail services are accessed using a Web browser instead of e-mail client software. You will learn more about using a Web-based e-mail service later in this chapter.

E-MAIL SERVERS AND PROTOCOLS   E-mail messages are sent over the Internet using the same packet-switching technology and TCP/IP suite that govern all communications over the Internet. An e-mail client might use a number of protocols, such as **POP (Post Office Protocol)**, **SMTP (Simple Mail Transfer Protocol)**, **IMAP (Internet Message Access Protocol)**, and HTTP (Hypertext Transfer Protocol) to interact with mail servers when sending and receiving messages. Figure 4-2 illustrates the steps involved in sending and receiving an e-mail message:

Step 1: The sender creates and sends the message.

Step 2: An outgoing mail SMTP server contacts a DNS name server to resolve the host domain name portion of the e-mail address to an IP address, determines the best route over the Internet to the message's destination, and sends the message on its way.

Step 3: The message is typically routed through multiple Internet routers until it reaches its final destination mail server (POP3, IMAP, or HTTP).

Step 4: The mail server receives the message and stores it in the recipient's mailbox, which is a folder on the server that is identified by the user ID portion of the e-mail address. Upon request from the user's e-mail client, the mail server sends the new message to the client.

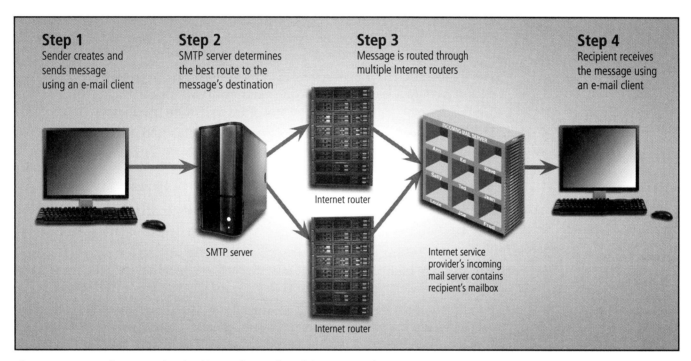

Step 1
Sender creates and sends message using an e-mail client

Step 2
SMTP server determines the best route to the message's destination

Step 3
Message is routed through multiple Internet routers

Step 4
Recipient receives the message using an e-mail client

SMTP server

Internet router

Internet router

Internet service provider's incoming mail server contains recipient's mailbox

Figure 4-2 Several steps are involved in sending and receiving an e-mail message.

E-mail clients, such as Microsoft Outlook and Windows Live Mail, use POP or IMAP incoming mail servers. Some free Web-based e-mail services, such as Windows Live Hotmail, use HTTP servers. While each type of server handles incoming messages, each server does so in a different way.

When there are incoming messages on a POP server, the e-mail client handles all mail management functions. For example, an e-mail client sends a request to a POP server, downloads all new messages, and stores the messages on the user's computer. The main disadvantage of a POP server is that after messages are downloaded to a user's computer, only that computer can be used to view and manage the messages.

In contrast, an IMAP mail server provides mail management functions on the server. The user's messages are stored and managed on the server. Although the user reads, deletes, or sorts the messages using his or her e-mail client, the action actually takes place on the IMAP server. The user also can work with messages locally on his or her computer by downloading the messages and reading them, marking them for deletion, or composing new messages. The next time the user's e-mail client connects to the IMAP server, the server synchronizes with the e-mail client, sending out any new mail messages and deleting messages on the server that were marked for deletion in the e-mail client. Unlike POP servers, where a user downloads his or her messages to a specific machine, a user can access an IMAP server from different computers to view his or her messages.

An HTTP server provides Web-based e-mail services that can be accessed through a Web site and a Web browser. The main advantage of an HTTP server and Web-based e-mail is that access to e-mail is available wherever access to the Internet and the Web are available. One disadvantage is that an e-mail client, such as Windows Live Mail, might not support access to incoming messages stored on an HTTP server.

Anatomy of an E-Mail Message

Most e-mail clients provide the same basic message window features, including the following elements, which are illustrated in Figure 4-3:

- The **To line** contains one or more e-mail addresses of the message's recipient or recipients. The e-mail addresses for multiple recipients are typically separated with semicolons or commas.

- The **Cc line** lists the e-mail addresses of recipients who will receive a courtesy copy of the message. A **courtesy copy** is a copy of the message that is sent as a courtesy to someone other than the primary recipients in the To line.

- The **Bcc line** contains the e-mail addresses of recipients who will receive a blind courtesy copy of the message. A **blind courtesy copy** is a copy of a message that is sent to a recipient without that recipient's name or e-mail address appearing in the message header. The Bcc line is visible only to the sender and the Bcc recipient.

- The **Subject line** contains a description of the message content.

- The **Attach line** contains the file names of any attachments. An **attachment** is a file that is transmitted along with the e-mail message.

- The **message body** contains the text of the message. In addition to text, a message body can include graphics, links to Web pages, or the contents of Web pages.

- The signature can be automatically inserted using a small **signature file** containing standard content, such as the name, title, and contact information of the sender.

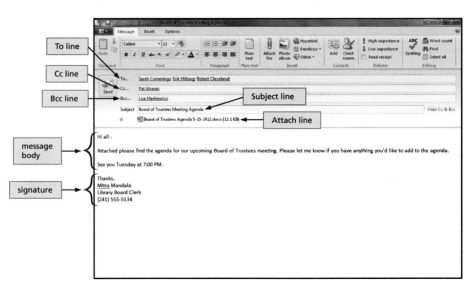

Figure 4-3 Typical components of an e-mail message window.

The To, Cc, Bcc, Subject, and Attach lines are all part of the **message header**. You can indicate whether to compose your message as plain text or as an HTML-formatted message. An **HTML-formatted message** contains formatting, such as different fonts, font sizes, and font styles, as well as bulleted lists, indented paragraphs, and so forth. If you specify an HTML-formatted message, a Formatting toolbar might appear above the message composition box, as it does in Figure 4-3. Most e-mail clients can read HTML-formatted messages, or can translate HTML-formatted messages into text-based ones. HTML-formatted messages are shown in this book.

In Windows Live Mail, to specify that all messages are composed in HTML format, click the Windows Live Mail button, point to Options, then click Mail to open the Options dialog box. Click the Send tab and click the HTML option below the Mail Sending Format group. To compose an individual message in HTML format, click the Rich text (HTML) button in the Plain text group on the Message tab in the New Message window.

E-Mail Etiquette

The very characteristics of e-mail that make it so popular and easy to use also can be disadvantages. For example, because e-mail is informal, messages might not be written clearly or worded carefully. The speed and ease with which an e-mail message can be sent create another potential problem. An individual might send an e-mail message when tired, upset, or uninformed without carefully thinking through the message's contents. Additionally, because e-mail is so easy to send, some individuals might send too many unnecessary, and often unwanted, e-mail messages to their friends, family, and coworkers.

One major drawback of e-mail, and of most text-based communications in general, is the potential for a message to be misunderstood. The composer of an e-mail message might write something with sarcasm in mind. The reader, however, might not interpret the language as sarcasm, instead reading the message as entirely sincere. The reader sees only the content of the message, and does not see the facial expressions, hear the tone of voice, or observe the body language of the sender. Following some basic e-mail etiquette guidelines can convey an idea clearly and avoid accidentally insulting someone or hurting feelings. E-mail etiquette guidelines include the following:

- When composing an e-mail message, do not use all capital letters for the entire message. All caps represent SHOUTING! and are read and interpreted as such.
- When responding to a message about which you have strong negative feelings, it is often a good idea to save your response for a few hours or a day before you send it. Responding with strong language or insults by e-mail (and other online communication tools) is sometimes called **flaming** and is considered improper in most online venues.
- When you want to convey a particular feeling or emotion in an e-mail message, you can make use of an **emoticon** such as typing a colon and a right parentheses character :) to convey a smile at appropriate points in the message to represent the emotion you are trying to convey. E-mail client (or instant messaging) programs might provide a set of emoticon icons you can use. Emoticons can help the message recipient get the full flavor of a message. Be careful, however, not to overuse emoticons: A message that contains one or more emoticons per sentence loses its appeal and impact. Additionally, emoticons generally are not appropriate for business e-mail messages.

Using Windows Live Mail

As you have learned, e-mail clients provide tools to send and receive messages; reply to and forward messages; and print, organize, and delete messages. In this section, you will review the Windows Live Mail e-mail client window and then receive, read, and reply to an e-mail message; open an attachment; compose and send a message with an attachment; and organize e-mail messages.

Note: Before sending and receiving e-mail using Windows Live Mail, you must first set up a Windows Live account, including a user ID, password, and the names of the POP or IMAP and SMTP servers to be accessed. Windows Live Mail does not offer access to HTTP servers. You must also create a Windows Live Mail e-mail account, or use another service, such as Gmail, and sync it to your Windows Live Mail e-mail account. For the projects in this section, it is assumed your e-mail account already has been set up. For more information about setting up Windows Live Mail, see Windows Live Mail Help.

Reviewing the Windows Live Mail Window

The Windows Live Mail 2011 window (Figure 4-4) includes common e-mail client elements, such as the Ribbon and viewing panes. At the top of the window is the title bar, which contains the name of the open mail folder and the application name, plus the standard Minimize, Restore Down or Maximize, and Close buttons. Below the title bar is the Ribbon, which contains tabs for common tasks such as sending, receiving, editing, viewing, and managing your e-mail messages.

The left pane contains links to your unread mail, your outbox, and the e-mail folders established by your e-mail client. The example in this chapter uses the Gmail Web-based e-mail service, which is accessed and managed using Windows Live Mail. One advantage of using Windows Live Mail is that you can organize mail from different e-mail accounts, such as the business e-mail address provided by your employer and a Web-based e-mail service you use for personal correspondence, in one window.

In the middle pane, you will see your Inbox messages and the Search box. You can use the Search box to search the address, subject, and body text of messages in the open mail folder.

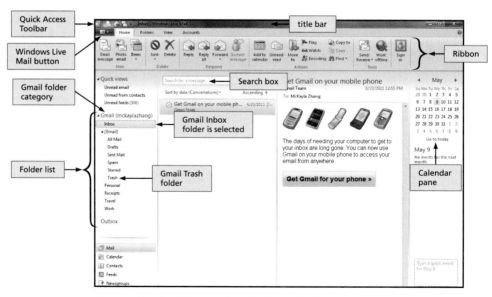

Figure 4-4　The Windows Live Mail e-mail client.

The Quick Access Toolbar is located next to the title bar and contains the following default buttons:

- New, which opens the New Message window that is used to address and compose an e-mail message
- Reply, which opens the Re: message window that is used to send a reply to a selected incoming message; the reply message is addressed to the original message's sender
- Update all, which updates Windows Live Mail with new e-mail messages, calendar items, RSS feeds, and newsgroups

The Windows Live Mail button (Figure 4-4) enables you to complete program-specific tasks, such as printing, saving, importing or exporting, setting program options, getting Help, and exiting the program.

The Ribbon is located below the title bar. The tabs, groups, and buttons on the Ribbon differ depending on what type of item you are currently viewing. When you are viewing mail items, the Ribbon contains the following tabs: Home, Folders, View, and Accounts. The Mail Home tab contains the following groups and default buttons (Figure 4-5):

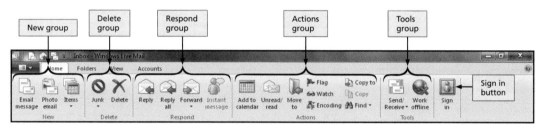

Figure 4-5 The Mail Home tab.

- The New group contains the Email message button that opens the New Message window that is used to address and compose an e-mail message; the Photo email button, which creates a photo album using Windows Live Photos on a Windows Live SkyDrive to send a message; and the Items button, which opens a menu of options you can create, such as events, contacts, and news messages.
- The Delete group contains the Junk button and Junk button arrow, which are used to move spam to the Junk mail folder as well as block senders and domains; and the Delete button, which is used to delete the selected message.
- The Respond group contains the Reply button and the Reply all button, which open the Re: message window and address the reply message to all addresses in the incoming message (the sender plus anyone receiving a copy of the message); the Forward button, which opens the Fw: message window that is used to forward an incoming message to one or more recipients; the Forward button arrow, which enables you to forward a message as an attachment; and the Instant message button, which is used to open an Instant Message window.
- The Actions group contains several buttons that you can use to manage messages, including the Add to calendar button, which creates a calendar item based on the selected message, as well as buttons you can use to move, flag, mark as unread, and copy a message. Also in the Actions group is the Find button, which is used to search for contacts, message folders, or the contents of the current message.
- The Tools group contains the Send/Receive button and the Work offline button, which disconnects Windows Live Mail from the Internet.

The Folders tab (Figure 4-6) contains buttons that enable you to move, flag, copy, and navigate through messages and folders. The View tab (Figure 4-6) can be used to change the layout of the panes in the Windows Live Mail window, sort or filter the current view or folder, or follow a conversation. You will learn about watching and ignoring conversations later in this chapter. The Accounts tab (Figure 4-6) contains buttons that help you manage your e-mail accounts and newsgroups.

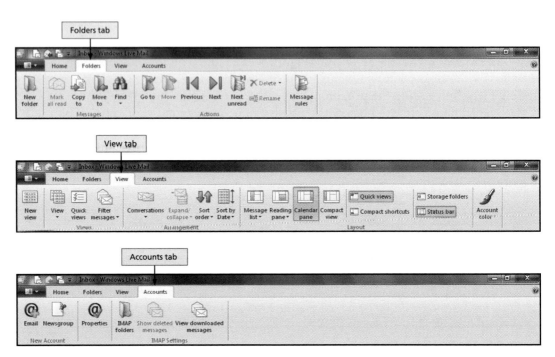

Figure 4-6 Additional Windows Live Mail tabs.

FACTS @HAND **Windows Live SkyDrive** is a file-hosting service that is a part of the Windows Live suite. SkyDrive is an example of cloud computing. Anyone who has a Windows Live ID has up to 25 gigabytes of free file storage, which can be used to store files for personal use, as well as to share with others. **Windows Live Photos** is part of SkyDrive, and can be used to create photo albums that you share with others. SkyDrive is also used to store documents created using **Office Web Apps**, which are free, scaled-down, online-only versions of Microsoft Word, Excel, PowerPoint, and OneNote.

Four viewing areas — the Folder list, Message list, Preview pane, and Calendar — appear below the Ribbon.

The Folder list contains the Windows Live Mail mail folders used to store messages. The Quick views category enables you to view all unread messages and newsgroup items. Each e-mail account appears as a separate category, such as in the example used in this chapter, which uses Gmail as the e-mail account connected to the Windows Live Mail client.

Depending on the account(s) you have installed, for each account you may have some or all of the following folders: Inbox, Outbox, Sent items, Deleted items, Drafts, and Junk e-mail folder, as well as other default folders or folders you create. Gmail by default creates folders for Personal, Receipts, Travel, and Work. You can delete or create folders to suit your own needs. An **Inbox folder** contains incoming messages. An **Outbox folder** is a temporary storage folder for outgoing messages. Once an outgoing message has been sent, a copy is placed, by default, in the **Sent items** or **Sent Mail folder**. The **Deleted items** or **Trash folder** contains deleted messages. Just as you can restore deleted files sent to the Windows Recycle Bin until you empty it, you can retrieve deleted messages from the Deleted items folder until you empty it manually. You also can set an option to have the folder emptied each time you close Windows Live Mail. The **Drafts folder** contains messages that you create and save to work on again, usually with the intention of sending them later.

Because the Folder list can be customized to add or delete folders, the folders you see in your Windows Live Mail window might vary from those shown in the figures in this chapter. The **Junk e-mail** or **Spam folder** contains messages marked as unsolicited commercial e-mail or spam based on the junk e-mail options you set. You will learn more about setting junk e-mail options later in this chapter. To access any folder, click it in the Folder list.

The **Message list** displays individual messages. The messages are organized in the Message list by date by default. Click the Sort by date button to change the sort order. The Preview pane displays a preview of the selected message in the Message list. As new e-mail messages are received, you also might see an e-mail notification icon in the notification area on the taskbar. The Calendar pane shows the current month, as well as a list of tasks, events, or appointments for that day.

You can change the layout of the Message list and control which messages are displayed in the list using the commands on the View tab.

Receiving and Replying to an Incoming E-Mail Message

Most e-mail clients check for new e-mail messages on the assigned mail servers at regular intervals and then display them in your Inbox. Windows Live Mail checks for new messages by default every 10 minutes; you can change this setting on the General tab in the Options dialog box. At any point, however, you can click the Send/Receive button on the Ribbon in the Tools group to check for new e-mail messages, or the Update all button on the Quick Access Toolbar to sync all mail and newsgroup items.

Q&A

What is the difference between email and e-mail?
Although Windows Live Mail uses the spelling, email (without a hyphen), within this text, e-mail (with a hyphen) is used. Both are considered acceptable spellings. As new words are developed, spelling usage can vary. In fact, eMail, Email, and EMail have also been used as common spellings. You can choose any as a preferred term. If asked to write to a particular style, such as *The Chicago Manual of Style* or to a company's style guide, such as Microsoft's, you should use whichever term is listed.

You can turn off the automatic downloading of messages by clearing the 'Check for new messages every X minutes' check box on the General tab in the Options dialog box. To open the Options dialog box, click the Windows Live Mail button, point to Options, and then click an option, such as Mail.

To Open Windows Live Mail

The following steps open Windows Live Mail using the Start menu.

- Click Start on the taskbar.

- Point to All Programs to display the menu.

- Scroll to view the Windows Live Mail command (Figure 4-7).

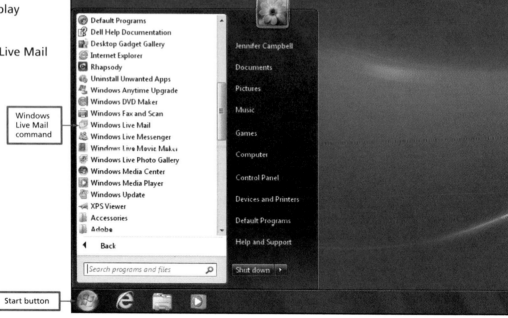

Windows Live Mail command

Start button

Figure 4-7

- Click the Windows Live Mail command to open Windows Live Mail (Figure 4-8).

Why do I see a dialog box telling me Windows Live Mail is not my default e-mail program?
Your computer might have a different e-mail client, such as Outlook, assigned as the default e-mail client. Follow the instructions provided by your instructor to click the Yes or No button in the dialog box.

Update all button

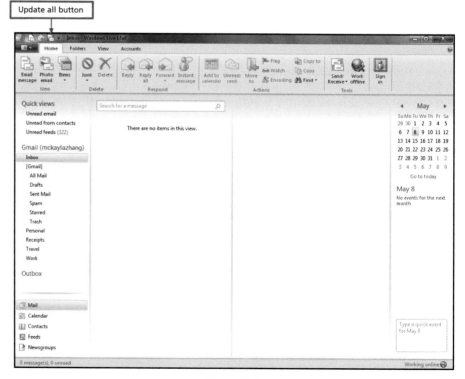

Figure 4-8

Other Ways

1. Double-click Windows Live Mail icon on desktop

To Check for Incoming Mail

The following step checks for incoming e-mail and review an e-mail message sent to you by your instructor. In this chapter, the default Windows Live Mail folders are illustrated and the incoming messages are downloaded from a POP3 server. If your Windows Live Mail folders are different or if your messages are stored on an IMAP server, your instructor will provide alternative instructions. The contents of your Windows Live Mail Message list might be different.

- Click the Update all button on the Quick Access Toolbar to download an incoming message from your instructor and send any outgoing messages temporarily stored in the Outbox folder.

- Click the message from your instructor to select it and view the message contents in the Preview pane (Figure 4-9).

What if I did not receive a message from my instructor?

If your instructor did not send a message to you, open any message in your Inbox that contains an attachment to complete the steps below. If you do not have any messages with an attachment, read through the next several sets of steps until you learn how to send a message with an attachment; send an e-mail to yourself that contains an attachment; and then complete the steps you read.

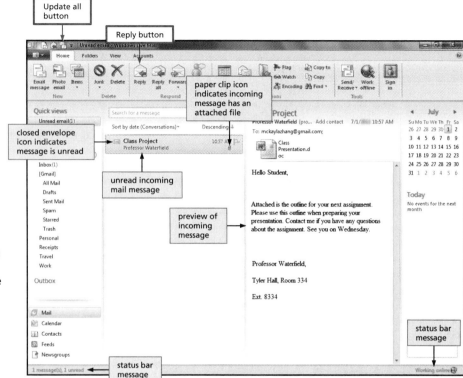

Figure 4-9

Other Ways

1. Click Send/Receive button (Tools group on Home tab)
2. Press F5

You can open your default e-mail client, such as Outlook or Windows Live Mail, by clicking the Read mail button on the Internet Explorer 9 Command bar. To specify your default e-mail client for Internet Explorer 9, open the Programs tab in the Internet Options dialog box and click the Set programs button. Then follow the instructions in the Control Panel window.

FACTS @HAND

A standard feature of any e-mail client is the reply feature, which allows you to respond to an incoming message. Replying opens an Re: message window addressed to the sender of the original message. The window includes, on the Subject line, a reference to the subject of the original message preceded by Re:. By default, the text of the original message is included for reference. The Re: message window also contains a Ribbon and a Quick Access Toolbar you can use to perform a variety of tasks, such as send the message; cut, copy, and paste message contents; check spelling; set message priority; undo a previous action; and more.

To Reply to an E-Mail Message

The following steps reply to the e-mail message you just received.

- Click the Reply button in the Respond group to open the Re: message window.

- Click the Maximize button on the Re: message window title bar, if necessary, to maximize the message window (Figure 4-10).

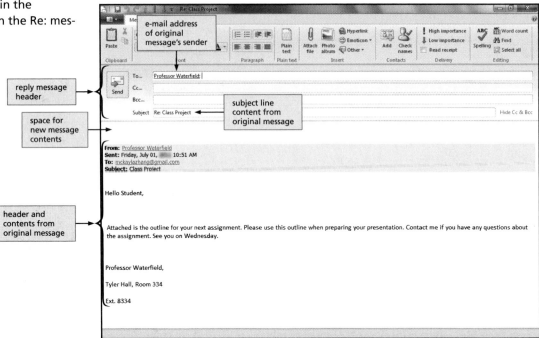

Figure 4-10

- Type **Received** at the insertion point on the blank line above the original message header and text.

- Press the ENTER key to move to a new line.

- Type your name on the current line.

- Press the ENTER key to complete the message (Figure 4-11).

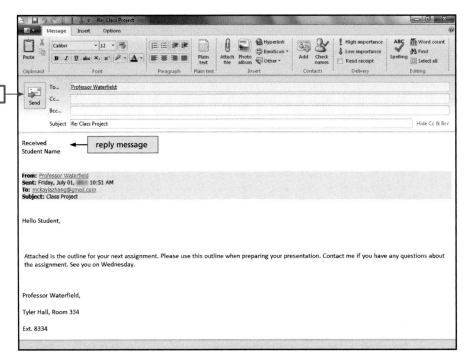

Figure 4-11

3

- Click the Send button to close the Re: window and send the message.

- Click the Sent Mail or Sent items folder to see the sent message (Figure 4-12).

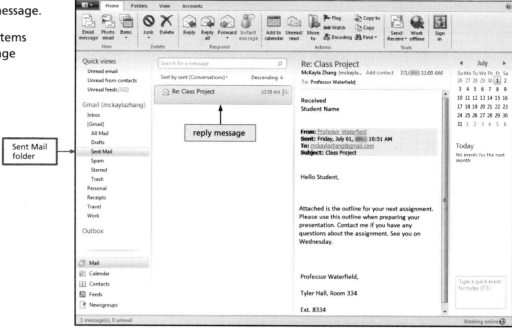

Figure 4-12

Other Ways

1. CTRL+R to reply to sender

You can change the settings that control how incoming messages are displayed and marked as read in the Message list using options on the Read tab in the Options dialog box. To open the Options dialog box, click the Windows Live Mail button, point to Options, and then click an option, such as Mail.

FACTS @HAND

VIEWING AND SAVING ATTACHMENTS   The message from your instructor has an attached file, indicated by the paper clip icon (see Figure 4-9). You can preview, save, and print an attachment by first opening the message with the attachment in a message window and then using a shortcut menu or menu commands to open the e-mail in the program in which it was created, such as Microsoft Word, or to save or print the attachment. When you open an attachment, the program associated with the attachment's file type automatically starts. By default, Windows Live Mail automatically blocks file attachments commonly used to spread e-mail viruses (for example, .exe, .pif, and .scr files). However, you should always use caution when opening attachments because of the risk of receiving attachments that contain damaging viruses. To protect against e-mail viruses, you should think twice about opening an attachment from an unknown source or an attachment even from a trusted source unless you are expecting the attachment.

> **FACTS @HAND** By default, Windows Live Mail automatically saves e-mail attachments in the Windows 7 Documents folder. To save attachments in a different folder, click the Browse button in the Save Attachments dialog box and select the desired folder. You can turn off the automatic blocking of suspicious attachments in the Security tab in the Safety Options dialog box; however, doing so is not recommended.

To View and Save an Attachment

The following steps view the file attached to your instructor's message and then save the attached file in a folder specified by your instructor. The message contents and attachment file name might vary from those shown in the figures.

- Verify that the Windows Live Mail window is open, click the Inbox folder icon, and select the message from your instructor in the Message list.

- Double-click the message from your instructor to open the message in its own window.

- Maximize the message window, if necessary (Figure 4-13).

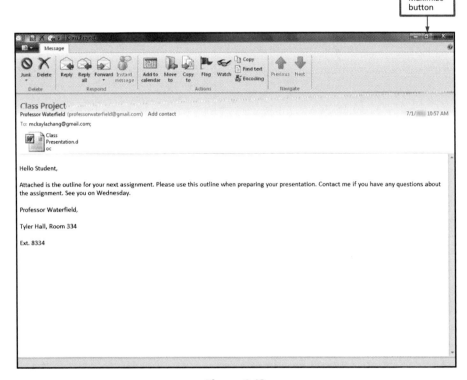

Figure 4-13

- Right-click the attachment's file name to display the shortcut menu (Figure 4-14).

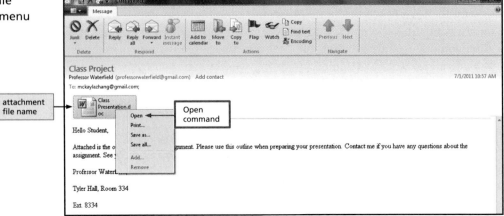

Figure 4-14

3

- Click the Open command on the shortcut menu to display the Mail Attachment dialog box (Figure 4-15).

Figure 4-15

4

- Click the Open button to open the attachment in your word processing program (Figure 4-16).

Q&A

Why does my word processing program window look different from the illustration?
You might have a different version of the word processing program installed, or you might have different features turned on or off.

Close button

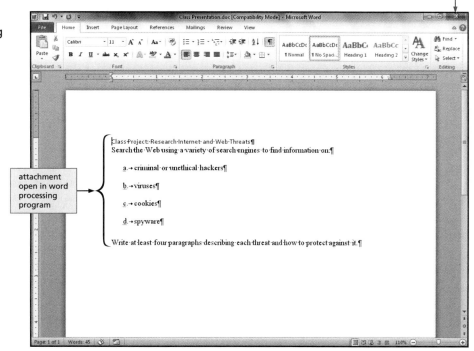

attachment open in word processing program

Figure 4-16

5

- Click the Close button on the word processing program title bar to close the document and return to Windows Live Mail (Figure 4-17).

Windows Live Mail button

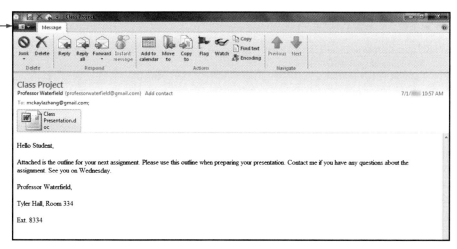

Figure 4-17

- Click the Windows Live Mail button, and then point to Save to view the save options on the Windows Live Mail menu (Figure 4-18).

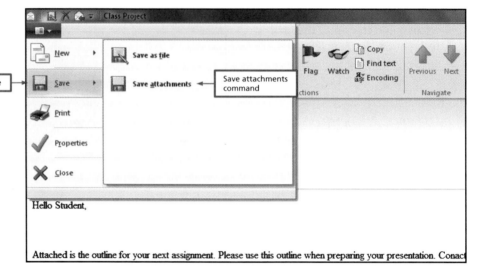

Figure 4-18

- Click the Save attachments command on the Windows Live Mail menu to open the Save Attachments dialog box (Figure 4-19).

- If necessary, click the Browse button to navigate to the drive or folder specified by your instructor.

- Click the Save button to close the Save Attachments dialog box and save the attachment.

- Click the Close button on the message window title bar and leave Windows Live Mail and the Inbox folder open.

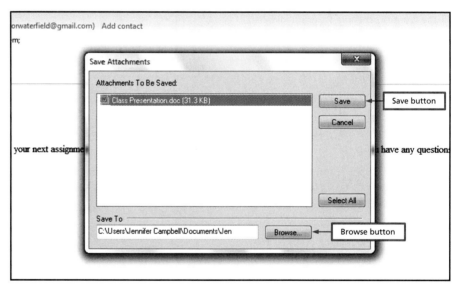

Figure 4-19

Other Ways

1. Double-click attachment icon in message header to open attachment

2. F5 to send and receive all messages

3. CTRL+O to open selected message in its own window

4. ENTER to open selected message in its own window

5. ESC to close message window

FORWARDING AN E-MAIL MESSAGE You might receive an e-mail message that contains information that should be shared with other users who were not addressed in the original message. For example, a message sent to one person with information about a rescheduled meeting might need to be shared either in part or in total with all meeting attendees. To **forward** a message means to send a message you receive to someone else. You can forward a message by selecting the message in the Message list and then clicking the Forward button on the Ribbon to open the Fw: window (Figure 4-20). You can also press CTRL+F to open the Fw: message window.

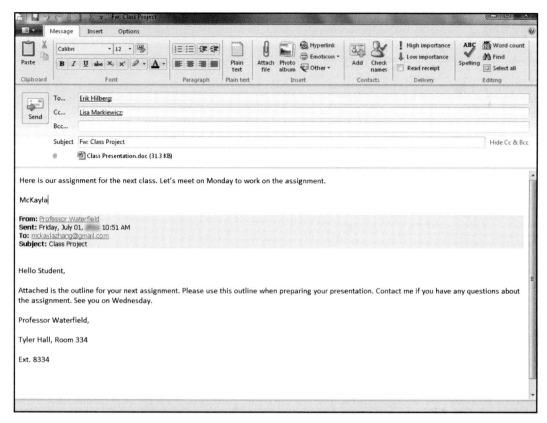

Figure 4-20   Use the Fw: window to send a received message to another person.

When the Fw: window opens, you can type the recipient's e-mail address in the To text box, type your message text in the message body area above the original message, and then click the Send button. By default, a forwarded message includes the original message and any attached files. Remember to use good judgment when forwarding messages to ensure that you include enough of the original message to preserve its integrity — but do not forward information not meant to be distributed freely. If only part of the original message is appropriate for forwarding, you can select and delete that portion of the original message that should not be shared before forwarding the message.

@ISSUE   Cyber Bullying

Cyber bullying includes any Internet activity that is intended to hurt or humiliate someone. Cyber bullying includes circulating cruel and spiteful e-mail, photos, instant messages, and social networking messages. Anything designed to hurt and humiliate the messages' target — perhaps a former girlfriend or boyfriend, a classmate, a coworker, or even a stranger — for entertainment or revenge is considered to be bullying and should not be sent. Examples of cyber bullying abound: The pictures of a young girl's horrific death in an automobile accident are widely circulated online, tormenting the girl's family; a student continually is harassed by other students with hateful messages until she is forced to leave school; a young girl commits suicide because of a social networking hoax; and intimate pictures circulated among classmates result in a teenager's prosecution for child pornography and a lifetime as a registered sexual predator.

The cyber bullying statistics for kids and teens are astounding. According to online safety educator i-SAFE, 42 percent of kids have been bullied online, 58 percent have had hurtful things said about them online, and 53 percent admit to saying hurtful things about others online!

Although protecting against cyber bullying can be difficult, some commonsense tips include asking for help from school officials and/or the police, blocking e-mail or instant messages, and keeping personal information private and out of the hands of bullies. For more information on protecting against cyber bullying, visit the *Discovering the Internet, Fourth Edition* @Issue Book Companion Site Web page at **www. cengagebrain.com**, and then click a link below Chapter 4, Cyber Bullying.

PRINTING AN E-MAIL MESSAGE   Although e-mail messages are stored and read electronically, many people prefer to work with paper and pen for certain tasks. Windows Live Mail and other e-mail clients provide printing capabilities that allow users to create a hard copy of an e-mail message. To print a message, select the message in the Message list, click the Windows Live Mail button, and click Print to open the Print dialog box (Figure 4-21). You also can press CTRL+P, or right-click the message and click Print on the shortcut menu to open the Print dialog box. In the dialog box, you can set various print options, such as the number of copies to print, and then click the Print button to send the message to the selected printer.

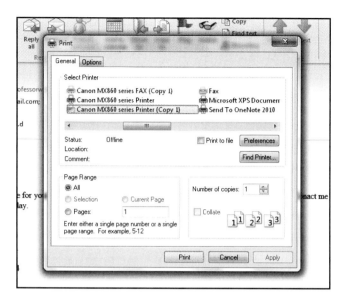

Figure 4-21   Print a message by selecting it, opening the Print dialog box, setting print options, and clicking the Print button to send the message to the printer.

Composing and Sending an Outgoing E-Mail Message

Although many of the e-mail messages you send will be replies to messages you receive, many times you will need to send an original message. As you compose a message, keep in mind the following guidelines to ensure that your messages are reader-friendly:

- Put a meaningful phrase in the Subject line to get the reader's attention or to identify the message's content.

- Add a greeting. Although the e-mail header shows the recipient's e-mail address or name, it still is considered good form to include a greeting on the first line. The greeting can be a formal one (Dear Ms. Patil:) or a casual one (Hi, Julia!), depending on the nature of the message.

- Keep the message brief, but make sure its wording is clear. Make the point quickly, but provide enough information so the recipient understands the required background information. If the message contains requests, clearly state them in the first sentence or two, if possible.

- Instead of typing or retyping information, use hyperlinks to link to a Web site or network folder you are referencing in your e-mail, or include an attachment file that contains information.

- When replying to an e-mail, you should leave the message to which you are replying at the bottom of your message. Maintaining a message thread in this way can provide background information and make it easier for the recipient to understand the latest message in the thread.

- Use a personalized closing and include a signature file in case the recipient needs to know alternative ways to contact you.

CREATING A SIGNATURE FILE   Windows Live Mail allows you to create a signature file, a file that includes standard information that is inserted automatically at the end of e-mail messages. For example, you often might need to provide your contact information and title, particularly with business e-mail. A signature file can contain basic contact information, such as your name, company, telephone number, fax number, and e-mail address; a confidentiality agreement; an inspirational quotation or motto; or any text that you want to add to the end of e-mail messages.

 FACTS @HAND You can use a word processing program to create a signature containing custom fonts or graphics, and then save the file as an HTML file. In the Windows Live Mail Options dialog box, select the HTML file in the Signatures tab to select the file as your signature file.

To Create a Signature File

The following steps create a signature file for your messages. If you are working in a computer lab, check with your instructor before setting up a signature file.

- Verify that Windows Live Mail and the Inbox folder are open.

- Click the Windows Live Mail button to view the Windows Live Mail menu, and then point to Options (Figure 4-22).

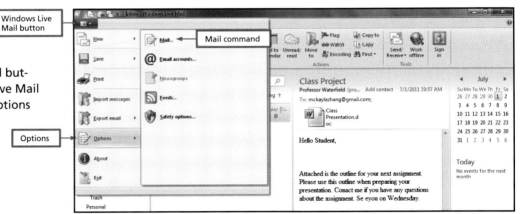

Figure 4-22

- Click Mail to display the Options dialog box (Figure 4-23).

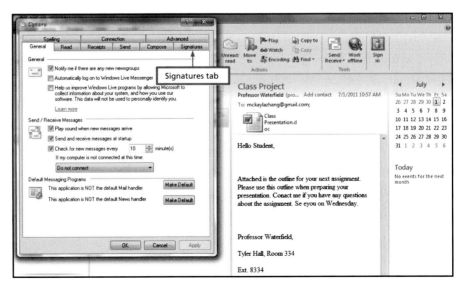

Figure 4-23

3

- Click the Signatures tab.

- Click the New button to create a new signature file.

- Click the Text option button to activate the Edit Signature text box.

- Type your name and telephone number in the Edit Signature text box, pressing the ENTER key to insert a line break.

- Click the 'Add signatures to all outgoing messages' check box to add the new signature to all outgoing messages.

- If necessary, click the 'Don't add signatures to Replies and Forwards' check box to select it (Figure 4-24).

- Click the OK button to create the signature and close the dialog box.

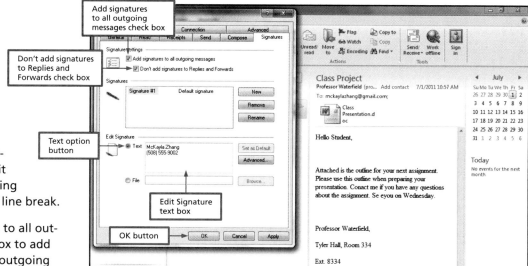

Figure 4-24

Now, whenever you create a new message, Windows Live Mail automatically appends the signature file to the message. When deciding whether to create and include a signature in your e-mail messages, consider how you usually use e-mail. If most messages you create do not need a signature, then you might prefer to include a signature on a message-by-message basis, instead of automatically including it in all e-mail messages. Some e-mail clients, including Windows Live Mail, also allow you to set up multiple signatures so that you can use one for business communications, one for personal messages, and so on. If you want to insert a signature file on a message-by-message basis or be able to select from multiple signatures, do not turn on the option to add the signature file to all new messages. Instead, create the signature file or files. Then, after composing a new message, click the Insert tab on the new message window's Ribbon, click the Signature button, and select the desired signature from the Signature submenu. You also can press CTRL+SHIFT+S to insert the default signature file in a message.

COMPOSING A NEW MESSAGE WITH AN ATTACHMENT   You can send an electronic file — such as a document, spreadsheet, or photo — to someone by attaching the file to an e-mail message. Be aware, however, that some mail servers limit attachment sizes to ensure that extremely large files do not bog down the e-mail system. Additionally, some networks block incoming e-mail messages that have certain types of attachments to reduce the risk of viruses. To send e-mail to someone, you need to know his or her e-mail address. As you have learned, you can look up an e-mail address in an online white or yellow pages directory. In most cases, however, the best way to find out an e-mail address is to simply ask the intended recipient.

FACTS @HAND

It is a good idea to check the spelling of your message before you send it. To check the spelling, you can click the Spelling button in the Editing group on the message window Ribbon to open the Check Spelling dialog box and correct any spelling errors. You also can press the F7 key to open the Check Spelling dialog box.

To Compose and Send a Message with an Attachment

The following steps compose a new e-mail message and attach a small file as an attachment. For these steps, assume that you have asked a classmate, John Olivero, for his e-mail address. Then compose a new e-mail message to John Olivero, attach the file, and send the message.

- Verify that the Windows Live Mail window and Inbox folder are open.

- Click the Email message button and, if necessary, maximize the message window (Figure 4-25).

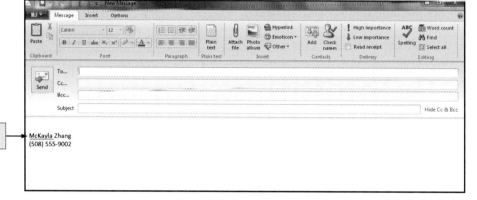

Figure 4-25

- Type **John.Olivero@course. com** in the To text box.

- Type **Class Assignment** in the Subject text box.

- Type **Hi John,** as the greeting line in the message body area, and then press the ENTER key twice.

- Type **Let's get together before class to work on the attached assignment.** as the message body, and then press the ENTER key (Figure 4-26).

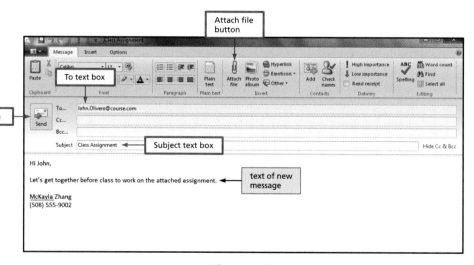

Figure 4-26

3

- Click the Attach file button in the Insert group to display the Open dialog box.

- Open the Documents folder or navigate to the location in which you saved the attachment from your instructor.

- Double-click the Class Presentation file name to attach the document to the message (Figure 4-27).

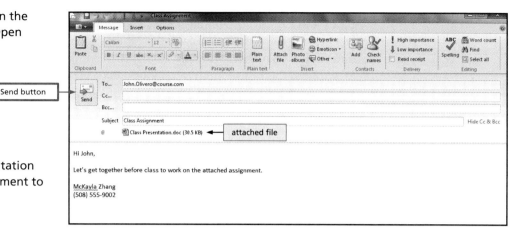

Figure 4-27

4

- Click the Send button. You should receive John's reply soon. Click the Update all button if necessary to view the incoming reply message from John Olivero (Figure 4-28).

Q&A

Is John standing by to return my message?

No. The reply you receive from John is an automated reply. An automated reply is sent in response to an e-mail. You can set up an automated reply to inform people that you will be out of the office and provide alternate contact information, or to inform them of a change to your e-mail account.

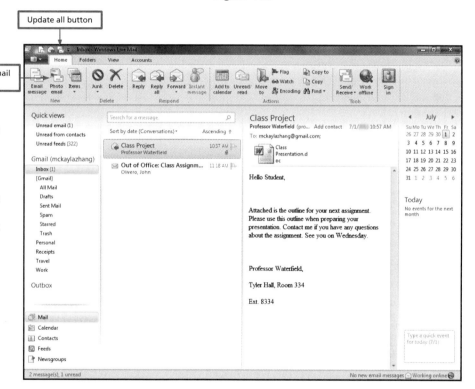

Figure 4-28

Other Ways	
1. Click New button on Quick Access Toolbar	3. CTRL+ENTER to send message
2. CTRL+N to open New Message window	4. ALT+S to send message

You can change the default font for message text and set other options for message composition on the Compose tab in the Options dialog box.

FACTS @HAND

COMPOSING A PHOTO MESSAGE WITH AN ATTACHMENT Although you can send photos as an attachment to an e-mail, doing so can fill up space in the recipients' Inbox and hard drive with large files. Windows Live Mail 2011 has a new feature that enables you to send a link to a photo album, where the high-resolution file sizes are stored on Windows SkyDrive. Recipients can click a link to view the files without downloading anything to their own computer. Windows SkyDrive is one of the many free services that enable you to do this; others, such as Shutterfly and Kodak Photo Gallery, are discussed later in the chapter.

To Compose a Photo Message

The following steps compose a new photo e-mail message using a picture uploaded to SkyDrive. You will open a new photo e-mail message, sign in to Windows Live with your Windows Live ID, address it to John Olivero, select a photo, and then send it.

- Verify that the Windows Live Mail window and Inbox folder are open.

- Click the Photo email button in the New group to display the Windows Live Mail sign in dialog box (Figure 4-29).

Q&A **Why am I not prompted to sign in to Windows Live Mail?**
If you are using a Windows Live Mail account, you will not be prompted to sign in. Skip step 2 if necessary.

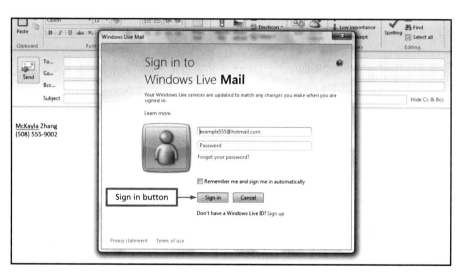

Figure 4-29

- Type your Windows Live ID name and password, and then click the Sign in button to sign in to Windows Live and display the Add photos dialog box (Figure 4-30).

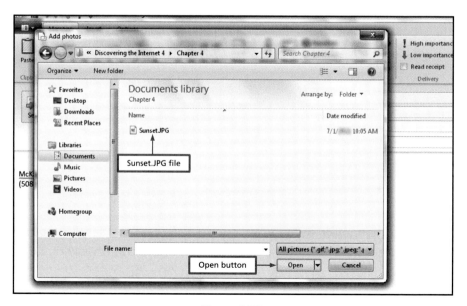

Figure 4-30

- Navigate to the location in which you stored the Sunset.JPG file from your instructor, and then double-click the file to add it to the photo album that Windows Live Mail automatically creates using Windows SkyDrive.

- Type **John.Olivero@ course.com** in the To text box.

- Type **Sunset Photo** in the Subject text box, and then add a short message describing the picture (Figure 4-31).

- Click the Send button to send the message.

Q&A

Why did I not receive another reply from John Olivero?
Most servers set up auto-reply messages so that a sender will only receive one auto-reply for an out-of-office message, such as the one you previously received from John Olivero.

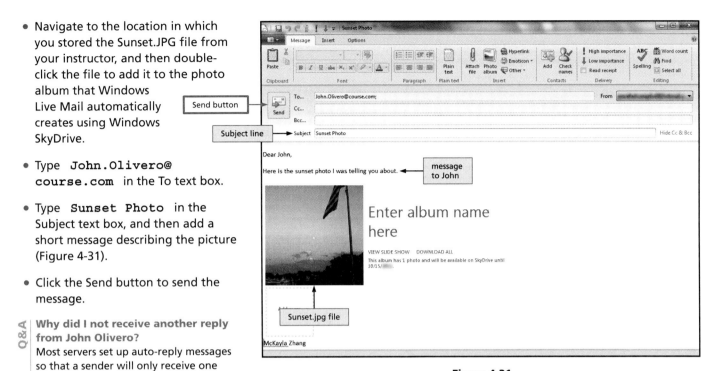

Figure 4-31

Managing Messages

As the number of e-mails you receive from friends, family members, business associates, and others grows, keeping track of them all can be a challenge. You can organize the messages to find specific messages more quickly, delete messages you do not need, and indicate which new messages need your immediate attention. With Windows Live Mail, you can create folders in which you can store your messages, access options for deleting messages, and create rules by which incoming messages automatically are moved into specific folders. You also can flag incoming messages for follow-up and mark message conversations — multiple messages on the same topic — as watched conversations. Finally, you can rearrange messages in the Message list by sorting them in a specific order.

You can mark a message as either read or unread despite any previous action with the message. To mark an unread message as a read message, right-click the message and click Mark as read. To mark a read message as an unread message, click Mark as unread on the shortcut menu. You also can mark a message as read by pressing CTRL+ENTER or CTRL+Q, or by using commands in the Actions group on the Home tab.

FACTS @HAND

CREATING MESSAGE FOLDERS   The first step in organizing your incoming e-mail messages is to create message folders. You then can move your messages into the folders. Creating and using message folders with meaningful names makes finding a particular message much easier.

To Create a New Message Folder

The following steps create a new folder for incoming messages about class assignments.

- Verify that Windows Live Mail and the Inbox folder are open.

- Right-click the Inbox folder in the Folder list to display the shortcut menu (Figure 4-32).

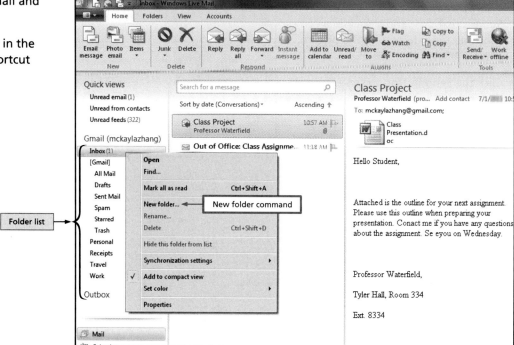

Figure 4-32

- Click the New folder command to display the Create Folder dialog box.

- Type **Assignments** in the Folder name text box (Figure 4-33).

- Click the OK button to create the folder.

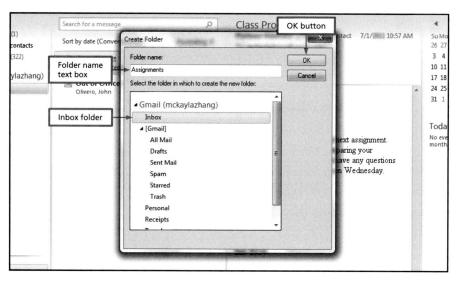

Figure 4-33

- Click the Inbox folder arrow to view the Assignments subfolder as a subfolder of the Inbox folder, if necessary (Figure 4-34).

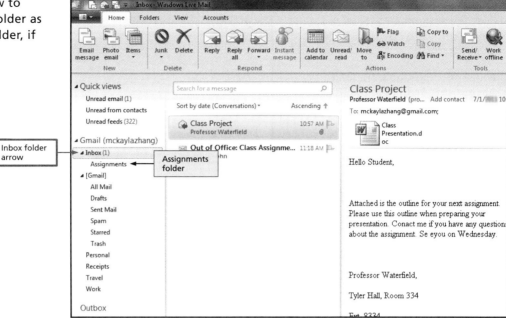

Figure 4-34

Other Ways

1. CTRL+J to select Inbox folder
2. CTRL+Y to open Go to Folder dialog box

To Move a Message from the Inbox Folder into the Assignments Folder

After you create message folders, you can move incoming messages from the Message list (or from any folder) into the appropriate folder. The following steps drag your instructor's message into the Assignments folder.

- Verify that Windows Live Mail and the Inbox folder are open.

- Click the Class Project message from your instructor in the Message list to select it, if necessary.

- Drag the message from the Inbox folder and drop it into the Assignments folder in the Folder list (Figure 4-35).

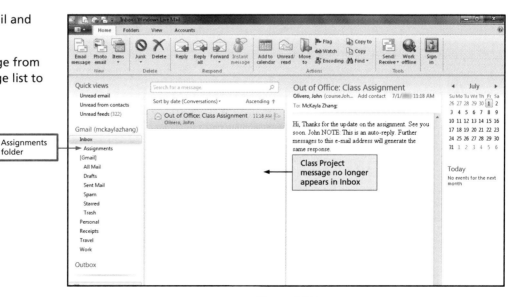

Figure 4-35

2

- Click the Assignments folder in the Folder list to open the folder (Figure 4-36).

Q&A

Why is the message from John Olivero now marked as read?
If the Olivero message is the only message in your Inbox folder, it will appear in the Preview pane and be marked as read.

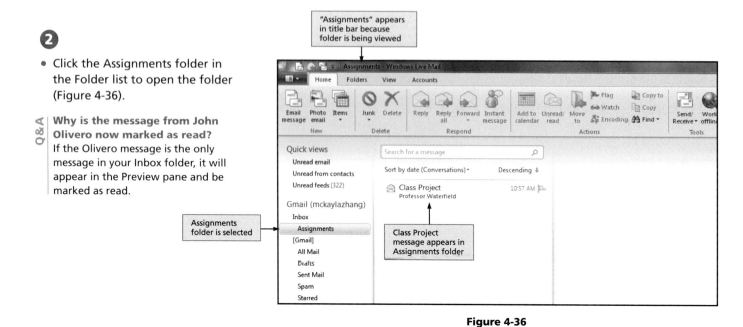

Figure 4-36

USING RULES TO ORGANIZE MESSAGES   You can specify a **message rule** that instructs Windows Live Mail to automatically move certain messages to specific folders. For example, you might choose to have all incoming messages from a business colleague automatically moved into a folder named for the colleague. To set rules for incoming messages, click the Folders tab, and then click the Message rules button to open the New Mail Rule dialog box (Figure 4-37). If you have any mail rules set up, the Rules dialog box will open when you click the Message rules button. If this happens, click the New button in the Rules dialog box to open the New Mail Rule dialog box. In the New Mail Rule dialog box, you can select conditions and set actions for a rule.

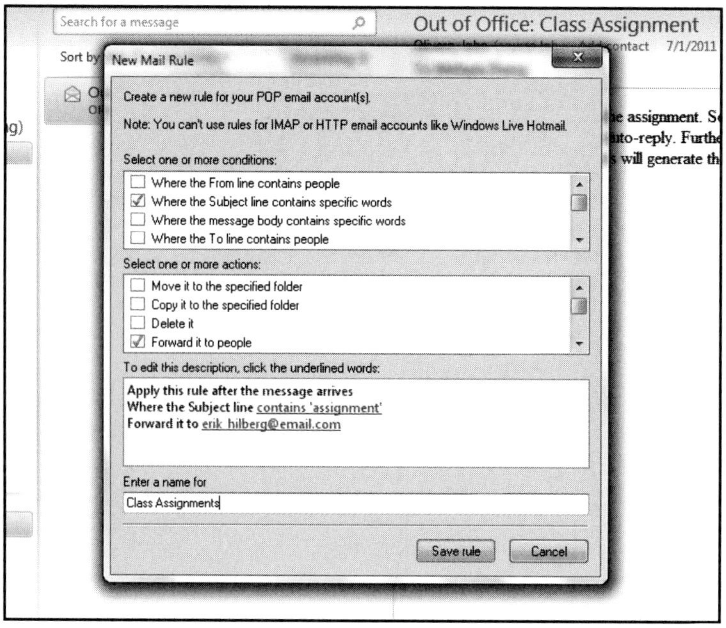

Figure 4-37   You can set rules for incoming messages in the New Mail Rule dialog box.

DELETING A MESSAGE   In addition to keeping messages organized using folders, you can keep the number of incoming messages manageable by deleting selected messages when you no longer need them. You can delete selected messages by clicking the Delete button in the Delete group on the Home tab. To select multiple adjacent messages for deletion, click the first message, press and hold the SHIFT key, and click the last message. To select nonadjacent messages, press and hold the CTRL key and click each message to be deleted. Deleted messages are moved to the Deleted items folder.

You can retain messages in the Deleted items folder and then retrieve them, as necessary, by moving them to another folder, such as the Inbox folder. You can empty the Deleted items folder by clicking the Empty 'Deleted items' folder command on the short-cut menu that is displayed when you right-click the Deleted items folder. Once you empty the Deleted items folder, however, you no longer can retrieve any of the messages stored in the folder.

To retrieve a message from the Trash or Deleted items folder, open the folder and drag the message to another folder. You also can right-click a message in the Trash or Deleted items folder and click the 'Move to folder' command on the shortcut menu.

FACTS @HAND

To Delete a Message

The following steps delete a message from your Inbox folder.

- Verify that Windows Live Mail is open, and then click the Inbox folder.

- Double-click the message from John Olivero to open it (Figure 4-38).

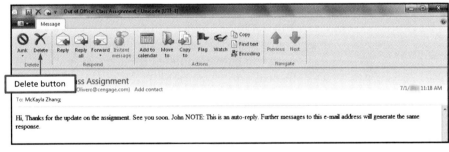

Delete button

Figure 4-38

- Click the Delete button on the Message tab in the Delete group to move the message to the Deleted items folder.

- Close any open message windows, if necessary.

- Click the Deleted items or Trash folder to verify that it contains the Olivero message (Figure 4-39).

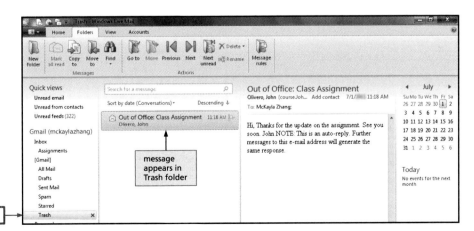

Trash folder

message appears in Trash folder

Figure 4-39

3

- Click the Inbox folder to open it and confirm that the Olivero message is deleted (Figure 4-40).

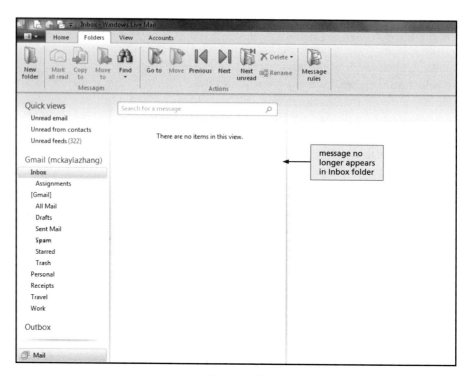

Figure 4-40

FLAGGING AND WATCHING MESSAGES Some messages require further action. You can mark an incoming message with a flag icon, indicating that the message requires your attention. You then can leave the flagged message (Figure 4-41) in your Inbox folder until you have completed the required action. To **flag** or unflag a message, click in the flag column to the right of the message in the Message list or click the Flag button in the Actions group on the Home tab.

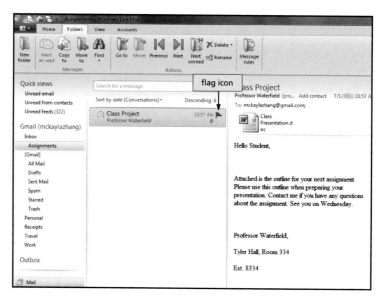

Figure 4-41 You can flag a message for further action.

FACTS
@HAND

It is common for people to exchange multiple messages on the same topic or in the same conversation by replying and forwarding messages. To more easily identify all the messages in a conversation, you can mark the original message and all of its replies as part of a **watched conversation**. To mark a selected message as part of a watched conversation, select the message, and then click the Watch button in the Actions group on the Home tab. To stop watching a conversation, click the Watch button again to toggle it off. Messages in a watched conversation appear in color in the Message list. You also can add a Watch/Ignore column to the Message list to display a watch symbol or an ignore symbol for each message in a watched conversation.

By default, Windows Live Mail organizes all messages that originate from the same message (such as replies and forwards) into a conversation. This helps you keep your Inbox organized by subject. To turn conversation view on and off, click the View tab, click the Conversations button in the Arrangement group, and then click On or Off.

PRIORITIZING MESSAGES   Windows Live Mail allows you to assign one of three action priorities to an outgoing message: High, Normal, and Low Priority. By default, all outgoing messages are assigned a Normal Priority. If you want a message recipient to take immediate action when he or she receives the message, you can mark it High Priority by clicking a button, such as the High importance button, in the Delivery group on the Message tab of the New Message window (Figure 4-42). You can indicate that a message has a low priority for action by clicking the Low importance button.

If the message recipient is using Windows Live Mail, a red exclamation point appears in the Priority column in the Message list when a high-priority message is downloaded into his or her Inbox folder. A low-priority incoming message is represented by a downward-pointing blue arrow. As with any feature, think carefully before setting the importance of a message. What is important to you may not seem as urgent to the recipient, and marking it as a high priority does not guarantee that he or she will respond immediately. If you send all of your messages with High importance, eventually people will ignore the indicator.

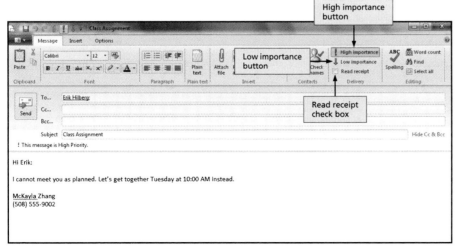

Figure 4-42   You can specify a High or Low importance status for an outgoing message. An incoming message's High or Low importance indicator appears in the Priority column in the Message list.

ADDING A READ RECEIPT   A third option in the Delivery group is the Read receipt check box. Clicking this check box causes Windows Live Mail to send you a message when the recipient opens the e-mail. This feature can help track when a recipient receives the message and when the response is delivered. Usually the recipient is notified that the read receipt has been sent to the original sender. This feature should also be used sparingly. With the prevalence of smartphones, a recipient could check your message while he or she is on personal time or otherwise busy. One benefit of e-mails is that recipients can respond on their own time. A recipient may need time to research or respond to the original message, and might not appreciate the notification.

SORTING MESSAGES   You also can rearrange messages in the Message list by sorting the messages in a specific order. The most common way to sort is by the date the messages were received — either most recent or earliest — according to the Received column. To select a different sort order and/or column, click the Sort order button in the Arrangement group on the View tab. You also can click the Sort by button in the message pane, and then click an option (Figure 4-43). The sort order is based on the contents of the column — for example, by A–Z or Z–A order for From or Subject names, most recent or oldest order for Received dates, highest to lowest or lowest to highest for importance, and so forth.

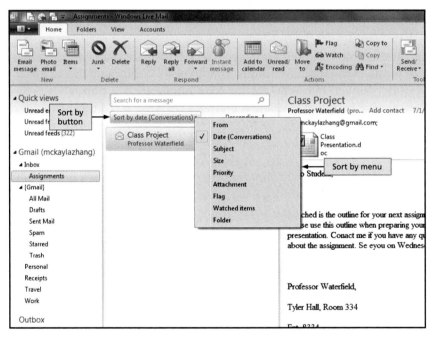

Figure 4-43   You can sort a folder by date, priority, sender, and more.

Managing Contacts

All e-mail clients have an electronic address book in which you can store the e-mail addresses and other information for your contacts. The **Contacts folder** is the electronic address book for Windows Live Mail. In the Contacts folder, you can enter names, addresses, e-mail addresses, and other important information about those with whom you correspond using Windows Live Mail. Other e-mail clients have similar contact management tools.

CREATING CONTACTS   You can open the Contacts folder by clicking the Contacts button in the left pane of the Windows Live Mail window. When the Contacts folder opens, you can add, modify, or delete a contact.

Most e-mail clients and Web-based e-mail services allow you to create a nickname or an alias for a contact. You then can simply enter the nickname in the To line instead of typing the entire e-mail address or selecting a contact from the Contacts folder. Additionally, e-mail clients and Web-based mail services often provide an AutoComplete-style feature that remembers commonly typed text, such as e-mail addresses. The AutoComplete-style feature offers a list of suggested e-mail addresses as you begin to type in the To, Cc, or Bcc lines of a message header.

FACTS @HAND

To Create a Contact

The following steps open the Contacts folder and add John Olivero as a contact.

1

- Verify that Windows Live Mail and the Inbox folder are open.

- Click the Contacts folder icon in the left pane to open the Contacts folder (Figure 4-44).

Why does my Contacts folder look different from Figure 4-44?
In the illustrations in this section, the Folder list in the left pane is hidden and the right pane, which shows the contents of the Contacts folder, is displayed in List view. Your Contacts folder display settings might be different. Additionally, your list of contacts will be different.

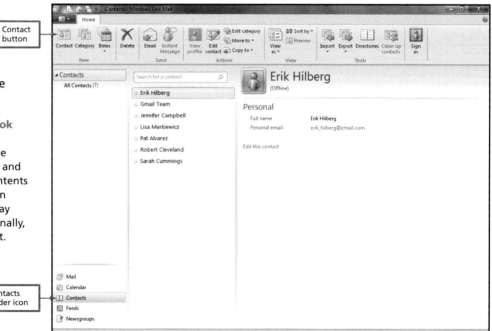

Figure 4-44

②

- Click the Contact button in the New group on the Home tab to display the Add a Contact dialog box (Figure 4-45).

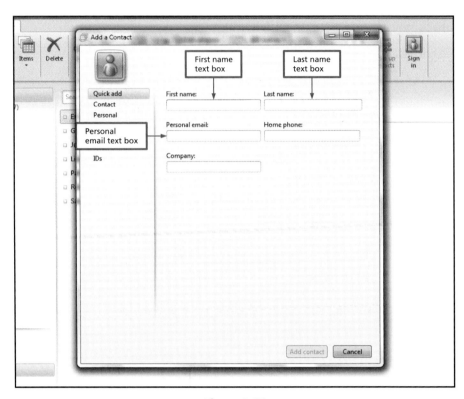

Figure 4-45

③

- Type **John** in the First name text box.

- Type **Olivero** in the Last name text box.

- Type **John.Olivero@course. com** in the Personal email text box (Figure 4-46).

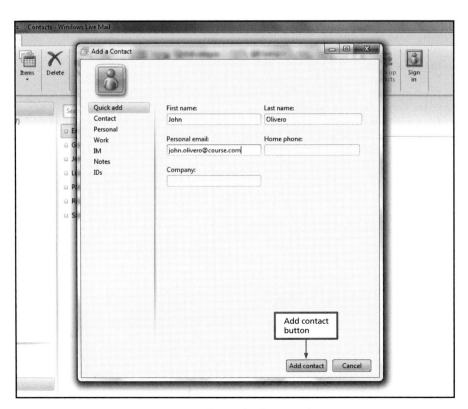

Figure 4-46

- Click the Add contact button to add the new contact and view the new contact in the Contacts folder (Figure 4-47).

- Click the Mail folder icon in the left pane to return to the Mail folder.

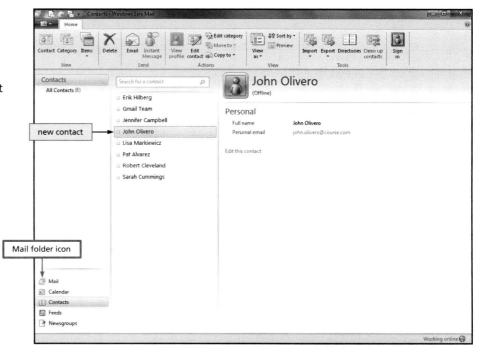

Figure 4-47

Other Ways

1. CTRL+SHIFT+C to open the Add a Contact dialog box

To Send an E-Mail Message to a Contact

You can create a new message and click the To button to open the Send an Email dialog box to select a contact's e-mail address. The following steps send an e-mail message to John Olivero using the Contacts folder.

- Verify that Windows Live Mail and the Inbox folder are open.

- Click the Email message button in the New group on the Home tab and maximize the New Message window, if necessary.

- Click the To button in the message header to open the Send an Email dialog box (Figure 4-48).

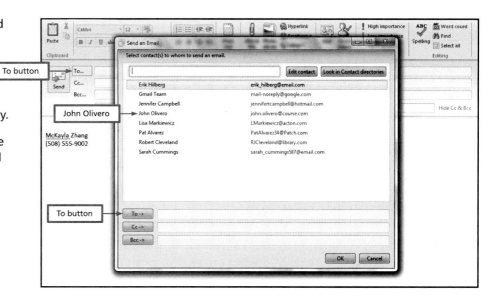

Figure 4-48

2

- Click John Olivero to select the contact.

- Click the To button in the lower part of the dialog box to add John Olivero to the To text box (Figure 4-49).

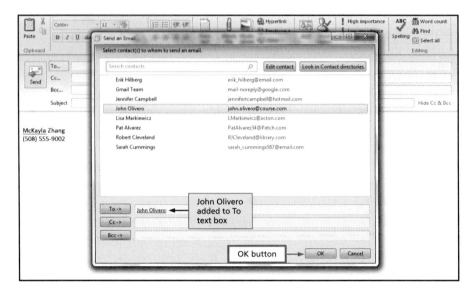

Figure 4-49

3

- Click the OK button to add John Olivero's address to the To text box in the message header (Figure 4-50).

- Compose the message of your choice by typing a subject in the Subject text box and a short message in the message body area.

- Click the Send button.

- Close Windows Live Mail.

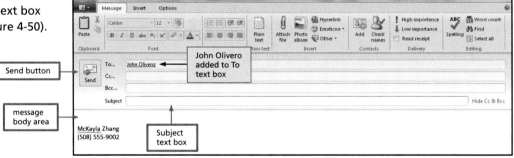

Figure 4-50

EDITING AND DELETING CONTACTS You might need to edit a contact's information or to delete a contact. You can view a contact's properties quickly and then edit the information — for example, to update his or her e-mail address or telephone number — by right-clicking the contact's name in the Contacts folder and clicking Edit contact. You also can double-click a contact in the Contacts folder to open the contact's Edit Contact dialog box.

You can delete a contact by selecting the contact's name in the Contacts folder and then pressing the DELETE key, or by right-clicking the contact's name in the Contacts folder and clicking the Delete Contact command on the shortcut menu. In each case, you will be asked to confirm the deletion before the contact is removed.

CREATING CONTACT CATEGORIES A **contact category** is a list of contacts to which you can refer collectively by a single name and to whom you can easily address a single e-mail. A contact category is sometimes called a contact group, mailing list, or distribution list. For instance, a contact category named Team could contain the e-mail addresses and contact information for everyone involved in a specific school or work project. When you need to send an e-mail message to everyone on the team, you use the Team contact category name in the To text box instead of entering individual e-mail addresses. To create a contact category, open the Contacts folder, click the Category button in the New group on the Home tab to open the 'Create a new category' dialog box. Next, type a name for the category and select the contacts to be included in the group. After you create the category, the category's name appears in the Contacts folder. Sending an e-mail message to a contact category follows the same process as sending an e-mail message to an individual contact.

E-Mail Viruses and Worms

@ISSUE

For all its benefits, e-mail has the distinction of being a primary method of spreading computer viruses and worms. One way a computer virus can be distributed is through e-mail attachments. Viruses and worms that arrive in an e-mail message might damage files on the hard disk, copy themselves to other computers on a network, or hijack an infected computer's address book and replicate themselves by sending out infected messages.

Viruses also can be distributed through e-mail **worms**. Unlike a virus, which attaches itself to programs and documents, an e-mail worm is self-replicating. A mass mailing worm harvests the e-mail addresses stored on an infected computer and then sends an infected e-mail message to each address it harvests.

An e-mail message also might include, as an attachment, a program that appears to be something useful, but actually does something harmful, such as creating a way for a hacker to breach network security. This type of threat is called a **Trojan horse**. Spyware is a different type of threat. In Chapter 2, you learned about spyware, which is software installed on your computer without your permission and used to gather personal information. Spyware usually is downloaded unknowingly as part of other software or by clicking a link at a Web site, but spyware also can be distributed as a script attached to e-mail formatted as HTML.

Because of the risk of e-mail viruses, worms, Trojan horses, and spyware, you always must be cautious when opening e-mail messages. Make certain that you install virus protection software on your computer and keep it updated. Set the software options to scan all incoming e-mail. Do not open attachments unless they are from a trusted source. As an added precaution, open an attachment only from a trusted source and only if you are expecting the attachment. An e-mail system's address book can be hijacked by an e-mail worm without your trusted source's knowledge.

Unscrupulous people continually attempt to identify and exploit security flaws in e-mail client software. Because of this, e-mail client software manufacturers frequently publish security updates for their software. It is very important that you keep your e-mail client software updated as new security updates are released. You can generally download these security updates — called patches — from the manufacturers' Web sites.

Another area of concern is virus hoaxes. Sometimes unsuspecting people receive e-mail from family, friends, or other associates describing a new virus threat. Be aware that these types of e-mail warnings are often hoaxes. Before you send the message on to someone else or attempt to follow any instructions for removing the "virus," check it out. Antivirus software manufacturers, such as Symantec, maintain lists of legitimate viruses, worms, and other threats and hoaxes at their Web sites. You can also use sites such as snopes.com to search for and verify that an e-mail is a hoax.

For more information on e-mail viruses, visit the *Discovering the Internet, Fourth Edition* @Issue Book Companion Site Web page at **www.cengagebrain.com**, and then click a link below Chapter 4, E-Mail Viruses and Worms.

Junk E-Mail Options

Spam is the bane of Internet e-mail users. Because e-mail is inexpensive to send and easy to use, it is a perfect medium for bulk e-mail advertisements, and many people now suffer from Inboxes stuffed with misdirected and unwanted messages. The monstrous volume of unsolicited commercial e-mail strains computing resources, frustrates technical support personnel, and consumes bandwidth. Financial fraud perpetrated by spammers includes fraudulent requests for money and phony products or services for sale. Spam can be used for:

- **Phishing** — Attempts to collect personally identifiable information, credit card numbers, bank account numbers, and so forth
- **Stock-manipulation schemes** — Scams encouraging unwary investors to buy a specific stock, thereby artificially inflating the stock's value
- **"Nigerian Sting" operations** — Fraudulent requests for money

Other types of spam messages include advertisements for prescription drugs, mortgage or home refinancing, software, dating Web sites, and pornography. To protect against spam, many ISPs and most Web-based e-mail services now provide spam-filtering services — services that filter out messages that do not meet certain criteria, such as messages from senders whose addresses are not in the recipient's address book. Most e-mail clients, including Windows Live Mail, can be configured to filter spam. Additionally, businesses can install spam-filtering software for their networks, and individuals can install spam-filtering software on their home computers.

To set spam or junk e-mail options, you can click the Junk button arrow in the Delete group on the Mail Home tab, and then click the Safety options command to open the Safety Options dialog box (Figure 4-51). You can set options on the various tabs to block junk e-mail and to set exceptions to the blocking process.

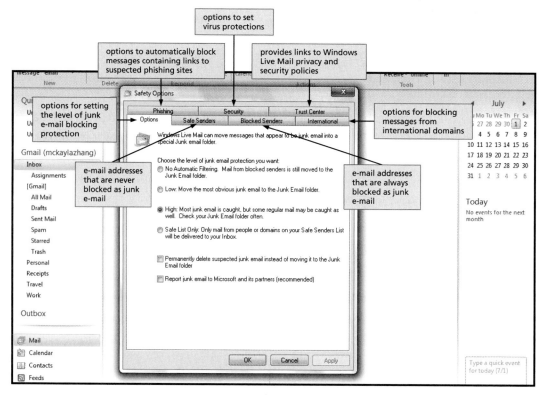

Figure 4-51   You can set options to block junk e-mail in the Safety Options dialog box.

By default, blocked messages are delivered to the Junk e-mail folder. You also can set Windows Live Mail to automatically delete blocked messages instead of delivering them to the Junk e-mail folder; this setting is available in the Options tab. Take care when automatically deleting blocked messages! Depending on the level of blocking you set in the Options dialog box, legitimate messages might be inadvertently deleted. It is also a good idea to periodically check the Junk e-mail folder for legitimate messages that have been blocked in error.

Mailing Lists

As you learned in Chapter 1, mailing list subscribers use e-mail to exchange information, opinions, and ideas about particular subjects with other subscribers who might be located anywhere in the world. Some mailing lists are one-way announcements or newsletters in which subscribers receive, but do not respond to, information on a specific topic. Other mailing lists, called two-way groups, allow subscribers to contribute to the ongoing discussion by sending e-mail to the list that then is distributed to the entire group. Mailing lists have diminished in popularity; with the rise in usage of social networking tools, many companies and groups rely on Facebook groups or their Twitter feed rather than e-mail to disseminate information. However, because they are easy to use, offer free or inexpensive options, and have none of the privacy concerns of social networking Web sites, they are still used.

Users can find mailing lists through work or professional associations or while searching the Web. Some Web sites provide mailing list directories, and most of these sites have a search tool you can use to find mailing lists on specific topics.

A server, called a **list server**, handles the job of directing the e-mail messages to all subscribers. In addition to the list server, a mailing list requires special software, referred to as **LISTSERV** or **Majordomo**, to facilitate the exchange of e-mail among members; the mailing list also must have a **moderator** or **list owner** who handles administrative tasks.

To receive e-mail from a mailing list, you first must join, or **subscribe** to, the list. To subscribe to a mailing list, you send an e-mail message to the list's administrative address asking to subscribe. The **administrative address** is an e-mail address used for administrative requests, such as subscribing to and unsubscribing from a list. E-mail sent to the administrative address is not sent to list members. When subscribing to an **open list**, the subscription begins automatically upon receipt of the subscription e-mail message. Subscriptions to a **closed list**, however, require approval by the list moderator. In either case, an accepted subscription is acknowledged by an e-mail reply. Figure 4-52 illustrates the sequence of events in subscribing to a mailing list.

@SOURCE

Spam and the CAN-SPAM Act
You might be wondering, because spam is such a problem, what are governments doing about it? The CAN-SPAM Act of 2003 set standards for defining spam, and authorized the Federal Trade Commission (FTC) to monitor spam. The acronym, CAN-SPAM, stands for Controlling the Assault of Non-Solicited Pornography And Marketing. The act has been largely unenforced, and does not prevent users from sending spam or allow for prosecution of spammers. Although intended to define, regulate, and lessen spam, it has had little effect on the volume of spam sent and received on the Internet. One major reason is that the bots used to gather e-mail addresses and send spam are located outside of the United States. For more information about spam, its costs, and how to protect against it, as well as the CAN-SPAM Act, visit the Book Companion Site Web page at **www.cengagebrain.com**. Under the Chapter 4 @Source links, click a link below Spam.

Figure 4-52 The process of subscribing to a mailing list includes sending an e-mail to a list administrator to subscribe. Some mailing lists require new subscribers to reply to a confirmation e-mail before the subscription is accepted.

@SOURCE

Mailing Lists
To see Web sites that offer a mailing list directory, visit the Book Companion Site Web page at **www. cengagebrain.com**. Under the Chapter 4 @Source links, click a link below Mailing Lists.

You also can send messages to the **list address**, which is an e-mail address used to send messages for distribution to list subscribers. If the list is an **unmoderated list**, the message goes out immediately to all subscribers who receive messages in individual message format and is appended immediately to the digest to be sent later. If the list is a **moderated list**, the moderator reviews the message and then either approves and sends it, edits and sends it, sends it back to the sender with comments, or discards it. Sending messages to the list is called **posting**. Each mailing list might follow different rules for posting messages; therefore, you should take time to become familiar with a mailing list's rules and instructions before posting to the list. Mailing list rules are intended to ensure that new subscribers can contribute to the list in a productive manner and do not offend other subscribers by sending inappropriate material to the list.

After reading a mailing list's postings for a while, you might decide that the information in the list does not meet your needs or that the volume of mail is too high. Therefore, you can choose to unsubscribe, or leave, the list by sending an e-mail message.

E-Mail Marketing and Online Survey Technologies

Other replacements for mailing lists include e-mail marketing and online survey technologies. Online marketing companies, including Constant Contact (Figure 4-53) and Lyris, are used by companies, schools, churches, and nonprofits. **E-mail marketing software** helps organizations send e-mail and track the success of a marketing campaign by keeping track of the number of times the e-mail was read, how many times the recipients clicked a link in the e-mail, and then finally how many times the recipients purchased a product or enrolled in a service. In addition to e-mail services, these services can help you reach customers using social media and promote events. Unlike spam, e-mail marketing relies on users to **opt-in** to receive e-mails. A user opts-in to an e-mail marketing list by providing his or her e-mail address during an enrollment, solicitation, or purchase, usually from the company or organization's Web site.

Figure 4-53 E-mail marketing enables the sender to disseminate information to a group who has opted in.

Online survey technology companies, such as SurveyMonkey (Figure 4-54) and LimeSurvey, offer companies and organizations the ability to send an online survey using e-mail. Recipients typically click a link in the e-mail to open the survey in their browser. Surveys can be used to collect and analyze opinions about products, services, or any other topic. Some survey companies allow you to create a free survey with limited functionality or to subscribe for a premium version of the service, which gives additional analytical and formatting capabilities.

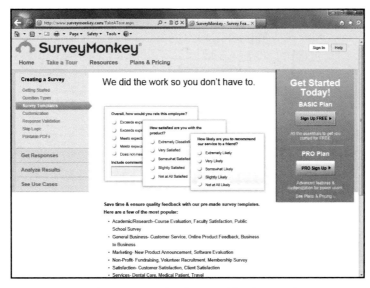

Figure 4-54 Online survey technology enables the creation, dissemination, and analysis of a survey.

Using Web-Based E-Mail Services

A **Web-based e-mail service** is an e-mail service available to a user through a browser and a Web site. Web-based e-mail services make personal e-mail available to people who do not own a computer but who have access to public computers connected to the Internet. Individuals who have Internet access at work but want to receive personal mail in an account other than one supplied by their employer also use Web-based e-mail services. In addition, some individuals set up separate Web-based e-mail accounts to use for specific types of e-mail, such as one for correspondence with family and friends and another for buying and selling at auction Web sites.

Web-based e-mail services typically offer the same e-mail functions as an installed e-mail client: sending and receiving messages, maintaining contacts, sending messages with attachments, and so forth. The primary advantage of using a Web-based e-mail service is portability. Because Web-based e-mail can be sent and received from any computer, users can access their e-mail accounts at cyber cafés, libraries, and other public venues that provide Internet and Web browser access. The primary disadvantage of Web-based e-mail is the inclusion of advertising on the e-mail service's Web pages that some users find annoying.

Basic Web-based e-mail services are generally free because they are supported by advertising. A premium Web-based e-mail service usually reduces or eliminates advertising and often provides additional advanced features, such as increased message storage space, typically for a small annual fee. Popular basic and premium Web-based e-mail services include Microsoft Windows Live Hotmail (basic), Microsoft Windows Live Hotmail Plus (premium), Yahoo! Mail (basic), and Yahoo! Mail Plus (premium).

Creating a Web-Based E-Mail Account

To create a Web-based e-mail account, you must have access to a computer with an Internet connection and a Web browser. The computer can be in a public facility, such as a library, because setting up an account does not store account-specific information on the computer. You access your account by signing in with your user ID and password on a Web page.

In this section, you will use Yahoo! Mail to send and receive e-mail messages. First, you will set up an e-mail account with a user ID and password. Take care to write down your user ID and password and keep them in a safe place in case you need them later. Next, you will access your new Yahoo! Mail account and read a Welcome message automatically sent to your account's Inbox folder. As with other activities in this text, your screen might look different from the figures in this section.

To Create a Yahoo! Mail Account

The following steps access the Yahoo! Mail Web site and create a new Yahoo! Mail account. If you already have a Yahoo! Mail account, your instructor might modify these steps. You will open all Yahoo! Mail Web pages in the same tab.

- Start Internet Explorer.

- Visit the *Discovering the Internet, Fourth Edition* Chapter 4 Steps Web page at **www.cengagebrain.com**.

- Right-click the Yahoo! Mail link, click the 'Open in new window' command on the shortcut menu to open the Yahoo! Mail Web page, and then maximize the window if necessary (Figure 4-55).

Q&A

What if I already have a Yahoo! Mail account?

If you already have a Yahoo! Mail account, your instructor will provide alternative instructions to sign in to your existing account or to create a new Yahoo! Mail account.

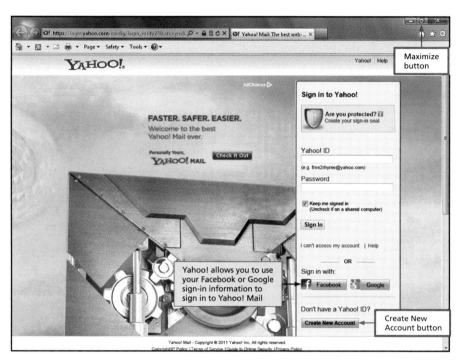

Figure 4-55

2

- Click the Create New Account button to open the Yahoo! registration page.

- Type your name and other requested information in the top section.

- Type a Yahoo! ID in the Select an ID and password section.

- Click the Check button to verify that the ID you selected is available.

- Type and verify a password, making sure the password you choose is rated Strong (Figure 4-56).

Q&A **What if I get a prompt that tells me that my chosen user ID is already taken?**
You might have to try several user IDs before you find one that is not already in use by someone else, or choose one of the suggested alternatives. Many e-mail services block or reserve common or generic names or word combinations to prevent your e-mail address from being randomly generated by spammers. Spam bots, mentioned earlier in this chapter, not only collect e-mail addresses but can also generate e-mail addresses to which to send spam. For example, a common first and last name likely has been used to create an e-mail address on Gmail and other Web sites. You can further protect yourself from spam by using initials and numbers to make your e-mail address more specific and less vulnerable to spammers.

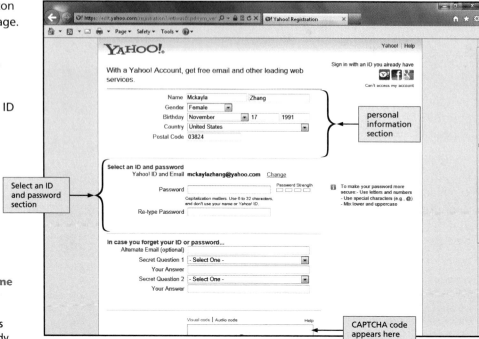

Figure 4-56

3

- Scroll the registration Web page to view the rest of the form.

- Type in the CAPTCHA code as it appears on the page.

- Select two security questions of your choice and type the related answers (Figure 4-57).

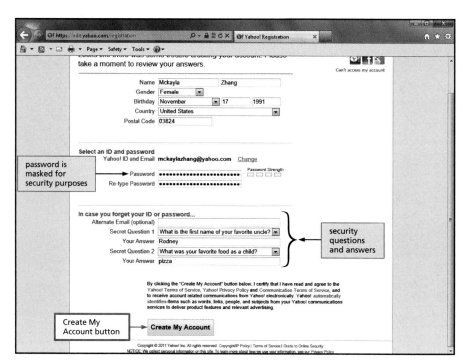

Figure 4-57

4

- Read the Terms of Service, Privacy Policy, and other links as desired.

- Click the Create My Account button to create the account and display the Yahoo! Mail Congratulations page (Figure 4-58).

- With your instructor's permission, print the Web page.

- Click the 'Make Yahoo! your homepage' check box to remove the check mark, if necessary.

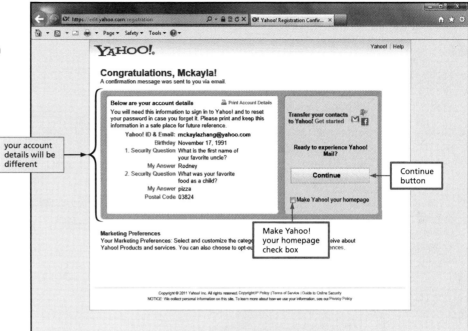

Figure 4-58

5

- Click the Continue button to view your e-mail account Web page (Figure 4-59).

Figure 4-59

To Display the Inbox Tab and Read and Delete a Message

The following steps display the Inbox folder tab, view the Welcome message from Yahoo! Mail in the Reading Pane, and then delete the message.

- Verify that you are viewing the What's New tab on your Yahoo! Mail account Web page.

- Click the Inbox folder tab to view the new Welcome message in the Inbox folder (Figure 4-60).

Q&A

Why is the content of the Subject line in bold?
Content in bold indicates an unread message.

Navigation bar

new message

Figure 4-60

- Click the Welcome to Yahoo! message Subject line to select the message and view it in the Reading Pane (Figure 4-61).

- Scroll the Reading Pane to read the message.

Delete button

Figure 4-61

- Click the Delete button to delete the selected message and view the empty Inbox folder (Figure 4-62).

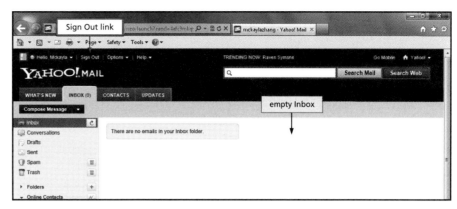

Figure 4-62

- Click the Sign Out link to sign out of your Yahoo! Mail account and view the Yahoo! portal page (Figure 4-63).

Figure 4-63

> **Other Ways**
> 1. Click Inbox folder shortcut icon in folder list in Navigation bar

Sending and Receiving Messages

You can log in to your Yahoo! Mail account at any time to send and receive e-mail messages. The messages you receive and copies of messages you send are stored on the Yahoo! Mail servers. Sending and receiving Web-based e-mail is very similar to sending and receiving e-mail using an e-mail client. When you log in to Yahoo! Mail, the HTTP servers immediately are checked for any new incoming mail, and new mail is directed to the Inbox folder. You can check for new incoming mail at any time by clicking the Check for new email button on your account Web page.

To Compose a Message and Check for New Mail

The following steps compose a message and check for new incoming mail. You will open all Yahoo! Mail Web pages in the same tab.

- Click the Sign In link to display the sign-in text boxes.

- Type your Yahoo! ID and password in the appropriate text boxes.

- Deselect the 'Keep me signed in' check box if necessary (Figure 4-64).

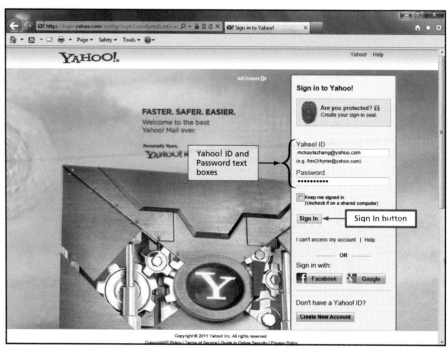

Figure 4-64

- Click the Sign In button to display the portal page.

- Click the Mail link on the portal page.

- Click the Inbox tab to display the Inbox (Figure 4-65).

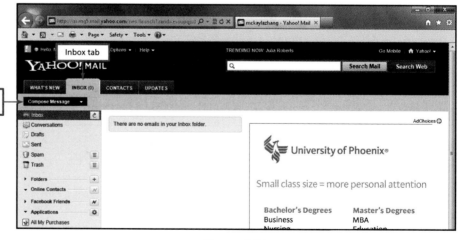

Figure 4-65

- Click the Compose Message button to open the new e-mail tab.

- Type **John.Olivero@course. com** in the To box.

- Type **Class Project** in the Subject text box (Figure 4-66).

- Click the Attachments tab if necessary.

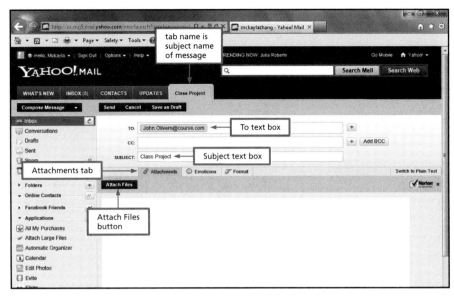

Figure 4-66

4

- Click the Attach Files button to display the 'Select file(s) to upload...' dialog box (Figure 4-67).

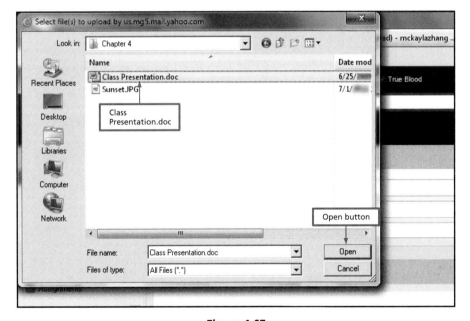

Figure 4-67

5

- Navigate to the folder that contains the Class Presentation document, and then click the document to select it.

- Click the Open button to attach the file to the new message.

- Type a short, appropriate message followed by your name and telephone number (Figure 4-68).

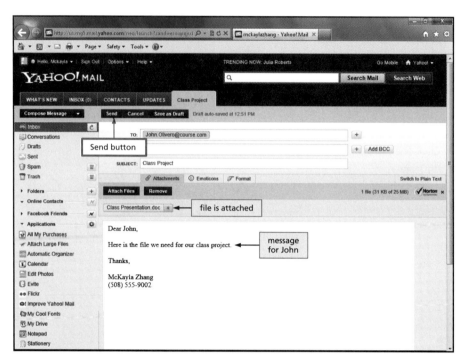

Figure 4-68

6

- Click the Send button to send the message, enter the CAPTCHA code, if necessary, and display the Class Project tab (Figure 4-69).

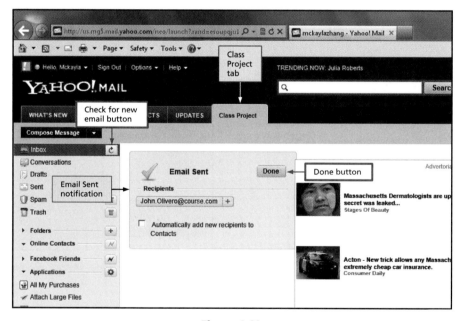

Figure 4-69

- Click the Done button to close the Class Project tab.

- Click the 'Check for new email' button to check for new incoming mail. Click the Inbox folder if necessary. You will receive the automated reply from John Olivero and any other messages in the Inbox folder (Figure 4-70).

- Click the Sign Out link to sign out from your Yahoo! Mail account.

- Close the browser.

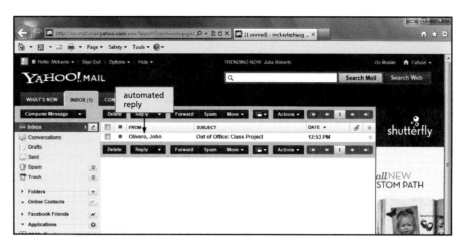

Figure 4-70

Other Ways

1. N to open New message tab
2. CTRL+ENTER to send message
3. M to check mail

Using Other Web-Based E-Mail Features

Yahoo! Mail and other Web-based e-mail services provide the same basic e-mail features offered by the e-mail clients you learned about earlier in the chapter, such as replying to and forwarding a message, using folders to organize your messages, creating and appending signature files, and managing your contacts.

REPLYING TO AND FORWARDING A MESSAGE To reply to a message, select the message and click the Reply button or press the R key to open the Re: (Reply) tab, and then type a reply and click the Send button. If you are replying to multiple recipients, click the Reply button arrow and then click Reply to All or press the A key.

To forward a message, click the Forward button to open the Fw: (Forward) tab, and type an e-mail address and forwarding message. Then click the Send button. Figure 4-71 illustrates the Yahoo! Mail Reply and Forward buttons for an open message. Message replies have Re: preceding the original subject text, and forwarded messages have Fw: preceding the original subject text.

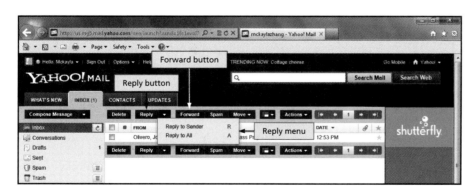

Figure 4-71 Click the Reply or Forward buttons to reply to or forward a selected message.

After you send a reply, the original message is marked with a blue left-pointing arrow or Reply icon. A forwarded message is marked with a green right-pointing arrow or Forward icon.

FACTS @HAND To direct incoming messages that match certain criteria into specific folders, you can create filter rules with one or more filtering criteria. To learn more about the Yahoo! Mail filtering features, click the Help link on the e-mail account Web page, and then use a keyword search or click links to find a topic called Using Filters to Sort Incoming il.

PRINTING A MESSAGE If you click the Print button on the Internet Explorer Command bar, the entire Web page — including ads, the folder list, and so forth — will be printed. To print only the message, click the Print button on the message tab toolbar or press the P key to open the selected message in the Print – Windows Internet Explorer window and open the browser's Print dialog box, as shown in Figure 4-72.

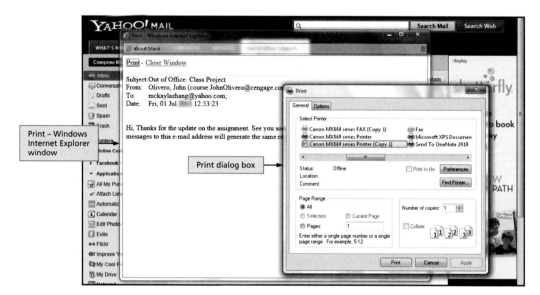

Figure 4-72 You can print only a selected message by clicking the message tab Print button or pressing P.

USING FOLDERS Folder organization is just as important when using Web-based e-mail services as it is when using an e-mail client. To create a new folder, click the Folders Add button to display the Add a New Folder dialog box, enter a name for the new folder in the Folder name text box, and then press the ENTER key. The new folder is added in the Folders custom folders section; click the Folders arrow to expand its contents, if necessary (Figure 4-73).

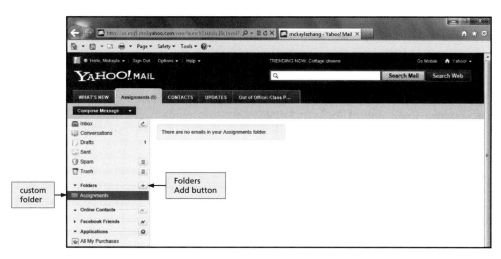

Figure 4-73 You can add custom folders to your Yahoo! Mail account.

You also can use a shortcut menu to manage your messages. Right-click a message to review the shortcut menu commands.

MOVING AND DELETING MESSAGES Yahoo! Mail also allows you to move a message from the Inbox into a different folder. To move a message from the Inbox folder to the Spam or Trash folder or a custom folder, click the check box next to the message (or messages) to be moved. Then click the Move button arrow to display a list of folders, and click the folder in which you want to store the message (Figure 4-74). You can select multiple messages simultaneously to move the messages into the same folder. You also can use drag and drop to move messages into different folders.

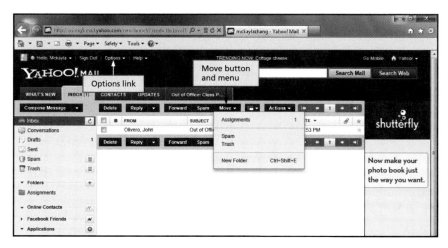

Figure 4-74 You can move selected messages from the Inbox folder to other folders.

To delete messages, click the check box next to each message to be deleted, and then click the Delete button or press the DELETE key to move the selected messages to the Trash folder. Deleted messages normally remain in the Trash folder until you click the Empty button, which permanently deletes the contents of the folder. Note, however, that Yahoo! Mail reserves the right to delete messages in the Trash folder at any time. Because

Yahoo! Mail limits the amount of space you can use to store your messages, you will want to empty the Trash folder often.

SIGNATURE FILES   Yahoo! Mail allows you to create a signature file to append to the end of every message. To create a signature file in Yahoo! Mail, click the Options link in the upper-left corner of the e-mail account Web page, and then click the Mail Options command in the menu to open the Yahoo! Mail account options page. Click Signature in the Navigation bar, click the 'Show a signature on all outgoing messages' option button, type the signature file text, and then click the Save Changes button (Figure 4-75). Click the Inbox tab to return to the e-mail account Web page. To stop adding a signature file to all outgoing messages, open the Signature Web page and click the 'Do not use a signature' option button.

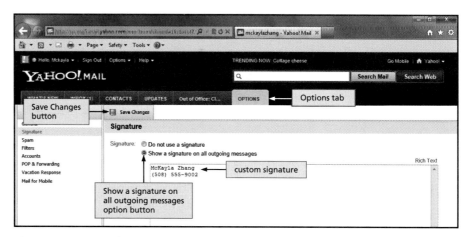

Figure 4-75   A signature file in Yahoo! Mail.

 For a complete list of Yahoo! Mail keyboard shortcuts, click the Help button on the e-mail account Web page to show the Help menu, and then click the Help command to open the Help Web page. Navigate to the Emailing: The Basics page. Click the Expand All link, if necessary, to expand the view of the Help topics, and then click the 'What are these shortcut keys I keep hearing about?' link.

MANAGING CONTACTS   Yahoo! Mail allows you to save names and e-mail addresses in the Contacts folder, as well as to import your contacts from Facebook or Web-based e-mail programs. To add a contact, click the Contacts tab, and then click the Add a New Contact button to display text boxes in which you can add the new contact information. Type the contact information and click the Save button to add the contact to the Contact list. You can also click the 'More actions for selected e-mails' button when viewing the Inbox or a message (Figure 4-76, left screen), and then click Add Sender to Contacts to open the Add to Contacts dialog box to add the sender to the Contacts folder. To manage your contacts, click the Contacts tab (Figure 4-76, right screen), click an option such as Gmail or Facebook, and then follow the steps to import contacts.

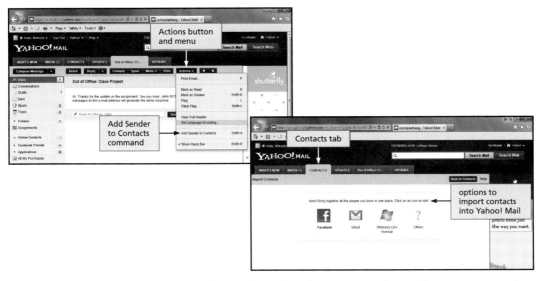

Figure 4-76 You can add a contact by clicking the Add Sender to Contacts icon and manage contacts in the Contacts tab.

A Yahoo! Mail distribution list is a list of contacts referred to collectively by a single name, and it fulfills the same purpose as a Windows Live Mail contact category. To create a distribution list, open the Contacts tab, click the New List button, and then enter the distribution list name and individual contact information.

To use a contact or distribution list when composing a message, click the Add recipients button to the right of the To, Cc, or Bcc button in the message header to open the Choose Contacts dialog box. Then select the individual contact or a distribution list and click the OK button.

You also can delete contacts and distribution lists. To delete contacts and lists, open the Contacts tab, select the contact or distribution list to be deleted, and then click the Delete button.

You can use the Yahoo! Mail SpamGuard feature to automatically filter suspicious incoming messages to the Spam folder. If you upgrade to the Plus version, you also can protect your e-mail address by using the Yahoo! Mail AddressGuard feature to create "disposable" e-mail addresses that you can use when you do not want to share your actual e-mail address — for example, when buying products or services online. For more information about the SpamGuard and AddressGuard features, click the Options button in the mail window, click Mail Options, and then click Spam in the Navigation bar (Figure 4-77).

FACTS @HAND

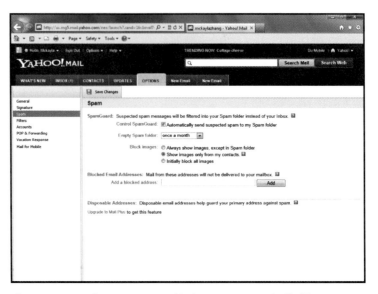

Figure 4-77 Yahoo! SpamGuard helps you automatically filter unwanted messages to your Spam folder.

Social Media

Social media tools are an integral part of the way Internet-connected individuals interact with family, friends, and others who share their professional, personal, or political interests. You were introduced to social media in previous chapters where you learned that **social media** can be broadly defined as online tools that allow people to communicate, collaborate, and share over the Internet.

Social networking Web sites such as Facebook, LinkedIn, Google+, and Memory Lane provide a medium in which friends, colleagues, and school alumni can share personal information or photographs, résumés and networking opportunities, or information about class reunions. Public figures, organizations, and businesses also use social networking Web sites and microblogging sites such as Twitter to build interest or connect with their fans, members, employees, and customers (Figure 4-78).

@SOURCE

Newsgroups
To learn more about newsgroups, visit the Book Companion Site Web page at **www. cengagebrain.com**. Under the Chapter 4 @Source links, click a link below Newsgroups.

Figure 4-78 Businesses use social networking Web sites to connect with customers.

Virtual meetings, video conferencing, and Internet telephony all enable professional and personal communications. You will learn more about these topics in Chapter 6.

FACTS @HAND

Social Networking

Individuals who maintain connections with other people in order to share information or participate in activities of common interest are involved in a process called **social networking**. Traditional social networking takes place in a physical space — for example, in the classroom, office, or other designated meeting area, such as a library, restaurant, gym, golf course, or athletic field.

Today, millions of individuals also participate in online social networking made possible by social networking Web sites, such as Google+, Myspace, Eons, Bebo, hi5, Facebook (Figure 4-79), and Friendster. Social networking sites typically offer a combination of online communication tools: e-mail, discussion groups, blogs, instant messaging, P2P networking, and real-time chat. Site members use these tools to build and maintain their own personal networks of friends.

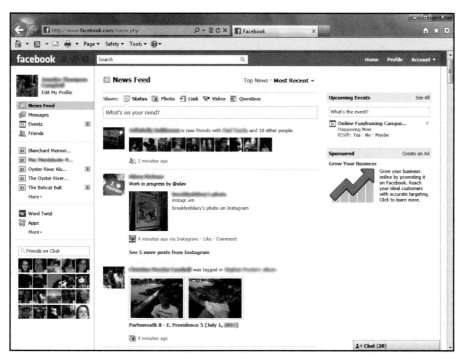

Figure 4-79   Social networking Web sites provide online venues in which people can connect with existing friends or make new friends.

@SOURCE

Social Networking
To learn more about the social networking Web sites discussed in this section, visit the Book Companion Site Web page at **www. cengagebrain.com**. Under the Chapter 4 @Source links, click a link below Social Networking.

Social networking Web sites use members' profiles as hubs for members' personal networks. When an individual joins one of these social networking sites, he or she first creates a personal profile that describes his or her hobbies and interests. This profile then becomes the center point from which the member builds his or her network of friends. Next, the new member uses the Web site's online communication tools to invite friends to join his or her network. Friends who join the new member's network then post messages to members' Web pages, post comments to discussion groups or blogs, chat with each other in real time, exchange digital files, and invite their other friends to join the network. The new member's personal network grows larger and larger as current friends connect to new friends and friends of friends.

According to a survey by the Pew Internet & American Life Project, 75 percent of online adults between the ages of 18 and 24 have a social network profile, as do 57 percent between the ages of 25 and 34.

Business, medical, and technology professionals are increasingly turning to online social networking to make new career contacts, find sales leads, locate job opportunities, and hire new employees. Social networking Web sites such as LinkedIn (Figure 4-80), Ryze, and Spoke focus on career networking. These sites offer online communication tools to create and build career-oriented personal networks plus information about offline educational and networking events, online job search tools, career tips, classified ads, and sales leads. Additionally, employers looking for new hires can join and search members' profiles to locate qualified prospective employees.

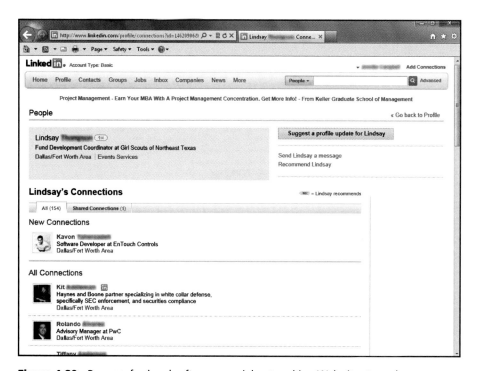

Figure 4-80 Busy professionals often use social networking Web sites to make career contacts, search for jobs, qualify sales leads, and hire new employees.

Smart and Safe Online Social Networking

A college student in Massachusetts is expelled. Several employees at an auto club in California are fired. A recent college graduate in Illinois is rejected for an important summer internship. A job hunter in North Carolina is never called for that critical and anticipated first interview. What do all of these people have in common? All were participants in online social networking, and all failed to recognize the dangers of posting inflammatory, harassing, or indiscreet comments and photos at social networking Web sites.

School administrators and employers are becoming increasingly aware of social networking sites, and they commonly review the sites' postings to assess reported inappropriate student activities or to gather information about prospective employees. In the previous examples, the Massachusetts college student was expelled for making inflammatory and, in the judgment of school administrators, threatening comments about a college security guard. The Illinois and North Carolina job applicants were rejected when prospective employers discovered comments about drug and alcohol use and explicit photos posted in the applicants' online profiles. The auto club employees were fired after an employee complained to management about workplace harassment through postings to a social networking blog.

The temptation toward unlimited self expression within a personal network of friends through social networking Web site postings can be great; however, social networking site postings — yours or the postings of friends who know you — might not be kept private, and the cost of indiscreet comments or photos posted at these sites can be very high indeed.

Personal safety is another issue for participants in an online social network. As you learned in Chapter 2, being online can expose you to certain safety risks, such as loss of personally identifiable information, exposure to objectionable material, or interactions with people who might not be who they say they are. Smart and safe participation in online social networking requires following a few simple rules, such as those outlined at the OnGuard Online Web site sponsored by the FTC and other federal agencies. For example, you should:

- Carefully review the type of participants allowed at a social networking Web site before you join.
- Control access to your profile, if possible, and be careful not to include any personally identifiable information in your profile.
- Post only those comments or photos you are willing to share with anyone, not just your network of friends.
- Keep in mind that with screen capturing software, anyone with access can take a picture of your profile or activity on a social networking Web site and post the picture to his or her blog or send it to the media.

For the complete list of the OnGuard Online safety tips plus more information about protecting yourself when participating in online social networking, visit the *Discovering the Internet, Fourth Edition* @Issue Book Companion Site Web page at **www.cengagebrain.com**, and then click a link below Chapter 4, Smart and Safe Social Networking.

Blogging and Microblogging

In Chapter 1, you learned about online diaries called weblogs or blogs. Although blogs had been around for some time, they gained national attention during the 2004 presidential election when news reporters and commentators, special interest groups, and candidates' supporters began hosting blogs. Today, blogs are highly popular and powerful tools for sharing thoughts and ideas across a wide spectrum of interests and audiences. To find blogs to which you want to contribute, you can use the search tools at blog portals or directories, such as iBlogBusiness, Bloghub, and Technorati (Figure 4-81). You also can create and publish your own blog using tools, such as Blogger, WordPress.org, and Windows Live Writer.

Figure 4-81 You can find blogs of interest or create and publish your own blogs using online tools.

@SOURCE

Blogging and Microblogging
To learn more about blogging and microblogging, visit the Book Companion Site Web page at **www. cengagebrain.com**. Under the Chapter 4 @Source links, click a link below Blogging and Microblogging.

Microblogging, which resembles a combination of blogging and instant messaging, involves broadcasting brief (typically 140 characters or less) messages to a public Web site or to the cell phones or computers of private subscribers. Individuals and professionals use microblogging to broadcast status updates about their thoughts, current activities, or current location to friends, family members, and other constituencies. Businesses, such as Priceline.com, Southwest Airlines, and IBM, use microblogging to broadcast special offers to customers, conduct informal customer surveys, provide customer service, and promote collaboration among employees. The most popular microblogging tool is Twitter; other microblogging tools include Tumblr, Jaiku, and Plurk. Figure 4-82 illustrates a Twitter page with microblogging posts by Barack Obama's reelection campaign staff. In addition to posting messages, users can employ **hashtags** to indicate that their message is part of a trending topic included in the service's search engine. Hashtags can appear within or at the end of a message.

Figure 4-82 Microblogging provides status updates to friends, family members, and other constituencies, and provides advertising messages to customers.

According to the Pew Internet & American Life Project, in June 2011, 13 percent of online adults in the United States were using Twitter, an increase of 5 percent over six months.

FACTS @HAND

Although discussed separately, microblogs, blogs, and social networking Web sites share many of the same features. For example, a microblog post on Twitter is called a tweet; Facebook uses status updates to enable users to share short thoughts or links; and LinkedIn offers ways for users to post microblogs. In addition, there are services that can share your microblog posts to multiple platforms at once, including one by Twitter that updates your Facebook status as you tweet. Vlingo enables you to speak your post into your phone and instantly update both your Twitter feed and your Facebook status.

FACTS @HAND

Newsgroups and Web-Based Discussion Groups

Most local communities have bulletin boards in public places. For example, laundromats, grocery stores, and student union buildings often have bulletin boards on which individuals can post information such as event notices, items for sale, properties for rent, want ads, and posters about causes or issues they support. These bulletin boards provide a venue where people can drop in to post information or read what others have posted. You do not have to belong to a group to read or post bulletin board messages; you just need access to the bulletin board. **Newsgroups** are online bulletin boards first made available in the 1980s over the distributed **Usenet network**. **Web-based discussion groups** are online discussion forums that are often hosted by a portal.

Usenet consists of a number of servers that use the **Network News Transfer Protocol (NNTP)** to send newsgroup messages over an IP network. Each Usenet server, also called a **news server**, acts as a host to a number of newsgroups. In addition, each news server subscribes to any number of newsgroups from other news servers. Figure 4-83 shows the relationships between the servers and the other groups to which the servers subscribe.

Each news server stores the messages of the newsgroups it hosts; the server also polls the other news servers at fixed intervals to find the new messages for its subscribed newsgroups from those servers. The servers then download the new messages to be able to provide them locally. Each group exists in a permanent home on one server, and copies of messages in other groups appear on other servers that subscribe to those groups. Some ISPs maintain a news server, or provide access to a news server, for their subscribers. An educational institution might provide access to news servers as well.

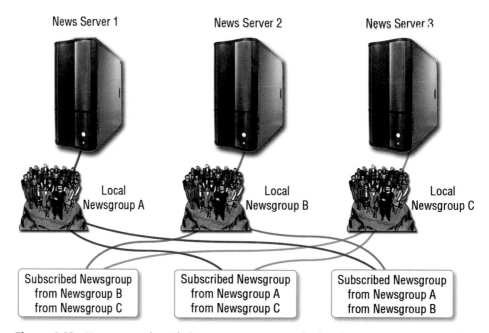

Figure 4-83   News servers host their own newsgroups and subscribe to newsgroups on other servers.

Newsgroup postings include text postings and image, video, and movie file postings. Some ISPs have limited or discontinued direct Usenet newsgroup services to avoid the increased cost of transmitting image, video, and movie file postings and to avoid the transmission of illicit images, such as pornography, or unauthorized copyrighted material, such as movies.

The basic organization behind newsgroups is simple. Each newsgroup has a unique name that identifies it, such as rec.pets.dogs or humanities.lit.authors.shakespeare. The names are multilevel, and each level provides more detail about the purpose of the newsgroup. The multilevel hierarchy is based on content. Figure 4-84 illustrates several top-level categories in the Usenet hierarchy.

Usenet Top-Level Categories

Category	Description
alt.*	Alternative topics
biz.*	Business
comp.*	Computers
humanities.*	Art and literature
k12.*	Education community
misc.*	Miscellaneous
news.*	Usenet information
rec.*	Recreation and entertainment
sci.*	Science
soc.*	Social issues and culture
talk.*	Current issues and debates

Figure 4-84 Several Usenet top-level categories.

FACTS @HAND

The Big-8 Management Board provides a board of directors to oversee the eight primary text-based newsgroups: comp.*, humanities.*, misc.*, news.*, rec.*, sci.*, soc.*, and talk.*.

Within each top-level category, additional levels are specified to define the group further. For example, within the rec.* category are subcategories — such as pets, sports, crafts, and music — to specify different types of recreational topics. To read newsgroup messages, a user needs an **NNTP client**. An NNTP client, also called a news client or **newsreader**, is software that allows a user to read newsgroup messages. Many e-mail clients, such as Windows Live Mail, use newsgroups or forums for users to communicate and troubleshoot problems. Additionally, some online newsgroup services, such as Newsville and Google Groups, provide access to newsgroups using a Web browser.

To Explore Newsgroups Using Google Groups

The following steps start the browser, open the Google Groups page in a new window, and then search for postings in the news.announce.newusers newsgroup. You will open all Google Groups pages in the same tab.

- Start Internet Explorer.

- Visit the *Discovering the Internet, Fourth Edition* Chapter 4 Steps Web page at **www.cengagebrain.com**.

- Right-click the Google Groups link, click 'Open in new window', and then maximize the window if necessary.

- Type **news.announce.newusers** in the Explore groups search box to quickly locate the specific newsgroup (Figure 4-85).

Figure 4-85

- Click the 'Search for a group' button to see a link to the news.announce. newusers newsgroup (Figure 4-86).

Figure 4-86

- Click the news.announce.newusers link to view the news.announce. newusers newsgroup postings (Figure 4-87).

- Read a few of the posts that interest you, and then close the browser.

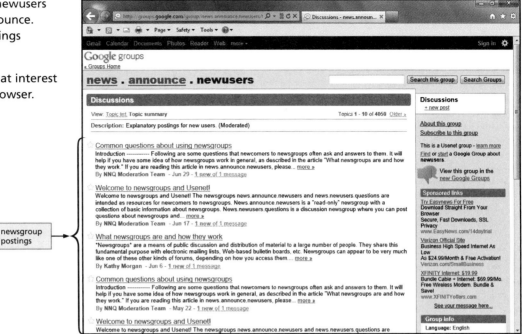

Figure 4-87

Asynchronous communication does not require users to be online at the same time and includes e-mail, mailing lists, and newsgroups. Chat is an example of **synchronous communication**, or real-time communication, in which two or more users are online at the same time.

Text Messaging and Chat

Text and multimedia messaging, also called **Short Message Service** (**SMS**) and **Multimedia Messaging Service** (**MMS**), respectively, allow users to send short messages containing text only or text, audio, and video to and from cell phones. Some wireless services, such as Verizon Wireless, allow users to send a text or multimedia message to a cell phone from a Web page (Figure 4-88). You also can find a number of online SMS services that provide messaging services from a Web page. Text messaging limits are typically 160 characters, including the address and subject line. The way text messaging services handle the character limit varies; some cut off the message once the character limit has been reached, and others break the message into multiple messages. Because the amount of text is so limited, short abbreviations are used to save space, such as keying "CU L8R K?" for "See you later, OK?".

Figure 4-88 Some wireless services, such as Verizon, allow you to send SMS messages to a cell phone from a Web page.

Chat is a facility that allows two or more people to exchange text or multimedia messages in real time, using either a special client or a Web interface. Before the Web, the earliest type of chat facility was **IRC**, or **Internet Relay Chat**, a text-based communications tool. To chat, users need a special client application on their computers and access to the Internet. Users connect to an IRC server, and, from that server, can chat with any other user on that IRC network. Several IRC networks exist; users cannot chat between networks.

Once connected to an IRC network, the user can use his or her IRC client to view a list of available channels or chat rooms and join one to chat with other users. A **channel**, or **chat room**, is a specific chat discussion that might be on a given topic or with a certain set of participants. Users also can set up private channels in which access is by invitation only, thus restricting who can participate. You can learn more about IRC clients, networks, and channels at Web sites such as QuakeNet.org. Many chat Web sites, such as Skype (Figure 4-89), include options to participate in text, video, voice, or some kind of combination.

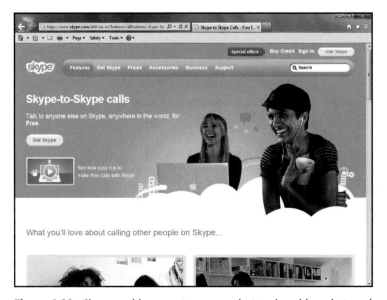

Figure 4-89 Skype enables users to communicate using video, chat, and voice calls.

Web-based chat allows for real-time communication using a Web browser instead of a special chat client. Opening a chat session is as simple as connecting to the Internet, starting your browser, and clicking a link on a Web page. Web-based chat allows users to exchange both text and multimedia messages. Some chat facilities also allow users with a microphone to exchange voice messages in a chat room instead of, or in addition to, text messages. Some Web-based chat sites provide the ability to share video between two participants who have Web cameras. Chat is very popular, but new users might find that it takes some time to learn how to follow a conversation online. If a chat room has many participants, many conversations might be going on at once, which makes following one particular chat thread very difficult.

Before jumping into a chat room discussion, a new user should read the rules and FAQs Web pages. Because many chat rooms have regular participants, a new member can become familiar with the group by **lurking**, remaining quiet, and not participating in the chat discussion at first. Because the exchange of text often is rapid, participants use many abbreviations and shorthand — for example, typing LOL instead of the phrase, "laughing out loud" — to express laughter in response to another's post. Flaming also can occur in a chat room, just as it does in asynchronous discussions taking place with e-mail, mailing lists, or newsgroups.

To maintain privacy and security, chat participants should adhere to these guidelines:

- Do not disclose your real name and address or any information of a sensitive nature. Use a nickname rather than your real name.
- Avoid using Web sites that display your IP address along with your nickname.
- Remember that other participants might misrepresent themselves — she might not be a woman, and he might not be a teen — and that some predators are online, seeking the unwary. Therefore, be careful about arranging to meet online chat participants in person.

Some e-commerce Web sites are using chat facilities for real-time customer service (Figure 4-90), providing the user with a chance to talk to a customer service representative electronically in real time.

@SOURCE

Chat Abbreviations
To learn more about common abbreviations used in chat, visit the Book Companion Site Web page at **www. cengagebrain.com**. Under the Chapter 4 @Source links, click a link below Chat Abbreviations.

@SOURCE

Chat
To learn more about chat and to locate a list of chat directories, visit the Book Companion Site Web page at **www. cengagebrain.com**. Under the Chapter 4 @Source links, click a link below Chat.

Figure 4-90 Some e-commerce Web sites are using live chat technologies for real-time customer service.

Another very popular form of chat is **instant messaging (IM)**, a private means of exchanging real-time messages with one or several people using the Internet. Several IM programs are in popular use, including AOL Instant Messenger (AIM), ICQ, Windows Live Messenger, Yahoo! Messenger, and Google Talk (Figure 4-91). Although all of these IM programs offer similar features, an individual using one IM program, such as AOL Instant Messenger, might not be able to communicate with another individual using a different IM program, such as Yahoo! Messenger. For this reason, many people choose to install and use several different IM programs so they can send instant messages to all of their contacts who use IM. Alternatively, users can install and use Trillian, an instant messaging program that consolidates messages from these dissimilar IM programs into a single interface.

Figure 4-91 Instant messaging is a popular form of real-time communications over the Internet.

FACTS @HAND According to a Pew Internet & American Life Project survey, more than 38 percent of Internet users report sending instant messages.

Collaboration and Sharing

Millions of people share their knowledge, research, opinions, photos, and video clips with others online using Web sites that allow them to collaborate on content, share favorite news stories, share image files, and share Web page bookmarks. Online tools for collaboration and sharing include wikis, social bookmarking, content-sharing, and opinion sites.

WIKIS Unlike standard Web pages that cannot be altered by viewers, a **wiki** consists of Web pages whose content can be edited, supplemented, or deleted by authorized users with access to the Internet. One popular example of a wiki is the free online encyclopedia Wikipedia (Figure 4-92). Other wikis include the LoudounPedia, a wiki sponsored by the Loudoun County Public Library in Virginia; Diplopedia, specializing in international relations and diplomacy and sponsored by the U.S. Department of State; and a Harry Potter wiki on the Wikia wiki service, which covers the mythology, characters, books, and movies from the popular series (Figure 4-92).

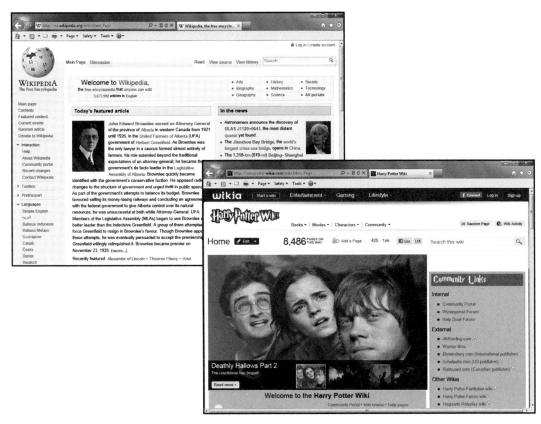

Figure 4-92   A wiki consists of Web pages whose content can be edited, added to, or deleted by approved contributors who are using a Web browser.

Businesses use wikis to build worker knowledge bases — a core of knowledge about the business contributed to by its employees. Professionals, such as accountants and attorneys, use wikis to share information. Technology vendors use wikis to allow customers to contribute to a knowledge base about their products or related topics of interest, such as computer security. Teachers use wikis to allow students to collaborate on projects. Many people whose lives are affected by a serious medical condition share information using wikis.

According to a survey by the Pew Internet & American Life Project, 53 percent of adult Internet users who are looking for information use the Wikipedia Web site. Despite the popularity of Wikipedia, users should take care to review the accuracy and authenticity of information posted to Web pages at the Wikipedia site just as they would any other Web site.

FACTS @HAND

SOCIAL BOOKMARKING   **Social bookmarking** and **content-sharing** sites, also called **social tagging** sites, allow users to post a Web page favorite or bookmark to a public Web site, and then tag the bookmark with keywords. Publishing bookmarks to a public Web site makes it easy to share bookmarks with others. Tagging the bookmarks with keywords helps organize them and makes it easy to search for bookmarks by topic. Evri (Figure 4-93) and Delicious are two examples of social bookmarking Web sites. The left screen in Figure 4-94 illustrates a menu of content-sharing and social bookmarking links on a ScienceDaily news story about brains. The right screen of Figure 4-94 illustrates a recommendation for the same news story posted at the Digg content-sharing site.

Figure 4-93 Social bookmarking Web sites allow you to tag your Web page bookmarks by keyword and share your bookmarks with others.

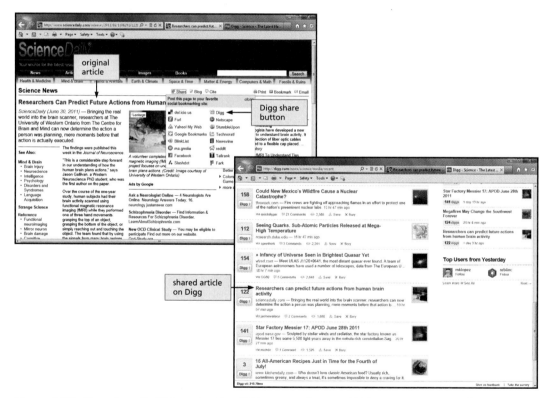

Figure 4-94 Share favorite Web content by clicking an option on a Web page menu to send a recommendation to a content sharing site.

Social bookmarking and content sharing Web sites are an example of a **folksonomy**. A folksonomy (word coined using "folks" and "taxonomy") is when users tag, share, and comment on articles and information. Using tags, such as a Twitter hashtag described earlier in the chapter, a poster or collaborator can indicate that an article, a video, or other content includes information about a certain topic. For example, an article shared to a social bookmarking Web site on the release of a new documentary about whales might include tags such as whales, ocean, documentary, and other tags that indicate where the documentary was filmed or other relevant information. Folksonomies and social tagging allow users to find information that is interesting and relevant to them, and to provide others with their opinions in the form of ratings and comments.

U.S. government agencies are successfully harnessing the power of social media to get their messages to the public and to improve internal operations. For example, the Centers for Disease Control (CDC) Web site offers multiple social media tools, such as microblogging, video blogging, and social networking, to broadcast information on critical health issues like the H1N1 Influenza A virus. Other examples include the Intellipedia site, a data-sharing wiki for the U.S. intelligence community sponsored by the Office of the Director of National Intelligence (not open to the public), and the Library of Congress's photostream project at the Flickr photo-sharing site.

FACTS @HAND

Many people go online to manage their photo collections using Web sites such as Flickr, Shutterfly (Figure 4-95), Snapfish, Picasa, and Kodak Gallery, and then share access to the photos and photo slide shows with family members and friends. The increase in broadband Internet access, together with access to inexpensive video equipment and webcams, has made creating personal video clips and sharing them online a very popular activity. So many people now regularly visit video-sharing Web sites, such as YouTube and Photobucket, that professionally created video clips are commonly posted to these sites to broadcast messages designed for a wide audience. In fact, the president of the United States posts political messages and weekly audio and video addresses to YouTube (Figure 4-96).

Figure 4-95   Web sites such as Shutterfly manage photo collections and share access to photos and photo slide shows.

Figure 4-96 Video-sharing Web sites offer a venue for sharing personal video clips as well as professionally created video designed to broadcast messages to a wide audience.

FACTS @HAND According to a Pew Internet & American Life Project survey, 69 percent of Internet users report watching a video on a video-sharing Web site, and 14 percent of Internet users report uploading videos to a video-sharing site.

@SOURCE

Social Bookmarking, Content Sharing, and Social Opinions
To learn more about the social collaboration and sharing Web sites discussed in this section, visit the Book Companion Site Web page at **www. cengagebrain.com**. Under the Chapter 4 @Source links, click a link below Social Bookmarking, Content Sharing, and Social Opinions.

SOCIAL OPINION   Consumers often augment their own research about products and services by asking neighbors, friends, and family members to share their experiences with the same or similar products and services. Today, consumers can visit **social opinion sites** to check out user reviews for products, movies, books, travel accommodations, local restaurants, and local service providers. Social opinion Web sites, such as Epinions and Yelp (Figure 4-97), aggregate thousands of individual reviews of products and services into well-organized and easily accessible categories. Some sites, such as Yelp, offer reviews of services by locality. Users who join social opinion sites can add their own reviews and rate the reviews posted by other users. E-commerce Web sites, such as Amazon.com and TripAdvisor, integrate social opinion features (reading list recommendations, book reviews, hotel and restaurant reviews) into their e-commerce operations to attract visitors.

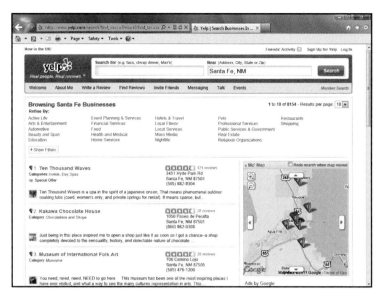

Figure 4-97 Social opinion sites compile multiple product and service reviews into categories.

Related to social opinion sites, knowledge-sharing Web sites offer community-based answers (generally free, but sometimes for a fee) to user questions on a variety of topics. Yahoo! Answers and Ask.com are examples of knowledge-sharing sites.

FACTS @HAND

Web-based interactive games, such as World of Warcraft and EverQuest, allow players from around the world to play together. People can create alternative identities in virtual worlds, such as Second Life, providing yet more ways to communicate and collaborate.

FACTS @HAND

Chapter Review

E-mail is one of the most popular online communication tools and now is indispensable for businesses and other organizations. An e-mail client, such as Windows Live Mail, is software installed on a computer that is used to send, receive, forward, and manage e-mail messages, and create and manage a list of contacts.

Mailing list subscribers use e-mail to exchange information, opinions, and ideas about particular subjects with other subscribers. E-mail marketing and online survey technologies enable organizations and companies to send, track, and analyze e-marketing and survey campaigns.

Many e-mail users prefer to use Web-based e-mail, such as Gmail or Yahoo! Mail. Web-based e-mail uses a Web browser and a Web page to send, receive, forward, and manage e-mail messages. The advantage of Web-based mail is portability; a user can access his or her Web-based mail account from any computer that has a Web browser installed and an Internet connection.

Social media — newsgroups, Web-based discussion groups, chat, blogs, microblogs, and wikis, along with social networking, bookmarking, content-sharing, and opinion Web sites — are an integral part of the way Internet-connected individuals interact with family, friends, and others who share their professional, personal, or political interests.

TERMS TO KNOW

After reading this chapter, you should know each of these Key Terms.

administrative address (209)
asynchronous communication (235)
Attach line (174)
attachment (174)
Bcc line (174)
blind courtesy copy (174)
Cc line (174)
channel (236)
chat (236)
chat room (236)
closed list (209)
contact category (206)
contact (174)
Contacts folder (202)
content sharing (239)
courtesy copy (174)
cyber bullying (188)
Deleted items folder (179)
Drafts folder (179)
e-mail client (172)
e-mail marketing software (210)
emoticon (175)
flag (200)
flaming (175)
folksonomy (240)
forward (186)
hashtags (230)
host name (171)
HTML-formatted message (175)
IMAP (Internet Message Access Protocol) (172)
Inbox folder (179)
instant messaging (IM) (238)
Internet Relay Chat (IRC) (236)
Junk e-mail folder (179)
list address (210)
list owner (209)
list server (209)
LISTSERV (209)
lurking (237)
Majordomo (209)
message body (174)
message header (175)
Message list (179)
message rule (198)
moderated list (210)

moderator (209)
Multimedia Messaging Service (MMS) (235)
Network News Transfer Protocol (NNTP) (232)
news server (232)
newsgroups (231)
newsreader (233)
"Nigerian Sting" operations (208)
NNTP client (233)
Office Web Apps (178)
online survey technology (211)
open list (209)
opt-in (211)
Outbox folder (179)
phishing (208)
POP (Post Office Protocol) (172)
posting (210)
Sent items folder (179)
Sent Mail folder (179)
Short Message Service (SMS) (235)
signature file (174)
SMTP (Simple Mail Transfer Protocol) (172)
social bookmarking (239)
social media (226)
social networking (227)
social opinion sites (242)
social tagging (239)
Spam folder (179)
stock-manipulation schemes (208)
Subject line (174)
subscribe (209)
synchronous communication (235)
To line (174)
Trash folder (179)
Trojan horse (207)
unmoderated list (210)
Usenet network (231)
user ID (171)
watched conversation (201)
Web-based chat (237)
Web-based discussion groups (231)
Web-based e-mail service (212)
wiki (238)
Windows Live Photos (178)
Windows Live SkyDrive (178)
worms (207)

Complete the Test Your Knowledge exercises to solidify what you have learned in the chapter.

True or False

Mark T for True and F for False. (Answers are found on page numbers in parentheses.)

___ 1. E-mail is an informal tool for personal communication and is not used to deliver important or official information. (171)

___ 2. Twitter is used for microblogging. (226)

___ 3. Yahoo! Mail and Gmail are examples of e-mail clients. (172)

___ 4. Windows SkyDrive is the premium version of Windows Live Mail. (178)

___ 5. You can open your e-mail client from Internet Explorer 9. (181)

___ 6. Content-sharing Web sites include Digg and Reddit. (239)

___ 7. A contact category allows you to send messages to multiple people at one time. (206)

___ 8. A wiki is an electronic bulletin board. (239)

___ 9. Google+ and Facebook are two examples of social bookmarking Web sites. (227)

___10. Yelp is an example of a social opinion Web site. (242)

Multiple Choice

Select the best answer. (Answers are found on page numbers in parentheses.)

1. The B in Bcc stands for _____. (174)

    a. before

    b. the letter, b, as in the second choice in a list

    c. blind

    d. beneficiary

2. Which of the following is *not* a communications protocol used to send e-mail? (172)

    a. IMAP

    b. HTML

    c. SMTP

    d. POP

3. To keep e-mail organized in your Inbox, you can _____. (198)

    a. print out each message

    b. create folders for different topics and move messages to them

    c. add a flag to each message

    d. attach electronic sticky notes to the messages

4. A valid e-mail address includes _____. (171)

   a. html://, the user ID, an @ symbol, and the host name

   b. http://, the user ID, the password, and the mail server name

   c. the user ID, an @ symbol, the password, and the mail server name

   d. the user ID, an @ symbol, and the host name

5. Examples of asynchronous communication include all of the following except _____. (235)

   a. IRC chat

   b. e-mail

   c. mailing lists

   d. newsgroups

6. A(n) _____ handles the job of directing messages to all mailing list subscribers. (209)

   a. HTTP server

   b. IMAP server

   c. list server

   d. host server

7. Which of the following is a photo-sharing Web site? (241)

   a. Wikipedia

   b. Delicious

   c. Epinions

   d. Flickr

8. comp.*, news.*, rec.*, sci.*, soc.*, talk.*, misc.*, and alt.* are associated with _____. (233)

   a. Usenet newsgroups

   b. list servers

   c. Web-based chat

   d. instant message chat

9. _____ is an example of a social bookmarking Web site. (239)

   a. Reddit

   b. Epinions

   c. Evri

   d. Twitter

10. The use of spam to attempt to collect personally identifiable information, credit card numbers, bank account numbers, and so forth is called _____. (208)

    a. spoofing

    b. phishing

    c. hacking

    d. a "Nigerian Sting" operation

Test your knowledge of chapter content and key terms.

Instructions: To complete the following exercises, please visit **www.cengagebrain.com**. On the CengageBrain home page, enter the book title *Discovering the Internet* and then click the Find button. On the product page for this book, click the Access Now button below the Study Tools heading. On the Book Companion Site Web page, click the drop-down menu, select Chapter 4, and then click the link for the desired exercise.

Chapter Reinforcement TF, MC, and SA

A series of true/false, multiple-choice, and short-answer questions that test your knowledge of the chapter content.

Flash Cards

An interactive learning environment where you identify chapter key terms associated with displayed definitions.

Practice Test

A series of multiple-choice questions that test your knowledge of chapter content and key terms.

Who Wants To Be a Computer Genius?

An interactive game that challenges your knowledge of chapter content in the style of a television quiz show.

Wheel of Terms

An interactive game that challenges your knowledge of chapter key terms in the style of the television show, *Wheel of Fortune*.

Crossword Puzzle Challenge

A crossword puzzle that challenges your knowledge of the key terms presented in the chapter.

Use the Exercises to gain hands-on Internet experience.

1 | Surveying Online Communications Choices

1. Survey five friends and ask them the following questions about their choices for online communications. Summarize the results, and include yourself in your summary.

   a. How often do you blog or read others' blogs?

   b. Do you microblog or subscribe to others' microblogs? What platform or service do you use? What device do you mainly use to read or post to a microblog?

   c. How often do you use IM to communicate with friends, family, coworkers, and classmates?

   d. How often do you participate in IRC chat or Web-based chat? Do you primarily chat or text using your phone or another device?

   e. Do you subscribe to mailing lists and newsgroups? How many? What type?

   f. Have you ever edited or contributed to a wiki? If yes, what type of wiki?

   g. Have you ever sent a text message to a cell phone using a Web page message center?

h. Do you have a profile at a social networking Web site? If yes, which one, and how big is your personal network?

i. Have you ever shared your bookmarks, photos, videos, and/or opinions at social media Web sites? If yes, how often, and which sites?

2. Use the results of your survey to describe how the survey group makes online communication choices.

2 | Surveying E-Mail Use

1. Survey five friends and ask them the following questions about their general e-mail use. Summarize the results, and include yourself in your summary.

   a. How many e-mail accounts do you use?

   b. How many messages do you receive daily, on average?

   c. How many messages do you send daily, on average?

   d. Do you access your e-mail accounts using multiple computers or a single computer, or using a smartphone or other mobile device?

2. Survey five friends and ask them the following questions about their use of folders in organizing e-mail. Summarize the results, and include yourself in your summary.

   a. Approximately how many messages are currently in your Inbox?

   b. Do you organize e-mail messages into folders or leave them all in the Inbox?

   c. If you use custom folders, how many custom folders do you have?

   d. How often do you delete unwanted messages?

   e. How often do you retrieve deleted messages?

3. Survey five friends and ask them the following questions about their experience with spam. Summarize the results, and include yourself in your summary.

   a. On average, how many spam messages do you receive daily?

   b. Have you ever received one of the following types of junk e-mail?:

      • "Nigerian Sting" operation

      • phishing

      • stock-manipulation schemes

   c. When you receive junk e-mail, do you ever recognize the supposed sender's e-mail or name? How do you know that the sender has been hacked?

   d. What measures do you take to avoid having junk e-mail affect your computer?

   e. Do you receive chain letters and forwarded messages from friends, and do you consider those to be spam? Do you forward these types of messages on to others?

4. Survey five friends and ask them the following questions about their experience with e-mail viruses. Summarize the results, and include your own experiences in your summary.

   a. How many e-mail viruses has your computer gotten in the past year?

   b. What virus protection do you use?

   c. How do you handle attachments on incoming messages?

5. Use the results of your survey to describe how the survey group uses e-mail.

3 | Exploring CAPTCHAs

1. Visit the *Discovering the Internet, Fourth Edition* Chapter 4 Exercises Web page at **www.cengagebrain.com** and click a link below Exercise 3 to search for information about CAPTCHAs. Use your research to answer the following questions:

   a. What is a CAPTCHA?

   b. Are there different types of CAPTCHAs?

   c. How are CAPTCHAs being used?

2. Print an example of a CAPTCHA.

4 | Evaluating Wikis

1. Visit the *Discovering the Internet, Fourth Edition* Chapter 4 Exercises Web page at **www.cengagebrain.com** and click the Wikia link below Exercise 4 to search for lists in which you might be interested.

2. Select one wiki of interest to you, and then read several links or articles. Evaluate the information for its credibility and think of information that might be missing or inaccurate.

3. Locate the Help link for Wikia to find guidelines for editing content and other rules for participation, and then read through them.

5 | Exploring Newsgroups and Web-Based Discussion Groups

1. Visit the *Discovering the Internet, Fourth Edition* Chapter 4 Exercises Web page at **www.cengagebrain.com** and click Google Groups below Exercise 5. Think of a topic that you would enjoy discussing with others, and then:

   a. Search Google Groups for that topic.

   b. Locate and read the rules for posting on Google Groups. Does this information encourage you to post a message or discourage you from doing so?

   c. Register for Google Groups and post a new thread or a reply in an existing group.

   d. Read the Google help information on how to delete your posting, and then delete it.

2. Visit the *Discovering the Internet, Fourth Edition* Chapter 4 Exercises Web page at **www.cengagebrain.com** and click Yahoo! Groups below Exercise 5. Think of a topic you would enjoy discussing with others. Use Yahoo! Groups to search for public discussion groups related to the topic. Visit two or more of the public discussion groups and review the types of postings in the groups.

6 | Evaluating Instant Messaging and Chat

1. Visit the *Discovering the Internet, Fourth Edition* Chapter 4 Exercises Web page at **www.cengagebrain.com** and click the links below Exercise 6 to research Yahoo! Messenger, Windows Live Messenger, and AIM (AOL Instant Messenger). Make a list of the features of each program, and then select the service you would most like to use. Give the reasons for your choice.

2. Visit the *Discovering the Internet, Fourth Edition* Chapter 4 Exercises Web page at **www.cengagebrain.com** and click Trillian below Exercise 6 to research the Trillian instant messaging service. Compare the benefits of using Trillian with the other IM programs you researched in Step 1.

3. With your instructor's permission, install an instant messaging service or use an already-installed instant messaging service to communicate with three classmates. Then write a brief description of the instant messaging service you used and how easy or difficult it was to communicate with your classmates using instant messaging.

4. Visit the *Discovering the Internet, Fourth Edition* Chapter 4 Exercises Web page at **www.cengagebrain.com** and click KidsCom.com below Exercise 6. Review the Chat and Buzz Safety Rules. Write a brief report on how this Web site keeps children safe in its chat rooms.

7 | Learning About Blogging and Microblogging

1. Visit the *Discovering the Internet, Fourth Edition* Chapter 4 Exercises Web page at **www.cengagebrain.com** and click links below Exercise 7 to learn more about the types of blogs in which you might be interested and how to contribute to them. Create a list of at least five blogs of interest to you.

2. Visit the *Discovering the Internet, Fourth Edition* Chapter 4 Exercises Web page at **www.cengagebrain.com** and click the links below Exercise 7 to visit the Twitter Web site.

   a. Join Twitter, if necessary, and view the postings of at least five people, including a local newsperson, a television or movie personality, a blogger, a politician, and an individual user (such as a friend or classmate).

   b. Write a one-page discussion of microblogging and how each person uses microblogging to communicate with his or her followers. For each person, include the following:

   • Example of a post

   • Average daily number of posts

   • Number of followers

   • Number of people the person follows

8 | Researching Social Networking

1. Start Internet Explorer, and then use the Search box and the search tool of your choice to:

   a. Research social networking Web sites that you might join for pleasure. Write a summary of your research.

   b. Research social networking Web sites that you might join to advance your career. Write a summary of your research.

   c. Research the dangers of participating in online social networks. Write a summary of your research.

9 | Exploring Social Bookmarking and Content Sharing

Visit the *Discovering the Internet, Fourth Edition* Chapter 4 Exercises Web page at **www.cengagebrain.com** and click links below Exercise 9 to learn more about social bookmarking and content-sharing Web sites and how you can use them. Write a brief report on the advantages and disadvantages of sharing your bookmarks and favorite content with others. Also discuss the benefits of reviewing other people's bookmarks and shared content.

10 | Investigating Social Opinions and Knowledge Sharing

Visit the *Discovering the Internet, Fourth Edition* Chapter 4 Exercises Web page at **www.cengagebrain.com** and click the links below Exercise 10 to learn more about social opinion and knowledge-sharing Web sites. Select four products or services: two products that can be purchased nationally (for example, consumer electronics or software) and two services that must be purchased locally (for example, restaurants, movie theaters, dog groomers, and so forth). Then use the social opinion sites of your choice to search for and read reviews and opinions on the product or service. Write a brief report about the usefulness of social opinion sites.

NOTES

NOTES

5 | Getting More Out of the Internet

Introduction

Web sites that you visit daily or multiple times a day likely contain complex, useful, interesting, and timely content. Possibly, some of your favorite sites are portal sites, similar to those you first learned about in Chapter 2. In this chapter, you will learn more about different types of portals and the role they play in ensuring that appropriate content is available to various target audiences: the public, employees, vendors, customers, and business partners. You also will learn how to get immediate notification of breaking news from a major news source, learn about traffic snarls that might make you late for school or work, listen to Internet radio, look up the definition of a new technical term, verify your bank balance and pay bills, and perform many more tasks using the Internet and the Web.

Objectives

After completing this chapter, you will be able to:

1. Describe and give examples of different types of portals and their target audiences

2. Identify and use online news, sports, weather, and traffic resources

3. Discuss streaming media, watch video clips, and listen to Internet radio

4. Use online research and reference tools

5. Explore health, entertainment, hobby, and other special-interest Web sites

6. Discuss online tools for managing personal finances

7. Describe online educational resources

8. Describe the consumer marketspace and online auctions

9. Identify types of online games

10. Download and share files over the Internet

Portals

In Chapter 2, you learned that a portal is a Web site that provides access to a wide variety of Web content and services. A portal can be a single Web-based interface to a company's general business information, intranet, and extranet, or a gateway to information about a specific area of interest or a specific industry. Portals are often classified by their targeted audiences; examples include general consumer portals, personal portals, vertical portals, industry portals, and corporate portals.

Consumer Portals

General consumer portals offer a broad range of content, including search tools, current news and weather, stock quotes, sports scores, links to reference tools, links to shopping, and perhaps an e-mail account. By offering varied content, a general consumer portal appeals to a very large audience, thus becoming a more attractive venue for other organizations wanting to advertise and promote their Web sites on the portal. Several popular general consumer portals evolved from more humble beginnings. For example, Yahoo! began as a list of links that developed into a search tool, while MSN originated from the default home page for the Internet Explorer Web browser. By expanding their content, these early search tool and default browser home page sites have increased their audiences by attracting new users and encouraging users to visit their sites repeatedly. Over time, these Web sites developed into general consumer portals.

Personal portals, also called **horizontal portals**, are consumer portals whose content you customize to meet your specific needs. Personal portals exploit the interactive nature of the Web to tailor Web page content to your specific interests. Using your personal preferences to customize a consumer portal makes the portal content more interesting and useful. My Yahoo! and My MSN (Figure 5-1) are examples of customized personal portals. As you learned in Chapter 2, you can change the settings in your Web browser to make a customized personal portal your browser's default home page.

@SOURCE

Portals
For more information about portals, visit **www.cengagebrain.com**. On the CengageBrain home page, enter the book title, *Discovering the Internet*, and then click the Find button. On the product page for this book, click the Access Now button below the Study Tools heading. On the Book Companion Site Web page, click the drop-down menu, select Chapter 5, and then click the @Source link. Click the links below Portals.

Figure 5-1 Personal portals allow viewers to customize content to their specific interests.

Vertical, Hyperlocal, and Industry Portals

Vertical portals, sometimes called **vortals**, provide a Web gateway for visitors with more specific interests, such as gardening, children's activities, social issues, ethnic interests, and government information. Examples of vertical portals include:

- USA.gov Senior Citizens' Resources and the Kids.gov sites (federal pages of interest to seniors and children)
- SuzySaid Acton (resources for the Acton, Massachusetts area)
- National Resource Directory (resources for U.S. service members, veterans, and their families)
- MSN Latino (Hispanic interests)
- Export.gov (export issues)
- City of Austin Environmental Portal (environmental issues)
- BlackVoices (African-American interests)

Hyperlocal portals are specific to a certain geographic location and provide content about that area, written for and by local citizens. Web sites such as Patch (Figure 5-2) and SuzySaid provide a platform where local citizens and businesses can advertise, blog, and write articles about their specific area.

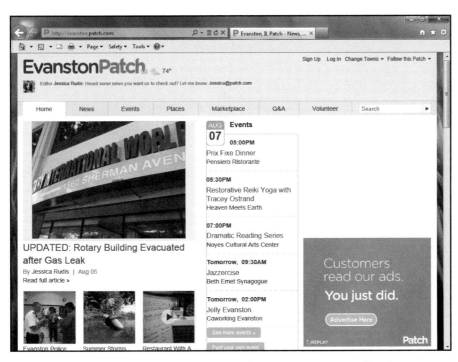

Figure 5-2 Hyperlocal portals provide content for and about a certain location.

Vertical portals that target viewers interested in a specific industry often are called **industry portals**. Some industry portals also aggregate information about a specific industry and provide a marketspace where businesses can buy from and sell to each other, creating a **B2B exchange**. Other industry portals simply provide industry information, news, links, and advertising.

Examples of industry portals include EARTHWEB (IT industry), Farms.com (agribusiness), Web Host Industry Review (Web hosting industry), MFG.com (manufacturing industry), COMMREX (commercial real estate industry exchange), and Business.gov (small business).

To Explore Vertical, Hyperlocal, and Industry Portals

The following steps explore vertical, hyperlocal, and industry portals, and the wide range of interests these portals cover. You will open each Web site's home page in a new tab. Linked pages at the same Web site will open in the same tab as the home page.

- Start Internet Explorer.

- Visit the Book Companion Site Web page for this text. Click the 'Select a chapter' list arrow, click the option for Chapter 5, and then click the Steps link on the left side of the page.

- Click the Kids.gov link to open the Web page in a new tab (Figure 5-3).

- Scroll the page and review its content.

- Click the links of your choice to review at least two subsidiary pages at the Kids.gov site.

Figure 5-3

- Close the tab and return to the Chapter 5 Steps page.

- Click the MSN Latino link to open the Web page in a new tab (Figure 5-4).

- Scroll the page and review its Spanish-language content.

- Click the links of your choice to review at least two subsidiary pages at the MSN Latino site.

Figure 5-4

3

- Close the tab and return to the Chapter 5 Steps page.

- Click the California Governor's Office of Economic Development link to open the Web page in a new tab (Figure 5-5).

- Scroll the page and review its content.

- Click the links of your choice to review at least two subsidiary pages at the California Governor's Office of Economic Development site.

Figure 5-5

4

- Close the tab and return to the Chapter 5 Steps page.

- Click the City of Austin Environmental Portal link to open the Web page in a new tab (Figure 5-6).

- Scroll the page and review its content.

- Click the links of your choice to review at least two subsidiary pages at the City of Austin Environmental Portal site.

Figure 5-6

- Close the tab and return to the Chapter 5 Steps page.

- Click the National Resource Directory link to open the Web page in a new tab (Figure 5-7).

- Scroll the page and review its content.

- Click the links of your choice to review at least two subsidiary pages at the National Resource Directory site.

Figure 5-7

- Close the tab and return to the Chapter 5 Steps page.

- Click the Farms.com link to open the Web page in a new tab (Figure 5-8).

- Scroll the page and review its content.

- Click the links of your choice to review at least two subsidiary pages at the Farms.com site.

Figure 5-8

- Close the tab and return to the Chapter 5 Steps page.

- Click the EARTHWEB link to open the Web page in a new tab (Figure 5-9).

- Scroll the page and review its content.

- Click the links of your choice to review at least two subsidiary pages at the EARTHWEB site.

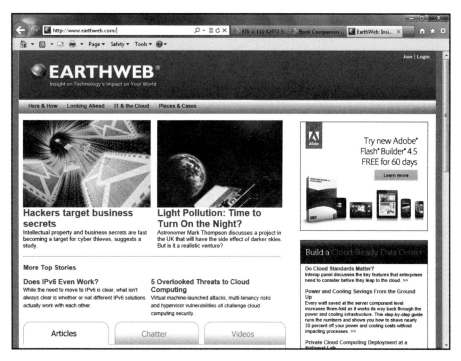

Figure 5-9

8

- Close the tab and return to the Chapter 5 Steps page.

- Click the SuzySaid link to open the Web page in a new tab (Figure 5-10).

- Scroll the page and review its content.

- Click the links of your choice to review at least two subsidiary pages at the SuzySaid site.

Figure 5-10

- Close the tab and return to the Chapter 5 Steps page.

- Click the BlackVoices link to open the Web page in a new tab (Figure 5-11).

- Scroll the page and review its content.

- Click the links of your choice to review at least two subsidiary pages at the BlackVoices site.

Figure 5-11

⑩

- Close the tab and return to the Chapter 5 Steps page.

- Click the SBA.gov link to open the Web page in a new tab (Figure 5-12).

- Scroll the page and review its content.

- Click the links of your choice to review at least two subsidiary pages at the SBA.gov site.

- Close the browser and close all open tabs.

Figure 5-12

Corporate Portals

Corporate portals also are called **enterprise information portals (EIPs)**. Employees, customers, vendors, and other business partners can use a single corporate portal to access a company's business information, work with others using e-mail and other internal collaboration tools, or conduct business transactions. Corporate portals control access to company information and business processes based on each user's personal profile. Some corporate portals also permit customization — news on specific job-related topics, stock trackers on specific stocks, and so forth — based on user preferences.

When an employee uses the corporate portal to log on to the company intranet, the content he or she sees is controlled automatically based on his or her employee profile. By personalizing portal content, an employee in the Accounts Payable Department, for example, can log on and track vendor invoices, company purchase orders, and company receiving reports; however, he or she cannot access any information from other departments, such as Accounts Receivable or Marketing. Other general information, such as industry and company news, company stock performance, links to search tools, and general employee information, also may be included in the employee's portal content. Similarly, when a customer, vendor, or business partner logs on through the corporate portal, personalized content allows access only to specific information based on his or her profile.

Companies such as Oracle and IBM (Figure 5-13) provide portal software packages that can be customized to fit a company's unique needs. Portal software enables customization, controlled access, and multisystem integration.

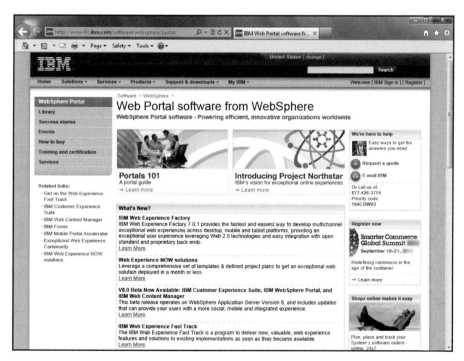

Figure 5-13 Portal software packages can be customized to fit a company's needs.

News, Sports, Weather, and Traffic Resources

Before the Internet became a source of readily accessible information, most people used newspapers, magazines, radio, and television to stay informed about current events, follow their favorite sports teams, keep an eye on the weather, or learn about traffic problems.

Today, users supplement these traditional print and broadcast news media sources with Web sites they access from computers at home, school, or work, or by using their smartphones (Figure 5-14).

Figure 5-14   Web sites can replace print resources for traffic resources and more.

In Chapters 2 and 3, you learned how to subscribe to RSS feeds for headline stories and other news articles, and you learned how to use online search tools to locate and read news stories from news-oriented Web sites. Most, if not all, U.S. and international newspapers publish online editions. Some offer a limited amount of free content; to read selected articles or access archived content, you must be a subscriber (for a fee, such as *The Wall Street Journal*) or register (for free, such as Boston.com, the site for *The Boston Globe*).

Web sites published by newspapers commonly include the same type of content found in the corresponding print versions: headline news, top stories, feature articles, current weather, sports scores, entertainment reviews, classified ads, editorials and opinion columns, and so forth. In addition to content available in the print editions, many sites offer frequently updated coverage on topics, enabling them to keep their audience continually informed. Some media Web sites include reader polls and most allow visitors to post comments on articles, which help them to track visitors' interest in and reaction to the news.

Television and radio networks, such as National Public Radio (NPR), NBC, CBC, BBC, CNN, FOX News, and local television network affiliates, publish Web sites that provide a combination of headline news, sports, weather, blogs, videos, podcasts, and other news and entertainment features. Often these Web sites include content that promotes their broadcast programming and on-air personalities.

While sports, weather, and traffic reports usually are available at news-oriented Web sites, you also can find a number of Web sites devoted specifically to sports, weather, and traffic. For example, online editions of ESPN, FOX Sports (television), and *Sports Illustrated* (magazine) cover a wide range of sports around the world, often in conjunction with existing cable news networks, such as CNN.

Web sites such as the Weather Channel, AccuWeather.com, and Intellicast.com provide local and worldwide weather forecasts, weather-related travel advisories, and weather maps. Web sites such as NAVTEQ, Google Maps, and local television station sites provide updated traffic reports that highlight routes with congestion, construction, or accidents that might cause delays.

According to the Pew Internet & American Life Project, 47 percent of American adults use mobile devices, such as tablet computers or smartphones, to get local news.

FACTS @HAND

Characteristics of News-Oriented Web Sites

Internet users access news, sports, weather, and traffic Web sites for the following reasons:

- Availability — They can be accessed easily from almost anywhere, at any time.
- Immediacy — They can be updated quickly with breaking news, sports scores, or weather and traffic updates.
- Interactivity — They provide features that allow their viewers to interact with the editorial staff by posting comments, and react or respond to articles.
- Customizability — They provide information customized for each viewer's locality and interests.
- Connectivity — They enable users to share news and articles with their contacts by posting links using social media.

The following sections review each of these characteristics in detail.

AVAILABILITY   Local, national, and international news-oriented Web sites often are more readily available than broadcast news sources. For example, if you are away from home, you might be unable to conveniently access television or radio, but you may have access to the Internet by using a computer at work or at school, or by using a mobile device. The ready availability of Internet access from multiple locations makes it very easy for you to check the latest news, sports scores, or changing weather quickly.

IMMEDIACY   News-oriented Web sites are updated quickly with breaking stories as the actual events unfold, thus providing you with immediate access to the latest information. Print news media, of course, cannot be constantly updated and distributed, and can contain only information about events that occurred prior to the last publication deadline.

INTERACTIVITY   Interactive features help to make any type of Web site stickier and more interesting. A **sticky Web site** is one that users visit often and browse for long periods of time. Many news-oriented Web sites provide interactivity by allowing you to submit questions and comments to their editorial staff, commentators, and reporters by e-mail, or to join other users in posting questions and comments in Web-based discussion groups or on blogs. If the Web site is associated with print or broadcast media, these questions and comments also may be addressed in print or on the air. Another way in which these Web sites provide interactivity and create stickiness is by allowing viewers to participate in an online survey on a current topic and then quickly see how their opinions compare with those of other viewers. Sports-oriented Web sites often use a similar technique to allow viewers to vote for a league's most popular players, or to vote for members of an All-Star team. Additionally, many of these Web sites allow viewers to subscribe to a mailing list so that they can receive brief e-mail messages about breaking news and a link to the Web site for more details, or to follow them on Twitter or Facebook.

CUSTOMIZABILITY The ability to customize Web site content plays a major role in the growing popularity of news-oriented Web sites. For example, the Web sites for MSNBC, CNN, and BBC allow you to customize content based on a series of preferences. These preferences can include the following:

- ZIP code or locality — Used to customize content for local news, weather, and traffic
- News region preference — Used to customize content for a specific geographic area, such as the United States, Europe, or Asia
- Sports preferences — Used to include news and scores for favorite sports or teams
- Stock portfolio — Used to include activity reports and current quotes on the individual investments in a personal portfolio

CONNECTIVITY By allowing users to link to articles using social networking tools, such as Twitter, Facebook, or Digg, users share and recommend content to others with similar interests, enabling the Web site to reach a wider audience.

To Explore News and Traffic Web Sites

The following steps explore several news and traffic Web sites to view the latest news and information. Many major print newspapers require that you subscribe to their Web site, generally for free, to access many of the site's features and subsidiary pages; therefore, in these steps, you will view only the home page of a print newspaper's Web site. You also will investigate the interactive and customizable features of a television news Web site.

You will open each Web site's home page in a new tab. Linked pages from the Web site's home page will open in the same tab as the home page. Because you are reviewing sites that contain current content, the content on your screen will vary from the illustrations in this section.

- Start Internet Explorer.
- Return to the Discovering the Internet, Chapter 5 Steps page.
- Click the The Washington Post link to open the Web site in a new tab.
- Scroll the page to review its major headlines and links to subsidiary pages (Figure 5-15).

Figure 5-15

- Close the tab to return to the Discovering the Internet, Chapter 5 Steps page.

- Click the The Dallas Morning News link to open the Web page in a new tab.

- Scroll the page to review its major headlines and links to subsidiary pages (Figure 5-16).

Figure 5-16

❸

- Close the tab to return to the Discovering the Internet, Chapter 5 Steps page.

- Click the CNN.com link to open the Web page in a new tab.

- Scroll to view the Quick vote area in the right margin of the page.

- Read the Quick vote question (Figure 5-17).

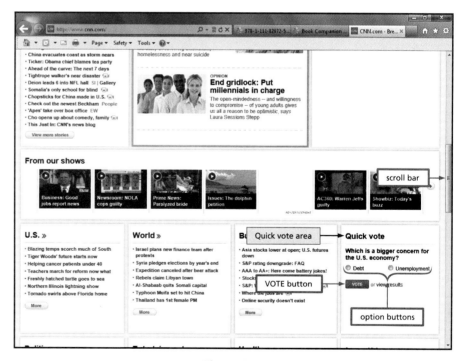

Figure 5-17

- Click an option button to vote on the question (your question will differ).

- Click the VOTE button to register your vote and display the cumulative results of all votes (Figure 5-18).

Figure 5-18

⑤

- Close the tab to return to the Discovering the Internet, Chapter 5 Steps page.

- Click the Google Maps: Live Traffic link to open the Web page in a new tab (Figure 5-19).

- Click the arrows on the Pan button to pan the U.S. traffic map up, down, to the right, or to the left, if necessary, to more easily view a traffic symbol indicating a major city in your state.

Q&A | **What if no major city is indicated on the map for my state?**
You can use Birmingham, Alabama as your city for these steps.

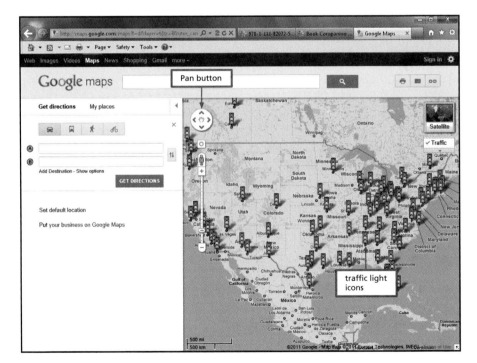

Figure 5-19

- Click the desired city's traffic light icon to display a message balloon (Figure 5-20).

- Click the Zoom In link in the message balloon to zoom in to your city's local traffic map.

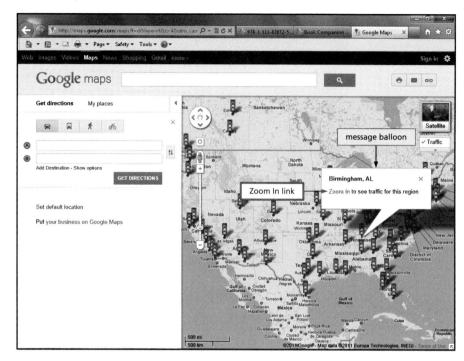

Figure 5-20

- Click a construction or other traffic issue icon on the map to view a message balloon containing information about the traffic issue (Figure 5-21).

- Click the message balloon's close button.

- Continue checking construction or other traffic issues. Note the traffic flow color indicators along highways and roads, and the traffic flow indicator color legend in the lower-left corner of the traffic map.

- Close the browser and all open tabs.

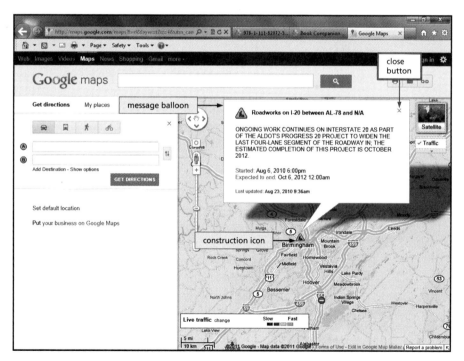

Figure 5-21

Streaming Media

Web site audio and video content can enhance text-based content by providing interviews and reports from newscasters, subjects, or eyewitnesses. Audio and video that is continuously delivered from a Web server to a Web browser is called **streaming media**. Many news Web sites, such as CNN.com, provide video clips of timely news commentaries or important newsmaker interviews, while sports Web sites provide video clips of game highlights or postgame interviews with players and coaches. Radio Web sites provide short audio clips of interviews or make entire broadcasts available as audio over the Internet. Television studios, such as ABC, show clips or entire episodes on their Web sites. Hulu is a site that collaborates with multiple entertainment studios to provide clips, episodes, and movies from a variety of sources (Figure 5-22).

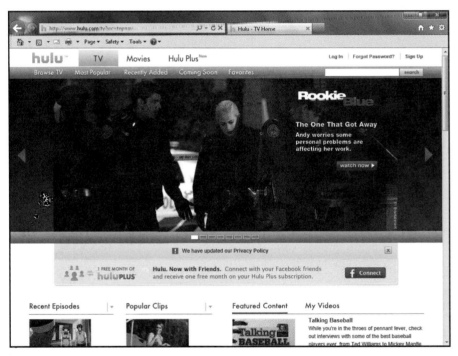

Figure 5-22   Streaming media includes audio and video continuously delivered from a Web server to a Web browser.

To enjoy streaming media, your computer must have a sound card, speakers, and a media player. The Windows 7 operating system comes with the Windows Media Player; other media players, such as RealNetworks' RealPlayer and Apple's QuickTime Player, are available as free downloads from the vendors' Web sites. A number of Web sites that offer video, such as CNN.com, MSNBC, and the TODAY show, stream the media in their own media player.

A fun way to experience streaming media is to listen to a radio broadcast over the Internet. A number of traditional radio station broadcasters, such as NPR, as well as local radio stations broadcast over the Internet directly from their Web sites.

To View a Web-Based Video and Listen to an Internet Radio Broadcast

The following steps allow you to experience streaming media by viewing a video using a built-in Web site media player and by listening to Internet radio.

- Start Internet Explorer.

- Visit the Discovering the Internet, Chapter 5 Steps page.

- Click the USA Today Video link to open the Web page in a new tab (Figure 5-23).

Figure 5-23

- Click the video clip of your choice to open the USA Today Video media player window and view the video (Figure 5-24).

- Continue clicking video clips in the list of available clips to view several clips of your choice.

- Click the media player window Pause button, and drag the arrows to fast-forward and rewind the videos.

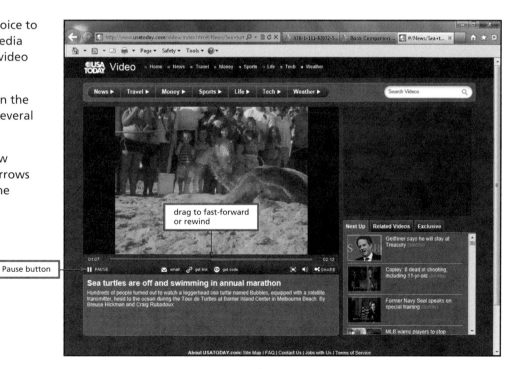

Figure 5-24

③

- Close the tab to return to the Discovering the Internet, Chapter 5 Steps page.

- Click the NPR Radio link to open the Web page in a new tab (Figure 5-25).

Figure 5-25

④

- Click the Hourly News button in the upper-right corner of the Web page to open the NPR media player in its own window (Figure 5-26).

 Why do I get a message that the window is blocked?
If necessary, turn off the Internet Explorer pop-up blocker to open the NPR media player in its own window. After you are done listening, turn on the browser's pop-up blocker, if necessary.

- Click the 24-Hour Program Stream link in the upper-right area of the page to listen to the broadcast stream.

- Click the media player window Close button.

- Close the browser and all tabs.

Figure 5-26

Research and Reference Tools

As you learned in Chapter 3, the Web includes numerous sites that provide access to specialized information collections, such as LexisNexis, FindLaw, and Hoover's (Figure 5-27), and government Web sites, such as the Library of Congress (Figure 5-27) and the Bureau of Labor Statistics. In addition to these specialized information collections, the Web also includes numerous general reference sites, such as online encyclopedias, dictionaries, reference desks, and trip planners. Remember to use the tools you learned about in Chapter 3 to evaluate the credibility of the content on reference sites.

@SOURCE

Online Reference Tools
To review the encyclopedia, dictionary, reference desk, and trip planner Web sites discussed in this section, visit the Book Companion Site Web page at **www. cengagebrain.com**. Under the Chapter 5 @Source links, click a link below Online Reference Tools.

Figure 5-27 Reference sites provide access to specialized information collections.

Online Encyclopedias

You are probably familiar with the process of looking up a topic in a printed encyclopedia at home, at your school, or at a public library. With an Internet connection, you can access a number of online encyclopedias, such as Encyclopedia.com (which aggregates information from multiple encyclopedias), Encyclopædia Britannica (a premium service), Bartleby.com, Infoplease, and Encyclopedia Smithsonian.

To Explore an Online Encyclopedia

The following steps use an online encyclopedia to perform a keyword search for a specific topic. You will open the Web site's home page link to open the Web page in a new tab. Linked pages from the home page will open in the same tab as the home page.

- Start Internet Explorer.

- Return to the Discovering the Internet, Chapter 5 Steps page.

- Click the Encyclopedia.com link to open the Web page in a new tab.

- Type **Molly Pitcher** in the Search box to find information about the American Revolutionary War heroine (Figure 5-28).

Q&A

Why do I see a drop-down list of search query suggestions?
Like some of the search engines you learned about in Chapter 3, Encyclopedia.com provides a list of search suggestions based on the characters you are typing in the Search box. You can click a search suggestion in the list to search using that search suggestion.

Figure 5-28

- Click the Search button to search for articles and other information about Molly Pitcher (Figure 5-29).

- Scroll the page to review its content, and then click an article to read it.

- Read the article.

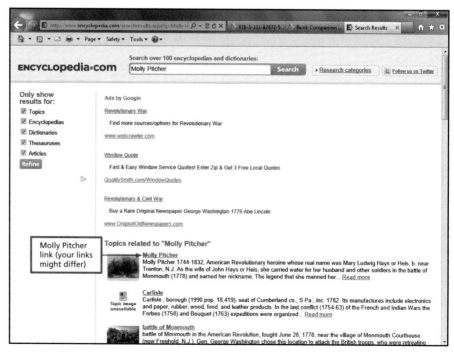

Figure 5-29

❸

- Click the Tools link to view online tools for printing, citing, and sharing the search results (Figure 5-30).

Figure 5-30

❹

- Click the 'Cite this article' link to view the citation styles tabs (Figure 5-31).

- Click the MLA, Chicago, and APA citation styles tabs in turn to review how to cite the Molly Pitcher article in a written report.

- Close the browser and all open tabs.

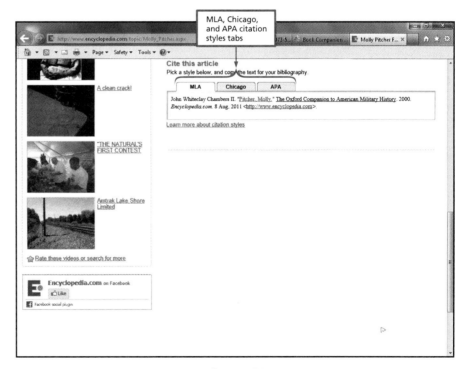

Figure 5-31

Online Dictionaries

You can use online dictionaries and thesauri to check the spelling and meaning of words or find synonyms in a number of languages. Examples include Merriam-Webster Online, OneLook Dictionary Search, Cambridge Dictionaries Online, and Thesaurus.com. You also can find dictionaries devoted to specific topics, such as law, biology, or technology. The NetLingo and Law.com dictionary sites, for example, provide definitions of thousands of technical and legal terms, respectively.

Some Web sites, such as OneLook, enable you to do **wildcard searches**. Wildcard searches use characters such as * or ? to replace letters, or use : (the colon character) to narrow your search by subject (Figure 5-32).

Wildcard Searches

Search Term	Finds Words or Phrases That
*ball	End with *ball*
ball*	Start with *ball*
b????? ball	Start with *b*, end with *ball*, and have five characters between, such as *basketball*
:ball	Are related to *ball*

Figure 5-32 Sample wildcard search terms and results.

To Explore an Online Dictionary

The following steps use an online dictionary to search for the definition, part of speech, and phonetic pronunciation of a specific word. You will open the Web site's home page link to open the Web page in a new tab. You also will perform wildcard searches.

- Start Internet Explorer.
- Return to the Discovering the Internet, Chapter 5 Steps page.
- Click the Merriam-Webster Online link to open the Web page in a new tab.
- Type **quinoa** in the Search box (Figure 5-33).

Figure 5-33

2

- Click the Search button to search for a definition.

- Review the main entry, which is the definition of quinoa as a noun (Figure 5-34).

Figure 5-34

3

- Click the sound icon to open the Merriam-Webster Pronunciation page in the same tab and hear the pronunciation (Figure 5-35).

- Close the Information Bar, if necessary, to open the page.

- Click the 'Listen to the audio pronunciation again' link on the Pronunciation page to listen to the pronunciation a second time.

- Click the pronunciation window Close button to close the window.

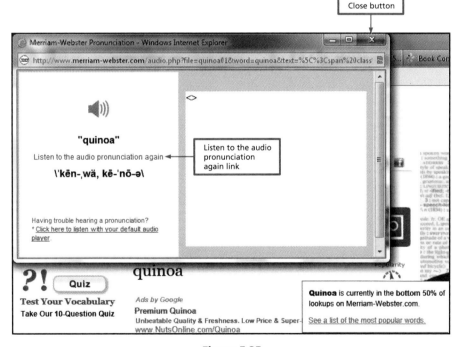

Figure 5-35

- Close the tab to return to the Discovering the Internet, Chapter 5 Steps page.

- Click the OneLook link to open the Web page in a new tab.

- Type ***grain** in the Search box (Figure 5-36).

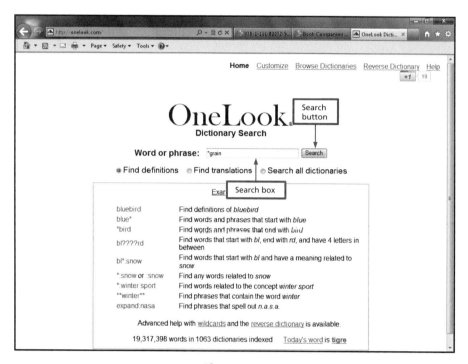

Figure 5-36

5

- Click the Search button to view the search results (Figure 5-37).

- Close the browser and all open tabs.

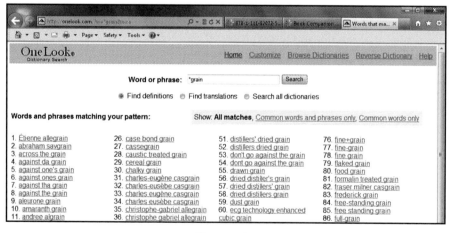

Figure 5-37

In Chapter 3, you learned several Google search engine shortcuts. Another Google shortcut is the define: shortcut, which you can use to return a search results list that contains Web pages with a definition for a specific word or phrase. Simply type the shortcut define: followed by a word or phrase in the Google keyword text box and click the Google Search button. Google then returns a search results list of Web pages containing a definition of the word or phrase, or a message indicating no Web pages meet the criteria.

To Use the Google define: Shortcut

The following steps open the Google search engine home page link to open the Web page in a new tab. You use the Google define: shortcut to find several Web page definitions for the phrase, Boolean operators. You must include the colon (:) in order for Google to return a list of Web pages with a definition, not just an ordinary search results list. The search results page will open in the same tab as the home page.

1

- Start Internet Explorer.

- Return to the Discovering the Internet, Chapter 5 Steps page.

- Click the Google link to open the Web page in a new tab.

- Type **define: boolean** in the Search box to open a list of suggested search terms (Figure 5-38).

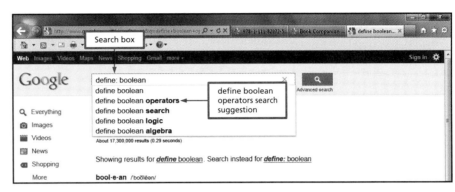

Figure 5-38

2

- Click 'define boolean operators' in the search terms list to open the search results.

- Review the Google Definition for boolean operators on the Web search results page (Figure 5-39).

- Click the link of your choice to review the definition's source.

- Close the browser and all open tabs.

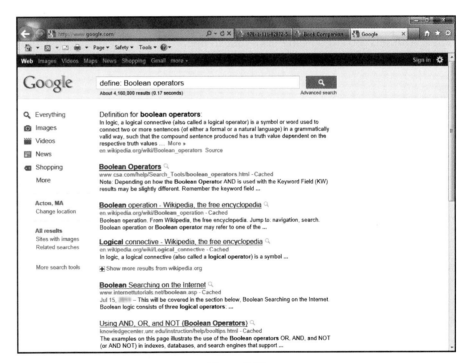

Figure 5-39

Online Reference Desks

One of the most comprehensive collections of online maps can be found in the Perry-Castañeda Library Map Collection at the University of Texas at Austin General Libraries Web site. To find a link to this map collection, visit the Book Companion Site Web page at **www.cengagebrain.com**. Under the Chapter 5 @Source links, click the Perry-Castañeda Library Map Collection link below Online Reference Tools.

Do you need to know what time it is in Bahrain? What important event took place on today's date in history? How to translate text into another language? You can find this information at an online reference desk Web site, such as the Internet Public Library, Refdesk, LibrarySpot.com, and iTools.

Online reference desks offer links to dictionaries, thesauri, language translators, fast fact finders, and other traditional library reference desk resources. Additionally, many college, university, public, and government libraries offer online reference desk resources. Examples include the Michigan eLibrary, the Duke University Libraries Reference and Research Services, and the Chicago Public Library Online Research Web sites.

To Explore an Online Reference Desk

The following steps explore an online reference desk, which is a collection of links to online resources. You will open the Web site's home page link to open the Web page in a new tab. Linked pages from the home page open in the same tab as the home page.

1

• Start Internet Explorer.

• Return to the Discovering the Internet, Chapter 5 Steps page.

• Click the Refdesk link to open the Web page in a new tab (Figure 5-40).

• Scroll the page to review the reference desk resources available.

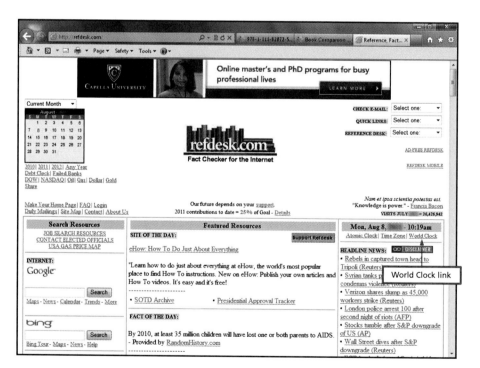

Figure 5-40

- Click the World Clock link to view the current day and time for a list of major cities around the world (Figure 5-41).

- Scroll the page to review the list.

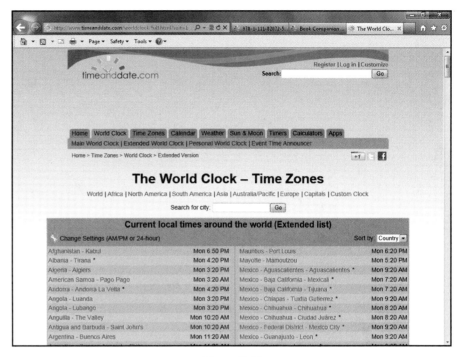

Figure 5-41

Back button

- Click the Back button to return to the Refdesk home page.

- Scroll down to locate the CIA World Fact Book link in the Facts-at-a-Glance section in the left margin of the page (Figure 5-42).

CIA World Fact Book link

Figure 5-42

- Open the CIA World Fact Book in a new tab (Figure 5-43).

- Scroll down the page and review the links to resources available at the Web site.

Figure 5-43

⑤

- Click the Select a Country or Location box arrow near the top of the page.

- Scroll the list to view the Sri Lanka link.

- Click Sri Lanka in the list to view the Sri Lanka information page (Figure 5-44).

- Scroll the page to review the data available for Sri Lanka.

- Close the browser and all open tabs.

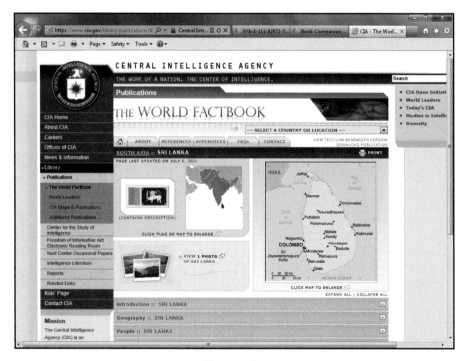

Figure 5-44

Most online dictionary, reference desk, and encyclopedia sites, such as the sites you explored in the previous sections, offer free information. Some Web sites, such as the Encyclopædia Britannica and the Britannica Kids sites, offer premium sites requiring a subscription fee to access some or all of the information available at the site.

Online Trip Planners

Planning an automobile trip used to require that you pore over printed maps and manually calculate the distance between your starting location and your destination. Often it was not clear where you could find overnight accommodations along the way. Now, you can plan your automobile trip in a snap with online trip planners such as FreeTrip, MapQuest, Google Maps, Yahoo! Maps, and Expedia Maps. When you use one of these online driving trip planners, you specify a starting location and an ending destination, and then indicate your preference for either a scenic route or the shortest-distance route. Some trip planners also provide information about restaurants, shopping, and motel, hotel, and bed-and-breakfast accommodations along the desired route.

To Explore an Online Driving Trip Planner

The following steps explore an online driving trip planner. You will open the Web site's home page link to open the Web page in a new tab. The trip itinerary page opens in the same tab as the home page.

- Start Internet Explorer.

- Return to the Discovering the Internet, Chapter 5 Steps page.

- Click the FreeTrip link to open the Web page in a new tab (Figure 5-45).

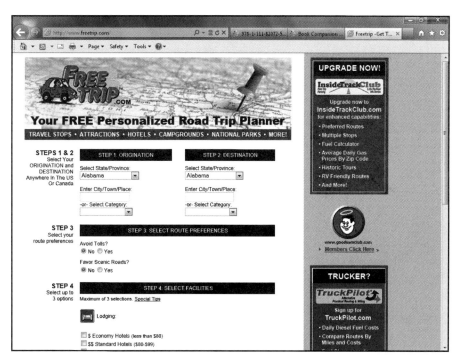

Figure 5-45

2

- Click the Step 1: Origination Select State/Province box arrow and click your state. If you do not live in the United States, click Oregon.

- Type the name of your city or type **Portland** in the Step 1: Origination Enter City/Town/Place text box.

- Click the Step 2: Destination Select State/Province box arrow and click Utah.

- Type **Moab** in the Step 2: Destination Enter City/Town/Place text box (Figure 5-46).

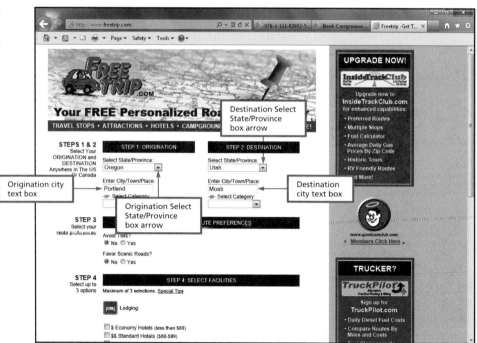

Figure 5-46

3

- Click the No option button, if necessary, in the Step 3: Select Route Preferences: Avoid Tolls? and Favor Scenic Roads? sections.

- Click the $$ Standard Hotels ($80–$99) check box in the Step 4: Select Facilities Lodging area (Figure 5-47).

Figure 5-47

- Click the No option button, if necessary, in the 'Step 5: Road advisory display options, Want displayed distance in kilometers?' section.

- Enter your e-mail address in the Step 6: Enter Your E-Mail Address text box to receive a copy of your itinerary by e-mail, if desired.

- Scroll to view the 'Step 7: Submit your trip request' area near the bottom of the page (Figure 5-48).

- Read the disclaimer about the accuracy of the trip planner's results.

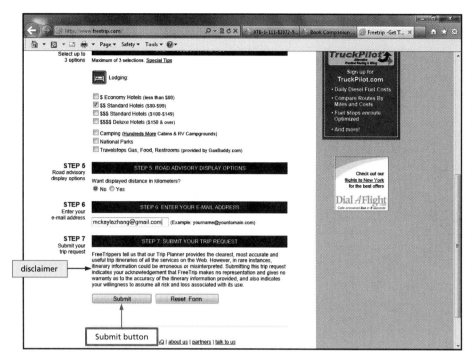

Figure 5-48

5

- Click the Submit button.

- Scroll your personal itinerary page to view the driving instructions and suggestions for accommodations (Figure 5-49).

- Close the browser and all open tabs.

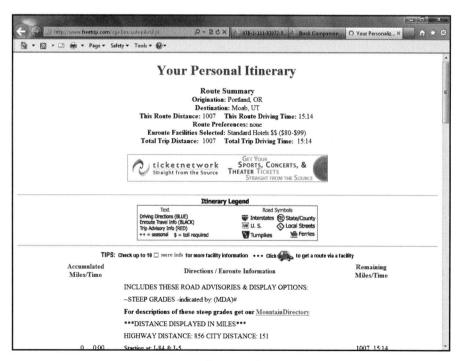

Figure 5-49

Special-Interest Web Sites

No matter how obscure your hobby or special interest might be, there is likely a Web site dedicated to it. Thousands of special-interest Web sites are devoted to topics such as health, diet, and fitness; entertainment news and movie reviews; home decorating and repair; museums; or genealogy. The next few sections explore just some of the wide range of health, entertainment, hobby, and other special-interest Web sites available online.

FACTS @HAND   According to the Do-it-yourself Information Data Memo by the Pew Internet & American Life Project, more than 50 percent of American adults have looked for how-to or do-it-yourself information online — and about 7 million adults do so on a typical day.

Health, Diet, and Fitness Information

The epidemic of obesity in the United States, coupled with rising health care costs, may have you thinking about ways to ensure that you are eating a healthy diet, getting the proper exercise, and staying informed on health, diet, and fitness issues. From time to time, you also may want to review information about a specific illness or medical condition. Your primary source of health, diet, and fitness information should be your doctor or another health care professional. If you are looking for general health, diet, and fitness information online, however, you can choose from hundreds of Web sites, such as Discovery Health, MayoClinic.com, and WebMD (Figure 5-50).

Several popular commercial diet and fitness Web sites, such as eDiets and WeightWatchers Online (Figure 5-50), are available for a monthly fee to help you plan and execute a personal diet and fitness program. These sites offer a variety of features, including:

- Restricted-calorie meal plans
- Grocery shopping lists
- Exercise plans, complete with text and graphic instructions
- Daily food and exercise diaries
- Electronic pantries or databases of frequently consumed food items used to select foods for daily food consumption diaries
- Support discussion groups

Everything you need to create a personal diet and fitness plan is available at one of these commercial Web sites for a fee. For free diet and fitness information, you can turn to government Web sites such as Fitness.gov, which is sponsored by the President's Council on Fitness, Sports and Nutrition, and Nutrition.gov.

@SOURCE

Health, Diet, and Fitness
To review the online health, diet, and fitness Web sites discussed in this section, visit the Book Companion Site Web page at **www.cengagebrain.com**. Under the Chapter 5 @Source links, click a link below Health, Diet, and Fitness.

Figure 5-50   Diet, fitness, and health-related sites provide general information.

A study by the Pew Internet & American Life Project indicates that 80 percent of American adults have gone online to research health, diet, and fitness information.

**FACTS
@HAND**

@ISSUE   Credibility of Online Health Information

Because of the large numbers of American Internet users who search for health information online, many health care professionals and Internet users are concerned about the credibility of online health information that might not have been professionally reviewed.

With these concerns in mind, how should you evaluate health-oriented Web sites? The credibility of the content at these Web sites first should be evaluated using the steps you learned in Chapter 3, including identifying the sponsoring organization or author, establishing that the content is timely and objective, and comparing the content with that from other, similar sites. Most people who go online to find health information rely on popular search tools to locate health-oriented Web sites; however, some health care professionals suggest that you ask a trusted source, such as your doctor or medical information professional, to recommend health-oriented Web sites. Another resource to help you evaluate health-oriented Web sites is the CAPHIS (Consumer and Patient Health Information Section) Web site. The CAPHIS Web site is sponsored and published by medical information professionals from the nonprofit Medical Library Association. CAPHIS evaluates health-oriented Web sites based on a number of criteria, including credibility, disclosure, sponsorship and authorship, and design, and

then lists the top 100 highest-evaluated Web sites as part of the CAPHIS Top 100.

Another alternative is to look for accredited Web sites. Two agencies that offer accreditation for health-oriented Web sites are the URAC Health Web Site and Health Content Vendor Accreditation program and the Health On the Net Foundation HONcode accreditation program. The Web site standards required by these agencies include the full disclosure of financial relationships, an editorial review process to ensure content accuracy, and internal processes to ensure privacy, security, and Web site quality. Web sites that adhere to the standards established by these agencies are entitled to display the URAC or HONcode symbols on their Web sites, as illustrated in Figure 5-51. For more information about the URAC and HONcode programs, visit the *Discovering the Internet, Fourth Edition* Book Companion Site Web page at **www.cengagebrain.com**, and then click a link below Chapter 5, URAC and HON.

Figure 5-51   The URAC and HONcode symbols indicate that the information at a health-oriented Web site meets strict quality standards.

In addition to researching specific health topics, you can review hospital Web sites to check out services or view pictures of newborns; go to health insurance provider Web sites to evaluate enrollment options and coverage; and fill prescriptions at online drugstores. Sites such as CarePages enable people with a health condition to create a Web page where they can post information about their health and treatments, and receive comments from friends and family. You also can go online to learn about and sign up for medical clinical trials or to locate a doctor in your area. Web sites such as CenterWatch, ClinicalTrials.gov, AMA DoctorFinder, and MedlinePlus offer these services. Many health care organizations, such as the American Diabetes Association, also provide online information about a specific disease and its treatment and how to find support groups.

To Explore Health-Related Web Sites

The following steps explore health-related Web sites. You will open each Web site's home page link to open the Web page in a new tab.

- Start Internet Explorer.

- Return to the Discovering the Internet, Chapter 5 Steps page.

- Click the MayoClinic.com link to open the Web page in a new tab.

- Type **peanut allergies** in the Search box (Figure 5-52).

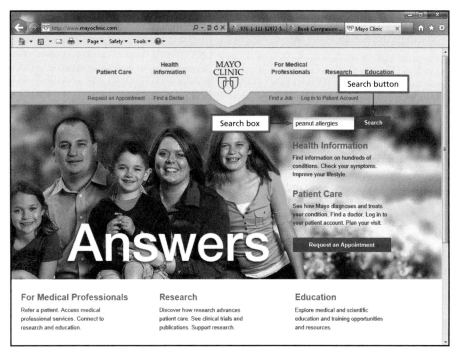

Figure 5-52

- Click the Search button to view a search results list for the keywords, peanut allergies (Figure 5-53).

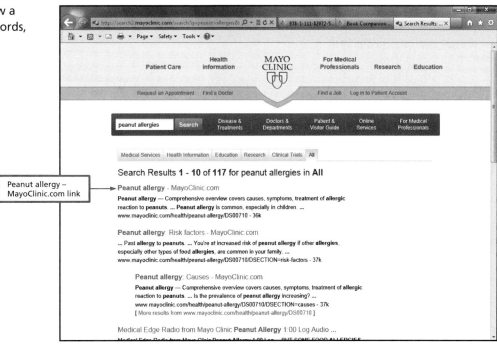

Figure 5-53

- Click the Peanut allergy – MayoClinic.com link or another link of your choice to learn more about peanut allergies.

- Read the article about peanut allergies (Figure 5-54).

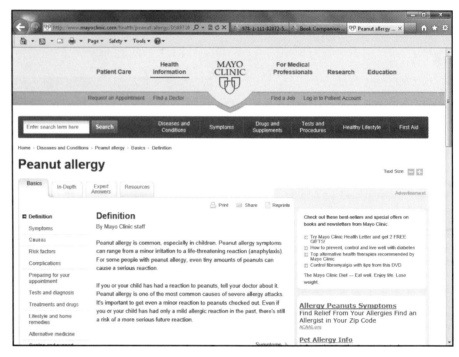

Figure 5-54

4

- Close the tab to return to the Discovering the Internet, Chapter 5 Steps page.

- Click the Nutrition.gov link to open the Web page in a new tab.

- Click the Smart Nutrition 101 link in the Browse by Subject area to display the Smart Nutrition 101 page (Figure 5-55).

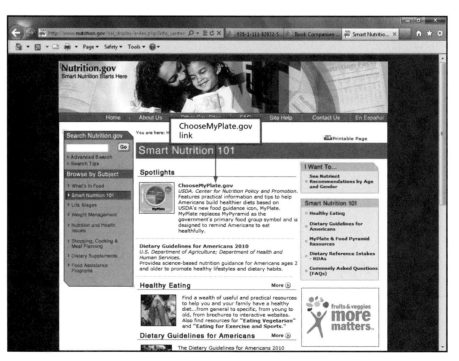

Figure 5-55

5

- Click the ChooseMyPlate.gov link in the Smart Nutrition 101 section to view links to information about the MyPlate food guide program (Figure 5-56).

- Scroll the page to view the resources for creating a healthy eating and fitness MyPlate plan.

- Close the browser and all open tabs.

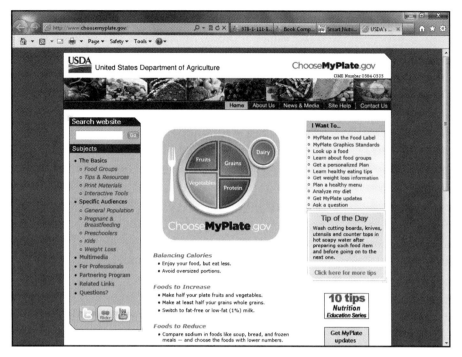

Figure 5-56

Entertainment, Hobby, and Other Special-Interest Web Sites

Whether your interest is cooking, learning about your family's genealogy, finding a job, making new friends, reading a movie review or the latest celebrity gossip, or visiting the world's great museums, thousands of entertainment, hobby, and other special-interest Web sites exist. For example, using one of the numerous entertainment, hobby, and other special-interest Web sites, you can:

- Learn to make gazpacho at VegWeb.com.

- Exchange family history with distant cousins at FamilySearch.org.

- Review résumé writing tips and post your résumé at Monster.com.

- Check out colleges, universities, graduate schools, and financial aid choices at Peterson's.

- Enjoy movie reviews at Rotten Tomatoes.

- Discover the beauty of Native American art by touring online exhibits at the National Museum of the American Indian.

@SOURCE

Special-Interest Web Sites
To review the special-interest Web sites discussed in this section, visit the Book Companion Site Web page at **www.cengagebrain.com**. Under the Chapter 5 @Source links, click a link below Special Interest.

FOOD AND COOKING   Just as news media publish related Web sites, food and cooking print and broadcast media also publish Web sites to promote their magazines and television shows, while famous chefs publish Web sites to promote their restaurants and cookbooks. Sites such as Emerils.com (Emeril Lagasse, world-famous chef and restaurateur), Epicurious (*Gourmet* and *Bon Appétit* magazines), and Vegetarian Times (*Vegetarian Times* magazine) (Figure 5-57) tempt you with recipes, easy-to-follow cooking tips, products to purchase at online stores, and information about associated restaurants.

If you love to cook and want to try something different, you can find a wide variety of food and cooking Web sites that offer recipes and cooking tips from around the world. For example, you can learn how to make vegetarian and nonvegetarian Indian dishes with recipes at the Sify Food Web site, or learn to cook specialties from Italy's Tuscany region at the Ciao Italia Web site (Figure 5-57).

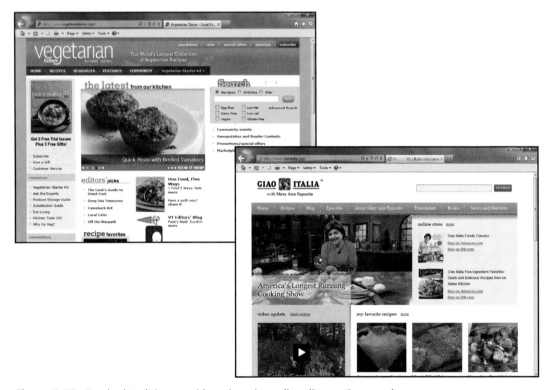

Figure 5-57 Food-related sites provide recipes, ingredient lists, reviews, and more.

MUSEUMS Perhaps you enjoy touring museums and viewing natural science exhibits, paintings, sculpture, or ancient artifacts from around the world. With Internet access, many of the world's museum exhibits — great and small — are as close as your computer screen. At museum Web sites, you can learn about current exhibits, operating hours, and membership opportunities. You also can view portions of ongoing special exhibits at many museum Web sites. Examples of online museum exhibits include the following:

- Archaeological and anthropological exhibits at the American Museum of Natural History in New York
- An art history timeline at The Metropolitan Museum of Art in New York (Figure 5-58)
- Fashion design featuring Hispanic designers at the Smithsonian National Museum of American History (Figure 5-58)
- An animated tour of treasures from the world's greatest libraries at the National Library of Australia
- An exhibit of American colonial coins at the Colonial Williamsburg Museum
- Illustrations of African American life in Philadelphia from colonial days to the middle of the nineteenth century at the African American Museum in Philadelphia

Figure 5-58 Museum sites provide information about exhibits, hours, and memberships.

GENEALOGY If you are interested in learning more about your family's history, you can use the Internet to find U.S. census data, federal land grant information, state and county court records, death and cemetery records, marriage records, immigrant ship manifests, diary transcripts, historical and genealogical society records, and other genealogical information online. Similar information from other countries around the world is available online as well.

For a subscription fee, commercial Web sites such as Ancestry.com allow you to access a variety of databases. Data recorded in these databases includes the U.S. and U.K. censuses, U.S. county and U.K. parish records, the U.S. Social Security Death Index, and family tree submissions by other subscribers. RootsWeb.com is a free genealogy site that focuses on surname searches and general information on how to research family history. Hobbyist-supported Web sites, such as Cyndi's List of Genealogy Sites on the Internet, publish free directories of online genealogical information from around the world. Many government archives, such as Canadian Genealogy and Family History on the National Archives of Canada Web site (Figure 5-59), Directgov, the National Archives of Australia, and the U.S. National Archives, publish Web sites offering a wealth of tips on how to gather genealogy information, including how to order copies of archived military pension, naturalization, and immigration documents.

Figure 5-59 Genealogy sites connect you with information about your family's history.

SENIORS Seniors use the Internet to enrich their lives by using social networking, e-mail, and chat to stay connected to family and friends; visiting news sites to keep up to date with world and local events; and staying informed about health and aging issues. A number of Web sites, such as the AARP site and SeniorNet (Figure 5-60), cater exclusively to the interests of older adults. Senior-oriented Web sites offer a variety of content, including articles on aging, continuing education courses, book clubs, retirement planners, and updates on legislation that affects seniors. Government sites, such as the USA.gov Senior Citizens' Resources site, the Public Health Agency of Canada Seniors Health site, and the Australian Seniors.gov.au site (Figure 5-60), offer information about health and aging and about government programs designed for seniors.

Figure 5-60 Senior-oriented sites include articles on aging, retirement planners, and more.

The range of informative and useful special-interest Web sites is virtually unlimited. Regardless of your age or interest, you likely can find any number of Web sites to enjoy.

According to the Pew Internet & American Life Project, participation in social networking among Internet users ages 50 and older grew from 22 percent in April 2009 to 42 percent in May 2010.

FACTS @HAND

To Explore a Special-Interest Web Site

The following steps explore a special-interest Web site on fitness. You will open the Web site's home page link to open the Web page in a new tab.

- Start Internet Explorer.

- Return to the Discovering the Internet, Chapter 5 Steps page.

- Click the Fitness.com link to open the Web page in a new tab (Figure 5-61).

- Scroll the page to view its contents.

Figure 5-61

❷

- Click the Healthy Recipes link to view the Web page (Figure 5-62).

- Scroll the page to view its contents.

Workouts link

Figure 5-62

❸

- Click the Workouts link.

- Scroll the page to review the list of resources for workouts (Figure 5-63).

- Close the browser and all open tabs.

Figure 5-63

Personal Finance Resources

Using online tools to help manage your personal finances — from checking your bank balance and paying your monthly bills to financing a new car or reviewing investment opportunities — makes managing your personal finances easier, faster, and more convenient. In this section, you will learn about online personal financial management tools and the benefits of using them.

Banking, Bill Presentment, and Bill Payment Services

Using online banking allows you to complete traditional time-consuming and paper-based banking activities, such as those required to transfer money from one account to another, quickly and easily. If you use your bank's or financial institution's online banking features, you already might be familiar with how easy it is to go online and check your bank balance, or view a list of paid items from your account.

In the past, a bank was largely a **brick-and-mortar business**, meaning that customers conducted transactions primarily in person at a physical location, over the phone, or using paper-based transactions. Today, large banks, such as Chase, Citibank, the RBC Royal Bank (Canada), and the National Australia Bank, as well as smaller regional banks, local banks, and credit unions are becoming **brick-and-click businesses** — that is, they offer online banking in addition to the services offered at the physical banks. A brick-and-click business is any business that allows customers to conduct business or complete transactions at a physical location as well as online at a Web site.

@SOURCE

Personal Finances
To review the online personal finance-oriented Web sites discussed in this section, visit the Book Companion Site Web page at **www.cengagebrain.com**. Under the Chapter 5 @Source links, click a link below Personal Finances.

According to the Generations Online in 2009 report by the Pew Internet & American Life Project, more than 50 percent of American Internet users now do some or all of their banking online.

FACTS @HAND

Online banking can allow you to complete some or all of the following tasks:

- View real-time account balances and recent transactions.
- View a history of account activity.
- Search for individual transactions.
- Pay your bills.
- Transfer funds between accounts.
- Download transactions into personal financial management software, such as Quicken.
- Issue a stop payment on a check.
- Order checks.
- Report a lost or stolen ATM card and request a replacement.
- Change personal information, such as your address, telephone number, and e-mail address.

Fees for online banking services vary from one institution to another. For example, some banks offer free online checking with no minimum account balance requirement, while other banks may require that you maintain a minimum balance to avoid paying service fees. Some banks also charge additional fees for specific types of online transactions, such as transferring money from account to account. Before you open an online bank account, you should compare the services and fees of several online bank services.

A common concern about online banking is related to the security of online banking transactions. Although no online transactions are 100 percent secure, and instances of online banking fraud have occurred, the banking industry has been involved with the security of electronic transactions for more than 40 years, starting with the electronic funds transfer (EFT) systems originating in the 1960s. Today, you can expect your bank to use sophisticated Internet security technologies to protect your personal information and to secure your online transactions. When shopping for an online bank, you should carefully review a bank's privacy policies and any security statements it provides.

Many financial industry analysts think the most valuable use of online banking is online bill payment services. A **bill payment service** allows you to log on to a Web site and pay any number of bills from a range of vendors. In addition to online banks, e-businesses such as MSN Bill Pay and PayTrust offer bill payment services. To pay a bill online using your bank or a bill payment service, simply log in to your account with the bank or service, select a vendor from a list you created when you first set up your bill payment service, enter a payment amount, and specify a payment date. On the scheduled payment date, your payment is debited from your bank account and transmitted to the vendor either by an electronic funds transfer or with a paper check. You also can set up recurring monthly payments so that bills, such as your cellular phone bill or car payment, can be paid automatically on a specific day each month.

Increasing numbers of utilities, credit card companies, auto finance companies, and other businesses are using **bill presentment**, the process of sending bills electronically, instead of mailing paper bills or statements to their customers. Using bill presentment to send electronic bills, also called **e-bills**, instead of sending paper bills can reduce a company's billing costs substantially, and is a more environmentally friendly approach. You can arrange to receive e-bills and then pay them electronically through your online bank account or bill payment service. For many consumers, receiving bills online is a convenient way to pay bills while on vacation or on a business trip. If you receive an e-bill while away from home, you can log on to your bill payment service from a laptop or mobile device and pay the bill on time.

Some banks offer online bill payment and bill presentment services for free, while others charge monthly service fees as well as transaction fees. You should research several banks and bill payment services and compare their fees before selecting an online bank.

One way to take advantage of the ease and speed of online bill presentment and payment without paying a fee is to pay your bill directly at the vendor's Web site. Many utility and credit card companies now allow you to set up payment information that includes a user ID, password, and bank account information at the company's own Web site. Then, you simply log on to the Web site each month, view your monthly statement, and make your payment. Although this method is less expensive than paying for a bill presentment and payment service, it lacks the advantage of using just one Web site to pay all your bills. For example, to pay bills directly at credit card company or utility company Web sites, you must remember multiple user IDs and passwords.

Financial Calculators, Insurance, and Credit Web Sites

Online information sources can help you make important personal financial decisions, such as buying a new automobile, selecting the right home mortgage, getting the best insurance value, or accepting a credit card offer. For example, online mortgage loan calculators and auto loan calculators can help you decide how much you can afford to pay each month for a home mortgage or how big of a down payment you should make when buying an automobile. Savings calculators can help you plan for a major purchase or your eventual retirement. These types of financial calculators are available at a number of financial institution Web sites, such as the Chase Web site, or at financial information sites, such as CardRatings.com (Figure 5-64) or Kiplinger.com. Note that unless you decide to do business with a company and have thoroughly checked out its reliability and security, you should not provide any personal, financial, or contact information to any site.

If you own a vehicle, auto insurance is likely one of your major expenses. Shopping for auto insurance offline often requires that you personally contact several different insurance agents and then manually compare each agent's policies, terms, and quoted rates. Web sites such as InsWeb (Figure 5-64), Insure.com, or Insurance.com make it easier to comparison shop for auto insurance by providing competing quotes from multiple insurance companies in just a few seconds. You simply submit your auto and personal information, along with the insurance coverage you want, using an online form. You also can get online comparative quotes on other types of insurance, such as homeowner's, renter's, and life insurance.

Figure 5-64 Online financial calculators, insurance agencies, credit card comparisons, and credit reporting agencies.

Web sites provide similar comparison shopping for credit cards. Because a wide range exists in the payment terms, fees, and services associated with different credit cards, it is a good idea to shop for a credit card in the same way that you shop for other products and services. You can compare credit card offers at comparison shopper sites, such as BillSaver.com, or credit card information sites, such as CardRatings.com (Figure 5-64). Additionally, before you accept a credit card offer, you may want to learn more about the advantages and disadvantages of using credit cards; learn how to protect yourself from credit card fraud; and learn how to budget your credit card spending. Online credit card education is provided by many credit card issuers; for example, banks Wells Fargo and Citibank include student financial services and credit education Web pages at their sites.

Protecting your credit also involves being aware of your credit history, which is maintained by credit reporting agencies, and knowing what to do if you are a victim of credit card fraud or identity theft. The three major U.S. consumer credit reporting agencies — TransUnion, Experian, and Equifax — provide options for reviewing your credit reports online. By quickly and conveniently reviewing your credit reports online, you easily can detect an error or an instance of possible fraud and take immediate action to have the error corrected or the fraud uncovered. If you are a victim of credit card fraud or identity theft, the U.S. Federal Trade Commission (FTC) Web site provides useful information on steps you should take to protect yourself and correct your credit records.

@ISSUE   Coupon Web Sites

When considering finances and saving money, couponing comes to mind. Printed coupons, available in weekly flyers from the grocery store or mailed as promotions, have been widely used since the early 1900s when the Post cereal company started printing them on cereal boxes. In the digital age, manufacturer or store coupons can be e-mailed to customers or made available on the vendor's Web site.

The use of electronic coupons is so prevalent that many sites exist for the sole purpose of sharing coupons or links to coupons. In order to take advantage of the coupons, sometimes you need to print a copy to bring to a brick-and-mortar store, or copy a code to enter when shopping online.

Examples of couponing sites include Coupons.com, CouponMom.com (Figure 5-65), and RetailMeNot.

For more information about coupon Web sites, visit the Book Companion Site Web page at **www.cengagebrain.com**. Under the Chapter 5 @Issue links, click a link below Coupons.

Figure 5-65   Couponing Web sites enable users to search for, review, print, and use coupons for groceries, clothes, and more.

Investing Online

The availability of quick access to online investment information and the proliferation of investment-oriented Web sites empower people to handle or receive advice on their own stock portfolios and other investments. Online sources such as MarketWatch (Figure 5-66), Hoover's, CNNMoney, Morningstar, MSN Money, and The Motley Fool (Figure 5-66) provide investors with current market information and stock quotes. Online brokers, such as E*TRADE and Charles Schwab, offer a variety of investment accounts, some with low start-up costs and small per-trade transaction fees. Most online brokers also offer premium financial services, including financial planning and market research.

Increasingly, online brokers are offering a full line of financial services, including e-bill presentment and payment from your investment account. If you are considering investing online, Web sites such as the Investing Online Resource Center (IORC) can help by providing tips on how to select an online broker and how to open an online account. The IORC Web site also provides an online investing simulation in which you can practice managing an investment account before you actually open one. Many investor information Web sites also offer a portfolio feature that you can use to create a mock portfolio and practice managing it over time.

Figure 5-66 Online investment sites enable people to manage their own stock portfolios, use online brokers, and research investments.

Education Tools

Today, ubiquitous Internet access is the leading technology behind an explosion in the popularity of online education. **Web-based learning**, also called **online learning** or **distance learning**, involves the delivery of educational material over the Internet to users, who view and use the material using a Web browser.

You can find Web-based learning opportunities in virtually every educational venue, from K–12 schools to adult continuing education at colleges and universities. Online adult professional development courses and employee training courses abound. Additionally, you can enjoy noncredit online courses on almost any topic for your personal enrichment or just for fun. In this section, you will learn how the Internet and Web-based learning are changing the face of K–12 schools, colleges, and universities; employee training and professional development; and adult continuing education.

K–12 and University Students

Web-based learning programs open up a broad vista of educational opportunities for K–12 and university students. Rural schools with limited enrollment and resources can offer their students more curriculum choices through Web-based learning. Web-based learning courses are available 24/7; you can participate from any place that has an Internet connection, and courses can be self-paced. Today, hundreds of colleges and universities offer online courses in which students interact with their instructors and other students through e-mail, chat rooms, blogs, podcasts, and online discussion groups. Students can even take exams online. Web-based learning allows colleges and universities to offer working adults courses that are flexible enough to fit into their busy lives, even allowing them to complete degree programs without setting foot on campus.

The same tools used to teach online classes also are being used to enhance the regular curriculum at all levels of education. Companies such as Blackboard (Figure 5-67) offer course management systems. Publishing companies often work with Blackboard and other similar companies to provide online content, testing, and games that correspond with textbook content.

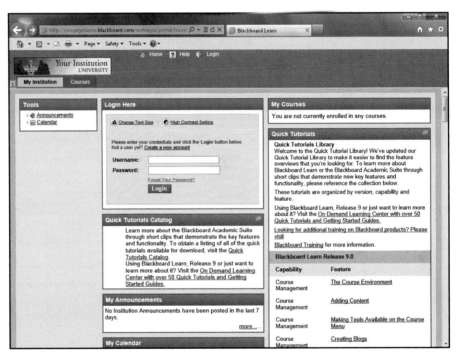

Figure 5-67 Online course management systems are used to manage virtual classes and enhance learning.

Online Employee Training and Professional Development

Diverse business, nonprofit, and government organizations use Web-based learning to deliver employee training programs. Using Internet, satellite, and video conferencing technologies, these organizations save millions of training dollars each year by reducing travel costs, keeping their employees on the job, reducing the need for trainers and centralized training facilities, and promoting customer service. For example, General Motors has used Web-based learning to introduce new vehicle models to auto dealership salespeople, and to train dealership mechanics on how to repair them. By delivering new vehicle training online, General Motors avoided the expenses involved in sending thousands of sales and service trainers to auto dealerships around the country each new model year. Additionally, General Motors provides Web-based drivers training for its large commercial van customers. The U.S. Army offers soldiers the chance to enroll in online courses and degree programs from colleges and universities around the country through the

Army's GoArmyEd Web-based learning program. The GoArmyEd program is designed to encourage new enlistments and keep enlistees in the service longer — thus reducing recruitment and turnover costs.

Busy accountants, doctors, and other professionals also are going online to meet their professions' continuing education requirements. For example, e-businesses such as Checkpoint Learning (Figure 5-68) offer online continuing professional education (CPE) courses for accounting and financial professionals, who are required by state licensing agencies to take several courses each year. Doctors and other health professionals can log on to the Medscape CME page (Figure 5-68) and take online courses to complete their continuing medical education (CME/CE) requirements.

Education
To review the education Web sites discussed in this section, visit the Book Companion Site Web page at **www.cengagebrain.com**. Under the Chapter 5 @Source links, click a link below Education.

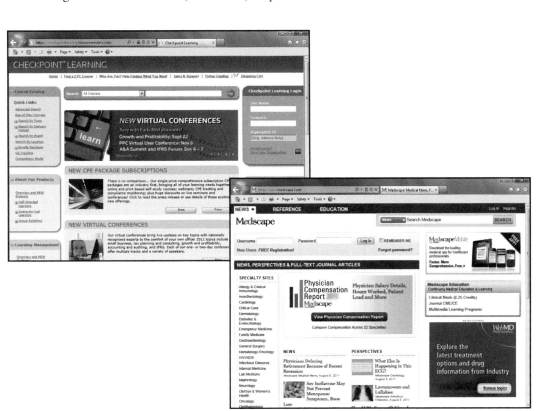

Figure 5-68 Online employee training and professional development sites enable users to keep up with their education.

Technical certification enhances career opportunities for information technology (IT) professionals and helps keep their skills up to date in today's highly dynamic technological environment. IT professionals can use online courses provided by colleges, universities, and training companies, such as SkillSoft and New Horizons (Figure 5-69 on the next page), to prepare for CompTIA A+ and Network+ certification, the Microsoft Certified Systems Engineer (MCSE) certification, the Cisco Certified Network Associate (CCNA) certification, and other technical certification examinations.

Figure 5-69　Online professional development and professional certification sites enable users to take classes and earn certifications.

Adult Continuing Education Web Sites

Learning for personal growth, lifestyle enrichment, and just plain fun is easy by participating in online courses. Many colleges and universities, such as the University of California, Berkeley, offer a variety of credit and noncredit courses online. Additionally, e-businesses such as lynda.com and Universal Class offer online courses on a wide range of topics, from ecological gardening to making salsa to getting your music compositions recorded and published. Fees for online courses at e-business Web sites such as these can range from free for short, noninteractive courses to around $100 for interactive, instructor-led courses. Fees for college- and university-sponsored online continuing adult education courses vary by the length of the course and whether you earn college credit.

Shopping Web Sites

@SOURCE

Shopping
To review the shopping Web sites discussed in this section, visit the Book Companion Site Web page at **www. cengagebrain.com**. Under the Chapter 5 @Source links, click a link below Shopping.

You can purchase, sell, auction, and bid on any type of item or service online: electronics, specialty foods, vehicles, flowers, and customized clothing to name a few. Online stores do not have to worry about renting storefronts, creating displays, or deciding what hours to run their business. Consumers around the world shop for products online more and more frequently for several reasons. For one, broadband Internet access allows consumers to view feature-rich Web stores, and permits online inquiries and transactions to be processed quickly. Online store sites are designed with shoppers' needs in mind and are easy to use. Additionally, shoppers enjoy the ability to compare products online without making trips to one or more brick-and-mortar stores. Finally, as consumers make frequent online purchases, they increasingly trust the online purchasing process and are satisfied with the results.

The Online Consumer Marketspace

The term **marketspace** is sometimes used to distinguish the virtual location in which e-business is conducted — such as an online bookstore — from the conventional physical marketplaces in which business takes place — such as the bookstore in the local mall. In the United States, consumers use the Web to purchase goods and services from pure-play or Internet-only e-retailers, such as Amazon.com, and brick-and-click retailers, such as Best Buy, Wal-Mart, and J.Crew. As you learned in Chapter 3, if you want to buy consumer electronics, such as an MP3 player or a digital camera, you can use a shopping bot or shopping aggregator to compare features and prices at multiple online retailers, avoiding traffic hassles and long checkout lines at brick-and-mortar stores. Additionally, online retailers may offer discounted prices, free shipping, and other incentives that could make your consumer electronics purchase a real bargain.

Some consumers shop online to compare product features and prices, and then buy the products at brick-and-mortar locations. Using the Internet and the Web to gather product information before making a buying decision leads to a power shift away from sellers and toward buyers. One example is the purchase of new or used cars and trucks. Online shoppers in the market for a new or used vehicle can use third-party automotive Web sites, such as Edmunds.com, Autobytel.com, Kelley Blue Book, and CARFAX, to get information on factory and dealer pricing, trade-in values, financing deals, auto owner-ship histories, and other factors that go into buying a new or used vehicle. Armed with this kind of information, vehicle buyers then are better able to negotiate with sellers at the point of sale — either online or at a dealership.

Auction, Discount, and C2C Web Sites

Online auction Web sites attract millions of individuals with something to sell or a desire to buy. Computer equipment, hand-crafted jewelry, quilts, collectible items, autos, books, and numerous other items can be found on sites that specialize in overstocked items, such as O.co (Figure 5-70 on the next page), on online auction sites, such as uBid.com and eBay (Figure 5-70), or on consumer-to-consumer sites such as Etsy. In addition to major auction Web sites, some companies such as Dell Auction conduct online auctions of refurbished, marked-down, and closeout computer equipment at their own Web sites. Other companies provide B2B auction sites where business buyers and sellers can use the online auction model to buy and sell equipment and other products.

@SOURCE

Auction Fraud
To learn more about reducing the risk of auction fraud, visit the Book Companion Site Web page at **www. cengagebrain.com**. Under the Chapter 5 @Source links, click the OnGuard Online: Internet Auctions link below Shopping.

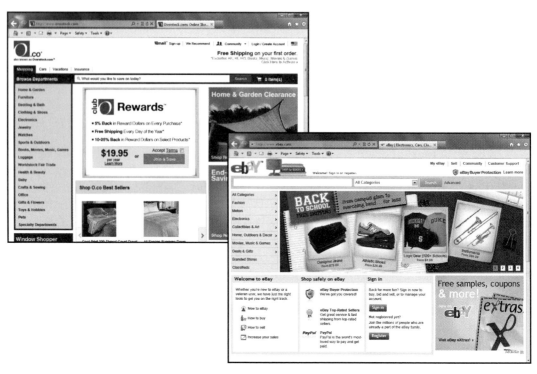

Figure 5-70　Online discount and auction sites are popular ways to shop online.

Even at different online auction sites, the general processes for selling and buying items are similar. First, you register at the Web site as a seller, a buyer, or both. As a seller, you post the items you want to sell and indicate the specific time period during which each item is available for purchase. Sellers also can set a **reserve price**, which is the lowest price at which a seller is obligated or willing to sell an item. As a buyer, you search the Web site for an item you want to buy. When you find the item, you indicate how much you are willing to pay for it, an amount called a **bid**. At the end of the specified time frame, the item is sold to the highest bidder. Finally, the seller and buyer arrange for payment and shipping.

The main advantages of buying items at an online auction include access to a variety of items, some of which may be hard to find elsewhere, and the opportunity to get products at lower prices. Unfortunately, a darker side to online auctions also exists. A 2008 report by the Internet Crime Complaint Center (IC3) indicates auction fraud — including nonpayment and nondelivery of merchandise — accounted for almost 26 percent of all IC3 complaints. Most reputable auction sites provide tips for their prospective sellers and buyers on how to reduce the risk of auction fraud; the OnGuard Online Web site also provides helpful tips on reducing this risk.

Online Gaming Web Sites

While early online gamers were likely to be males ages 15 through 30 involved in role-playing games, today, online gaming appeals to a much wider group of participants, including young women and older adults of both genders. You can play card games, arcade games, and word games, or you can log on to an online game room and join a friend — from across town or across the world — in playing a board or tile game. You can test your gaming skills by competing with other players in online game tournaments, or you can experience an exciting alternative universe by participating in a strategy or role-playing game.

@SOURCE

Online Gaming
To review the online gaming Web sites discussed in this section, visit the Book Companion Site Web page at **www. cengagebrain.com**. Under the Chapter 5 @Source links, click a link below Online Gaming.

Many online games are free. For example, some nongaming Web sites offer free word or trivia games as an incentive for viewers to return to their sites frequently, or include advertisements for their products or sell ads to other companies to generate revenue. Gaming portals, such as Yahoo! Games and MSN Games, offer free online and downloadable games for players who register at their sites. A number of sites directed toward children, such as PBS Kids and Webkinz, offer online games. Some online games are subscription based; gamers buy the software and install it on their computers and then pay a subscription fee for premium features or to play online with other players. Popular strategy or role-playing games, often called **massively multiplayer online games (MMOGs)**, in which thousands of players from around the world assume personas and play either on a turn-by-turn basis or in real time, are subscription-based games. A **virtual world**, such as Second Life, in which players assume a persona that lives in an alternate virtual existence, is another type of role-playing game. Figure 5-71 provides a sample of various types of online games.

Online Games

Category	Name
Arcade games	Zuma, Pebble Dash, Bubble Town
Board and tile games	Backgammon, Bingo, Chess, Checkers, Dominoes
Casino games	Blackjack, Poker, Baccarat, Roulette, Slots
Children's games	Undersea Underworld, Bionicle, Slapshot Mania, Candy Shot
Classic card games	Solitaire, Bridge, Canasta, Cribbage, Gin, Hearts, Spades
Sports games	Fantasy Auto Racing, Football, Golf, Baseball, Basketball
Strategy and role-playing games: MMOGs and virtual worlds	The Sims, EverQuest, Star Wars Galaxies, Civilization, Asheron's Call
Word and trivia games	Crossword, Bookworm, Word Mojo, Scrabble

Figure 5-71 Types of online games.

According to the Pew Internet & American Life Project, 73 percent of teens and 38 percent of adults play online games. Of online gamers, more than 20 percent participate in role-playing or MMOG games or virtual worlds.

FACTS @HAND

@ISSUE

Online Gambling

Online gaming should be about fun — enjoying the challenge of the game and interacting with other players in multiplayer games. When it comes to online gambling, however, the stakes and consequences can be much higher than simply losing a game to a friend. As losses mount, online gambling can have a detrimental effect on the personal lives of gamblers.

Regardless of your personal opinions about gambling, gambling Web sites — offering everything from virtual poker to betting on college football games — already exist on the Web. At least 50 countries now authorize Internet gambling; however, an ongoing controversy in the United States rages about the legality of online gambling, and it might be illegal in your area. In the fall of 2006, the U.S. Congress passed legislation that made it illegal for financial institutions, such as banks or credit card companies, to transfer money to online gambling sites. In 2009, some members of the U.S. Congress made an effort to legalize online gambling in the United States. In 2010, New Jersey became the first state to legalize certain forms of online gambling. As of this writing, the status of the effort to legalize online gambling in the United States is unsettled; therefore, before considering participating in online gambling, you should research its current legality.

Many Internet analysts and social scientists are concerned about the addictive quality of online gambling, specifically because gambling on the Web makes gambling more convenient; provides access to children, who are not allowed to gamble legally; and is not regulated like other forms of legal gambling, and thus is more open to fraud.

Before you begin gambling online, you should consider the ethical, social, and financial ramifications for you and your family. For more information on gambling issues, visit the *Discovering the Internet, Fourth Edition* @Issue Book Companion Site Web page at **www.cengagebrain.com**, and then click a link below Chapter 5, Online Gambling.

Download and File-Sharing Web Sites

Downloading paid content, such as music files, software, stock photos, and so forth, is one of the most popular Internet activities. For example, music download Web sites, such as Apple iTunes, Rhapsody, and Kazaa (Figure 5-72), typically offer either subscription-based services or pay-per-song services, while software vendors offer all types of software downloads for which you pay a licensing fee. In addition to paid content sites, the Internet also has numerous sites where you can search for and download freeware or shareware programs, including games, utilities, and screen savers.

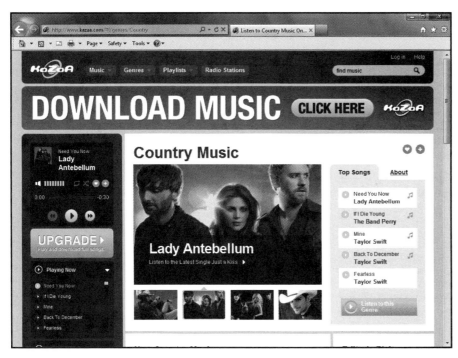

Figure 5-72 Music download sites offer subscription-based or pay-per-song services.

Transferring files between Internet-connected computers is another widely used and convenient activity. In Chapter 4, you learned how to transfer a file by attaching it to an e-mail message. Two other ways to transfer files over the Internet are by using FTP (File Transfer Protocol) or by using a peer-to-peer (P2P) file-sharing network. In this section, you will learn where to find freeware and shareware download sites, how to use FTP to download and upload files, and how P2P file-sharing networks are used.

Commercial file downloading might use HTTP (Hypertext Transfer Protocol), FTP (File Transfer Protocol), and other technologies specifically developed for file transmission over a network.

**FACTS
@HAND**

Download Web Sites

Freeware is software that the author allows you to download and use without charge; however, the software is protected by copyright law, meaning you can use it only in the ways permitted by the author, manufacturer, or copyright owner. For example, you cannot distribute it to someone else unless given permission to do so. **Shareware** is software that you can download and try out, but you are expected to pay for the software if you decide to use it on a permanent basis. You can search Web sites, such as Tucows, and CNET Download.com, for freeware or shareware screen savers, games, utilities, file compression programs, and more.

File Transfer Protocol (FTP)

As you learned in Chapter 1, FTP is an Internet standard that allows you to download or upload files to and from other computers connected to the Internet. You can use

FTP to view a directory of files located on a remote computer, called an **FTP site**, and then open or download a file. You also can upload a file to an FTP site.

To access an FTP site, you log on with a username and a password. Public FTP sites, such as those provided by government agencies, some colleges and universities, and other organizations, are called **anonymous FTP sites** because anyone can log on to these sites using "anonymous" as their username. As a courtesy to the site administrator, anonymous users often enter their e-mail addresses at the password prompt, although a password is not required for a public FTP site. Private FTP sites, such as those operated by a private company for its employees' use, restrict access to authorized users, who must enter a unique username and a unique password.

You can download or upload files using FTP by typing instructions using an FTP client program, using your Web browser, or using the Windows operating system's Document window or **Command Prompt window**.

An **FTP client**, such as SmartFTP (Figure 5-73) or WS_FTP Professional, is a program that offers an easy-to-use graphical user interface containing menu commands and toolbar shortcuts. FTP clients generally use an interface similar to other file management programs with which you already may be familiar, such as Windows Explorer. To upload or download files, you simply:

1. Start the FTP client. Select or enter the information for the FTP site to which you want to connect.

2. Enter your username and password, and connect to the site.

3. Specify the source location (where the file is stored) and the destination location (where the file is to be downloaded or uploaded).

4. Select a file or files.

5. Click a menu command or toolbar button to begin the download or upload process.

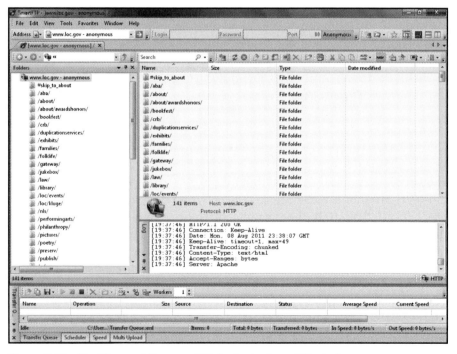

Figure 5-73 The Library of Congress FTP site in the SmartFTP window.

The FTP client automatically issues the necessary FTP commands to download or upload the selected file(s). To navigate to an FTP site using your Web browser, you type the FTP site's URL in the Address box in the same way in which you type a Web site's URL. FTP sites' URLs start with ftp://, to represent the File Transfer Protocol (FTP), instead of the http:// used for Web sites' URLs. The URL for an FTP site can include username and password information, or those can be prompted when necessary after the FTP site and folder have been opened.

The Command Prompt window included with the Windows operating system provides a nongraphical interface in which you can enter commands. To use FTP and the Command Prompt window, click the Run command on the Start menu to open the Run dialog box, and then enter the command, `ftp`. You then enter a series of commands to log on to the FTP site and download or upload your files.

<table>
<tr><td>You can add the Run command to the Windows 7 Start menu, if necessary, by right-clicking the taskbar and clicking Properties to open the Taskbar and Start Menu Properties dialog box. Click the Start Menu tab and click the Customize button. Click the Run command check box in the list of Start menu customization options and click the OK button. The Run command appears on the right side of the Start menu.</td><td>
FACTS @HAND</td></tr>
</table>

To Access the U.S. Census Bureau FTP Site

The following steps access the U.S. Census Bureau FTP site and view a PDF document using the Windows 7 Documents window. A PDF document is a document created using the Adobe Systems, Inc. Portable Document Format (.pdf). You must have the Adobe Reader® installed on your computer to view the PDF document. The Adobe Acrobat Reader is available as a free download from the Adobe Systems Inc. Web site.

After you view the PDF document, you then download a compressed file containing data that supports the text in the PDF file.

1

- Double-click the Documents short-cut folder icon on the desktop to open the Documents window.

- Click in a blank area of the Address box to select its contents.

- Type `ftp://ftp.census.gov/` in the Address box and press the ENTER key to connect to the Census Bureau FTP site (Figure 5-74).

Q&A | **What if I do not have a Documents shortcut icon on my desktop?**
You also can click Documents on the Start menu to open the Documents window.

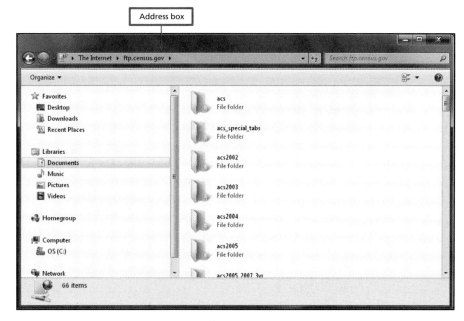

Figure 5-74

②

- Double-click the census_2010 folder icon to open the folder.

- Double-click the 03-Demographic_ Profile subfolder icon in the census_2010 folder to open the folder (Figure 5-75).

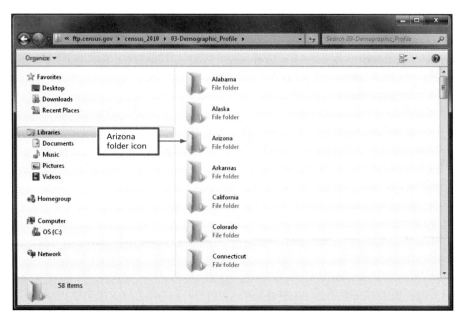

Figure 5-75

③

- Double-click the Arizona folder icon to open it (Figure 5-76).

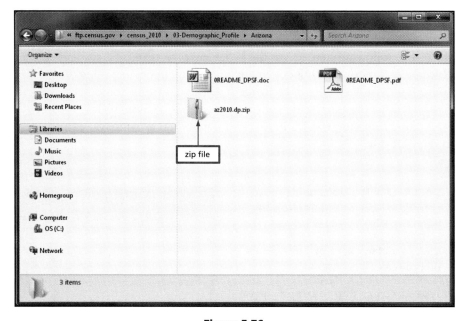

Figure 5-76

- Right-click the compressed file's file name ending in .zip to display the shortcut menu (Figure 5-77).

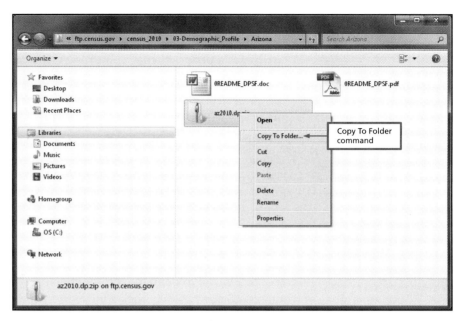

Figure 5-77

- Click the Copy To Folder command.

- Navigate to the local folder specified by your instructor and select it (Figure 5-78).

- Click the OK button to copy the zip file to your local folder.

- Close the Documents window.

Figure 5-78

A **compressed file** is a file that has been shrunk to a smaller size using a file compression utility, such as WinZip® or StuffIt®, or by using tools built into your operating system (Microsoft® Windows® 7, for example). A **file compression utility** is a program that compresses one or more files so that they require less storage space, and decompresses compressed files to restore them to their original sizes. Compressing a file often is referred to as **zipping a file**, while decompressing a file often is referred to as **unzipping a file**. To open and view or use a compressed file, such as the one you just downloaded from the U.S Census Bureau FTP site, you must decompress it using the file compression utility or your operating system's tools.

As shown in the previous steps, FTP sites use a directory structure of folders and subfolders. Depending on whether you log on to the site at the root folder or a subfolder, you might see a directory as a list of linked folder names or as a group of folder icons. You can click a linked folder name or double-click a folder icon to open a folder and view its contents. You can double-click a file icon to open the file at the site. Double-clicking some file icons, such as that for a compressed file, opens a dialog box that allows you to either open the file at the FTP site or download it.

P2P File-Sharing Networks

Another way to share or transfer files is over a peer-to-peer (P2P) file-sharing network. A **peer-to-peer (P2P) file-sharing network** allows files to be transferred between individual personal computers located on the same local area network (LAN) or between individual personal computers connected to the Internet. P2P file-sharing networks exploded in popularity as a means for individuals to share music, video, and other files stored on their personal computers. Unfortunately, many users of these P2P file-sharing networks might be sharing material — music, movies, and software — that is protected by U.S. copyright law. In fact, the music and movie industries, through the Recording Industry Association of America (RIAA) and the Motion Picture Association of America (MPAA), are working to stop the piracy of copyrighted material over P2P file-sharing networks.

Responsible Internet Access

Many workers assume that no one gets hurt if they spend time on the Internet for personal reasons while at work, and some companies allow moderate personal use of company computers. However, **cyberslacking**, or the excessive use of the Internet and the Web for personal use at work, can result in lost worker productivity and reduced IT network capacity. For example, downloading music and video files eats away at a company's expensive Internet access bandwidth, slowing down legitimate business activities. Sending and receiving personal e-mail and downloading files can expose a company's network to viruses and other security breaches. Viewing pornography sites or hate sites at work creates a hostile work environment and increases a company's liability for expensive and embarrassing lawsuits.

Increasingly, companies are protecting themselves from cyberslacking in several ways, including:

- Formulating clear Internet use policies
- Educating employees about Internet use policies, and then following through with appropriate action when an employee violates those policies
- Controlling which employees have Internet access
- Installing monitoring software that provides information on individual employees' Internet activities
- Installing filtering software that blocks access to nonbusiness sites and filters e-mail

What should you do to access the Internet at work responsibly? Carefully read and understand your company's Internet access policies and follow them. When in doubt, ask your supervisor for clarification on the policies. Resist the urge to shop, chat, play online games, send personal e-mail, visit social media sites, or send instant messages to friends during work hours, unless your company permits these kinds of activities. Remember that downloading copyrighted music, videos, and software — either at work or at home — without paying for the downloaded material is piracy and a violation of U.S. copyright law.

Music and video file sharing, while popular, are not the only uses of P2P networks. Commercial applications of P2P file-sharing networks include sharing product information among several thousand employees and researchers, and distributing training materials to employees. Many Internet analysts expect more organizations to use P2P technologies in the future to distribute network processes to individual users.

Chapter Review

Portals for every interest and need are available online, including general consumer portals, personal or horizontal portals, hyperlocal portals, vertical portals that focus on more narrow interests, and corporate portals.

Internet users go online to get news, weather, sports, and traffic information from news-oriented Web sites because these sites share five primary characteristics: availability, immediacy, interactivity, customizability, and connectivity. Streaming media is audio and video transmitted continuously from a Web server to your browser.

Online dictionaries, encyclopedias, reference desks, and trip planners provide you with convenient 24/7 access to information on specific topics, fast facts, word definitions, and driving directions. Internet users, including more and more seniors, are going online to find health, diet, and fitness information; enjoy entertainment information; practice their hobbies; look for jobs; make new friends; trace their family tree; and many other activities.

Managing your personal finances with online tools, such as online banking and bill payment, is fast, easy, and convenient. Web-based financial calculators help you determine how much you can afford to spend and estimate a monthly mortgage or auto payment.

Millions of people around the world are taking advantage of Web-based learning opportunities made possible by the Internet and the Web. K–12 schools and universities, employers, and professionals are embracing Web-based learning.

Consumers shop online because of the availability of Internet access, the design of online stores, greater trust in the online purchasing process, and increasing satisfaction with their shopping results. You can play card games, board games, casino games, word games, trivia games, arcade games, and strategy or role-playing games online — either alone, with a friend, or with thousands of other players.

Downloading paid content, such as music files, is a popular Internet activity. You also can download software from vendors' Web sites, and several popular Web sites offer freeware and shareware software downloads. You can use FTP to download and upload files. Another way to transfer files is over a P2P file-sharing network, where files can be transferred from one computer to another over a local area network (LAN) or the Internet.

After reading this chapter, you should know each of these Key Terms.

anonymous FTP sites (312)
B2B exchange (259)
bid (308)
bill payment service (300)
bill presentment (300)
brick-and-click businesses (299)
brick-and-mortar business (299)
Command Prompt window (312)
compressed file (316)
corporate portals (265)
cyberslacking (317)
distance learning (303)
e-bills (300)
enterprise information portals (EIPs) (265)
file compression utility (316)
freeware (311)
FTP client (312)
FTP site (312)
general consumer portals (258)
horizontal portals (258)

hyperlocal portals (259)
industry portals (259)
marketspace (307)
massively multiplayer online games
    (MMOGs) (309)
online learning (303)
peer-to-peer (P2P) file-sharing network (316)
personal portals (258)
reserve price (308)
shareware (311)
sticky Web site (267)
streaming media (272)
unzipping a file (316)
vertical portals (259)
virtual world (309)
vortals (259)
Web-based learning (303)
wildcard searches (278)
zipping a file (316)

Complete the Test Your Knowledge exercises to solidify what you have learned in the chapter.

True or False

Mark T for True and F for False. (Answers are found on page numbers in parentheses.)

____ 1. A Web site that viewers visit often and browse for longer periods of time is called a sticky Web site. (267)

____ 2. Many news-oriented Web sites provide the ability to customize content, which means they can display information tailored to the user's locality and interests. (268)

____ 3. A hyperlocal portal provides general information on global news, entertainment, and other topics. (259)

____ 4. All health information on the Web has been evaluated and certified as accurate by health care professionals. (290)

____ 5. An MMOG is a type of online trivia game. (309)

____ 6. Decompressing a file is often referred to as zipping a file. (316)

____ 7. A Command Prompt window, such as SmartFTP or WS_FTP Professional, offers an easy-to-use graphical user interface containing FTP commands and toolbar shortcuts. (312)

____ 8. A brick-and-mortar location is one that offers both an online store and a physical location, such as in a mall. (299)

___ 9. The term, marketspace, is used to distinguish the virtual location in which e-business is conducted from the conventional physical marketplaces in which business takes place. (307)

___10. Software you can download and use for free on a permanent basis is called shareware. (311)

Multiple Choice

Select the best answer. (Answers are found on page numbers in parentheses.)

1. File-sharing networks that allow users to transfer files between individual personal computers located on the same LAN or between Internet-connected individual computers are called _____ networks. (316)

    a. FTP

    b. P2P

    c. C2C

    d. NPR

2. A _____ portal can provide employee or client access, and can be used to manage a company's human resources or accounting activities. (265)

    a. corporate

    b. horizontal

    c. vertical

    d. customer

3. Which of the following is true about online gambling? (310)

    a. It is illegal in the United States.

    b. It is less open to fraud than other types of gambling.

    c. It is legal for banks to transfer money to online gaming sites.

    d. It is legal in more than 50 countries.

4. _____ is an example of a Web site where you are likely to find financial calculators. (301)

    a. PASS Online

    b. MFG.com

    c. CardRatings.com

    d. Merriam-Webster Online

5. FTP stands for _____. (312)

    a. File Transfer Protocol

    b. Free Transfer Portal

    c. Full Torrent Protocol

    d. Forward Telephone Packet

6. A reserve price is often used with _____. (308)

   a. consumer-to-consumer sales

   b. discount shopping

   c. brick-and-click sites

   d. online auction sites

7. _____ is an example of a company that provides online course management tools. (304)

   a. eSchool

   b. Blackboard

   c. Peterson's

   d. iTools

8. When evaluating a health care Web site, if it includes the _____ symbol, it is likely a credible source for general health information. (290)

   a. CAPHIS

   b. HONcode

   c. URAC

   d. either b or c

9. A public FTP site also is called a(n) _____. (312)

   a. anonymous FTP site

   b. open FTP site

   c. nameless FTP site

   d. unknown FTP site

10. Audio and video content transmitted continuously from a Web server to a Web browser is called _____ media. (272)

    a. downloaded

    b. virtual

    c. freeware

    d. streaming

Test your knowledge of chapter content and key terms.

LEARN IT ONLINE

Instructions: To complete the following exercises, please visit **www.cengagebrain.com**. On the CengageBrain home page, enter the book title *Discovering the Internet* and then click the Find button. On the product page for this book, click the Access Now button below the Study Tools heading. On the Book Companion Site Web page, click the drop-down menu, select Chapter 5, and then click the link for the desired exercise.

Chapter Reinforcement TF, MC, and SA

A series of true/false, multiple-choice, and short-answer questions that test your knowledge of the chapter content.

Flash Cards

An interactive learning environment where you identify chapter key terms associated with displayed definitions.

Practice Test

A series of multiple-choice questions that test your knowledge of chapter content and key terms.

Who Wants To Be a Computer Genius?

An interactive game that challenges your knowledge of chapter content in the style of a television quiz show.

Wheel of Terms

An interactive game that challenges your knowledge of chapter key terms in the style of the television show, *Wheel of Fortune*.

Crossword Puzzle Challenge

A crossword puzzle that challenges your knowledge of the key terms presented in the chapter.

EXERCISES

Use the Exercises to gain hands-on experience working with the Internet and the Web.

1 | Identifying Vertical Portals

1. Use the Internet Explorer Search box and the search engines of your choice to search for at least one example of a vertical portal focused on each of the following interests:

   a. chess

   b. gardening

   c. teaching

   d. parenting

   e. running

2. Write a brief paragraph giving the URL for each example and a description of the portal's contents.

2 | Customizing a Personal Portal

1. Visit the Discovering the Internet, Fourth Edition Chapter 5 Exercises Web page at **www.cengagebrain.com** and click Yahoo! below Exercise 2.

2. On the Yahoo! home page, click the My Yahoo! link to view preference settings.

3. Click the Sign In link and sign in to My Yahoo! using the Yahoo! ID and password you created in Chapter 4.

4. Use links on the My Yahoo! page to change content, appearance, location, and other options for your personal My Yahoo! page. Sign out from your My Yahoo! page when finished.

3 | Customizing a News-Oriented Web Site

1. Visit the Discovering the Internet, Fourth Edition Chapter 5 Exercises Web page at **www.cengagebrain.com** and click MSNBC below Exercise 3.

2. Change the settings for the Local News and Weather box for your ZIP code, and change the number of items listed in the Local News and Weather box. (*Hint*: Click

the change link on the Local News and Weather box header to change the ZIP code, and click the Show option links to change the number of items shown in the box.)

3. Explore expanding, collapsing, and moving other category boxes, such as Politics, Entertainment, or Travel, to suit your preferences.

4 | Using Online Resources to Research a Report Topic

1. Visit the Discovering the Internet, Fourth Edition Chapter 5 Exercises Web page at **www.cengagebrain.com** and click any of the online encyclopedia and reference desk links below Exercise 4 to find answers to the following questions:

   a. Where is Argentina located? Who are its geographical neighbors? Where can you find a map of Argentina and its geographical neighbors? What are its major cities and towns?

   b. List three major events in Argentina's history.

   c. What is the current population of Argentina?

   d. What is the basis of Argentina's economy?

2. Write a short, one- or two-page report describing the geography, history, population, and economy of Argentina. Follow the directions provided by your instructor on how to cite your online sources.

5 | Planning an Automobile Trip Using Online Resources

1. Visit the Discovering the Internet, Fourth Edition Chapter 5 Exercises Web page at **www.cengagebrain.com** and click the links below Exercise 5 to plan a road trip or get directions.

2. Plan a road trip from your location to Albany, New York. If you do not live in North America, plan a trip from Boise, Idaho, to Vancouver, British Columbia. Select options to include scenic routes and references to camping locations along the way, if available.

3. Use the personal itinerary created by the trip planner to answer the following questions:

   a. How many miles will you drive?

   b. What is the total driving time to arrive at the destination?

4. Print the itinerary page.

5. Plan the trip a second time, but do not select scenic routes. Use the personal itinerary to compare the new itinerary's miles and hours driven with the original itinerary.

6. Print the new itinerary page.

6 | Evaluating the Credibility of Online Health Information

1. Visit the Discovering the Internet, Fourth Edition Chapter 5 Exercises Web page at **www.cengagebrain.com** and click the URAC: Consumers link below Exercise 6.

2. Use the navigational links and the search feature at the URAC Web site to answer the following questions:

   a. What is URAC's mission and how is the organization structured?

   b. What services does URAC provide?

   c. Which of the following health-oriented Web sites are accredited by URAC: Medscape, WebMD, or MDAdvice.com? (*Hint*: Use the Accreditation Directory link in the Consumer Resource Center to search for Web site accreditation.)

3. Visit the Discovering the Internet, Fourth Edition Chapter 5 Exercises Web page at **www.cengagebrain.com** and click the HON link below Exercise 6.

4. Use the information, search feature, and navigational links at the Health On the Net Foundation (HON) Web site to answer the following questions:

   a. Where is HON located and what is its mission?

   b. What global organization is affiliated with HON?

   c. Which of the following health-oriented Web sites are accredited by HON: KidsHealth, WebMD, MayoClinic.com, or DrWeil.com? (*Hint*: Click the Patient/ Individual link on the HON home page; then click the Trustworthy medical information link under the HONsearch icon to search for accredited Web sites.)

5. Visit the Discovering the Internet, Fourth Edition Chapter 5 Exercises Web page at **www.cengagebrain.com** and click the CAPHIS link below Exercise 6.

6. Follow various navigational links to identify at least five Web sites that meet the CAPHIS standards.

7 | Exploring Special-Interest Web Sites

1. Visit the Discovering the Internet, Fourth Edition Chapter 5 Exercises Web page at **www.cengagebrain.com** and click the Monster link below Exercise 7.

   a. Point to the Advice link at the top of the page.

   b. Click the Resumes & Letters link and review tips on writing a résumé.

2. Visit the Discovering the Internet, Fourth Edition Chapter 5 Exercises Web page at **www.cengagebrain.com** and click the RootsWeb link below Exercise 7.

   a. Enter your last name in the Search RootsWeb.com Last Name text box and click Search. Use the Search Results page to respond to the following:

   • List the featured databases that contain your last name.

   • List at least three vital records indexes that contain your last name.

   • List two additional Web site searches that include your last name.

3. Visit the Discovering the Internet, Fourth Edition Chapter 5 Exercises Web page at **www.cengagebrain.com** and click Peterson's below Exercise 7.

   a. Use the information on the Peterson's home page and the navigational links to learn which online practice tests are available for graduate admissions.

   b. Create a list of the available tests.

8 | Managing Your Personal Finances Online

1. Visit the Discovering the Internet, Fourth Edition Chapter 5 Exercises Web page at **www.cengagebrain.com** and click Bankrate.com below Exercise 8.

2. In the Calculators area, use Mortgage and Auto Calculators to answer the following questions based on your own personal data, whether real or fictitious:

   a. How much can you afford to spend on a car?

   b. How much can you afford to spend on a home?

3. Visit the Discovering the Internet, Fourth Edition Chapter 5 Exercises Web page at **www.cengagebrain.com** and click FTC: Identify Theft below Exercise 8.

   a. Click the Identity Theft link. Using the information and links on the Identity Theft home page:

      • Test your knowledge about identity theft by taking an online quiz, if one is available.

      • Review what you should do if you think you are a victim of identity theft.

4. Visit the Discovering the Internet, Fourth Edition Chapter 5 Exercises Web page at **www.cengagebrain.com** and click IORC below Exercise 8.

   a. Click the Online Trading graphic link and then complete the Find Out What It's Like To Trade Online simulation. Using the information in the simulation, answer the following questions:

      • What are market orders?

      • What are limit orders?

9 | Shopping for an E-Reader

1. Visit the Discovering the Internet, Fourth Edition Chapter 5 Exercises Web page at **www.cengagebrain.com** and click links below Exercise 9 to shop for a new or used e-reader (choose one brand, such as the Amazon Kindle or Sony Reader, for example) priced under $200.

2. Create a list of at least three available e-readers, including the online store or auction seller, manufacturer, model, features, and price. For auction site items, include the reserve price, if any, and the duration of the auction. Read the reviews of each e-reader. If visiting an auction site, read the reviews and ratings for the sellers as well.

10 | Downloading Files and File Sharing

1. Visit the Discovering the Internet, Fourth Edition Chapter 5 Exercises Web page at **www.cengagebrain.com**. Click the Tucows and CNET Download.com site links below Exercise 10 to locate a freeware screen saver program and download the file. If you are working in a computer lab or on a school computer, ask your instructor's permission before you download the file.

2. Visit the Discovering the Internet, Fourth Edition Chapter 5 Exercises Web page at **www.cengagebrain.com** and click the TechWeb: TechEncyclopedia link below Exercise 10. Search the TechWeb: TechEncyclopedia for information you can use to answer the following questions:

   a. What is cloud computing?

   b. What is a peer-to-peer network?

PHOTO CREDITS

Figure 5-1: © 2011 Microsoft

Figure 5-2: Copyright © 2011 Patch. All Rights Reserved

Figure 5-3: SOURCE: Kids.gov

Figure 5-4: © 2011 Microsoft

Figure 5-5: Copyright © 2010 State of California

Figure 5-6: © 1995 City of Austin, Texas. All Rights Reserved

Figure 5-7: U.S Department of Defense, U.S Department of Labor and U.S Department of Veterans Affairs

Figure 5-8: Copyright © 1995–2011 Farms.com, Ltd. All Rights Reserved

Figure 5-9: Copyright 2011 QuinStreet Inc. All Rights Reserved

Figure 5-10: © 2011 Suzy Said, LLC

Figure 5-11: © Drew Reece

Figure 5-12: U.S. Small Business Administration

Figure 5-13: SOURCE: IBM.com

Figure 5-14: © 2010 NAVTEQ All rights reserved

Figure 5-15: © 1996–2011 The Washington Post

Figure 5-16: ©2011, The Dallas Morning News, Inc. All Rights Reserved

Figure 5-17: © 2010 Cable News Network. Turner Broadcasting System, Inc.

Figure 5-18: © 2010 Cable News Network. Turner Broadcasting System, Inc.

Figure 5-19: © Google

Figure 5-20: © Google

Figure 5-21: © Google

Figure 5-22: Copyright © 2011 Hulu. All rights reserved

Figure 5-23: Copyright 2011 USA TODAY, a division of Gannett Co. Inc.

Figure 5-24: Copyright 2011 USA TODAY, a division of Gannett Co. Inc.

Figure 5-25: Copyright 2011 NPR

Figure 5-26: Copyright 2011 NPR

Figure 5-27a: Copyright © 2011 LexisNexis. All rights reserved

Figure 5-27b: SOURCE: Library of Congress

Figure 5-28: SOURCE: encyclopedia.com

Figure 5-29: SOURCE: encyclopedia.com

Figure 5-30: SOURCE: encyclopedia.com

Figure 5-31: SOURCE: encyclopedia.com

Figure 5-33: © 2011 Merriam-Webster, Incorporated

Figure 5-34: © 2011 Merriam-Webster, Incorporated

Figure 5-35: © 2011 Merriam-Webster, Incorporated

Figure 5-36: OneLook® Dictionary Search

Figure 5-37: OneLook® Dictionary Search

Figure 5-38: © Google

Figure 5-39: © Google

6 | Understanding Internet Technologies and Security

Introduction

The Internet and the Web include the networking technologies that make it possible to use Internet-based services. In Chapters 1 and 2, you were introduced to circuit switching, packet switching, the TCP and IP protocols, the Domain Name System (DNS), IP addresses, URLs, and other fundamental networking and Internet technologies. In this chapter, you will learn about local, metropolitan, and wide area networks and the devices that connect them; how IP addresses are structured; how the DNS server hierarchy resolves domain names to IP addresses; and how network service providers facilitate the exchange of data across the Internet backbones. You also will learn about wireless Web location-based services, how the Internet works with traditional telephony and conferencing technologies, and about network security threats and security technologies.

Objectives

After completing this chapter, you will be able to:

1. Discuss basic networking technologies

2. Describe the infrastructure of the Internet, including network service providers, the TCP/IP stack, IP addresses, and the Domain Name System (DNS)

3. Discuss GPS and identify wireless location-based services

4. Explain the convergence of the Internet with telephony and conferencing

5. Discuss internal and external network security threats, transactional risks, and virtual private networks

Networking Basics

To better understand Internet technologies, it is helpful to begin with basic networking technologies. As you have learned, a computer network connects two or more computers, printers, or other devices using cables or wireless media. A computer network makes it possible for users to share data, peripheral devices, and other network resources such as an Internet connection. Computer networks can be simple or complex, local or worldwide. A simple computer network for a small business or home office might have only two or three computers and a single printer, often connected by cable or, more and more frequently, using wireless transmission. A large, complex computer network can have thousands of computers in multiple worldwide locations communicating with each other using a combination of transmission media.

Local, Metropolitan, and Wide Area Networks

Modern networks can be categorized by the physical area they cover: a local area, a metropolitan area, or a wide area.

LOCAL AREA NETWORKS   As discussed in Chapter 1, a local area network (LAN) is a computer network supporting users in a small geographical area, such as a home, an office, a single building, or several buildings, such as on a college campus. Each computer or other device on a LAN is called a **node**; these nodes communicate with each other with cables or wireless media, such as radio waves. LANs are configured in one of two basic structures: peer-to-peer or client/server.

In Chapter 5, you learned about peer-to-peer (P2P) file-sharing networks that allow Internet-connected users to transfer files between individual computers. The term, peer-to-peer, also is used to describe the way in which computers and other devices are connected in a simple LAN. A **peer-to-peer LAN** consists of a small number of personal computers (generally 10 or fewer) linked together. One or more of the computers also might have a printer, a scanner, or an external storage device attached to it (Figure 6-1). To connect to the peer-to-peer LAN, each computer must have a network interface card, or have networking capabilities built into the motherboard. A **network interface card (NIC)**, sometimes called a **network card**, is an internal expansion card that enables a computer or other device to access a network. Many computers come with Ethernet standards built in. You will learn more about Ethernet, a common network access method, later in the chapter. The computers on a peer-to-peer LAN can be connected to each other with one main cable. More commonly, however, the computers on a peer-to-peer LAN are connected at a common connection point on the network, using a hub. A **hub** is an inexpensive hardware device used to connect multiple nodes on the same network.

Users on a peer-to-peer LAN can access files stored on any of the networked computers and use any peripheral devices connected to the computers. For example, if your computer is part of a peer-to-peer LAN, you can open a file stored on another user's computer, save it to your hard drive, and then send the file to a printer attached to a different user's computer. Access to files and printers is controlled by setting options in the desktop operating system of the individual computers connected to the peer-to-peer LAN.

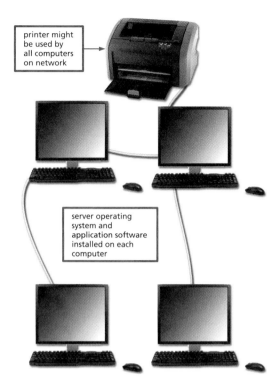

printer might be used by all computers on network

server operating system and application software installed on each computer

Figure 6-1 A small number of personal computers can be connected in a peer-to-peer LAN.

A peer-to-peer LAN is an attractive networking choice for a home office or for a small business or other organization with minimal computer networking needs because it is simple to configure and inexpensive to use. A peer-to-peer LAN is not a practical option to connect more than a few computers or devices, however. An organization thus may outgrow a peer-to-peer LAN quickly, as more computers need to be added or file- and device-sharing becomes more complex. Additionally, a peer-to-peer LAN lacks robust security options.

Most larger organizations use a client/server LAN. In Chapter 2, you were introduced to client/server computing, in which client computers request resources from servers. A **client/server network** consists of multiple personal computers or workstations (clients), one or more servers, and other devices such as printers (Figure 6-2, on the next page).

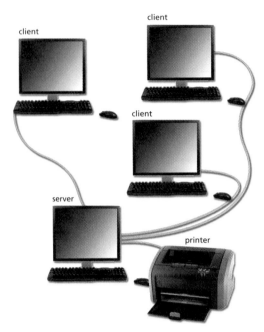

Figure 6-2   Multiple personal computers, servers, and printers can be connected on a client/server network.

The servers enable the clients to share data, file storage space, peripheral devices, and an Internet connection. A client/server LAN uses a **network operating system** to manage data storage, printer access, communications, Internet connections, security, and network administration. Examples of network operating systems include Microsoft® Windows® Server®, Mac OS® X, Novell® NetWare®, UNIX®, and Linux®. Figure 6-3 describes the different types of services provided by a network operating system.

Network Operating System Services

Services	Benefit
File	Permit the centralized storage of files on a file server, which can be accessed by any authorized user on the network. Maintain backup copies of critical files and protect against accidentally deleted files, damaged files, or files lost due to natural or man-made disasters. Files stored centrally on a file server are backed up more easily than files stored on individual computer hard drives.
Print	Enable users to share printers across a network. Replacing multiple individual printers with one or two high-speed networked printers can reduce equipment costs and increase productivity.
Mail	Manage the sending, receiving, routing, and storage of e-mail messages. E-mail is now a critical component of any organization's communications with employees, clients, and vendors. Enable e-mail communications to flow smoothly.
Communications	Allow authorized users to connect to the network when out of the office. Network users may need to keep up with their e-mail messages or work with their data files when they are not in the office. Communications services permit remote users to connect to the network.
Internet	Manage internal Web-based services, external Internet access, and other Internet-based services such as Web servers, Web browsers, and Internet-based e-mail. Organizations use Internet-based e-mail to send and receive messages from clients or vendors outside the organization. Many organizations also use internal Web pages to support internal business operations. External Web pages are used to sell products and services and provide customer support. Internet services help manage these critical operations.
Management	Enable network administrators to manage the health and operation of the network by determining the level of network activity, detecting and solving network hardware and software problems, and distributing software to users.

Figure 6-3   A network operating system provides a variety of services on a client/server network.

The ability of a client/server LAN to support shared data storage, provide network maintenance tools, and promote more efficient data backups offers advantages over a peer-to-peer LAN. Client/server network operating systems also offer extensive built-in security features. Setting up and maintaining a client/server network, however, can be more difficult and more expensive than setting up and maintaining a peer-to-peer LAN, and can require much more technical expertise to manage. For these reasons, a client/server LAN is the best networking choice for an organization with multiple users and the technical staff and financial resources to develop and maintain the LAN.

METROPOLITAN AREA NETWORKS   A **metropolitan area network (MAN)** connects clients and servers in a region that is larger than a single office or building (Figure 6-4). A MAN might connect multiple buildings across a city or multiple educational, research, or government facilities across a state. MANs generally are owned by a consortium of users or by a single network provider that sells high-speed network services to multiple users.

Figure 6-4   A metropolitan area network connects multiple buildings across a city or region.

WIDE AREA NETWORKS   A **wide area network (WAN)** — a network covering a very wide geographical area — can be a single network or multiple connected LANs located across the country or around the world (Figure 6-5, on the next page). For example, a business with branch offices in England, Australia, Canada, and the United States could use a WAN to connect the individual LANs in each branch office. Most WANs are corporately owned and private. The Internet, which is the world's largest WAN, is a public WAN.

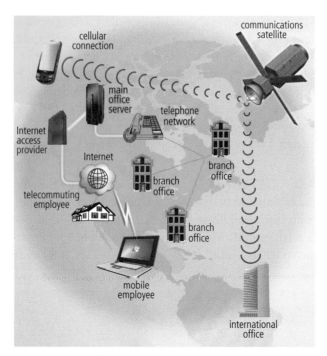

Figure 6-5 A wide area network can be a single network or can connect LANs around the world.

Network Topologies, Access Methods, and Transmission Media

A network's **physical topology** is the layout in which its computers, printers, and other devices are arranged. A network's **access method** specifies how data is transmitted from node to node across the network, and its **transmission media** are the communication media — physical or wireless — used to carry these transmissions. These three characteristics help define a network's **throughput** — that is, the amount of data that can be transferred from one node to another node in a specified amount of time.

PHYSICAL TOPOLOGIES Three basic LAN physical topologies are the bus, the ring, and the star (Figure 6-6). Today, however, many LANs use a hybrid physical topology that combines some elements of these three basic physical topologies.

Network Topologies

Topology	Description	Layout
Bus	Connects all nodes on a peer-to-peer LAN to a single connection, called a bus, shared by all nodes. Only one transmission is allowed at a time.	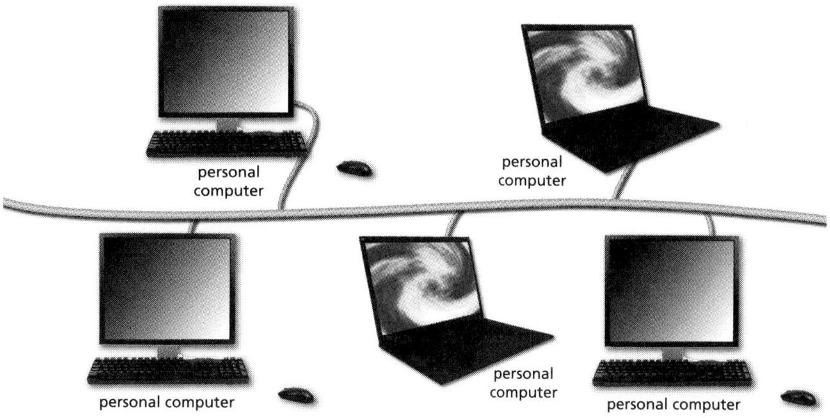
Ring	Connects each node to the next node using a single circle of cable. A transmission moves from node to node around the circle in a clockwise direction.	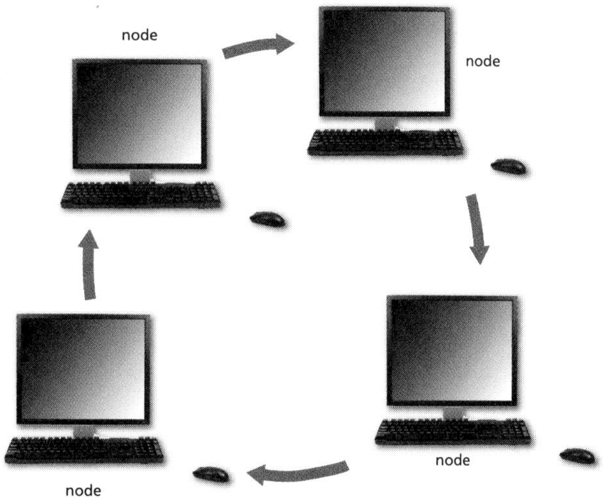
Star	Connects each node to a central device, such as a hub or switch. A transmission passes from the originating node, through the hub, directly to the destination node.	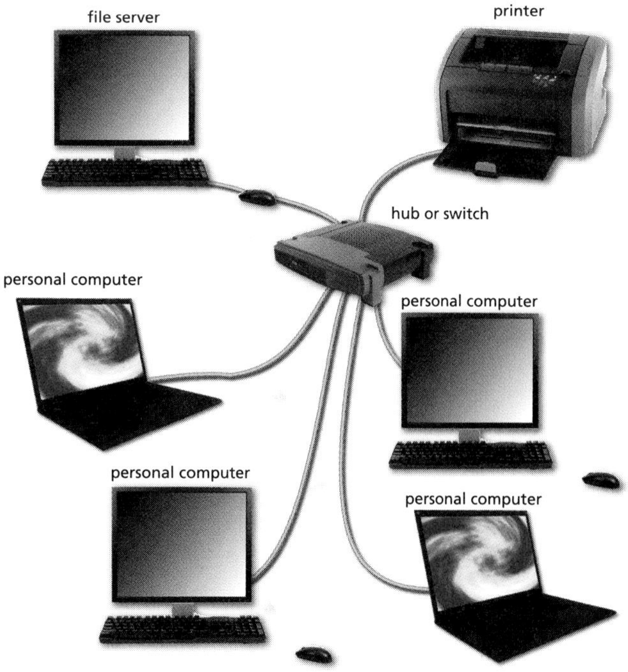

Figure 6-6 Overview of three LAN topologies.

Networking Standards
For information on organizations that set networking standards, visit **www. cengagebrain.com**. On the CengageBrain.com home page, enter the book title, *Discovering the Internet,* and then click the Find button. On the product page for this book, click the Access Now button below the Study Tools heading. On the Book Companion Site Web page, click the drop-down menu, select Chapter 6, and then click the @Source link. Click the links below Networking Standards.

ACCESS METHODS   A network's access method (sometimes called its **logical topology**) is the way in which data is transmitted between nodes. The two most common network access methods are Ethernet and token ring. **Ethernet** is a network access method in which a node that is attempting to transmit data first must determine if any other node is sending a transmission. If so, the node waits a short period of time and then checks again. When the network is available, the node sends its transmission. When two nodes check and then transmit at the same time, their two transmissions collide. Both nodes then stop transmitting, wait a random amount of time, check again, and then send their transmissions.

Networks using a bus or star topology commonly use the Ethernet access method, which can transmit data from 10 Mbps to 100 Mbps. High-speed networks might use Gigabit Ethernet, which can transmit data at 1, 10, 40, or 100 gigabits.

A **token ring** network uses a token-passing access method. A **token** is a small packet that moves clockwise in a circle from node to node. Only one free or unused token is available per network; a node cannot transmit until it has the token. When a node is ready to transmit, it intercepts the token, adds data and the destination node's address, and then sends the token on to the next node. The token moves from node to node around the network until it reaches the destination node, which intercepts the token and sends an acknowledgment back to the originating node. The originating node then reissues a free token and sends it to the next node. Because a node cannot transmit unless it has the token, two nodes cannot transmit at once, avoiding the transmission collisions that may occur on an Ethernet network. A token ring network generally is more expensive to install, however.

FACTS @HAND   Some researchers and IT analysts predict terabit (1,000-gigabit) Ethernet standards and technologies will be available by 2015.

TRANSMISSION MEDIA   As you learned in Chapter 1, data is transmitted over modern networks using a variety of physical media, such as cable, and wireless media, such as radio waves.

Examples of wireless media used in networks include microwave, infrared, and radio frequency. As you learned in Chapter 1, microwave transmissions are used to provide high-speed connectivity to the Internet where DSL and cable are not available. Microwaves transmitted by satellite also are used for WAN transmissions.

Infrared (IR) transmissions use infrared light-wave signals as a short-range transmission medium between computers or other devices equipped with infrared ports (Figure 6-7). IR transmissions are line-of-sight transmissions, meaning that the sending and receiving devices must be positioned or aligned so that the infrared signal's path is unobstructed.

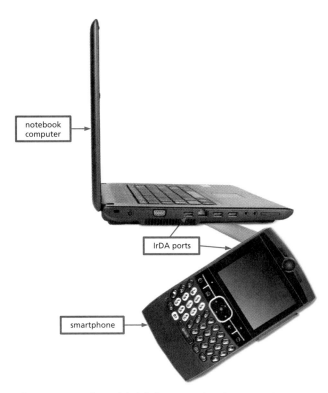

Figure 6-7 Infrared (IR) light-wave signals are used as a short-range transmission medium between computers or other devices equipped with an infrared (IrDA) port.

Radio frequency (RF) transmissions use broadcast radio waves to transmit data over short distances, such as between two handheld computers or between a notebook computer and a printer. RF transmissions require a transmitter for sending data and a receiver for receiving it. They are not line-of-sight transmissions. Some wireless devices send and receive RF transmissions using a **transceiver** — a single component that both sends and receives transmissions.

Bluetooth is an example of a short-range RF technology that sends and receives wireless transmissions between devices such as personal computers, personal digital assistants (PDAs), headsets (Figure 6-8), and smartphones or cell phones. A Bluetooth-enabled device contains a transceiver that sends and receives radio transmissions in the 2.4 GHz radio frequency band with a throughput of up to 1 Mbps. Bluetooth devices, which are designed for small **wireless personal area networks (WPANs)**, have a range of approximately 33 feet (10 meters) or less.

Figure 6-8 Bluetooth is a short-range RF technology that sends and receives wireless transmissions between devices such as a headset and a smartphone.

A **wireless LAN (WLAN)** uses a wireless medium — such as radio frequency transmissions — to connect computers, printers, and other devices. A wireless LAN in an office, for example, can use radio frequency transmissions to allow computers and printers equipped with wireless network interface cards (NICs) or built-in wireless capabilities to communicate. To ensure that the devices on the network communicate, wireless LANs follow IEEE 802.11 wireless networking standards, the latest iteration of which is IEEE 802.11n, which was published in 2009. The IEEE 802.11 family of wireless LAN standards specifies data transmission speeds and the radio frequencies over which the WLANs can communicate.

FACTS @HAND

802.11 was the original standard, but is now obsolete. Each subsequent version (starting with 802.11a in 1999) is an amendment to the standard, which is voted upon by members of the IEEE Standards Association. Each amendment includes not only updated standards, but also the original standards and the requirements of the previous amendments.

Some wired LANs also provide wireless access for notebooks, handheld computers, and other devices through wireless access points (Figure 6-9). As you learned in Chapter 1, a wireless access point is a hardware device with an antenna that sends and receives radio signals to and from a mobile device and a wired LAN.

In addition to wireless networks set up for home or office use, libraries, coffee shops, and other public spaces offer free access to their WLAN for customers or patrons. Laptops and mobile devices can recognize when they are near a wireless network, and either connect automatically or prompt the user for a password to access the WLAN.

@SOURCE

Wireless Networking
For more information on Bluetooth, Wi-Fi, IEEE 802.11 standards, and other wireless networking technologies, visit the Book Companion Site Web page at **www. cengagebrain.com**. Under the Chapter 6 @Source links, click a link below Wireless Networking.

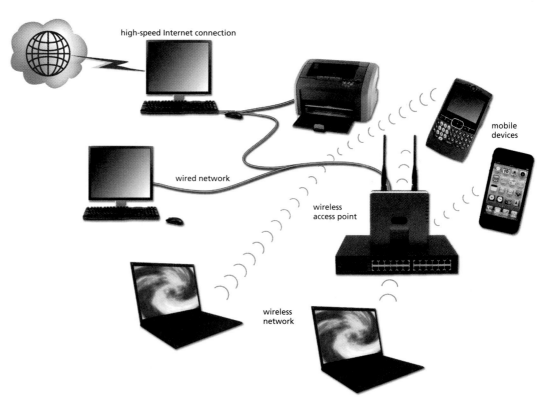

Figure 6-9 A wired LAN can also provide wireless access to computers, printers, and other wireless devices through a wireless access point.

Examples of physical media used in networks include coaxial, twisted-pair, and fiber-optic cable. Coaxial cable was the transmission medium of choice for many early networks and still is used for cable television connections. **Coaxial cable** (Figure 6-10), commonly called coax (KO-ax), consists of a single copper wire surrounded by insulating material, woven or braided metal, and a plastic outer covering. Coaxial cable can carry network traffic for long distances and is resistant to interference. It is not used in most modern networks, however, because it does not transmit data as fast as other media.

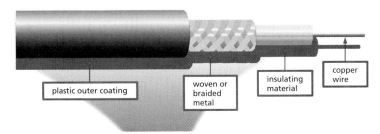

Figure 6-10   Coaxial cable can carry network traffic for long distances and is resistant to interference, but does not transmit data as fast as other media.

Twisted-pair cable (Figure 6-11) consists of insulated copper wires twisted around each other in pairs and then enclosed in a plastic covering. Twisted-pair cable originally was used for telephone transmissions; today it commonly is used as a LAN transmission medium because it is easier to install than other types of cable and can handle the faster transmission speeds required by modern networks.

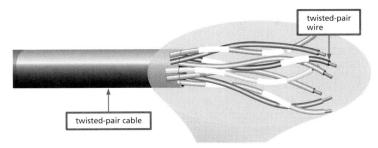

Figure 6-11   Twisted-pair cable is commonly used as a LAN transmission medium because it is easy to install and can handle faster transmission speeds.

Fiber-optic cable (Figure 6-12, on the next page), which contains glass fibers surrounded by a layer of glass cladding and a protective outer jacket, is used to carry voice, video, and data transmissions over very long distances. Because of its capacity and reliability, fiber-optic cable is a popular transmission medium for high-speed long-distance transmissions. While fiber-optic cable is too expensive to be used as a transmission medium for a small LAN, it is the transmission medium of choice for MANs and WANs.

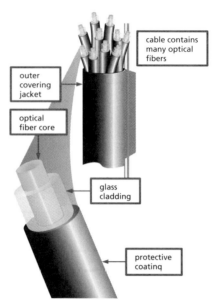

Figure 6-12   Fiber-optic cable is a popular transmission medium for high-speed long-distance transmissions.

Connectivity Hardware and Software

As discussed in Chapter 1, packet switching involves breaking up data into packets at its source and then transmitting the individual packets across various networks to their destination, where the packets are reassembled. Hardware connectivity devices, such as hubs, bridges, data switches, and routers, and hardware or software gateways are at the heart of this process. These devices and software are used to connect nodes on the same network, to connect across multiple networks, and to forward packets between nodes.

Large modern networks often are broken up into **segments**, or multiple groups of computers that share a common function. For example, in a business LAN, the Marketing Department computers might be on one segment and the Sales Department computers might be on another segment. Bridges, data switches, routers, and gateways connect different network segments and control transmissions between segments (Figure 6-13). Most large networks use a combination of network hardware and software to help move packets efficiently and quickly to their destinations.

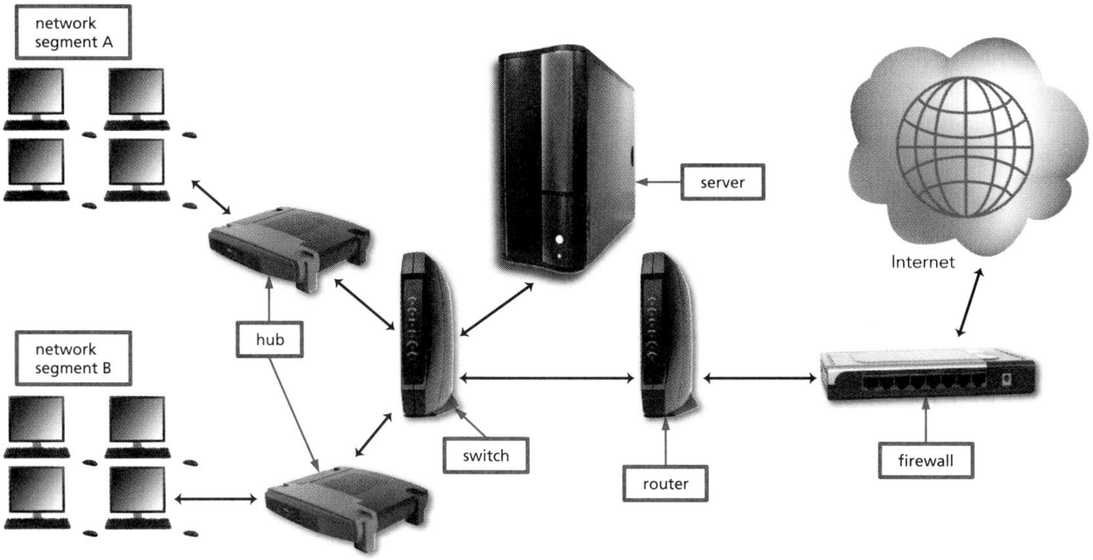

Figure 6-13 Large modern networks are often broken up into network segments.

HUBS As you learned earlier in this chapter, a hub is an inexpensive hardware device used to connect multiple nodes on the same network. A **passive hub** cannot determine how to direct a packet; it simply sends the same signal to all the nodes or segments to which it is connected. An **intelligent hub**, however, can perform a variety of tasks, such as filtering data or permitting a network administrator to monitor hub traffic.

BRIDGES A **port** is an opening in a device that is used to connect it to another device. A **bridge** is an intelligent connectivity device with one input port and one output port that connects two segments on the same LAN or two separate LANs. Each node on a network has a unique physical address called its **MAC (Media Access Control) address**, which is assigned to its network interface card (NIC) by the card's manufacturer. A bridge creates a database of all the MAC addresses for nodes on its segment or LAN. It then uses the database to determine if a packet should be forwarded to another segment or LAN. Bridges originally were able to connect only segments or LANs that used the same access method — either Ethernet or token ring. Today, more sophisticated bridges can connect, forward packets, and translate the packets between Ethernet and token ring LANs. In some cases, however, bridges are being replaced by modern data switches and routers.

DATA SWITCHES A **data switch** is an intelligent device that also interprets MAC addresses and filters and forwards packets to other network segments. A data switch has multiple ports, with each port acting as a bridge. Using multiple ports to direct packets helps ease congestion and makes a data switch a less-expensive choice than a bridge for networks with a large number of nodes.

ROUTERS Like a data switch, a **router** is an intelligent device with multiple ports. A router, however, is much more powerful than a switch. In fact, a router is a specialized computer that can connect LAN segments, two LANs, or multiple LANs on a WAN — all transmitting at different speeds and using different protocols. In addition to keeping track of all the nodes on a network, a router can determine the best route for a packet to take to its destination and switch the packet to an alternate route, if necessary.

@SOURCE

Seven-Layer OSI Model
The Seven-Layer OSI Model illustrates the flow of data in a network and defines the networking protocols at each step in the flow. To learn more about the Seven-Layer OSI Model, visit the Book Companion Site Web page at **www.cengagebrain.com**. Under the Chapter 6 @Source links, click a link below Seven-Layer OSI Model.

A router can use one of two methods of directing packets: static routing and dynamic routing. A router using **static routing** is programmed by a network administrator to route packets over specific paths between nodes. **Dynamic routing** allows a router to determine the best route between two nodes automatically and then store this information in a **routing table**, which is a data table stored on the router or on a network computer that includes a list of routes to network addresses. To route a packet dynamically, an incoming packet is opened, the packet's destination address is compared with the routing table, and then the packet is sent on to its destination using the route specified in the routing table. Dynamic routing also allows a router to detect trouble on a specific route and reroute packets when necessary.

The routers used to route packets on the Internet are complex, fast, and expensive devices that can search through routing tables quickly enough to correctly forward millions of packets per second. Internet routers ensure that packets reach their destination — across town or across the world — by sending packets from one router to another until the packets reach their destination network. Forwarding a packet to the next Internet router is called a **hop**. The more hops, the longer it takes for data to go from the sending computer to the destination computer.

Most operating systems provide a utility that you can use to trace hops from your computer to another computer over the Internet. In the Windows operating system, this program is called the **tracert utility**. The tracert utility can be used to test the path to a destination Internet site and see if any problems exist with making a connection at a particular point along the route.

To Use the Tracert Utility to Trace Hops

The following steps use the Command Prompt window and the Windows tracert utility to identify the number of hops from your computer to a Cengage Web server.

- Click the Start button on the Windows taskbar.

- Point to All Programs on the Start menu.

- Click Accessories.

- Click Command Prompt to open the Command Prompt window (Figure 6-14).

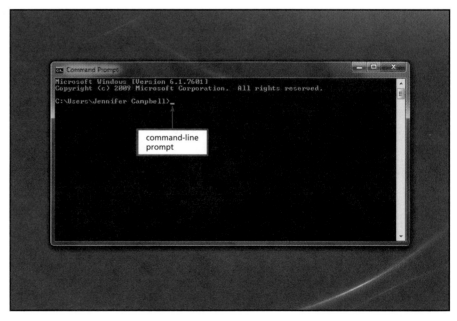

Figure 6-14

Type `tracert www.cengage.com` at the command-line prompt to instruct the operating system to trace the number of hops between your computer and the destination computer (Figure 6-15).

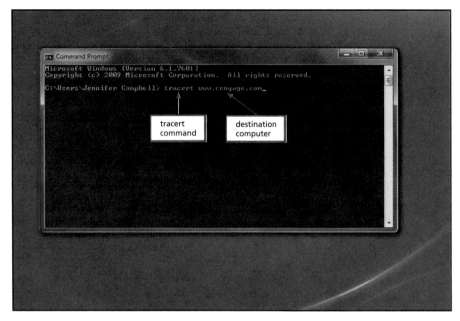

Figure 6-15

Press the ENTER key to view the path from your computer to the Cengage destination server as packets are sent from router to router over the Internet (Figure 6-16).

Click the Close button on the Command Prompt window title bar.

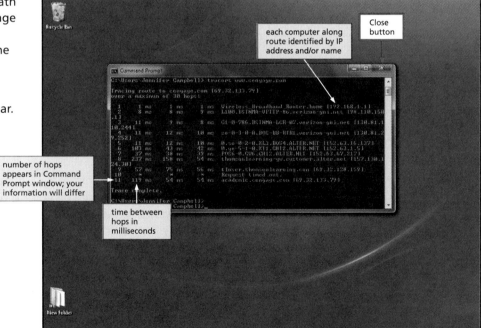

Figure 6-16

GATEWAYS A **gateway** is a hardware device or software that runs on a mainframe computer, a server, an individual workstation, or a router. Gateways are used to connect two or more networks or network segments that use different packet formatting, different communication protocols, and different access methods. Gateways not only forward packets, they also translate packets so that those packets can be read by the destination network. Because of this translation capability, gateways are more expensive than routers and transmit packets more slowly than do bridges, switches, or routers. Most routers have a gateway, although a PC or network server can be programmed to act as a gateway. Figure 6-17 lists different types of gateways.

Types of Gateways

Name	Description
E-mail	Converts e-mail messages created by one type of e-mail system so that they can be read by a different type of e-mail system.
Internet	Allows LAN users to access the Internet. May be used to define which users have Internet access or to restrict access to certain Internet services or Web sites.
LAN	Connects LAN segments that use different access methods and communication protocols.
Voice/data	Allows data packets to be sent over a voice network, or voice to be sent over a data network by translating between voice circuit switching and data packet switching.
Wireless	Integrates wireless devices such as laptops, PDAs, and cell phones with a wired network.

Figure 6-17 Gateways can connect two or more divergent networks.

Internet Infrastructure

From a user's perspective, accessing the Internet and downloading a file, viewing a Web page, or sending an e-mail may seem quite simple. In a few seconds, the file is downloaded, the Web page is loaded into your browser, or the e-mail message reaches its destination. The processes that occur behind the scenes, however, are quite complex and rely on the ability of your computer to communicate with computers on other networks. Each computer must be operational and have the proper protocols, programs, and gateways to complete the process. The processes also rely on the ability of your Internet service provider (ISP) to exchange data with other providers, and on the ability of network hardware and software to break down data into properly addressed packets that are delivered error-free and reassembled correctly at their destination.

In this section, you will learn about network service providers and how they interact to exchange data at specific points on the Internet backbones. You also will learn more about the TCP/IP suite of protocols that is instrumental in addressing and delivering data packets, how IP addresses are constructed, and how the DNS resolves domain names to IP addresses.

Network Service Providers (NSPs)

Recall that the original Internet backbone was provided by the NSFnet, which used transmission media from AT&T. In the mid-1990s, the NSFnet Internet backbone was replaced by interconnected backbones or networks provided by several telecommunications companies, including AT&T. Today, AT&T, Sprint, Verizon, Level 3 Communications, Century Link, and others, called **network service providers (NSPs)**, provide the public and private network infrastructure for the Internet.

INTERNET EXCHANGE POINTS   An **Internet exchange point (IXP)** is a physical infrastructure that enables ISPs to communicate among their networks, which limits the upstream traffic an ISP must handle. Each ISP has at least one network switch, to which each participating ISP connects. The use of an IXP reduces the costs for running an ISP because it uses a shared connection. IXP usage also improves an ISP's bandwidth. The costs for operating an IXP are typically shared by the participating ISPs.

IXPs range in size from around 10 members to several hundred. One of the largest IXPs in operation is the Equinix Internet Exchange, which connects several European cities (including London, Paris, and Zurich) to ISPs in the United States (Dallas, Los Angeles), Asia (Tokyo, Singapore), and Australia (Sydney). The Equinix Internet Exchange was established in 1998 and had 768 members in 2011.	**FACTS @HAND**

A specific type of IXP — called a **Metropolitan Area Exchange (MAE)** — is a high-speed Ethernet connection within a metropolitan area. The list of MAEs available around the world is long; three regional U.S. MAEs owned and operated by Verizon, as shown in Figure 6-18, are MAE West (San Jose and Los Angeles, California), MAE East (New York City, the Washington, D.C. area, and Miami, Florida), and MAE Central (Dallas, Texas and Chicago, Illinois). Verizon also owns and operates MAEs in Europe.

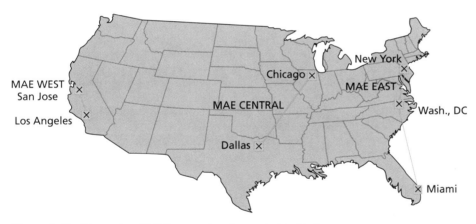

Figure 6-18   The regional MAEs owned and operated by Verizon.

Network service providers (NSPs) provide the public and private network infrastructure (backbones) for the Internet. ISPs sell Internet access to individuals, businesses, and other organizations. An ISP may sell Internet access locally to individuals and businesses, regionally to other ISPs, or worldwide to a varied customer base. An ISP may or may not be an NSP; several NSPs, however, are also ISPs.	**FACTS @HAND**

PEERING   **Peering** is the exchange of Internet traffic and router information between NSPs and ISPs at an exchange point, such as an IXP. Peering agreements specify the terms under which NSPs exchange data and can include how much traffic can be peered or exchanged, the type of network the peering entities must have, and other requirements such as transit fees. Public peering involves exchanging Internet traffic at a public connection, such as an IXP. Because network access points (NAPs) can become very congested during the Internet's peak traffic periods, some NSPs and ISPs set up **private peering** connections, which are dedicated connections to each other's networks. These private peering arrangements and connections enable Internet traffic to bypass congested public peering points.

TCP/IP Stack

As you learned in Chapter 1, the Transmission Control Protocol/Internet Protocol (TCP/IP) suite, also called the **TCP/IP stack**, is the de facto set of standard Internet protocols on which communications across the Internet and many private networks rely. The TCP/IP stack encompasses multiple subprotocols, many of which are shown in Figure 6-19. Of these protocols, TCP, IP, and UDP are the core subprotocols required for all TCP/IP transmissions. Other subprotocols accomplish various network communication tasks such as downloading files or sending and receiving e-mail.

TCP/IP Stack

Subprotocol	Description
Transmission Control Protocol (TCP)	Breaks data into packets, verifies packet integrity, and reassembles error-free packets at their destination.
Internet Protocol (IP)	Sends packets and provides routers with the address information needed to deliver the packets.
User Datagram Protocol (UDP)	Sends packets without checking for errors or verifying receipt of the packets. UDP is used to broadcast live video or audio over the Internet.
Address Resolution Protocol (ARP)	Converts a computer's IP address to its physical MAC address.
Reverse ARP (RARP)	Converts a computer's physical MAC address to its IP address.
Internet Control Message Protocol (ICMP)	Sends error messages to routers and host computers when problems occur with data transmissions.
Dynamic Host Configuration Protocol (DHCP)	Automatically assigns IP addresses to network devices.
Hypertext Transfer Protocol (HTTP)	Allows Web servers and Web browsers to communicate.
Post Office Protocol version 3 (POP3)	Manages storage of e-mail messages on a mail server and forwarding of e-mail messages from a mail server to a user's mailbox.
Simple Mail Transfer Protocol (SMTP)	Routes e-mail messages from mail server to mail server across an IP network such as the Internet.
Internet Message Access Protocol version 4 (IMAP4)	Provides remote access to a mail server, allowing users to manage their stored messages; functions similar to POP3.
File Transfer Protocol (FTP)	Enables uploading and downloading of files between a local and remote computer.
Telnet	Allows a computer to act as a terminal for logging on to remote devices such as a computer or router.

Figure 6-19 The TCP/IP stack includes several subprotocols on which communications across the Internet and private IP networks rely.

Most current network operating systems use the TCP/IP stack as their default networking protocols. A network running TCP/IP is often called an IP network.

IP Addresses

Every network node must have its own individual and unique identifier to ensure that data transmitted over a private or public IP network reaches its correct destination. Earlier in this chapter, you learned that each network device has a MAC address, which is a physical address set in its network interface card (NIC). In addition to a physical address, each node on an IP network also has a **logical address**, called an IP address. The IP subprotocol uses this address to deliver packets to the correct destination.

The current IP standard, called **IPv6**, lengthens IP addresses from 32 bits to 128 bits and thus increases the number of available IP addresses from the IPv4 standard, which it replaced. Figure 6-20 compares IP addresses based on the IPv4 and IPv6 standards.

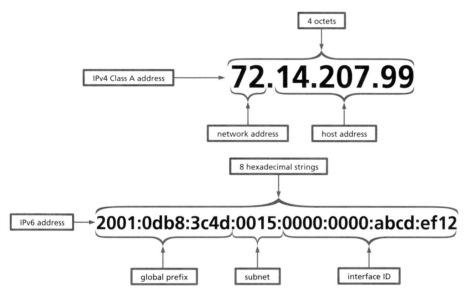

Figure 6-20   The IPv6 standard lengthens IP addresses to 128 bits, increasing the number of available IP addresses.

An IPv6 address includes eight 8-bit numbers. Each 8-bit number in the IP address is called an **octet**. In IPv6, each octet is separated by a colon (:). IPv6 was established to enable more nodes, networks, and domains to have a unique logical address. A node that has an IPv4 address does not need to update to an IPv6 address; the two are compatible.

The IP address for any node on a network is made up of two components: one that identifies the network to which the node is connected, and one that identifies the node itself. The IP addresses for nodes on the same network have the same network identification component, while each has a unique node component. Originally, a **classful routing system** was used to assign IP addresses by classifying networks as Class A through Class E networks to maximize the number of available IP addresses for each network. The network class defined which octets in the IP address identified the network, and which octets identified the specific node. However, most networks were not using the full amount of IP addresses available to them, making the classful system wasteful.

@SOURCE

IPv6
For more information about IPv6, visit the Book Companion Site Web page at **www. cengagebrain.com**. Under the Chapter 6 @Source links, click a link below IPv6.

The explosive demand for IP addresses strained the capabilities of this classful routing system, leading to the development of a **classless routing system**, called **Classless Inter-Domain Routing (CIDR)**. CIDR is a notation system that allows network administrators to expand the number of network nodes assigned to an IP address. CIDR is used extensively on the Internet and in large private networks. CIDR address blocks are assigned to an ISP, which then can use one IP address for thousands of customers by assigning them subnetwork addresses. By using subnetworks, the number of unique IP addresses needed is reduced, yet each node has its own identifier based on an IP address and a subnetwork prefix.

FACTS @HAND

Some IP addresses are reserved for special uses. For example, 127.0.0.1 is used to troubleshoot TCP/IP-related problems on an individual computer, and 255.255.255.255 is reserved for broadcasting messages to multiple computers. Other groups of IP addresses, such as 192.168.0.0 through 192.168.255.255, are internal IP addresses reserved for private networks.

To View a Networked Computer's IP Address

As previously discussed, every computer on a network has a unique IP address. You can use the Command Prompt window and the **ipconfig /all** command to display your own computer's IP address. The following steps use the Command Prompt window to view the IP address of your computer. To complete the steps, your computer must be connected to a network. The contents of your Command Prompt window will be different from the figures in these steps.

1

- Open the Command Prompt window.

- Type **ipconfig /all** at the command-line prompt to instruct the operating system to display all IP information about your networked computer (Figure 6-21).

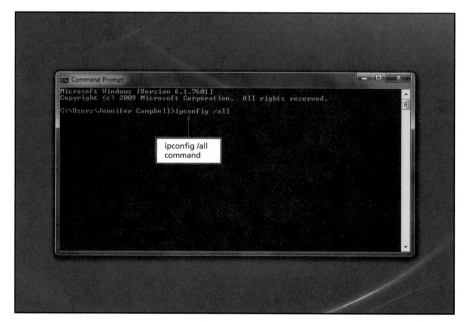

Figure 6-21

2

- Press the ENTER key to display your computer's host name, IP address, and other IP information (Figure 6-22).

Q&A

Why do I not see IP information?
If your computer is not connected to a network, no IP information appears.

- Scroll the Command Prompt window, if necessary, to view the information.

- Click the Close button to close the Command Prompt window.

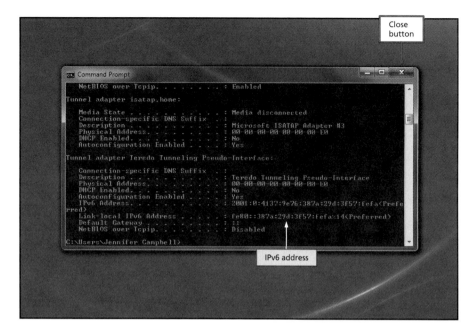

Figure 6-22

Domain Name System (DNS)

In Chapter 2, you were introduced to domain names, ICANN, and the DNS. ICANN, through its agreement with the U.S. Department of Commerce, oversees the assignment of IP addresses, the accreditation of domain name registrars, and contracts with TLD (top-level domain) registries as part of the DNS. The DNS also consists of a hierarchy of servers used to translate domain names into IP addresses in a process called **resolving** the domain name.

DNS SERVERS At the top of the DNS hierarchy (Figure 6-23, on the next page) are the DNS **root name servers** that publish a directory of the next level of DNS servers, called the **root zone file**. The root zone file lists the addresses of all the TLD and ccTLD (country code top-level domain) DNS servers. Twelve different organizations, including VeriSign, NASA, the University of Maryland, and the University of Southern California, operate the root name servers.

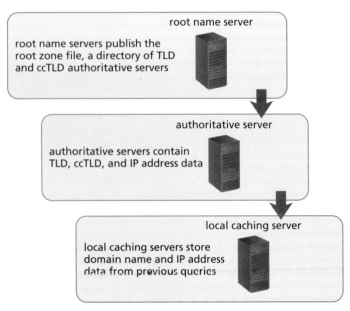

Figure 6-23 DNS servers consist of root name servers, authoritative servers, and local caching servers.

At the next level are the DNS **authoritative servers**, which contain the IP information for the TLD and ccTLD domains and their registrants. At the bottom of the hierarchy are thousands of local DNS **caching servers** operated by ISPs and company IT departments containing stored domain name and IP address information developed from previous domain name resolution inquiries. All of the information in the DNS databases — including the top-level domain, country code top-level domain, domain name, and IP address information — is sometimes called the **DNS namespace**.

The process of resolving a domain name to an IP address (Figure 6-24) begins with a local caching server, which may be located at your company or at your ISP. In most cases, a local caching server can quickly resolve a domain name to its IP address based on the server's cached or stored resolution inquiries. In some cases — for example, the first time the caching server attempts to resolve a specific domain name or if the caching server has just been started and its cache is empty — the caching server must contact authoritative or root name servers in the DNS to resolve a domain name.

Assume you have entered the URL mynewsite.biz in your browser. Your browser first contacts the local caching server to resolve the mynewsite.biz domain name to its IP address. If the local caching server cannot resolve the domain name, it can contact the authoritative server for the .biz TLD for a list of other authoritative servers that can resolve the mynewsite.biz domain name. The caching server then queries one of the appropriate authoritative servers for the mynewsite.biz domain and returns the IP address to the browser. If the caching server does not know the address for the .biz TLD authoritative server, it can contact a root name server for the address. Figure 6-24 illustrates the process of resolving the mynewsite.biz domain name assuming the local caching server cannot resolve the domain name and does not know the address of the appropriate authoritative server.

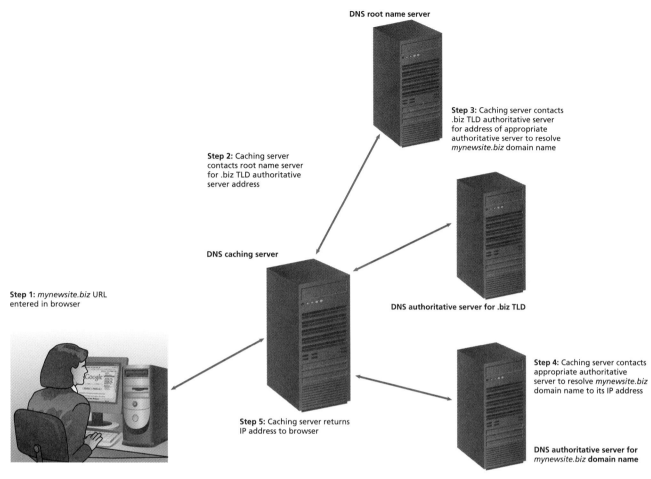

Figure 6-24 The process of resolving a domain name using the DNS begins with a local caching server.

You can use the Command Prompt window and the **nslookup** command to find the numeric IP address that corresponds to a domain name and vice versa.

To Look Up Corresponding IP Addresses and Domain Names

As you have learned, IP addresses are the numerical equivalent of domain names. The following steps use the Command Prompt window to look up corresponding IP addresses and domain names.

1

• Open the Command Prompt window.

• Type **nslookup cnn.com** at the command-line prompt to display the IP address or addresses for the cnn.com domain name (Figure 6-25).

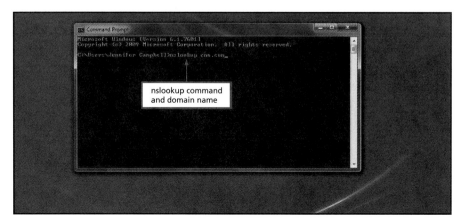

Figure 6-25

- Press the ENTER key to see that the cnn.com domain name corresponds to multiple IP addresses (Figure 6-26).

Figure 6-26

- Type **`nslookup 207.171.182.16`** at the command-line prompt.

- Press the ENTER key to see that the IP address 207.171.182.16 corresponds to the Amazon.com domain name (Figure 6-27).

- Close the Command Prompt window.

Figure 6-27

DNS REGISTRATION   The **Shared Registration System (SRS)** is the registration system that allows private companies to handle the registration of domain names. These private companies, called **accredited registrars**, ensure that an organization's unique domain name is maintained on the appropriate DNS servers, for a small annual fee. Examples of accredited registrars include Network Solutions, NameSystem, Safenames, and Register.com (Figure 6-28). ICANN is responsible for managing the SRS.

Figure 6-28 Accredited registrars.

The process of registering a domain name online is very easy. You simply:

1. Visit an accredited registrar's Web site.

2. Enter a desired domain name including the top-level domain, such as .com, .net, or .biz. The Web site searches a database of registered domain names to determine whether the domain name you entered is available.

3. Select an available domain name and enter the purchaser information, which usually consists of the name, address, telephone number, and e-mail address of the person responsible for the domain name.

4. Provide the IP address(es) of the Web servers of the company or ISP hosting the Web site, if necessary. (See your network administrator or contact your ISP for this information, if necessary.)

5. Pay for the domain name using a credit card.

To Search for an Available Domain Name

If you are considering registering a domain name, you first may want to search a domain name database to see what appropriate domain names are available. The following steps show how to search an accredited registrar's database for an available domain name. You will open the Web site's home page in a new tab in the foreground. Linked pages from the home page will open in the same tab as the home page.

- Start Internet Explorer.

- Visit the Discovering the Internet, Fourth Edition Chapter 6 Steps page at www.cengagebrain.com.

- Click Network Solutions to open it in a new tab (Figure 6-29).

Do all domain name registrars have access to the same domain names?
Network Solutions, Go Daddy, and others are ICANN-accredited registrars. They pay ICANN fees in order to access the list of available domain names and help their clients secure the proper names.

WebAddress text box and domain check boxes

Figure 6-29

- Type **my-new-business** in the Search for a Domain Name text box.

- Click the .net check box to deselect it and click the .biz check box to select it (Figure 6-30).

Why do I type a hyphen instead of a space in my domain name?
You cannot use spaces in a domain name; instead, use a hyphen where you normally would use a space.

.co, .com, and .biz domains selected

proposed domain name

Search button

Figure 6-30

3

- Click the Search button to determine whether the my-new-business.com, my-new-business.co, or my-new-business.biz domain names are available (Figure 6-31).

- Close the browser.

Q&A | The search results might include a few choices of extensions. Your results may vary.

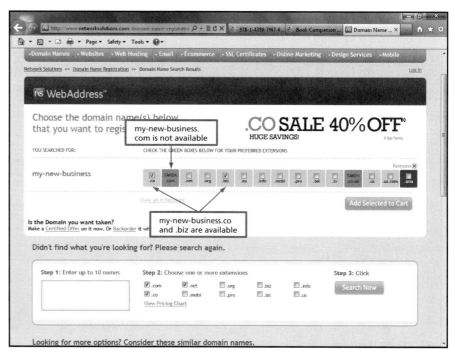

Figure 6-31

Selecting a Domain Name

Careful selection of a domain name is critical, whether your business is online-only or if you have an established presence beyond the Web. Most likely, you will need to purchase or reserve multiple domain names to help protect your brand, decrease market confusion, and reach more customers.

E-business domain names are used both to identify and to market e-businesses. When choosing an e-business domain name, select a short, easy-to-remember name that ties in to the products or services the e-business sells.

Consider any alternative names or abbreviations for your company, or marketing slogans, and purchase those domain names as well. You can reroute the alternate names to the main company Web site to ensure that your customers can reach you. For example,

BN is a common nickname for the bookstore Barnes & Noble. If you type www.bn.com in the Address bar and press the ENTER key, the Web site www.barnesandnoble.com is displayed. If you type www.adiamondisforever.com, you are redirected to the De Beers Web site.

You should also purchase a mobile Web site domain at the same time, regardless of whether your site currently requires a separate mobile site, to ensure that it is available for future use. The .mobi top-level domain is specifically for mobile Web sites.

For more tips on selecting a domain name, visit the *Discovering the Internet, Fourth Edition* Chapter 6 @Issue Web page at **www.cengagebrain.com** and click a link below Domain Names.

Location-Based Services and GPS

Handheld wireless devices, such as smartphones and tablets, are ubiquitous in today's modern mobile societies (Figure 6-32). You might already use one or more of these devices to communicate with friends and coworkers, connect to the Internet and check your e-mail, download games, get driving instructions, or view other Web content or access location-based services.

Figure 6-32   Handheld wireless devices are used to access content and services.

FACTS @HAND   According to the Pew Internet & American Life Project, 35 percent of American adults own a smartphone, and 25 percent of American adults do most of their online activities using a smartphone. Sixty-six percent of smartphone users sleep with their smartphones nearby.

A **location-based service (LBS)** is a wireless service offered to customers based on their physical location. An example of a noncommercial location-based service is the wireless 911 emergency service mandated by the FCC in its Enhanced 9-1-1 (E9-1-1) initiative. The E9-1-1 initiative allows emergency call centers to use a location-based service to identify the location of the caller accurately, thus helping to eliminate the delay caused by asking users to describe their location. Other uses of LBS include vehicle navigation systems, such as Garmin, that can pinpoint your location and provide you with step-by-step directions to a new location.

At the heart of this and other LBSs are the **Global Positioning System (GPS)** satellite network and receivers mounted in automobiles or placed in cell phones or other handheld devices. The GPS is a navigation system that consists of one or more Earth-based receivers that accept and analyze signals sent by small satellites orbiting approximately 11,000 miles above the Earth. There are at least 24 satellites operating at any time. Four to six satellites are always visible above the horizon, and each of these satellites constantly beams down a signal containing the exact time and its own position in the sky. A GPS receiver in a ship, airplane, pet collar or other wearable device, automobile, or smartphone uses these signals to calculate the receiver's location on Earth to within a few feet (Figure 6-33).

Figure 6-33   A GPS receiver in a ship, airplane, pet collar or other wearable device, automobile, or smartphone uses satellite signals to calculate the receiver's location to within a few feet.

Using the GPS satellite network, a service provider can identify the physical location of a person with a GPS-enabled device, such as a smartphone, and then offer services or information to which the person has subscribed based on that location. For example:

- Information services: "What is the traffic problem at I94 exit 187?"
- Social networking services: "We are at the Art Festival in Doverville. Catch up with us at 3 p.m."
- Tracking services: "Service truck #10 is en route to Job 23."
- Advertising services: "Gino's Pizzeria is immediately to your left. Use the coupon code 'HALF' to get any pizza at half price."
- Entertainment services: "Check out these coordinates for today's hidden treasure box. Good luck on your treasure hunt!"
- Navigation services: "Turn left at the corner of Evans Street" (Figure 6-34).
- Billing services: "You are now in Call Zone 3; all calls are billed at the Zone 3 rates."

Figure 6-34   GPS.

LBS
To learn more about location-based services, such as geosocial networking, visit the Book Companion Site Web page at **www. cengagebrain.com**. Under the Chapter 6 @Source links, click a link below LBS.

Geosocial networking is a term used to describe the combination of LBS with social networking providers. For example, Foursquare is a smartphone application that pinpoints a user's location using a GPS, and enables the user to "check in" to the location, such as a restaurant, and alert others using social networking tools, such as Facebook or Twitter. Using geosocial networking tools, such as Yelp (Figure 6-35), users can provide information to others about their current location, including reviews, menus, photos, and their own activities. Google Latitude enables users to track the locations of their friends who also use the Latitude feature. Geosocial networking, like all social networking, has some privacy concerns. For example, by sharing information about your whereabouts, you are not only enabling others to find you, but are also alerting them that you are not home, exposing yourself to potential home robberies.

Figure 6-35 Yelp is a geosocial networking application.

Internet Telephony and Web Conferencing

In addition to its large-scale computer networking function, the Internet is also used to enhance two traditional modes of communication: the telephone and business conferencing. In this section, you will learn how telephone calls are transmitted over the Internet, and how the Internet has changed the way many businesses conduct employee and client meetings and conferences.

Internet Telephony

In Chapter 1, you were introduced to the circuit-switching technologies that establish and maintain private circuits for telephone calls over the Public Switched Telephone Network (PSTN). A private circuit connection is maintained for the duration of a call even during conversation pauses when neither party is talking. **Internet telephony**, also called **IP telephony** or **Voice over IP (VoIP)**, uses TCP/IP and packet switching to send voice transmissions over a private or public IP network. Using IP packet-switching technologies to make telephone calls is more efficient than old circuit-switching technologies because packet switching minimizes the connection time for each call, thus allowing more calls to be transmitted during the same time period in which a single circuit-switched call must maintain its connection. VoIP customers can make calls from their computer or telephone by installing a VoIP router or adapter between their cable or DSL modem and their computer or telephone, as shown in Figure 6-36, and subscribing to a VoIP service.

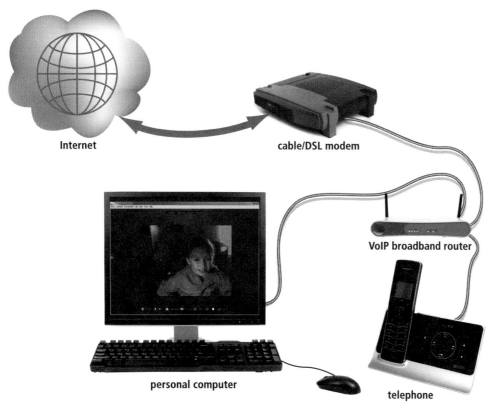

Internet   cable/DSL modem

VoIP broadband router

personal computer

telephone

Figure 6-36 VoIP customers can make calls from their computer or telephone by installing a VoIP router or adapter between their cable or DSL modem and their computer or telephone, and subscribing to a VoIP service.

VoIP is a popular option for home telephone service because of reduced service costs and free or inexpensive long-distance calls. VoIP is also an increasingly popular way for businesses to take advantage of packet-switching efficiencies, centralize the management of their private voice and data networks, increase productivity, and save money by avoiding the long-distance phone charges associated with traditional telephone service. VoIP business services typically include a PBX (private branch exchange) switching service that manages incoming and outgoing calls and calls between extensions. VoIP service providers, such as Vonage, Nextiva inTALK (Figure 6-37), Jive, and Phone Power offer telephone services to homes and businesses over broadband Internet connections.

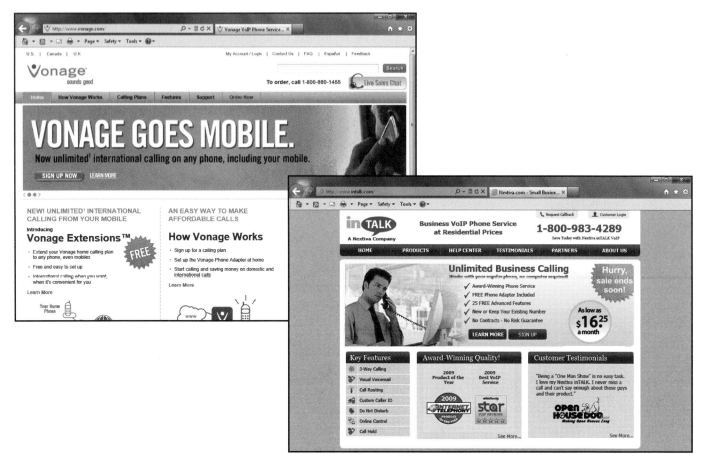

Figure 6-37 VoIP is an increasingly popular way for businesses and individuals to save money on telephone communications.

In addition, you can use a private or public IP network to make computer-to-computer or computer-to-telephone calls. With a properly equipped computer, you can participate in a toll-free conversation with someone using a similarly equipped computer, or you can make low-cost calls from your computer to any telephone around the world (Figure 6-38). To make such a call over the Internet, you need a computer equipped with a microphone and speakers or a headset, a sound card, special software provided by vendors such as Net2Phone or Skype, and an Internet connection.

FACTS @HAND The communications industry continues to develop technologies that allow voice, data, and video to be delivered simultaneously across the same network using a combination of computers, telephones, and television. Network engineers refer to these modern networks as **converged networks**.

Figure 6-38 Low-cost computer-to-telephone calls and toll-free computer-to-computer calls are possible over an IP network.

Virtual Meetings and Web Conferencing

A **virtual meeting** allows collaboration between participants, such as a group of employees, by allowing invitees to log on to their network and sign in to a meeting in which they communicate with each other as well as view, share, and work collaboratively on files. Virtual meeting participants typically communicate with each other using a combination of text, audio, whiteboard, and video.

Video conferencing, an expanded virtual meeting sometimes involving hundreds or thousands of participants, involves the real-time transmission of video and audio between two locations. Today, most video conferencing uses streaming video over a private or public IP network. Because of transmission quality concerns, commercial video conferencing over an IP network (video over IP) most frequently occurs over private IP networks, which have more control over traffic and bandwidth availability. Examples of commercial video conferencing include employee training sessions, customer support activities, and meetings involving employees who work in different locations (Figure 6-39, on the next page). Government agencies, colleges, and universities with access to Internet2 use it for video conferencing and for broadcasting instructors' lectures to numerous different classrooms.

Figure 6-39 Video conferencing is the real-time transmission of video and audio between two locations.

To listen and watch a video conference using your computer, your computer must be equipped with speakers, a monitor, a sound card, and video conferencing software. If you are going to participate in the video conference, your computer also must have a microphone or headset and a camera.

Web conferencing is a virtual meeting conducted using a browser and the Web. Web conferencing can save time and money and improve productivity by allowing participants at various geographic locations to come together online to communicate as though they were all sitting around the same physical conference table. In addition to the video, chat, and audio capabilities of video conferencing, Web conferencing provides a controlled meeting interface. Using the interface, participants can view another user's screen in order to follow a software demonstration or Microsoft® PowerPoint® presentation, or even enable one user to take control of another participant's screen to troubleshoot a computer problem. Major providers of Web conferencing software and services include Adobe Systems (Adobe® Connect™), Citrix Systems, Inc. (GoToMeeting™) (Figure 6-40), Microsoft (Lync™), and Cisco (WebEx®) (Figure 6-40).

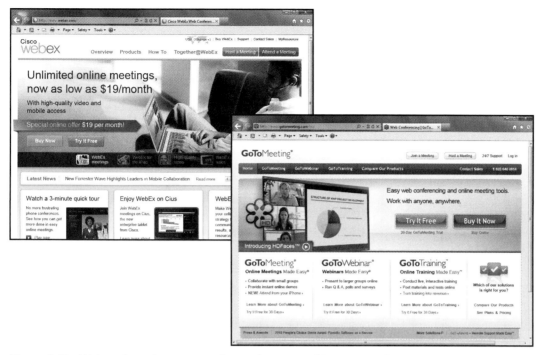

Figure 6-40 Web conferencing can save time and money and improve productivity.

Network Security Issues and Technologies

Network security involves protecting network equipment and data from accidental or deliberate damage. Threats to network and Web site security can originate both internally from within the organization and externally from outsiders. If business transactions are conducted over the network, fraudulent transactions and failure to protect transaction information pose additional risks. In this section, you will learn about the internal and external threats to network security, transactional security risks, and network security practices and technologies.

Most security analysts agree that the greatest threat to network security is from human ignorance and error. One simple but amazingly effective strategy for gaining unauthorized access to a network or network facilities is called social engineering. **Social engineering** simply relies on a network user divulging his or her username or password to someone, or allowing someone to enter a network facilities room without the proper authorization.

FACTS
@HAND

Internal Network Security Threats

Internal threats to network security can include management failure to support organization-wide security awareness, inadequate security policies, security procedures that are not enforced, unhappy employees or disgruntled former employees, failure to make backup copies of critical data or failure to store the copied data off-site, and missing or untested disaster recovery plans. These are just a few examples of the failure to protect against threats to internal network security and data security — the results of which can be catastrophic. Two important ways to protect against internal network security threats are (1) clearly stating and enforcing network security policies and procedures, and (2) ensuring that network access is restricted to authorized users. Equally important is ensuring that critical data is backed up and taken off-site for secure storage, and that plans for coping with a natural or human-caused disaster are in place.

SECURITY POLICIES AND PROCEDURES   After a thorough assessment of an organization's network security risks, management should develop appropriate security policies and procedures, and then ensure that both are understood and enforced. All employees should receive the training necessary to understand fully an organization's network security policies and how to implement specific security procedures. These procedures might be as simple as not divulging the physical location of network facilities to visitors, or they could be more complex, such as requiring all users to encrypt sensitive e-mails sent outside the organization.

AUTHORIZED NETWORK ACCESS   Network operating systems have built-in security features that allow network administrators to restrict user access to the network or to specific network functions. For example, a network administrator can configure the network so that each user must enter a unique user ID and password before he or she can log on to the network. As you learned in Chapter 4, a user ID is necessary to access an e-mail account. A user ID is also a unique identifier used along with a password to log on to a network. A password is a group of secret characters that identifies you as an authorized network user. When a network user leaves an organization, the network administrator eliminates that user's logon information.

Unauthorized internal users or outside intruders often attempt to guess legitimate passwords to break into a network. Passwords that contain a mix of at least six letters and numbers are much more difficult to guess than those with fewer characters or with only letters. Mixing uppercase and lowercase letters or adding some nonreserved special characters (such as & or $) also can help to make a password more secure. Additionally, passwords consisting of names, birth dates, and common words that might be easy to guess should be avoided. Finally, passwords should be changed regularly. Figure 6-41 illustrates some effective passwords.

Effective Passwords

Do This	Do Not Do This
Z89$33Q	Wilson (last name)
D33f084	012664 (birthday)
66G13b9	apple
7y3MF98F	user

Figure 6-41   Passwords containing a mix of letters, numbers, and special characters are harder to guess.

Other methods used to restrict network access are biometric identification and smart card identification. **Biometrics** involves using devices to measure biological data to identify a user. A user's fingerprints, voiceprints, iris or retina image, or other biological data can be read by biometric devices and software to allow network logon or permit entrance to a network's physical facilities (Figure 6-42). Authorization for a remote user to access a network or for an employee to enter a network's physical facilities can be provided by a smart card. A **smart card** (Figure 6-43), a plastic card the size of a credit card, contains memory chips that can store special access codes or biometric information.

Figure 6-42 Biometric devices measure biological data that can be used to identify a network user.

Figure 6-43 A smart card contains memory chips that can store special access codes or biometric information.

WIRELESS NETWORK SECURITY Wireless networks should be secured using the same tools, such as encryption and passwords, and for the same reasons, such as privacy and risk of exposure to malicious code, as wired networks. Wireless networks are vulnerable to more threats than traditional wired networks. One of these threats is **LAN jacking**, or **war driving**, which is the act of driving around with a laptop, antenna, and wireless card, looking for unsecured wireless networks to access. LAN jacking not only exposes a network to viruses and other risks, but can tie up a network's bandwidth and impact its performance. **Spoofing** is when a hacker accesses a network in order to set up a fake Web site or send mail that looks like it is coming from an internal server. In addition, a hacker can create a **rogue WLAN** by installing a wireless router that uses network resources and exposes the network to security threats.

DATA BACKUP AND RESTORE   Data backup and restore policies and procedures identify how and when copies of critical data and software are made and how backed-up data is restored to a network following an equipment failure or loss of data. Backup copies of critical data and software can be copied to magnetic tape, optical discs, or other storage media, which should then be stored off-site (Figure 6-44). Increasingly, businesses and individuals are turning to **cloud storage**, which involves backing up data to off-site server storage accessed using a browser and a Web page. A number of companies, such as IDrive®, Mozy®, and Carbonite™, provide cloud storage services.

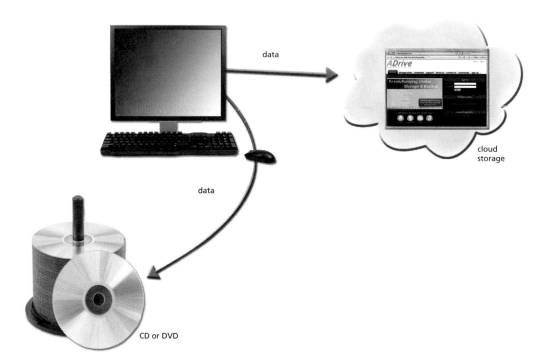

Figure 6-44   Backup copies of critical network data and software should be stored off-site using cloud storage, optical discs, magnetic tape, or other storage devices.

Data backup procedures should be a normal, regularly scheduled part of network operations, and data restore procedures should be tested periodically to ensure that the correct data is being backed up and the storage media is not damaged. Data backup and restore policies and procedures are an important part of an organization's disaster recovery planning.

DISASTER RECOVERY PLANNING   Networks and data are also at risk for physical damage from natural causes such as fire or flood, as well as from deliberate destruction by employees or outside intruders. IT managers and network administrators use a variety of techniques to protect against accidental or deliberate physical damage to network equipment and data; including storing equipment in locked, tightly controlled, and monitored rooms; removing room numbers and door signs so that network facilities are not marked clearly; using specially designed fire suppression systems; providing backup electrical power; and following sound data backup and restore procedures. Additionally, very large organizations might maintain duplicate network facilities in different geographical areas.

Despite the use of these techniques, disasters that compromise network operations still can occur. A **disaster recovery plan** covers how an organization deals with a natural or man-made disaster to ensure the organization's viability. The portion of a

disaster recovery plan that covers network operations should define how an organization plans to manage equipment failure, electrical outages, data loss, security breaches, and damage to physical facilities. Components of a disaster recovery plan should be tested periodically to make certain the plan covers new contingencies.

External Network Security Threats

External network security threats are those that originate from outside the network, such as natural disasters, hackers, viruses, worms, and Trojan horses. The best preparedness for natural disasters is a sound, tested disaster recovery plan. To help protect against hackers, viruses, worms, and Trojan horses, organizations should use virus protection software and perform regular security audits to ensure network security policies are in place.

UNAUTHORIZED NETWORK ACCESS   In Chapter 1, you were introduced to the term, hacker, which typically describes a person who uses his or her programming skills to gain unauthorized access to a computer network. A hacker might attack a network for any number of reasons, including accessing and perhaps stealing valuable information or planting malware.

To attack a network, a hacker might break into a home computer or break into multiple computers on a corporate network to plant software that allows the hacked computers to launch difficult-to-trace attacks on other networks. These types of attacks, called **distributed denial of service (DDoS)** attacks, involve sending a continuous stream of server requests that ultimately overload a server's capacity to respond. DDoS attacks have been launched by some hackers just for fun and bragging rights. Other DDoS attacks have been launched by criminals attempting to extort businesses with threats of further attacks or for revenge against business rivals.

Hackers may also break into a network to steal account information, such as credit card numbers, user passwords, and other personal information that can be used to steal a person's identity, make unauthorized purchases using a credit card, or open accounts in a user's name that can be used for illegal purposes.

@SOURCE **Security Threats**
To learn more about network security threats, visit the Book Companion Site Web page at **www. cengagebrain.com**. Under the Chapter 6 @Source links, click a link below Security Threats.

The term hacker was originally used to describe any especially gifted software programmer. Today, the term refers to malicious hackers, also called crackers or black-hat hackers, who compromise networks to steal information or disrupt network services. Some hackers who voluntarily use their skills to find network vulnerabilities and publicize them prefer to be called ethical hackers or white-hat hackers.

 FACTS @HAND

COMPUTER VIRUSES   Hackers often exploit well-known security vulnerabilities in popular software to spread destructive programs such as viruses, worms, and Trojan horses. As you have learned, a computer virus is a small, destructive program that infects other files on a computer. Viruses, which usually infect executable program files, spread to other files when the infected program is executed; viruses, however, also can be spread by e-mail headers or files attached to e-mail messages, or can be part of a computer worm.

A computer worm is a special kind of virus that spreads across a network, such as the Internet, by replicating itself. A worm does not attach itself to other programs; instead, the worm replicates continuously, ultimately consuming network resources, slowing server response, and crashing infected networks. For example, the W32.Sober.0@mm mass mailing worm and other Sober worm variants flew across the Internet harvesting e-mail addresses on compromised computers and then sending themselves to the addresses, spewing spam — up to 5 percent of all e-mail traffic at the time by some estimates — across the Internet as it moved from one infected computer to another.

Another type of destructive program that can be distributed as part of a virus or worm is a Trojan horse. A Trojan horse is a program that appears to do something useful or fun, but actually does something destructive, including destroying files, creating a way for a hacker to breach network security, stealing passwords, downloading files to the user's computer and then executing them, or recording user keystrokes. A Trojan horse program can be distributed as part of a standard virus, an infected Web page, a worm, an e-mail message, or a downloaded file. An example of a Trojan horse is the JS/Downloader-BNL Trojan that downloads and executes files from a remote Web site.

Protecting individual personal computers connected to the Internet or network computers, servers, and routers involves a combination of security tools, including hardware and software designed to guard against intruders and software designed to detect and destroy viruses, worms, and Trojan horses. Additionally, network administrators must be vigilant about installing software patches that plug security holes, and management should consider periodic security audits to detect network security vulnerabilities.

Several vendors, such as Symantec Corporation and McAfee, sell software that can detect a known virus, worm, or Trojan horse program as a file is downloaded or as an e-mail message is received, and then clean the infected file or e-mail message by removing the destructive program. To be effective, virus protection software must be updated continually with information on recently discovered viruses. Most virus protection software programs perform automatic virus definition updates through downloads over the Internet.

Viruses, Worms, and Trojan Horses
To learn more about virus, worm, and Trojan horse threats and hoaxes, visit the Book Companion Site Web page at **www.cengagebrain. com**. Under the Chapter 6 @Source links, click a link below Viruses, Worms, and Trojan Horses.

FACTS @HAND   Another element in disaster recovery planning is the development of a formal network security plan. A security plan identifies policies and procedures designed to prevent an attack, determines how to respond in the event of an attack, and documents how the business will interact with employees, clients, and other interested parties as it handles the consequences of an attack.

To Review Current Virus, Worm, and Trojan Horse Threats

The following steps review current virus, worm, and Trojan horse threats. You will open the Symantec Web site's home page in a new tab in the foreground. Linked pages from the home page will open in the same tab as the home page.

- Start Internet Explorer, if necessary.

- Visit the Discovering the Internet, Fourth Edition Chapter 6 Steps page at www.cengagebrain.com.

- Open Symantec Threat Explorer below Chapter 6 in a new tab in the foreground (Figure 6-45).

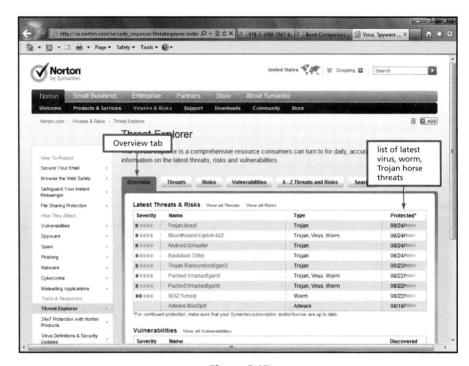

Figure 6-45

- Scroll down to view a list of vulnerability threats.

- Scroll the page to view its contents (Figure 6-46).

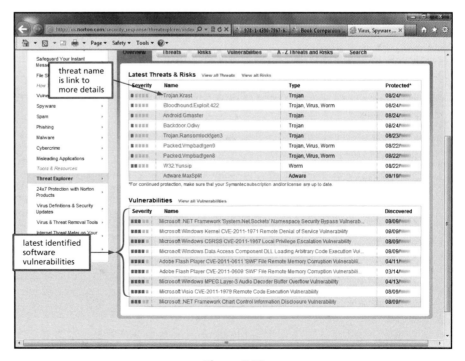

Figure 6-46

3

- Click the linked threat name for the first item in the Threats list to view its details.

- Scroll the page to review the specific threat details (Figure 6-47).

- Close your browser.

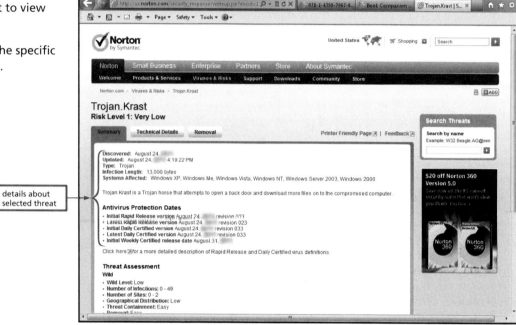

details about selected threat

Figure 6-47

WEB PAGE HACKING Web pages or databases accessed from Web pages are also targets for hackers. For example, hackers have done the following:

- Manipulated a *TIME Magazine* online poll
- Hacked the USAJOBS government Web site and stole personally identifiable information from a jobs database
- Distributed microblogging worms targeting celebrities' Twitter postings
- Hacked the *Wired* magazine site and planted a false story about a famous corporate executive
- Stole donor information by hacking a U.S. Senate candidate's Web site

During the 2008 U.S. presidential primary campaign, a hacker used the community blog section of the Barack Obama Web site to redirect traffic to the Hillary Clinton Web site, and hackers stole Social Security numbers from an Oklahoma state government Web site. A good resource for learning about Web application security and recent hacker attacks is the Web Application Security Consortium and its sponsored Web Hacking Incidents Database (Figure 6-48).

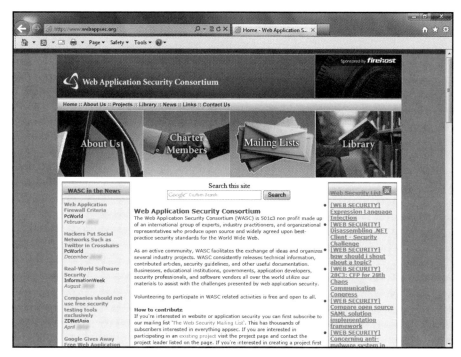

Figure 6-48 Reading about Web hacking incidents can help prepare you to take necessary security measures.

FIREWALLS AND PROXY SERVERS   In Chapter 2, you learned about personal firewall software, such as ZoneAlarm® PRO, which is used to protect home computers with DSL or cable modem "always on" Internet connections. A **network firewall** is a combination of hardware and software that filters traffic between private networks or between a private network and a public network, such as the Internet (Figure 6-49). Network firewalls can monitor and report suspicious network traffic, and can filter out or block incoming or outgoing network traffic based on a set of predetermined rules established by the network administrator. For example, a network firewall might block outgoing server requests for certain Web pages or block incoming e-mail from specific sources.

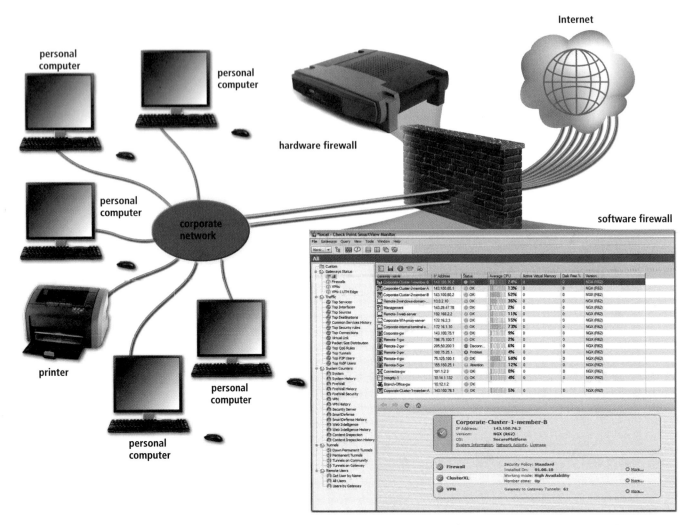

Figure 6-49 A network firewall is a combination of hardware and software that filters traffic between private networks or between a private network and a public network, such as the Internet.

A common type of network firewall is a **packet-filtering firewall**, which compares information contained in an IP packet header, such as the packet's source and destination IP addresses, with a set of predetermined filtering rules. The firewall allows packets that agree with the filtering rules to pass through to the network; packets that do not agree with the filtering rules are blocked. Another security device often used in conjunction with a packet-filtering firewall is a proxy server.

A **proxy server** is a computer or software application that hides an internal IP address from the outside world by substituting its own IP address for a source computer's IP address before sending outgoing e-mail or Web page requests. For example, an outgoing Web page request first would pass through the proxy server, which substitutes its own IP address for the original source's IP address (Figure 6-50). The proxy server then sends the request on to the packet-filtering firewall, which validates that the source IP address (now the proxy server's IP address) and the destination IP address meet its filtering rules before sending the request on to the destination Web server.

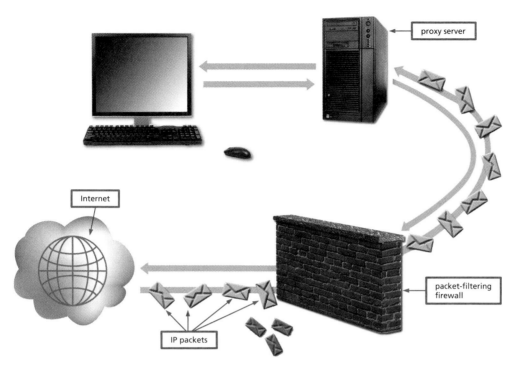

Figure 6-50 A proxy server hides an internal IP address by substituting its own IP address, and a packet-filtering firewall blocks packets that do not agree with its filtering rules.

INTERNET FILTERING SOFTWARE As you have learned, employees' inappropriate use of Internet access can increase a company's potential liabilities and network security risks. Vendors such as WebSpy and Websense sell Internet-filtering software that monitors and restricts employee Internet access.

SECURITY AUDITS Network administrators and IT managers use network security audits, conducted by third-party auditing firms, to expose network vulnerabilities. A **network security audit** reviews overall network security policies, employee security policy and procedure training, data backup and restore policies and procedures, and the physical security of the network equipment and data. A security audit may also involve **penetration testing**, in which security audit personnel try to hack into the network. The security audit results then are used to revise security policies and procedures, improve employee training, and make necessary updates to the network's hardware and software.

Transactional Risks

When a company conducts business transactions over the Internet, risks associated with online transactions are an additional security concern. The company must ensure that all parties are really who they say they are (authentication), that transactions cannot be intercepted or corrupted during transmission (integrity), that no party to a transaction can deny its participation (nonrepudiation), and that transaction information is kept private (confidentiality). The primary tools used to provide transaction authentication, integrity, nonrepudiation, and confidentiality are encryption and digital certificates.

Encryption is the process of translating readable data into unreadable data to prevent unauthorized access or use. Encrypted data is decoded at its destination using a special key, which can be created, for a fee, by a **certification authority (CA)**, such as VeriSign. When an organization wants to use encryption, it requests a set of associated public and private keys from a CA. The **public key** is used by others to encrypt data being sent to the organization and is posted by the CA to a publicly accessible directory. The **private key** is known only to the organization and is used to decrypt the incoming data.

A **digital certificate** electronically authenticates an organization's or individual's identity. A digital certificate is issued, for a fee, by a CA and contains the issuer's name, a certificate number, an expiration date, the requesting entity's public key information, and the issuer's digital signature, which validates the certificate's legitimacy (Figure 6-51). A digital certificate is posted to a public directory or registry so that interested parties can look up public keys.

Figure 6-51 A digital certificate issued by a certification authority electronically authenticates an organization's or individual's identity.

A **public key infrastructure** is the combination of organizations or individuals sending and receiving encrypted data, their public and private keys, and the CAs that issue the keys and digital certificates. Figure 6-52 illustrates sending and receiving encrypted data.

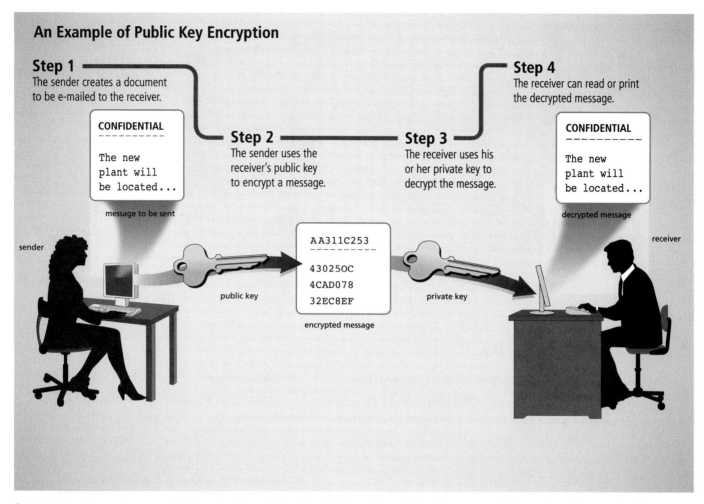

An Example of Public Key Encryption

Step 1
The sender creates a document to be e-mailed to the receiver.

Step 4
The receiver can read or print the decrypted message.

CONFIDENTIAL

The new
plant will
be located...

message to be sent

Step 2
The sender uses the receiver's public key to encrypt a message.

Step 3
The receiver uses his or her private key to decrypt the message.

CONFIDENTIAL

The new
plant will
be located...

decrypted message

sender

AA311C253

43025OC
4CAD078
32EC8EF

encrypted message

public key

private key

receiver

Figure 6-52 The sender encrypts data using the recipient's public key and sends the data over a public or private IP network to its destination, where it is decrypted using the recipient's private key.

Virtual Private Networks

A **virtual private network (VPN)** is a private network that uses a large public network, such as the Internet, to transmit its data (Figure 6-53, on the next page). **Tunneling** is a process that encapsulates one protocol inside another protocol. VPNs use tunneling to hide encrypted data, IP addresses, and a tunneling protocol inside IP packets that are routed over the public network using the IP protocol. When the IP packets reach their destination LAN, VPN firewall software removes the IP protocol information, and the tunneling protocol transmits the packet to its final destination computer. VPNs also use public and private key encryption, digital certificates, and special security protocols to secure their data transmissions.

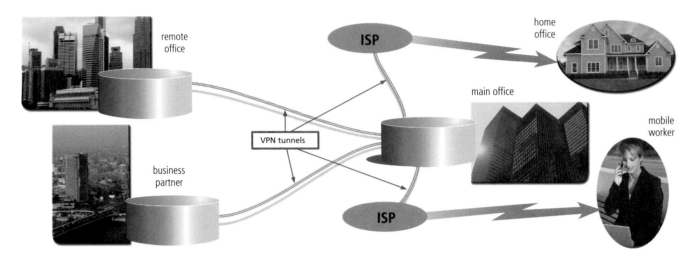

Figure 6-53 A virtual private network (VPN) sends encrypted data and a tunneling protocol inside IP packets over a public IP network, such as the Internet.

@ISSUE Cyber Security

In our interconnected world, the need for **cyber security** — preventing, identifying, and responding to attacks on persons or information through malicious Web sites, phishing, hacking, viruses, Trojan horses, worms, cyber bullying, and other threats — is an ever-present fact of daily life. According to a survey by Harris Interactive:

- 64 percent of respondents have (or know someone who has) received e-mail from an unknown sender requesting personal information.
- 58 percent of respondents have had (or know someone who has had) a computer infected by a virus.
- 51 percent of respondents have (or know someone who has) downloaded malware to their computer.

Like businesses, individuals also must recognize threats and risks and then take necessary steps to mitigate them. For example, individuals using home desktop or notebook computers should take care to follow the same safety practices that are used by businesses: back up critical data, choose passwords carefully, consider biometric authentication tools for logon, filter out junk e-mail, install virus protection software, and so forth. Additionally, individuals enjoying the mobility of notebook computers and other mobile devices also should be aware of the need to physically secure the device when it is not in use.

For more tips on cyber security, visit the Book Companion Site Web page at **www.cengagebrain.com**. Under the Chapter 6 @Issue links, click a link below Cyber Security.

Chapter Review

Networks are categorized by the physical area that they cover, and include local area, metropolitan area, and wide area networks. The Internet is the world's largest public WAN. LANs are configured in one of two basic structures: peer-to-peer or client/server.

The three most common physical topologies are the bus topology, the ring topology, and the star topology. The two most common LAN access methods are Ethernet and token ring. Networks use both physical transmission media, such as twisted-pair and fiber-optic cable, and wireless transmission media, such as infrared (IR) and radio frequency (RF) transmissions. The hardware devices and software that connect network segments and multiple networks to each other are hubs, bridges, data switches, routers, and gateways.

Network service providers (NSPs) provide the interconnected Internet backbones and networks at Internet exchange points (IXPs), and the three regional U.S. Metropolitan Area Exchanges (MAEs). Peering is the exchange of Internet traffic at a public or private exchange point. NAPs and NSPs create peering agreements that regulate the exchange of Internet traffic bound for each other's networks.

The TCP/IP stack is a group of subprotocols that provides the de facto standard protocols for communications across the Internet and for many private networks. An IP address is used by the IP protocol to deliver a data packet. The DNS consists of a hierarchy of servers: root name servers, authentication servers, and local caching servers.

ICANN manages the Shared Registration System (SRS), which allows private companies, called accredited registrars, to participate in the registration of domain names.

IP telephony or voice over IP (VoIP) uses TCP/IP and packet switching to send Voice over an IP network. Web and video conferencing permit the real-time transmission of images and sounds between two locations, and are used for activities such as employee meetings and training, new product introduction, and customer support activities.

Network security involves protecting network equipment and data from internal and external threats.

TERMS TO KNOW

After reading this chapter, you should know each of these Key Terms.

access method (334)
accredited registrars (352)
authoritative servers (349)
biometrics (364)
Bluetooth (337)
bridge (341)
caching servers (349)
certification authority (CA) (373)
classful routing system (347)
Classless Inter-Domain Routing (CIDR) (348)
classless routing system (348)
client/server network (331)
cloud storage (366)
coaxial cable (339)
converged networks (360)
cyber security (376)
data switch (341)
digital certificate (374)
disaster recovery plan (366)
distributed denial of service (DDoS) (367)
DNS namespace (349)
dynamic routing (342)
encryption (373)
Ethernet (336)
fiber-optic cable (339)
gateway (343)
geosocial networking (358)
Global Positioning System (GPS) (356)
hop (342)
hub (330)
infrared (IR) transmissions (336)
intelligent hub (341)
Internet exchange point (IXP) (345)
Internet telephony (358)
IP telephony (358)
ipconfig /all (348)
IPv6 (347)
LAN jacking (365)
location-based services (LBS) (356)
logical address (347)
logical topology (336)
MAC (Media Access Control) address (341)
Metropolitan Area Exchange (MAE) (345)
metropolitan area network (MAN) (333)
network card (330)
network firewall (371)
network interface card (NIC) (330)
network operating system (332)
network security audit (373)

network service providers (NSPs) (344)
node (330)
nslookup (351)
octet (347)
packet-filtering firewall (372)
passive hub (341)
peering (345)
peer-to-peer LAN (330)
penetration testing (373)
physical topology (334)
port (341)
private key (374)
private peering (346)
proxy server (372)
public key (374)
public key infrastructure (374)
radio frequency (RF) transmissions (337)
resolving (349)
rogue WLAN (365)
root name servers (349)
root zone file (349)
router (341)
routing table (342)
segments (340)
Shared Registration System (SRS) (352)
smart card (365)
social engineering (363)
spoofing (365)
static routing (342)
TCP/IP stack (346)
throughput (334)
token (336)
token ring (336)
tracert utility (342)
transceiver (337)
transmission media (334)
tunneling (375)
twisted-pair cable (339)
video conferencing (361)
virtual meeting (361)
virtual private network (VPN) (375)
Voice over IP (VoIP) (358)
war driving (365)
Web conferencing (362)
wide area network (WAN) (333)
wireless LAN (WLAN) (338)
wireless personal area networks
   (WPANs) (337)

Complete the Test Your Knowledge exercises to solidify what you have learned in the chapter.

True or False

Mark T for True and F for False. (Answers are found on page numbers in parentheses.)

____ 1. The HTTP stack of subprotocols is the de facto set of communication protocols for the Internet and many private networks. (346)

____ 2. A peer-to-peer LAN is an appropriate networking choice for a medium-sized organization with 45 users. (331)

____ 3. A proxy server sits between a user and the Internet and forwards HTTP requests using its own IP address rather than the user's IP address. (372)

____ 4. War driving is the act of driving around with a laptop, antenna, and wireless card, looking for unsecured wireless networks to access. (365)

____ 5. A virtual private network is another name for a wireless LAN. (375)

____ 6. VoIP uses TCP/IP and packet switching to send voice over an IP network. (377)

____ 7. Geosocial networking uses LBSs and tools such as Facebook to connect users. (358)

____ 8. An IXP is used by ISPs, but is expensive and has a negative impact on a network's bandwidth. (345)

____ 9. A DNS root name server publishes a directory of the next level of DNS servers. (349)

____10. Each 8-bit number in the IP address is called a byte. (347)

Multiple Choice

Select the best answer. (Answers are found on page numbers in parentheses.)

1. The transmission media of choice for MANs and WANs is _____. (339)

    a. coaxial cable

    b. infrared (IR)

    c. fiber-optic cable

    d. radio frequency (RF)

2. The Shared Registration System of domain name registrars is overseen by _____. (352)

    a. ISPs

    b. accredited registrars

    c. NSPs

    d. ICANN

3. _____ transmissions use light-wave signals as a short-range transmission medium. (336)

   a. radio frequency (RF)

   b. Wi-Fi

   c. infrared (IR)

   d. none of the above

4. The process of translating readable data into unreadable data to prevent unauthorized access or use is called _____. (373)

   a. decryption

   b. encryption

   c. tunneling

   d. private key

5. A _____ is an intelligent connectivity device with one input port and one output port that connects two network segments or two LANs. (343)

   a. bridge

   b. data switch

   c. router

   d. gateway

6. MAN stands for _____ area network. (333)

   a. megabyte

   b. managed

   c. multiple

   d. metropolitan

7. _____ is when a hacker accesses a network in order to set up a fake Web site or send mail that looks like it is coming from an internal server. (365)

   a. war driving

   b. LAN jacking

   c. spoofing

   d. cracking

8. Large modern networks often are broken up into _____, or multiple groups of computers that share a common function. (340)

   a. LANs

   b. segments

   c. VPNs

   d. servers

9. The IPv6 standard lengthens IP addresses to _____ bits. (347)

   a. 128

   b. 32

   c. 10^6

   d. 8

10. A _____ is a kind of virus that spreads across a network, such as the Internet, by replicating itself. (367)

   a. Trojan horse

   b. worm

   c. backdoor

   d. DDoS

Test your knowledge of chapter content and key terms.

Instructions: To complete the following exercises, please visit **www.cengagebrain.com**. On the CengageBrain home page, enter the book title *Discovering the Internet* and then click the Find button. On the product page for this book, click the Access Now button below the Study Tools heading. On the Book Companion Site Web page, click the drop-down menu, select Chapter 6, and then click the link for the desired exercise.

Chapter Reinforcement TF, MC, and SA

A series of true/false, multiple-choice, and short-answer questions that test your knowledge of the chapter content.

Flash Cards

An interactive learning environment where you identify chapter key terms associated with displayed definitions.

Practice Test

A series of multiple-choice questions that test your knowledge of chapter content and key terms.

Who Wants To Be a Computer Genius?

An interactive game that challenges your knowledge of chapter content in the style of a television quiz show.

Wheel of Terms

An interactive game that challenges your knowledge of chapter key terms in the style of the television show, *Wheel of Fortune*.

Crossword Puzzle Challenge

A crossword puzzle that challenges your knowledge of the key terms presented in the chapter.

Use the Exercises to gain hands-on experience working with the Internet and the Web.

1 | Looking Up Corresponding Domain Names and IP Addresses

1. Open the Command Prompt window and use the nslookup command to identify the domain names that correspond to the following IP addresses:

   a. 161.225.130.163

   b. 149.48.228.139

   c. 18.7.21.110

   d. 192.168.1.1

   e. 74.125.113.106

2. Use the Command Prompt window and the nslookup command to identify the IP addresses that correspond to the following domain names:

   a. verisign.com

   b. zazzle.com

   c. blogger.com

   d. yelp.com

   e. garmin.com

3. Close the Command Prompt window.

2 | Analyzing Security Threats

1. Visit the Discovering the Internet, Fourth Edition Chapter 6 Exercises Web page at **www.cengagebrain.com** and click links below Exercise 2 to research cyber security issues and tips.

2. Make a list of all the locations and situations in which you regularly access Internet resources.

3. Determine which three access methods or situations you use the most.

4. For each of the three scenarios, identify the greatest threat to security and describe the best method for protecting against each threat.

3 | Considering a Home Network

You are considering installing a home network to connect your personal computer, laptop, and printer. You need to weigh the pros and cons, make a list of hardware, and read about common networking issues. To learn more about whether and how to set up a network, you will take an online tutorial.

1. Visit the Discovering the Internet, Fourth Edition Chapter 6 Exercises Web page at **www.cengagebrain.com** and click the Home Networking Tutorial link below Exercise 3.

2. Use the links in the tutorial to answer the following questions:

   a. What are the benefits of setting up a home network? What is the difference between a wired and wireless network?

   b. What hardware resources do you need to set up a home network?

   c. How can a computer network enable you to share files and software applications between computers?

   d. Read the list of 10 most common networking problems. Make a list of the three that are your top concerns, and explain how you would fix them.

   e. What steps would you take to keep your network secure?

4 | Searching for an Available Domain Name

You want to register a domain name for your small photography supply business. The first step is to identify suitable and available domain names from which to choose. You need the domain name to be short, easy to remember, and appropriate for a photography supply business.

1. Visit the Discovering the Internet, Fourth Edition Chapter 6 Exercises Web page at **www.cengagebrain.com** and click the links below Exercise 4 to search for an appropriate domain name that meets your criteria: short, easy to remember, and appropriate for a photography supply business. Do not forget to search in multiple top-level domains (TLDs). Make sure to investigate the availability of a mobile address and any other domain names you might need at this time.

2. Print the search results page that provides available, appropriate domain names and indicate which name you prefer.

5 | Identifying Wireless Location-Based Services

1. Using the search engine of your choice, search for examples of wireless location-based services.

2. Write a one- or two-paragraph summary of at least five currently offered location-based services. Which of the services do you find the most useful? Why? Which of the services do you find least useful? Why?

6 | Using the Windows Tracert Utility to Trace Hops

1. Open the Command Prompt window and use the tracert command to identify the number of hops between your computer and the following locations:

   a. www.wm.edu

   b. www.cisco.com

   c. www.bbc.co.uk

   d. www.rackspace.com

   e. www.loc.gov

2. Which location required the most hops? Which location required the fewest hops?

7 | Identifying Current Virus, Worm, and Trojan Horse Risks

1. Visit the Discovering the Internet, Fourth Edition Chapter 6 Exercises Web page at **www.cengagebrain.com** and click the links below Exercise 7 to identify 10 current viruses, worms, and Trojan horses.

2. Create a table that lists the following information for each threat:

   a. Name

   b. Risk level

   c. Description

   d. Date discovered

   e. Source of information

8 | Reviewing Wireless Security Issues

1. Visit the Discovering the Internet, Fourth Edition Chapter 6 Exercises Web page at **www.cengagebrain.com** and click the links below Exercise 8 to research wireless security issues.

2. Using your wireless security research, write a one-page paper that describes current wireless security issues. Be sure to include the following topics in your discussion:

   a. Wireless viruses, worms, and Trojan horse risks

   b. Wireless LAN security risks

   c. Descriptions of suggested solutions or methods for handling identified threats

9 | Researching Past and Current Cyber Attacks

1. Use the search engines of your choice to research the following security hackers: Gordon Lyon, Eric Corley, Rafael Nunez, and Kevin Mitnick. Then write a brief paragraph about each hacker, including his contributions to security hacking.

2. Use the search engines of your choice to identify two network attacks that have occurred during the past 12 months. Write a short paragraph describing each attack. Remember to cite your sources correctly.

10 | Reviewing International Standards Organizations

1. Use the search engine of your choice to identify the mission of each of the following organizations that contribute to the development of networking technologies and standards:

   a. ANSI

   b. ETSI

   c. ITU-T

   d. IEC

   e. IEEE

   f. ISO

2. Write a short paper that includes one paragraph for each organization describing the organization and its mission.

Figure 6-1a: Robert Milek /Shutterstock.com

Figure 6-1b: Kitch Bain /Shutterstock.com

Figure 6-2a: Kitch Bain /Shutterstock.com

Figure 6-2b: Robert Milek /Shutterstock.com

Figure 6-4: kukuruxa /Shutterstock.com

Figure 6-6a: iStockphoto.com/Sirgunhik

Figure 6-6b: Robert Milek /Shutterstock.com

Figure 6-6c: tuanyick /Shutterstock.com

Figure 6-6d: Kitch Bain /Shutterstock.com

Figure 6-7a: Christian Delbert /Shutterstock.com

Figure 6-7b: alexkar08 /Shutterstock.com.com

Figure 6-8a: Diego Cervo /Shutterstock.com

Figure 6-8b: ©2011 Jupiterimages Corporation

Figure 6-9: Christian Delbert /Shutterstock.com

Figure 6-9a: Robert Milek /Shutterstock.com

Figure 6-9b: iStockphoto.com/macroworld

Figure 6-9c: David Brimm/Shutterstock.com

Figure 6-9d: Kitch Bain /Shutterstock.com

Figure 6-9e: iStockphoto.com/Sirgunhik

Figure 6-13a: Kitch Bain /Shutterstock.com

Figure 6-13b: tuanyick /Shutterstock.com

Figure 6-13c: tuanyick /Shutterstock.com

Figure 6-13d: prism68 /Shutterstock.com

Figure 6-13e: Pavel Kirichenko /Shutterstock.com

Figure 6-13f: Fesus Robert /Shutterstock.com

Figure 6-28a: Copyright ©1998–2011 Safenames Ltd.

Figure 6-28b: © 1995–2011 by Register.com®

Figure 6-29: Copyright © 2011 Network Solutions, LLC All rights reserved.

Figure 6-30: Copyright © 2011 Network Solutions, LLC All rights reserved.

Figure 6-31: Copyright © 2011 Network Solutions, LLC All rights reserved.

Figure 6-32a: iStockphoto.com/macroworld

Figure 6-32b: iStockphoto.com/duckycards

Figure 6-32c: Christian Delbert /Shutterstock.com

Figure 6-33a: Daniel Padavona /Shutterstock.com

Figure 6-33b: iStockphoto.com/macroworld

Figure 6-33c: Olga Gabay /Shutterstock.com

Figure 6-33d: robcocquyt /Shutterstock.com

Figure 6-33e: © Fredrik Broman/Getty Images

Figure 6-33f: Yuri Arcurs /Shutterstock.com

7 | Understanding E-Business

Introduction

As you learned in Chapter 1, the term e-commerce is sometimes used to describe the process of conducting business transactions over the Internet, while the term e-business is sometimes used to describe the broader scope of maintaining partner, customer, and employee business relationships using the Internet. However, many people use these terms interchangeably. This chapter uses the term e-business to describe business activities of all types supported by Internet technologies.

In this chapter, you will learn about the early origins of e-business and the unique factors that underlie its amazing growth, as well as individual e-business successes. Multiple real-world examples will help you learn about different e-business models. Finally, you will focus on business-to-consumer retailing by learning about online store software, merchant accounts, and how credit card transactions are authorized and processed.

Objectives

After completing this chapter, you will be able to:

1. Describe the origins of electronic business transactions, including the electronic funds transfer (EFT) system, the electronic data interchange (EDI) standard, and value-added networks (VANs)

2. Discuss unique e-business factors and identify e-businesses that use them

3. Define common e-business models and explain how each model generates revenue

4. Describe the e-retailing storefront software, merchant accounts, and payment-processing services needed to create and operate an online store

E-Business Origins

You might be surprised to learn that some types of business transactions have been conducted electronically for more than 40 years — long before the Internet became a popular and useful business channel. Electronic business activities actually originated in the 1960s and 1970s with the banking industry's electronic funds transfer system and the electronic data interchange (EDI) networks used by large companies.

Electronic Funds Transfer

Electronic funds transfer (EFT) allows money to be transferred between banks electronically — without the exchange of paper currency. In the 1960s, banks began exchanging money electronically through a network that connects all U.S. financial institutions, called the **Automated Clearing House (ACH)** network. EFT continues to play an increasingly important role in business today. Having your payroll check deposited directly to your bank account; paying your federal income taxes, utility bills, or credit card bills online; and using an ATM are all examples of EFT (Figure 7-1) in action.

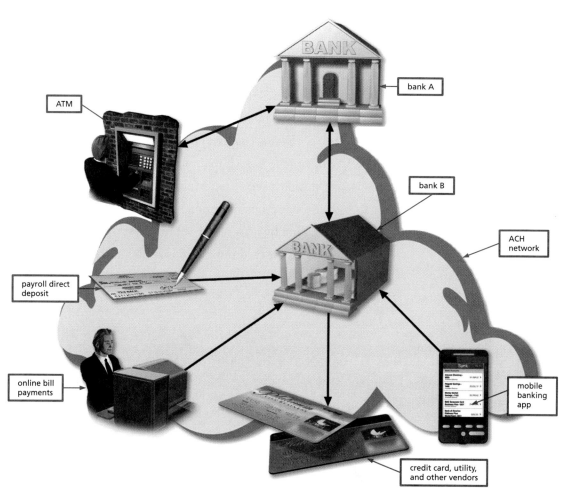

Figure 7-1   Paying bills online, having a paycheck deposited directly into an account, and using an ATM are examples of the electronic funds transfer (EFT) system in action.

Electronic Data Interchange

The **electronic data interchange (EDI)** standard specifies the layout or format a company uses to exchange electronic business data — such as purchase orders, receiving reports, and invoices — with its suppliers and customers. For example, a manufacturing company could use specific EDI formats to automate the process of ordering parts from its suppliers. The participants in an EDI exchange of business data are called **trading partners**. Before the Internet became a viable alternative for transmitting data, EDI exchange of business information between trading partners occurred over private telecommunication networks called **value-added networks (VANs)**. Traditional VANs are very expensive to set up and maintain, and require the creation of expensive, customized interfaces for exchanging data with trading partners. For these reasons, EDI exchanges (Figure 7-2) primarily have been used only by very large companies.

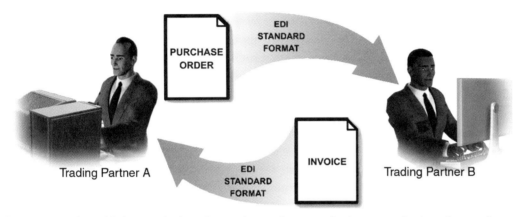

Figure 7-2   Value-added networks (VANs) are private telecommunication networks that allow trading partners to exchange business data.

The Internet is a much less expensive network alternative to creating and maintaining VANs, and many small, medium, and large companies use it rather than VANs to exchange business data. Companies can send purchase orders and invoices over the Internet to their trading partners using the XML document format and the HTTP protocols. The processes served by VANs are now more generally called grid computing. **Grid computing** combines resources from many sources to reach a common goal. For example, the software, hardware, and network capabilities of a group of companies in a business process — from resource procurement to manufacturing to sales — all combine to create a grid. Companies such as Microsoft and Telvent are working to create grid networking capabilities that use the Internet to help companies manage and distribute assets and provide and share other services.

Unique E-Business Factors

Companies that conduct their business activities online enjoy a host of business advantages, including worldwide sales opportunities, reduced transaction and purchasing costs, and access to small, niche markets. At the same time, individual and business consumers also enjoy similar advantages: access to a global electronic marketspace, wider product availability, improved customer and product support, and easy comparison shopping.

Beyond these advantages, other factors unique to conducting business activities online play an important role in the ongoing growth and success of e-business. In this section, you will learn about some of these factors, including the effects of geography, time, and space on the online marketspace; the network effect; the ability of individual e-businesses to redefine a market; and the power of personalization and customization.

Geography, Time, and Space

Geography, time, and space are limiting factors for any brick-and-mortar business. The following is a look at the role geography, time, and space can play in the operation of a brick-and-mortar store, such as a bookstore:

- Geography — A brick-and-mortar bookstore must be physically located within a modest driving distance of its targeted customer base. In addition, the store should be located in a high-traffic area to increase its visibility and attract new customers.

- Time — A brick-and-mortar bookstore is likely to maintain the same operating hours as other stores in its area, which might be only peak shopping hours. In most areas, it is uncommon to find a brick-and-mortar bookstore open 24 hours a day.

- Space — The inventory of books available at a brick-and-mortar bookstore is limited to the store's available storage and shelf space. Because of space restrictions, a brick-and-mortar bookstore might stock only the most recently published books in the most popular categories — perhaps carrying only a few hundred titles.

Now consider the effect of geography, time, and space on the online bookstore marketspace. Suppose you just read a review of the latest book by your favorite British mystery author, and you want to purchase a copy of the book. The book currently is available only in the United Kingdom and will not be available in U.S. bookstores for several months. No need to wait — geography and time no longer matter. WHSmith, one of the leading booksellers in the United Kingdom, operates an e-business Web site. You can simply visit the Web site and order the book any time it is convenient for you. You also might be able to purchase an electronic copy of the book from WHSmith, called an **e-book**, which can be downloaded to your computer or handheld device, such as an e-book reader (Figure 7-3), tablet computer, or smartphone.

Figure 7-3 E-book readers, like the Sony Reader, enable you to download books instantly from the Internet.

Perhaps you need to find an inexpensive used copy of a classic nineteenth century novel that is currently out of print, but the nearest used bookstore is several miles away and has a poor selection of these types of books. No problem. Infinite shelf space is available on the Web. Several e-business Web sites — such as Amazon.com, Abebooks.com, and Alibris (Figure 7-4) — aggregate information about the used, out-of-print, and rare book inventories held by individual book resellers located all over the world. You can even use Amazon.com to sell your own used books, or trade them with other book readers using services such as PaperBackSwap.com (Figure 7-4).

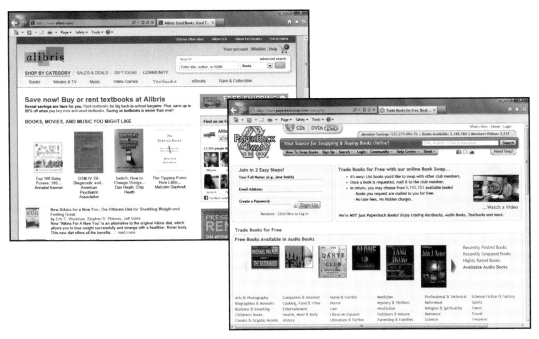

@SOURCE

Unique E-Business Factors
To learn more about the e-businesses discussed in this section, visit **www. cengagebrain.com**. On the CengageBrain home page, enter the book title, *Discovering the Internet*, and then click the Find button. On the product page for this book, click the Access Now button below the Study Tools heading. On the Book Companion Site Web page, click the drop-down menu, select Chapter 7, and then click the @Source link. Click a link below Unique E-Business Factors.

Figure 7-4   Online bookstores and trading sites enable you to find used or rare books from individuals or booksellers around the world.

The Network Effect

An important e-business success factor, called the **network effect**, refers to the increasing value of a network as the network grows. The analogy often used to describe the network effect is a telephone network. Assume that your telephone is the only telephone connected to a telephone network. Your single telephone and the telephone network to which it is connected have little or no value because you cannot call anyone else, and no one can call you. Connect a second telephone and user to the network, however, and the value of the network increases — now you and the other user can call each other. As additional telephones and users connect to the network, the network's value continues to increase.

The network effect also is known as Metcalfe's law and is named for Robert Metcalfe, an early pioneer in the development of Ethernet networking technologies and the founder of 3Com Corporation, an Internet technologies provider.

The rate at which the Internet has grown and the related explosion in e-businesses is an example of the network effect (Figure 7-5). For example, the value of the Internet to individual users and to the business community continues to grow as the number of people with Internet access grows. E-business continues to become an increasingly valuable part of the global economy as more businesses and consumers participate in the online marketspace.

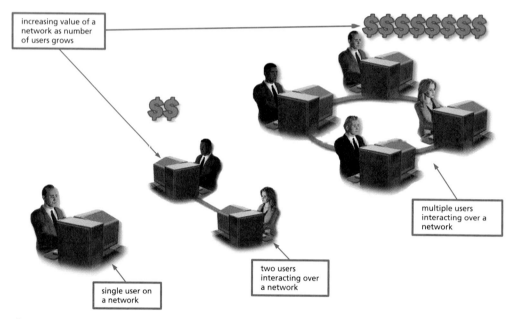

Figure 7-5 The network effect ensures that e-business will continue to become a more valuable part of the global economy as the number of e-businesses and their online customers grows.

Hotmail and the Network Effect

Perhaps one of the better-known examples of the network effect in the success of an individual e-business is Hotmail. Hotmail, an e-mail service now owned by Microsoft, was launched on July 4, 1996. Because little money was available to promote Hotmail's free e-mail service, Hotmail added a message with a link to the Hotmail Web site to the bottom of each outgoing e-mail message sent from its system. The added message encouraged the e-mail's recipient to click the link to the Hotmail Web site and subscribe to the free e-mail service.

Using the network to promote the Hotmail service — a process now called **viral marketing** because news of the Hotmail service traveled from user to user like a human virus — resulted in spectacular success. Within just a few days of its launch, hundreds of new users, mostly at colleges and universities, subscribed to the Hotmail service. First, a single user from a college or university would subscribe and then, over the next several days, thousands of users from the same school would subscribe. Back in 1996, many people had not yet begun to use e-mail as a regular form of communication between family, friends, and business associates. As each new Hotmail subscriber signed up for the Hotmail service, its value to all subscribers grew because there were more and more people with whom to exchange free e-mail.

Quickly, Hotmail spread to other colleges and universities, where the process began all over again. It was not long before users all around the world began subscribing to the Hotmail service. Eighteen months after its initial launch, Hotmail had 12 million worldwide subscribers. Did the value of the Hotmail e-business increase by exploiting the network effect? Yes, indeed. Not long after Hotmail reached 12 million subscribers, Microsoft bought it (Figure 7-6) from its founders for $400 million!

To learn more about Hotmail, visit the Book Companion Site Web page at **www.cengagebrain.com**. Under the Chapter 7 E-Biz Case Study links, click the Hotmail link.

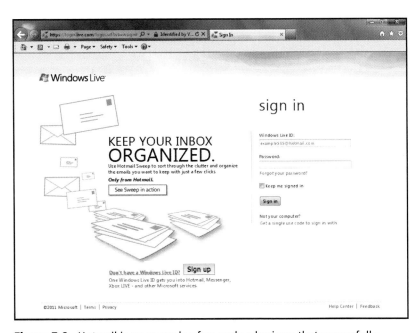

Figure 7-6 Hotmail is an example of an early e-business that successfully exploited the network effect.

Redefining Markets

Another important e-business factor is the opportunity an individual e-business might have to redefine a market. Market redefinition generally takes place in one of two ways: (1) by removing traditional marketplace intermediaries or (2) by creating new ways to add value to business transactions, often by introducing new types of intermediaries to the marketplace.

DISINTERMEDIATION   An **intermediary**, or middleman, is a business entity that brings sellers and buyers together. Examples of traditional marketplace intermediaries include:

- Sporting goods industry — A retail store, selling manufactured goods to consumers
- Real estate industry — A real estate agent, marketing home owners' properties to potential buyers
- Travel industry — A travel agent, working with individuals to purchase plane tickets or reserve hotel rooms and rental cars
- Insurance industry — An insurance broker, providing clients with options from home, life, and car insurers

An individual e-business can redefine a market by allowing consumers to bypass the market's traditional intermediaries and purchase products or services directly from the e-business's Web site. Redefining a market by removing its traditional intermediaries is called **disintermediation**. Dell arguably is one of the more famous examples of disintermediation. Dell built its business by bypassing retail computer stores to sell directly to customers. Dell uses its Web sites to sell thousands of personal computers, printers, servers, and other consumer electronics directly to consumers around the world.

The travel industry is another example of disintermediation, in which the growth of travel-related e-business is redefining the market. Traditionally, planning a vacation or business trip involved calling or visiting a local travel agent who made all the arrangements, including purchasing airline tickets, reserving a car, and booking a hotel room. In turn, the agent earned a fee or commission from the airline, auto rental companies, and hotel. Today, the travel agent intermediary often is bypassed by consumers who book and pay for their travel arrangements directly at e-business Web sites operated by airlines, auto rental companies, and hotels, such as those illustrated in Figure 7-7.

Figure 7-7   Examples of airline, auto rental, and hotel company Web sites contributing to travel industry disintermediation.

Dell Inc. and Disintermediation

Dell Computer Corporation (now Dell Inc.) was founded in 1984 by Michael Dell, while he was still an undergraduate at the University of Texas at Austin. Michael Dell recognized that a business opportunity existed in the huge difference between the cost of individual personal computer components and the price of an assembled personal computer purchased from a retail store. He decided that by eliminating the retail store middleman, he could sell personal computers directly to consumers for much lower prices and still generate a profit (Figure 7-8). And he was right. By 1993, Dell was a Fortune 500 company and one of the top five computer manufacturers in the world.

As the overall growth in PC sales flattened over the past several years, Dell has experimented with a variety of sales channels in addition to the Web, including shopping mall kiosks and retail stores. In 2008, Dell announced it was closing all of its U.S. shopping mall kiosks to focus on direct sales and retail partnerships. In 2011, Dell had $61.1 billion in sales and more than 100,000 employees worldwide, and the company appeared as number 41 on the Fortune 500 list.

For more information about Dell Inc., visit the Book Companion Site Web page at **www. cengagebrain.com**. Under the Chapter 7 E-Biz Case Study links, click the Dell link.

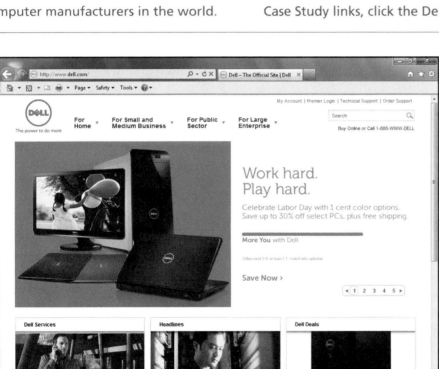

Figure 7-8 Dell sells personal computers directly to consumers.

REINTERMEDIATION   Some e-businesses are eliminating traditional intermediaries and, in the process, redefining markets. Other e-businesses also are redefining markets through a different process called **reintermediation**. Reintermediation occurs when an e-business introduces a new type of intermediary into the marketspace. Dell, Hewlett-Packard, and even the online versions of stores such as Best Buy are examples of e-business reintermediation in the computer industry. Although it is likely that online computer sales have contributed to the failure of some brick-and-mortar computer stores, such as Circuit City (with limited shelf space, and the higher business costs of renting store space and hiring store staff), disintermediation is not the culprit. E-business disintermediation in the computer industry occurs when computer manufacturers, such as Hewlett-Packard, sell computers directly to individual consumers from their Web sites. Online computer sales simply are a new type of technology industry intermediary that uses the Internet and the Web to provide value to the marketspace in new ways.

Two examples of reintermediation in the travel industry are Orbitz Worldwide and Hotels.com. Orbitz (Figure 7-9) was originally founded as an e-business partnership among five major airlines: American, Continental, Delta, Northwest, and United. Today, Orbitz Worldwide is a publicly traded company on the New York Stock Exchange and is a major provider of travel distribution services. Orbitz is a travel industry intermediary that uses its Web site to provide consumers with quick access to low fares for airline tickets and low rates on auto rentals and hotel accommodations.

Hotels.com, another travel industry intermediary, purchases large blocks of hotel rooms at a big discount from properties around the world. Hotels.com then marks up the discounted room rates and resells the rooms directly to consumers from its Web site.

Figure 7-9 Online travel intermediary Web sites contribute to reintermediation in the travel industry.

Personalization and Customization

The unique interactive nature of the Web that allows buyers and sellers to communicate directly, and in ever-changing ways, is another important e-business factor. E-businesses can exploit Web interactivity by personalizing and customizing Web content to increase sales, provide better customer support, and encourage customer loyalty.

The terms, personalization and customization, sometimes are used interchangeably. However, some analysts define **personalization** as an automatic process that tailors Web page content to fit the profile of a specific target audience, or that automatically tailors Web page content for an individual visitor based on his or her actions at a site. You experience the benefits of personalization each time you shop at an online store that acknowledges you by name and suggests new items — books, CDs, DVDs — for purchase based on your previous purchases at the site.

Customization is a manual process that allows a visitor to manage Web page content by selecting viewing preferences or by creating and updating a personal profile. In Chapter 5, you learned how visitors could customize the news, sports, and weather content at a major news-oriented portal Web site by indicating preferences or postal codes. Customization also allows e-business customers to create custom products, such as clothing or diet and fitness programs, designed specifically for them by indicating size, style, goals, or other preferences. Personalization and customization work together to create a unique viewing or shopping experience by using general customer purchase histories, product reviews, and target audience profile data. Personalization and customization also use individual visitor profiles to create uniquely targeted Web pages with specific content, including item recommendations and new products, based on the customer's past purchases.

E-businesses that sell directly to individual consumers and to other businesses use personalization and customization to develop a closer relationship with their customers that promotes increased customer loyalty. E-retail e-businesses, such as eDiets.com, provide customized diet and fitness plans based on consumer profiles, and then track and report each subscriber's results as he or she follows the plan. At the Lands' End custom design page (Figure 7-10), customers can complete an online profile to order jeans customized for their preferences and body type. E-businesses, such as Physician Sales & Service and Staples (Figure 7-10), that sell to other businesses also use personalization and customization. Physician Sales & Service, which sells medical supplies to physicians, uses personalization to create purchasing histories, inventory reports, and replenishment purchase orders that help a physician and his or her office staff manage the office's medical supply inventory. Online office supply vendors, such as Staples, also use personalization to provide their business customers with customized purchasing and office supply inventory control services.

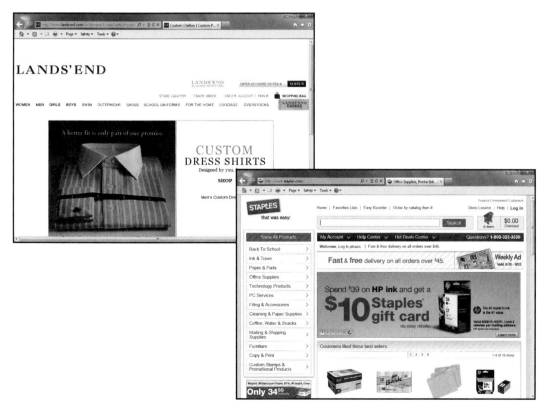

Figure 7-10   E-businesses use personalization and customization to attract and keep customers.

E-Business Models

As you browse the Web, you likely encounter many different types of commercial Web sites. From time to time you might ask yourself how a site makes money, because exactly how a commercial Web site generates revenue might not be obvious. The answer lies in the business model followed by the company that publishes the site. A **business model** is the way a company operates to generate revenue, create profits (the excess of revenue over expenses), and continue as a viable business entity. The business model adopted by a company doing business online often is called its e-business model. In Chapter 1, you were introduced to several different e-business models, as described in Figure 7-11.

E-Business Models

Targeted Customer	E-Business Model	Description	Example
Consumers	Business-to-Consumer (B2C)	An e-business sells products or services directly to consumers.	Lands' End Amazon.com
Consumers	Consumer-to-Consumer (C2C)	A consumer sells products or services directly to another consumer.	eBay Etsy
Businesses	Consumer-to-Business (C2B)	A consumer names a price for a product or service that competing businesses accept or decline.	Priceline.com
Businesses	Business-to-Business (B2B)	An e-business sells products or services to other businesses; brings multiple buyers and sellers together in a central online marketspace; sells e-business technologies; or transacts business activities over the Internet with trading partners.	Physician Sales & Service Storage Guardian
Government agencies and other businesses	Business-to-Government (B2G)	An e-business provides information about government agencies currently accepting bids for products and services; brings sellers and government agency buyers together in an online marketspace; or sells bidding and procurement technologies.	Fedmarket Onvia

Figure 7-11 E-business models can be defined by customer group.

Individual e-businesses optimize factors — such as geography, time, space, the network effect, personalization, and customization — within the framework of their e-business model. E-business models are classified in a number of ways, but the most common way is by targeted customer groups, such as consumers, other businesses, and government agencies. Although an individual e-business might seem to fit into one of the primary e-business model categories, many e-businesses actually operate using a mix of e-business models and revenue-generation methods. For example, an e-business's primary e-business model might emphasize selling products or services directly to consumers; however, the e-business also might generate revenue by doing one or more of the following:

- Offering subscription-based content
- Selling advertising space at its Web site

- Earning referral fees by providing links to other e-business Web sites
- Selling proprietary e-business technologies to other companies
- Providing a channel for business partners to sell their products
- Participating in an affiliate marketing program

In this section, you will use multiple real-world e-business examples to explore common e-business models.

Business-to-Consumer (B2C)

The business-to-consumer (B2C) e-business model generates revenue in several ways, including retail sales directly to consumers, often called e-tail or e-retail, selling Web site advertising space, and charging subscription or membership fees for premium content.

E-RETAIL   Most large, traditional brick-and-mortar retailers and catalog merchants, such as Williams-Sonoma (Figure 7-12), The Container Store (Figure 7-12), and JCPenney, take advantage of their retailing experiences and existing product distribution centers to combine e-retailing Web sites successfully with their physical stores and catalog operations — in the process, becoming brick-and-click businesses, or e-retailers. By adding e-retailing Web sites to existing operations, these companies create a new business channel mix that provides increased sales opportunities and improved customer service.

@SOURCE

E-Business Models
To learn more about the e-businesses discussed in this chapter, visit the Book Companion Site Web page at **www.cengagebrain.com**. Under the Chapter 7 @Source links, click a link below E-Business Models.

Figure 7-12   Most large brick-and-mortar retailers and catalog merchants are also brick-and-click e-retailers.

According to research firm eMarketer, U.S. retail e-commerce revenue will exceed $200 billion by 2013.

FACTS @HAND

Some early B2C e-retailers, however, started life in the online marketspace as completely new businesses with no existing brick-and-mortar stores or catalog operations.

These online-only retailers, called **pure-play e-retailers**, have met with mixed success. Amazon.com is, of course, the most famous example of a pure-play e-retailer. Many other early pure-play e-retailers, such as Pets.com and the original eToys.com, were never able to rival Amazon.com's volume of sales or market dominance and ended as spectacular e-business failures.

A **niche market** is a small segment within a larger market. Some pure-play e-retailers, such as FlirtyFinds, succeed by avoiding competition with larger e-businesses and, instead, target a niche market. Founded in 2008, FlirtyFinds specializes in accessories — such as jewelry, handbags, and wraps — that are high in quality, on-trend, and reasonably priced.

To Explore a Pure-Play E-Retailer

The following steps explore offerings at a pure-play e-retailer that targets a niche market. You will open the FlirtyFinds home page in a new tab. Linked pages from the home page will open in the same tab as the home page.

- Start Internet Explorer.

- Visit the Book Companion Site Web page for this text. Click the 'Select a chapter' list arrow, click the option for Chapter 7, and then click the Steps link on the left side of the page.

- Click the FlirtyFinds link to open the Web page in a new tab (Figure 7-13).

Figure 7-13

2

- Scroll the page to review its contents.

- Click the Jewelry link to view the current jewelry offerings (Figure 7-14).

- Close the browser and all open tabs.

Figure 7-14

ADVERTISING REVENUES   Some B2C e-businesses offer free content — information, links, games, and so forth — and generate revenue by selling advertising at their sites. Web site ads (Figure 7-15, on the next page) usually are linked to the advertiser's own Web site; therefore, visitors can go directly to the advertised Web site by clicking an ad in a process called a **click-through**. The effectiveness of a particular Web site ad often is measured by the number of visitors who use it to click-through to the advertised Web site; this method of revenue generation is called **per-click**. Another way to generate revenue or measure an ad's success is the **cost per impression (CPI)** method. CPI counts the number of times a page that includes an ad is loaded in the browser; reimbursement for CPI is often for a certain number of impressions, such as a thousand.

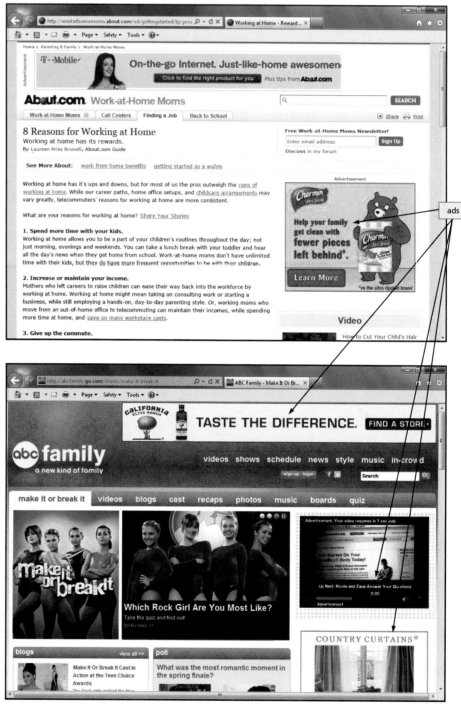

Figure 7-15   Examples of ads that generate revenue for a Web site.

Google AdSense (Figure 7-16) is an example of an application that Web site owners can implement to include targeted advertisements on their sites. Google administers and maintains the advertisements, and site owners can include text, video, or image advertisements. Because Google works with the advertisers, this is an effective option for small e-business companies that do not have an advertising department, or individual Web site hosts who want to generate revenue by hosting banner ads.

Cheap hotels
Find Hotels By Price, Star Rating Or
Location. Cheap hotels

Save on Las Vegas Hotels
Amazing Las Vegas hotel discounts.
Easily book your room today.

Ads by Google

Figure 7-16 Google AdSense enables Web site owners to add targeted advertisements.

SUBSCRIPTION FEES Another way the B2C e-business model generates revenue is through subscription fees for premium content. Some e-businesses that generate revenue from advertising, such as Yahoo!, also might charge subscription fees for certain premium services, such as résumé posting and job search, posting personals ads, or participating in an online community.

For example, WebmasterWorld (Figure 7-17) provides access to information on Web design, online marketing, and other relevant topics, such as domain names. Much of the content is generated by discussions among subscribers in forums; the forums are mostly free to visitors. For an annual subscription fee, members can contribute to forums, as well as access some discussion groups that are only open to members.

Some nonprofit organizations also follow the B2C subscription e-business model. For example, the Consumers Union is an independent consumer product testing organization that publishes *Consumer Reports* magazine and its online version, ConsumerReports.org (Figure 7-17). For an annual subscription fee, you can read reviews and test results on thousands of consumer products at the ConsumerReports.org Web site.

Figure 7-17 Some B2C e-businesses generate subscription-based revenue.

E-BIZ CASE STUDY

Netflix and the B2C Subscription Model

In 1997, Reed Hastings, a computer software entrepreneur, recognized a business opportunity in the emerging popularity of DVDs. To capitalize on this popularity, he cofounded the DVD rental e-business Netflix (Figure 7-18). Hastings wanted to operate a movie rental business in a very new way by having DVD rentals inexpensively delivered and then returned using a postage-paid envelope sent through the U.S. Postal Service, eliminating trips to a movie rental store. Originally, Netflix charged its customers a per-movie rental fee much like its brick-and-mortar competitors. Then, Hastings hit upon the idea of removing specific return dates and the threat of late fees. As the story goes, Hastings had rented a movie from a video store, watched it, and then forgot to return it on time, which resulted in whopping late fees. From that costly experience was born the next Netflix e-business idea — DVDs rented on a subscription basis. Hastings envisioned Netflix customers paying a monthly subscription fee to rent as many DVDs as they wanted and keep them as long as they wanted without incurring late fees.

Netflix's original model charged customers monthly fees, which differed depending on the level of service, such as the number of movies rented at a time, Blu-ray rentals, and streaming video. Movies on DVD are mailed to the customer and then returned in a postage-paid envelope. Many movies and TV episodes can be streamed directly to a customer's computer or television. Customers are encouraged to rate the movies they rent using its Cinematch five-star rating system. Netflix then uses a customer's movie ratings together with collaborative filtering software to create a list of movie recommendations based on the customer's viewing preferences.

Netflix keeps its inventory costs low by participating in rental revenue-sharing partnerships with a number of movie studios, which allows Netflix access to the studios' film libraries, and by increasingly relying on streaming video as a subscription type. Today, Netflix has an estimated 25 million subscribers and an ever-expanding inventory of movie titles on DVD, including new releases, classics, hard-to-find documentaries, independent films, plus thousands of movies and TV episodes available for streaming. In 2011, Netflix announced subscribers would be able to choose between streaming-only or DVD rental options or a combination.

For more information about Netflix, visit the Book Companion Site Web page at **www.cengagebrain.com**. Under the Chapter 7 E-Biz Case Study links, click the Netflix link.

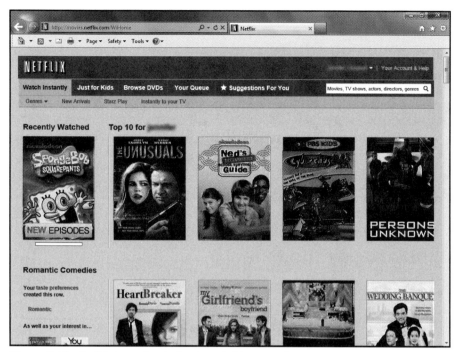

Figure 7-18 Netflix is a subscription-based video rental company.

SOCIAL MEDIA In previous chapters, you learned about the impact of Web-based social media — social networking, social opinion, social tagging, microblogging, and so forth — on personal communication. Businesses also are exploiting the benefits of social media, including the network effect, to promote individual businesses and specific industries, to sell products and services to their customers, or to generate revenue by selling advertising space. For example, the social networking sites Facebook and Myspace sell ad space; businesses actively solicit reviews of their sites by participants at StumbleUpon and other social bookmarking or tagging sites in order to build traffic to their sites; and Twitter (Figure 7-19) is used to broadcast a variety of business messages, or **tweets**, announcing everything from pizza specials, to new offerings in a specific real estate market, to CEO business status updates.

Figure 7-19 Business also are exploiting social media sites to generate ad revenue, build traffic to their sites, and sell products and services.

Squidoo (Figure 7-20) and HubPages are platforms for user-generated Web sites. Without needing to know HTML, users create topic pages, which are available on the platform. For example, Squidoo pages are called lenses, and page creators are called lensmasters. While lenses are informative, Squidoo pages also include click-through ads and links to generate revenue. Squidoo retains 50 percent of the revenue generated by each lens; the remainder is split between the lensmaster and any charities the lensmaster specifies.

Figure 7-20 Squidoo relies on ads and links on user-generated content pages.

Twitter and the Social Media Business Model

Evan Williams is a Silicon Valley entrepreneur who, in March 2006, joined with Biz Stone and Jack Dorsey to develop Dorsey's original idea for a new text-only messaging service based on Web syndication and SMS messaging technologies. To use the messaging service, individuals would first create an account and then broadcast messages to their Web page and to the cell phones of friends, family members, and others, who subscribed to or "followed" the individual's message feed.

In a few short years, the new messaging service, originally named Twttr and now called Twitter (Figure 7-21, on the next page), has turned the social media world on its ear. In 2011, Twitter had 200 million users and generated 200 million tweets a day. Twitter's effect on interpersonal communications has been so rapid and powerful that in 2009, the three Twitter founders were named to the TIME 100, *TIME Magazine*'s list of the world's most influential people.

Despite its popularity with users, as of this writing, Twitter is a free service surviving mostly on cash provided by investors, called venture capitalists, who have taken an ownership share of the company. In 2010, Twitter introduced paid advertisements, called "promoted tweets"; in 2011, it was expected that Twitter would receive $150 million in revenue from advertisements that year, according to eMarketer, compared with $4 billion in ad revenue by Facebook.

Some analysts suggest Twitter might capitalize on its popularity in a variety of other ways including charging a premium for commercial tweets, becoming involved in location-based marketing, joining in revenue-sharing arrangements with companies that are creating applications that enhance the way Twitter is used, or by selling the company. As of this writing, it remains to be seen what combination of revenue-generation methods Twitter's management will ultimately adopt.

For more information about Twitter, visit the Book Companion Site Web page at **www.cengagebrain.com**. Under the Chapter 7 E-Biz Case Study links, click the Twitter link.

Figure 7-21   Twitter uses venture capital funding and promoted tweets to generate revenue.

Consumer-to-Business (C2B)

A consumer-to-business (C2B) e-business allows a buyer to name his or her own price for specific goods or services, such as airline tickets or hotel accommodations, in a process sometimes called a **reverse auction**. The C2B e-business accumulates buyer offers and then presents them to competing sellers. A buyer's offer is considered binding; therefore, when a seller accepts a buyer's offer, the buyer's credit card is charged immediately. The C2B e-business generates revenue by earning booking fees and commissions on accepted offers. As you learned in Chapter 1, Priceline.com pioneered the C2B e-business model.

Consumer-to-Consumer (C2C)

The consumer-to-consumer (C2C) e-business model, which brings individual buyers and sellers together in an online marketspace, generates revenue in several ways, including transaction fees, sales commissions, subscription or membership fees, and personal ad fees. C2C e-businesses, such as eBay (Figure 7-22), offer the auction services you learned about in Chapter 5 and generate revenue from listing fees, sales commissions, and advertising. These auction services sometimes are called **forward auctions** because many buyers are bidding for an item offered by a single seller. Other C2C e-businesses offer reverse auctions, similar to the C2B model. In a C2C reverse auction, a single buyer makes an offer for a specific item, and multiple sellers compete to sell the item at the buyer's offer price.

Another type of C2C e-business, such as PaperBackSwap.com and SwapaDVD.com (Figure 7-22), allows members to list items of equal value they want to exchange — for example, exchanging a book for a book, or a DVD for a DVD. This type of C2C e-business might generate revenue by charging a small subscription or membership fee, selling advertising, or charging small fees for extra services, such as providing mailing labels and downloadable postage.

Still other C2C e-businesses, such as TraderOnline.com, sell online classified ad space to individuals trying to sell boats, cars, and other items.

Figure 7-22 C2C auction, swap, and classified ad sites allow consumers to buy from and sell to each other.

To Explore a C2C E-Business

The following steps explore an e-business Web site that follows the C2C e-business model. You will open the Web site's home page in a new tab in the foreground. Linked pages will open in the same tab.

- Start Internet Explorer.

- Visit the Discovering the Internet, Fourth Edition Chapter 7 Steps page at www.cengagebrain.com.

- Open PaperBackSwap.com in a new tab in the foreground (Figure 7-23).

Figure 7-23

- Click a left or right Browse arrow to browse recently posted books.

- Scroll to view the Printable Postage section (Figure 7-24).

Figure 7-24

- Click the Get Instant Credits! button to view information about the postage program (Figure 7-25).

- Follow the links of your choice to explore other pages at the Web site.

- Close the browser.

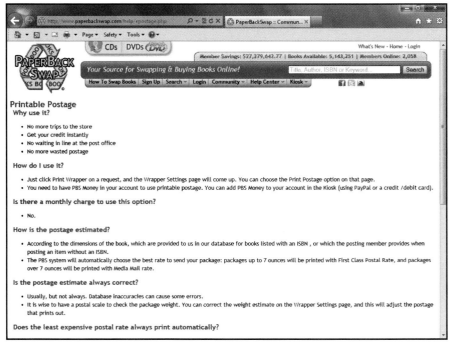

Figure 7–25

eBay and the C2C Marketspace

In the summer of 1995, Pierre Omidyar, a young Silicon Valley programmer, was thinking of ways to exploit the new and exciting online marketspace created by the Internet and the Web. Omidyar wanted to create a "perfect marketspace" in which people connected with others in an online community to buy and sell a wide variety of items. In this online community, all buyers would have the same information on items for sale, and prices would be set by the marketspace based on the supply of and the demand for each item. Omidyar's solution? An online auction.

In his spare time, Omidyar began creating the software to allow online sellers to post items for sale and online buyers to bid on those items. On Labor Day 1995, Omidyar launched AuctionWeb, a free online auction, as part of his personal Web site. Taking advantage of the network effect, Omidyar began advertising his free online auction through newsgroups as "The most fun buying and selling on the Web." Group participants discussed the auction service and e-mailed their friends with the news. The first items posted for sale at the site included used computer equipment, a few health-club memberships, a couple of automobiles, and some autographed posters and other collectibles, such as Pez dispensers. Because of the effective exchange of information about the new online auction from newsgroups and e-mail, traffic at AuctionWeb grew rapidly. In its first three months, AuctionWeb hosted hundreds of individual auctions and garnered several thousand buyer bids.

During 1995, Omidyar operated the free AuctionWeb service as a hobby. In February 1996, however, his ISP complained about the level of traffic to the site and began charging Omidyar a monthly fee for hosting a commercial site. To cover his increased expenses, Omidyar began charging sellers a fee based on a percentage of the final sales price for each item — and the money rolled in. By the end of February, the AuctionWeb site had generated enough in fees to more than cover its hosting expenses. AuctionWeb's fee revenue continued to grow, and a new profitable e-business — with no inventory, no warehouse, no responsibility for order fulfillment, and no liability for item returns — was born.

On September 1, 1997, AuctionWeb became eBay; and by October 1998, eBay was hosting new auctions at the rate of more than 1,000 per day. eBay now posts millions of items for auction in thousands of auction categories on any given day at its U.S. and international sites in countries such as Australia, Britain, Belgium, China, Sweden, and Germany.

eBay is one of the few early e-businesses to enjoy profitability almost from inception. Over time, the original eBay C2C e-business model has evolved to include both individual consumer and business auction participants, as well as revenue generation from listing fees, sales commissions, advertising, and more from its varied subsidiaries, such as Half.com, Skype, and StubHub (Figure 7-26). In 2010, eBay's revenue totaled more than $9 billion and it had more than 17,000 employees.

For more information about eBay, visit the Book Companion Site Web page at **www.cengagebrain.com**. Under the Chapter 7 E-Biz Case Study links, click the eBay link.

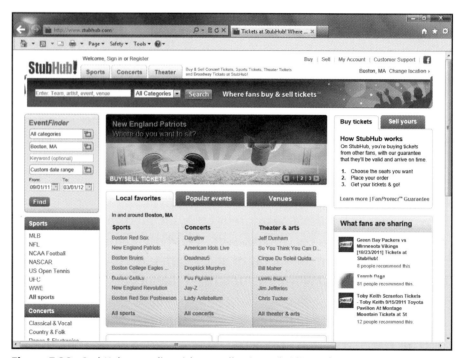

Figure 7-26 StubHub, an online ticket reseller, is a subsidiary of eBay.

<table>
<tr><td>E-BIZ
CASE
STUDY</td></tr>
</table>

Amazon.com and the Evolving E-Business Model

First, think about South America's Amazon River — huge, with thousands of branches and tributaries, completely dominating its rain forest environment. Now think about Amazon.com, the e-business named after the river — huge, selling thousands of products from books to bath soap, toys to tools, and DVDs to dresses, completely dominating its online retail environment.

In 1994, Amazon.com's founder, Jeff Bezos, reportedly observed the huge growth in the number of people using the Web and decided to create an e-business that could capitalize on that growth. Bezos then made a list of several different products that could be sold online. After considerable research, Bezos picked books for a number of reasons, including the enormous selection of available book titles. Bezos also reasoned that because books were inexpensive, his market risk was lower than with other products; that information about each book would fit nicely into a Web page format; and that books were easy to ship. With his research completed, Bezos quit his job as a vice president of D. E. Shaw, a New York investment firm, and headed to Seattle, where his new e-business would be close to technology innovators and a huge book distribution center. Following a business-to-consumer (B2C) e-business model that focused on product selection, customer service, personalization, and discount pricing, Amazon.com opened its virtual doors in July 1995, and within two years registered its one millionth customer account.

But growing Amazon.com into "Earth's Biggest Bookstore" was only a short-term objective. Bezos's long-term objective was to grow Amazon.com into the online store with "Earth's Biggest Selection." In 1998, Amazon.com added music, videos, and DVDs to its offerings, and the next year it added other retail products, including video games, toys, and electronics. To exploit the online auction craze, Amazon.com also opened its auction site in 1999. By 2009, the product offerings at Amazon.com also included power tools, sports equipment, clothing, and much, much more (Figure 7-27).

Because of acquisitions and partnerships with other retailers, such as Toys"R"Us and Target, Amazon.com has climbed to number 130 in the list of Fortune 500 companies. Amazon.com also continues to support the development of new technologies, such as the Kindle e-book reader, for which content is available exclusively from Amazon.com. According to a March 2011 study by International Data Corporation (IDC), the Kindle accounted for 48 percent of the $12.8 million total e-book sales worldwide in 2010. In 2007, Amazon.com acquired the social cataloging site Shelfari, which enables users to list, rate, and review books, and to purchase books based on others' recommendations and reviews. In 2005, Amazon.com launched its Prime service, which offers free, fast shipping, and streaming video options for its subscribers.

Along the way, Amazon.com's e-business model evolved from a single-product B2C e-retailer to a mix of e-business models that allows the company not only to sell products directly to consumers, but also to develop innovative e-business technologies and sell them to other businesses, and to provide a retailing channel for other companies. This successful mix of e-business models led to annual sales in excess of $34 billion in 2010, 33,700 employees, and millions of customers in more than 200 countries around the world.

For more information about Amazon.com, visit the Book Companion Site Web page at **www.cengagebrain.com**. Under the Chapter 7 E-Biz Case Study links, click the Amazon.com link.

Figure 7-27   Amazon.com successfully evolved to incorporate a mix of e-business models.

Business-to-Business (B2B)

While B2C and C2C might be the most familiar e-business models, online transactions between businesses, called business-to-business (B2B) transactions, account for an ever-increasing share of total e-business revenue. Like other e-business models discussed earlier in this section, the B2B e-business model takes a variety of forms, and B2B revenue is generated in a number of ways, including:

- Business directory listing fees
- Web site advertising
- Subscription or membership fees
- Referral fees
- Transaction fees
- Sales commissions
- Web site hosting fees
- File storage fees
- Software licensing and rental fees
- Affiliate marketing programs

Some B2B e-businesses aggregate business information for other businesses and generate revenue from directory listing fees and advertising. Examples include the Business.com business search engine and directory and the B2B Yellow Pages (Figure 7-28) that provide business-to-business information similar to a printed telephone business directory.

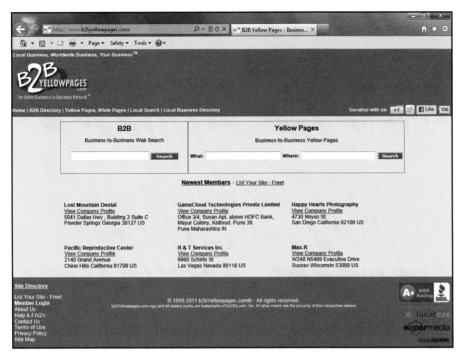

Figure 7-28 Some B2B e-businesses aggregate business information for other businesses.

The term infomediary refers to an e-business that gathers and organizes large amounts of data and information, and then acts as an intermediary between those who want the information and those who supply the information. Infomediary examples include several B2C e-businesses, such as Edmunds.com, Autobytel, AbeBooks.com, and Shopzilla. B2B infomediaries include Business.com and the B2B Yellow Pages.

FACTS @HAND

Other B2B e-businesses create online marketspaces in which to bring buyers and sellers together, operate reverse or forward auctions, participate in revenue-generating affiliate marketing programs, sell Web hosting services, sell file storage space, or develop and sell e-business technologies.

B2B EXCHANGES　As you learned in Chapter 5, B2B exchanges create online marketspaces in which businesses can buy and sell with each other following a predetermined set of exchange rules. These rules determine how buyers and sellers communicate with each other throughout the exchange, how they negotiate prices with each other, how payment is made, and how products are delivered. B2B exchanges usually generate revenue by charging subscription or membership fees, transaction fees, and sales commissions. Examples of B2B exchanges include CATEX (Figure 7-29, on the next page), a B2B exchange for the insurance and reinsurance industries, and Automotix Car Exchange, a B2B exchange for the auto industry.

Figure 7-29   B2B exchanges bring buyers and sellers together in an online marketspace.

AFFILIATE MARKETING PROGRAMS   B2B revenue is also generated by participating in an affiliate program. An **affiliate marketing program**, sometimes called an affiliate or associate program, is a referral marketing program designed to drive visitor traffic to a Web site. An affiliate program is a marketing tool for the e-business that sponsors it and a source of revenue for an e-business that participates in the program. Participants in an affiliate program are called affiliates or associates.

When an e-business joins an affiliate program, it places links on its Web site to the program operator's Web site. When a visitor to the affiliate's site clicks-through to the sponsoring e-business's site and takes some action, the affiliate earns a commission or referral fee. The commission or referral fee might be based on just the click-through, or it might be based on a resulting purchase or some other action taken by the visitor after he or she clicks-through to the sponsoring e-business's Web site.

Amazon.com popularized affiliate programs when it created its Amazon Associates program. Participants in the Amazon Associates program are paid a referral fee each time a visitor to their site clicks-through from their e-business Web site to the Amazon.com site and makes a purchase.

TECHNOLOGY PROVIDERS   A portion of total B2B e-business is conducted between e-businesses and their technology providers — companies that develop and sell the technologies that make e-business possible. Technology providers include ISPs and NSPs — such as AOL, EarthLink, Verizon, Level 3 Communications, and AT&T — that provide the Internet communications infrastructure. Other technology providers — such as Oracle, Microsoft, IBM, HP, SAP, and Cisco Systems — develop and sell the networking hardware and application software that enable buyers and sellers to conduct business activities online.

Many early B2C or B2B e-businesses, such as Amazon.com, modified their original e-business plans to include selling their proprietary e-business technologies. Other innovators, such as Yahoo!, added B2B technology sales to their business mix as their original e-business models matured. Still other B2B technology providers, including Web hosting companies, online storage companies, application service providers (ASPs), and content delivery networks, have created completely new kinds of businesses that use Internet technologies to provide new e-business services.

Thousands of **Web hosting** companies, such as Yahoo! Web Hosting and Hosting.com (Figure 7-30), provide e-businesses with Web and database server storage and server administration services at secure, temperature-controlled storage facilities. Many e-businesses — especially smaller e-businesses — find it more convenient and less expensive to pay for services at a hosting company than to operate Web and database servers at their own facilities. Monthly Web hosting fees can range from a few dollars for a shared hosting service to several hundred dollars for dedicated hosting or colocation services (colocation is described below).

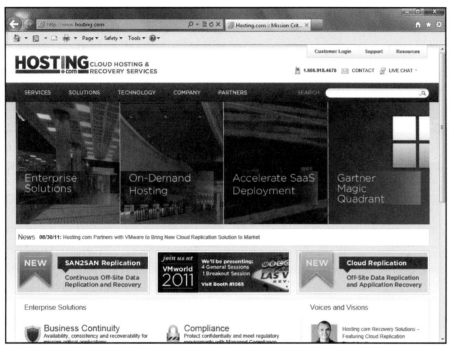

Figure 7-30 Web hosting companies provide storage and server administration for e-businesses.

In a **shared hosting** arrangement, multiple e-businesses share a single Web server owned by the hosting company. Shared hosting services are inexpensive and attractive for small e-businesses that lack the facilities and expertise to manage their own Web servers. Larger e-businesses with hundreds of complex transactions might choose to contract for **dedicated hosting** services, in which they have exclusive use of an entire server or servers. Other e-businesses might own their own servers, yet contract with a Web hosting company to store their servers at the hosting company's facilities. This arrangement, called **colocation**, allows e-businesses to reduce server facility costs. Some Web hosting companies, such as Rackspace, provide complete **managed hosting** services by building, customizing, managing, and supporting dedicated e-business servers for which their clients pay a flat monthly fee.

Rackspace and a New B2B E-Business Idea

In 1998, when Web hosting was in its infancy, three technologically savvy friends from San Antonio, Texas had a great idea for a new e-business — managed hosting. Richard Yoo, Dirk Elmendorf, and Patrick Condon were former classmates at Trinity University in San Antonio, and were all pursuing careers in IT when they came together to discuss creating a new e-business that would lease and administer customized, dedicated Web servers located in a secure, central data center. They named their new company Rackspace Managed Hosting.

Needing to acquire additional funding for their new e-business, the trio pitched their new hosting company to two experienced San Antonio businessmen, Graham Weston and Morris Miller, who immediately liked the managed hosting concept. Weston and Miller invested their own money in the new company and soon took responsibility for its overall management, allowing Yoo, Elmendorf, and Condon to concentrate on the technical aspects of the business.

One of the first problems faced by the new management team at Rackspace was how to differentiate Rackspace from the hundreds of other companies that were entering the Web hosting marketspace. To do this, the Rackspace management team asked themselves "What do our customers really want?" Surprisingly, the answer was not rooted in server technologies. The answer was "extraordinarily responsive customer support." The Rackspace management team then developed the company's trademark — Fanatical Support — to express its commitment and unique approach to serving its customers. The Fanatical Support approach includes a 99.999 percent server uptime guarantee, and 24/7 customer support provided by highly trained and qualified technicians. The commitment to Fanatical Support paid off handsomely, and Rackspace has been profitable since 2001.

From its early beginning serving small to medium-sized e-businesses, the company (now called Rackspace) has grown into one of the largest Web hosting companies in the market. Today, Rackspace (Figure 7-31) provides managed hosting services to more than 150,000 customers around the world — from state-of-the-art secure data centers located in San Antonio, Dallas, Virginia, Illinois, England, Australia, the Netherlands, and Hong Kong — and is a publicly traded company.

For more information about Rackspace, visit the Book Companion Site Web page at **www.cengagebrain.com**. Under the Chapter 7 E-Biz Case Study links, click the Rackspace link.

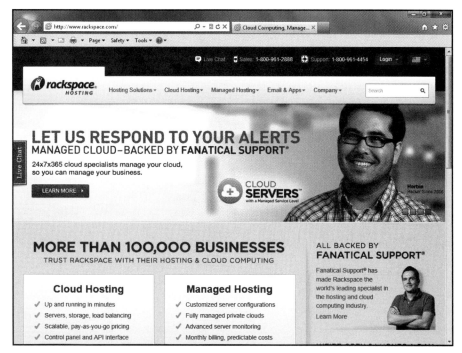

Figure 7-31 Rackspace.

In Chapter 6, you learned how important it is to create regular backup copies of critical files and then store those files off-site. Storing critical files off-site used to require manually carrying backup disks and tapes to an off-site storage warehouse. Today, for a monthly fee, an individual or business can store backup copies of critical files using an **online storage service** provided by e-businesses such as IBackup, i365, and Carbonite (Figure 7-32).

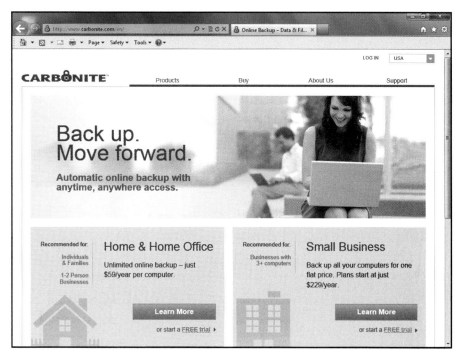

Figure 7-32 Online file storage can be accessed using a Web browser.

Developing e-business software applications in-house is very expensive; therefore, many e-businesses elect to save time and money by using business software created by an application service provider. An **application service provider (ASP)** develops and maintains its own business application software — such as accounting, marketing and sales management, personnel management, and employee collaboration software — and then provides it to its customers using several business models, including pay-per-use, or an annual or monthly fee. Customers access the software over the Internet using their Web browsers. ASP examples include AdminiTrack (software development tracking systems) and Salesforce.com (Figure 7-33).

Figure 7-33 ASPs develop and maintain business applications delivered over the Web.

Employee collaboration software allows employees to share documents, calendars, contacts, tasks lists, and other information, and is very popular and useful. You might be familiar with employee collaboration software, such as Microsoft® Outlook®, which is part of the Microsoft® Office® suite. E-businesses also can rent employee collaboration software from an ASP, such as WebEx.

To Tour an Application Offered by an ASP

The following steps explore how an ASP works by taking a tour at the WebEx WebOffice site. You will open the WebEx WebOffice home page in a new tab in the foreground. Linked pages from the home page will open in the same tab as the home page. (This online tour requires a high-bandwidth Internet connection.)

 1

- Start Internet Explorer.

- Visit the Discovering the Internet, Fourth Edition Chapter 7 Steps page at www.cengagebrain.com.

- Click the WebEx WebOffice link to open the Web site in a new tab (Figure 7-34).

Figure 7-34

2

- Click the View WebOffice Tour link to take an online tour of the WebOffice product (Figure 7-35).

- Continue to view the tour until you are ready to stop.

- Close the browser.

Figure 7-35

A **content delivery network (CDN)** is a dedicated network of servers located in different geographical areas of the country that store, or cache, Web page content from high-traffic Web sites for a fee. The content delivery network's servers quickly serve up the cached content on request. For example, high-traffic Web sites, such as Facebook, Netflix, and JCPenney, eliminate traffic congestion at their sites by distributing their Web page content over the Akamai content delivery network. When a visitor requests a Web page from one of these sites, that request is redirected to the Akamai server geographically closest to the visitor, allowing the content to be served up more quickly.

SUPPLY CHAIN MANAGEMENT   B2B transactions go far beyond selling products and services. Internet technologies are fostering a revolution in the way businesses interact with their partners, particularly their suppliers. Businesses can connect with their suppliers using the Internet to exchange product information, purchase orders, shipping reports, invoices, payments, and other B2B transactions. A **supply chain** consists of all the entities — raw material providers, manufacturers, distributors, wholesalers, retailers — involved in creating and distributing products to end users. Many businesses conduct B2B transactions across their supply chains over an extranet. An **extranet** is a private network that uses Internet technologies to connect a business with its suppliers and business partners. Using Internet technologies and extranets to exchange information among trading partners is a less expensive option than the value-added networks (VANs) you learned about earlier in this chapter.

Business-to-Government (B2G)

The business-to-government (B2G) e-business model includes online businesses that market and sell directly to government agencies. It also includes online businesses that create a marketspace, similar to a B2B exchange, that provides other businesses with information on bidding opportunities for government agency contracts, and sell the technologies used to manage the bidding and procurement process. Onvia (Figure 7-36), BidNet (Figure 7-36), Bidmain, and Fedmarket all participate in the B2G online marketspace.

Figure 7-36   B2G e-businesses provide other businesses with government contract bidding opportunities.

An intranet is an internal network that offers employees access to resources using a Web site or a software interface. Because of the prevalence of remote employees, or to accommodate offices spread out over multiple sites or locations, many intranets are accessed using the Internet. Internal business activities that are related to employees and are conducted over a company intranet sometimes are called business-to-employee, or B2E, transactions.

FACTS @HAND

Creating an Online Store

An entrepreneur is someone who both assumes the risks and responsibilities associated with starting his or her own business, and receives the opportunity to earn a profit from this business. Evan Williams (Twitter), Jeff Bezos (Amazon.com), Michael Dell (Dell Inc.), and Reed Hastings (Netflix) are famous entrepreneurial successes you learned about earlier in this chapter. Thousands of other men and women become e-business entrepreneurs each year, many by starting and operating their own online businesses, such as a B2C or e-retail store. In this section, you will learn about the basic elements required to operate an online store: storefront software, a payment-processing service, and a merchant account.

Storefront Software

A typical e-retail transaction (Figure 7-37, on the next page) consists of several steps. First, you access the online store's Web site and view the store's product catalog, which is a listing of products complete with descriptions and pricing. Next, you select items from the product catalog, provide your billing and shipping information, and specify a payment method — usually by credit card. Before the order can be filled, the online store must verify that your credit card number is valid and have the transaction authorized. After the transaction is authorized, the online store then must process your credit card payment, fulfill your order, and ship it. Creating and maintaining a complex online store that can handle all these steps can be very expensive. Some very large e-retailers spend thousands of dollars to develop their own custom online store software in-house. Other e-retailers choose to outsource that development by licensing storefront software packages from third-party vendors.

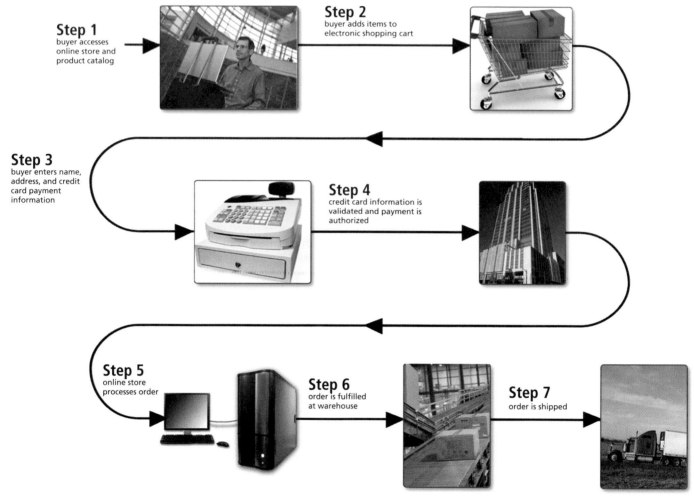

Figure 7-37 The path of an authorized e-retail transaction.

Online Stores
To learn more about the e-businesses discussed in this section, visit the Book Companion Site Web page at **www. cengagebrain.com**. Under the Chapter 7 @Source links, click a link below Online Stores.

Storefront software, sometimes called **e-commerce software**, is used to build and maintain Web pages and the underlying product databases that contain product images, descriptions, and prices. Storefront software also contains shopping cart software. **Shopping cart software** tracks items selected for purchase and handles the checkout process, including summarizing the order, calculating shipping and taxes, calculating the order's total, and processing the order's payment. High-end storefront software also might provide a number of other features, such as an interface to the e-business's order fulfillment and accounting systems or personalization features. Less-expensive storefront software might be limited to a product catalog and shopping cart.

FACTS @HAND

An e-business Web site that already has product pages but lacks online shopping capability can add the necessary shopping features by purchasing just the shopping cart software instead of a complete storefront software package. Adding shopping cart functionality to existing Web pages sometimes is called "bolting on" the shopping cart software.

Choosing the right storefront software package depends on the complexity of the online store and the specific features required. Medium- to large-sized e-retailers might license storefront software from vendors, such as Actinic, MerchandiZer, and ecWare (Figure 7-38), for a few hundred dollars. Sometimes called **installed storefront software**, this customizable storefront software is installed on an e-retailer's Web server, and then the e-retailer uses it to create and manage a complex e-retail site.

Figure 7-38 Installed storefront software is customizable software installed on an e-retailer's server.

Smaller e-retailers with simple online store requirements often choose to use **hosted storefront software** offered by vendors such as Yahoo! Small Business, Microsoft Office 365, and Homestead (Figure 7-39, on the next page). Hosted store-front software is designed around easy-to-use Web page templates that allow you to create a store and add products to your online catalog in just a few minutes. You access hosted storefront software using your Web browser. Fees for building and maintaining a hosted storefront can include monthly Web hosting fees, per-item fees for adding prod-ucts to the store's online catalog, and transaction fees.

Figure 7-39 Smaller e-retailers with simple online store requirements often choose hosted storefront software.

Some hosted storefront software vendors provide software demos or allow you to review their software on a free trial basis.

Credit Card Authorization and Processing

Most online store purchases — more than 90 percent by some reports — are paid for by credit card. A direct credit card payment at an online store is not the only way to pay for a purchase, however. Online auction sites and many online stores accept payments through a third-party payment processor, such as PayPal or Google Checkout. For example, a consumer can set up a personal account with PayPal that is linked to his or her credit card or bank account, and then choose PayPal as the payment option when making an online purchase. PayPal processes the payment by drafting on the consumer's bank account or charging a credit card and remitting the funds to the online store's account. Online stores also might accept electronic checks and prepaid cards, such as those provided by a bank or credit card, as well as store-specific gift cards.

Electronic cash, micropayments, smart cards, and other online payment methods, which were expected to change the e-retail payment process, have not yet caught on in the United States, where online shoppers continue to prefer to pay for their purchases with a credit card. E-shoppers in other countries, such as Japan, are not as reliant on credit cards to pay for e-commerce transactions. To accept credit card payments, an e-retailer must have two things: an account with a financial institution for credit card receipt deposits and a service that authorizes and processes credit card transactions.

MERCHANT ACCOUNT An e-business account with a financial institution into which the money from credit card purchases is deposited is called a merchant credit card account, or more simply a **merchant account**. Any business — whether brick-and-mortar or online — that accepts credit cards must have a merchant account. While an e-business can withdraw funds from a merchant account, nothing can be deposited to the account except credit card receipts.

@SOURCE

Alternative Payment Methods
To learn more about alternative online payment methods, visit the Book Companion Site Web page at **www. cengagebrain.com**. Under the Chapter 7 @Source links, click a link below Alternative Payment Methods.

An e-business applies for a merchant account at a financial institution — generally a bank that specializes in e-business merchant accounts — by providing general business information, such as its size, how long it has been in business, its credit history, and the type of cards the business will accept. Fees for an approved e-business merchant account might include one-time setup fees, monthly access fees, per-item transaction fees, and a **discount rate**, which is the percentage of each transaction that the financial institution will charge the e-business. The actual fees paid by an individual e-business for its merchant account are based on the financial institution's perceived level of risk on the account.

Before approving a merchant account, a bank first assesses its level of risk on the account based on the e-business's financial and operational history. The bank also evaluates its own chargeback history with similar e-business merchant accounts. A **chargeback** is a return of funds to a credit card company resulting from a card holder's refusal to pay a credit card charge. If a chargeback is processed after the bank has released merchant account funds to the e-business, the bank must recover the funds from the e-business. The bank faces a risk that it will not be able to recover the funds from the e-business. In assessing its chargeback risk, the bank also considers the kinds of products and services the e-business sells. For example, some types of online credit card transactions — such as payments for gambling, pornographic, or other such products or services — historically generate more chargebacks than other credit card transactions. An e-business offering these types of products or services generally is considered a higher risk and, if approved for a merchant account, is likely to pay higher fees.

Another merchant account risk inherent in online credit card transactions occurs because neither the credit card nor the credit card holder is physically present during the transaction. This situation increases the risk of credit card fraud and potential chargebacks. Because of the **card not present/card holder not present risk**, e-businesses typically are charged a higher discount rate than similar brick-and-mortar stores, where the card and card holder are present during the transaction.

PAYMENT GATEWAY   An online store also must be able to connect to a payment-processing service that can verify, authorize, and process secure credit card transactions (Figure 7-40, on the next page). You witness a payment-processing service in action when you use your credit card to pay for products or services at a brick-and-mortar store or restaurant. At these businesses, your card is passed through a card-swipe machine, and the transaction authorization is transmitted back to the store or restaurant electronically. Although it is possible to use a similar manual process to access a payment-processing service for online credit card transactions, most e-retailers use an online payment-processing service that authorizes the transaction while the customer is waiting. Online payment-processing services, called **payment gateways**, are offered by a number of vendors, such as Authorize.Net and iTransact (Figure 7-41).

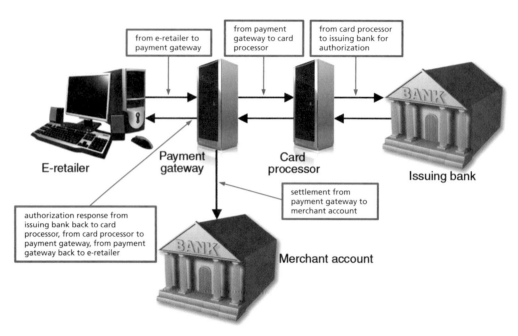

Figure 7-40　A payment gateway service verifies, authorizes, and processes secure credit card transactions.

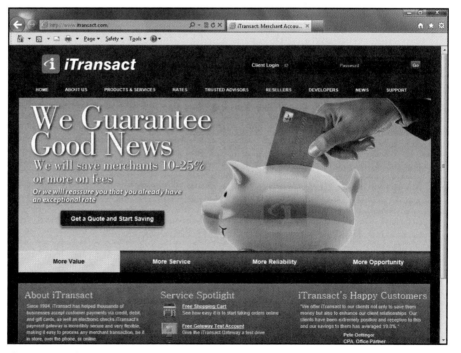

Figure 7-41　iTransact is a payment gateway vendor.

An important step in selecting storefront software, a payment gateway, and a merchant account is to be certain that all three are compatible. Most storefront software packages come complete with a connection to one or more payment gateway services. Hosted storefront software services, designed for small e-retailers with limited resources and experience, often provide access to both a merchant account and a payment gateway service for an additional fee.

E-retailers also must have a process for packaging and shipping products, called **order fulfillment**. Brick-and-click retailers can take advantage of existing fulfillment operations for fulfillment of online orders, while some large pure-play e-retailers build and manage their own fulfillment operations. Many e-retailers save time and money, however, by contracting with third-party fulfillment or logistics companies to warehouse, package, and ship their orders.

Chapter Review

Electronic business transactions began with the EFT system and the Automated Clearing House (ACH) network used by financial institutions to transfer money without the physical exchange of paper money. Other early electronic business transactions between trading partners were processed over private value-added networks (VANs).

The unique factors inherent in doing business online include the effects of geography, time, and space; the network effect; the ability of individual e-businesses to redefine their markets; and the power of personalization and customization.

E-businesses can capitalize on the interactive nature of the Web by using Web site personalization and customization features to offer tailored Web page content, products, and services.

Common business models include business-to-consumer (B2C), consumer-to-business (C2B), consumer-to-consumer (C2C), business-to-business (B2B), and business-to-government (B2G). Within each e-business model classification, an individual e-business might generate revenue in a variety of ways.

To create an online store, you need installed storefront software or hosted storefront software, a merchant account to accept credit card receipts, and a payment-processing service to authorize and process credit card transactions.

@SOURCE

Fulfillment Companies
For more information about fulfillment companies, visit the Book Companion Site Web page at **www. cengagebrain.com**. Under the Chapter 7 @Source links, click a link below Fulfillment Companies.

TERMS TO KNOW

After reading this chapter, you should know each of these Key Terms.

affiliate marketing program (418)
application service provider (ASP) (422)
Automated Clearing House (ACH) (390)
business model (400)
card not present/card holder not present risk (429)
chargeback (429)
click-through (403)
colocation (419)
content delivery network (CDN) (424)
cost per impression (CPI) (403)
customization (399)
dedicated hosting (419)
discount rate (429)
disintermediation (396)
e-book (392)
e-commerce software (426)
electronic data interchange (EDI) (391)
electronic funds transfer (EFT) (390)
extranet (424)
forward auctions (410)
grid computing (391)
hosted storefront software (427)

installed storefront software (427)
intermediary (396)
managed hosting (419)
merchant account (428)
network effect (393)
niche market (402)
online storage service (421)
order fulfillment (431)
payment gateways (429)
per-click (403)
personalization (398)
pure-play e-retailers (402)
reintermediation (397)
reverse auction (410)
shared hosting (419)
shopping cart software (426)
storefront software (426)
supply chain (424)
trading partners (391)
tweets (407)
value-added networks (VANs) (391)
viral marketing (395)
Web hosting (419)

TEST YOUR KNOWLEDGE

Complete the Test Your Knowledge exercises to solidify what you have learned in the chapter.

True or False

Mark T for True and F for False. (Answers are found on page numbers in parentheses.)

____ 1. Someone who assumes the risks and responsibilities associated with starting his or her own business is called an entrepreneur. (425)

____ 2. Shopping cart software is used to build and maintain Web pages containing an online store's product catalog. (426)

____ 3. Redefining a market by removing its traditional intermediaries is called disintermediation. (396)

____ 4. An intranet is a private network that uses Internet technologies to connect a business with its trading partners. (425)

____ 5. A business model is the way a company operates to generate revenue and profits and remain a viable business entity. (400)

____ 6. A CDN is a dedicated network of servers that cache Web page content for a fee. (424)

____ 7. A chargeback is a fee paid by an e-business to participate in a B2B auction. (429)

____ 8. Squidoo hosts advertiser-generated topic pages, called tweets. (408)

_____ 9. Colocation is when a business stores its servers at a hosting company's facility. (419)

_____10. A B2B exchange is an online marketspace in which businesses can buy from and sell to each other following a predetermined set of exchange rules. (417)

Multiple Choice

Select the best answer. (Answers are found on page numbers in parentheses.)

1. The term often used to describe how the growth in the number of online buyers and sellers increases the value of the online marketspace is the _____ effect. (393)

   a. network

   b. personalization

   c. affiliation

   d. infomediary

2. The process that allows money to be transferred between banks electronically is called _____. (390)

   a. ACH

   b. EDI

   c. CDN

   d. EFT

3. An example of a B2C e-business that generates revenue by charging subscription fees is _____. (406)

   a. Rackspace

   b. Yahoo!

   c. Netflix

   d. Twitter

4. The C2B e-business model is sometimes called a(n) _____. (410)

   a. reverse auction

   b. forward auction

   c. e-procurement model

   d. subscription model

5. Any retailer or e-retailer that accepts credit cards must have a _____. (428)

   a. chargeback

   b. merchant account

   c. sales channel

   d. vendor account

6. An example of a pure-play e-retailer is _____. (402)

   a. CNN.com

   b. Amazon.com

   c. Hosting.com

   d. JCPenney

7. The program designed to drive traffic to an e-business Web site by paying referral fees to other e-businesses is called a(n) _____. (418)

   a. supply chain

   b. shared hosting arrangement

   c. B2B exchange

   d. affiliate marketing program

8. A chargeback is _____. (429)

   a. charged to an affiliate for its marketing services

   b. the percentage of each transaction charged to an e-business by a bank as part of its merchant account fees

   c. the return of funds to a credit card company

   d. the cost of doing business

9. In a _____ hosting arrangement, multiple e-businesses share a single Web server owned by the hosting company. (419)

   a. shared

   b. colocation

   c. managed

   d. dedicated

10. Which of the following is *not* true about value-added networks? (391)

    a. They are private telecommunication networks used for EDI exchange.

    b. They require custom interfaces for exchanging data between business partners.

    c. Extranets are an alternative to VANs.

    d. They are less expensive than Internet-only options.

LEARN IT ONLINE

Test your knowledge of chapter content and key terms.

Instructions: To complete the following exercises, please visit **www.cengagebrain.com**. On the CengageBrain home page, enter the book title *Discovering the Internet* and then click the Find button. On the product page for this book, click the Access Now button below the Study Tools heading. On the Book Companion Site Web page, click the drop-down menu, select Chapter 7, and then click the link for the desired exercise.

Chapter Reinforcement TF, MC, and SA

A series of true/false, multiple-choice, and short-answer questions that test your knowledge of the chapter content.

Flash Cards

An interactive learning environment where you identify chapter key terms associated with displayed definitions.

Practice Test

A series of multiple-choice questions that test your knowledge of chapter content and key terms.

Who Wants To Be a Computer Genius?

An interactive game that challenges your knowledge of chapter content in the style of a television quiz show.

Wheel of Terms

An interactive game that challenges your knowledge of chapter key terms in the style of the television show, *Wheel of Fortune*.

Crossword Puzzle Challenge

A crossword puzzle that challenges your knowledge of the key terms presented in the chapter.

Use the Exercises to gain hands-on experience working with the Internet and the Web.

1 | Evaluating Hosted Storefront Software

You are thinking about opening an online store to sell your custom ski apparel. You have no experience running an online store, so you ask a friend how to get started. Your friend suggests that you consider using hosted storefront software to create and manage your store. (You may assume any other facts not stated here.)

1. Visit the Discovering the Internet, Fourth Edition Chapter 7 Exercises Web page at **www.cengagebrain.com** and click the links below Exercise 1 to review Yahoo! Small Business, Microsoft Office 365, and Homestead hosted storefront software and services. Create a table that compares the three companies' services and fees.

2. Choose one of the three for your online store and list the reasons for your choice.

2 | Identifying E-Business Models and Revenue-Generation Methods

1. Visit the Discovering the Internet, Fourth Edition Chapter 7 Exercises Web page at **www.cengagebrain.com** and click the links below Exercise 2 to review the following e-business Web sites:

   a. Bag Borrow or Steal

   b. GradeBeam.com

   c. Hometown Favorites

   d. Etsy

   e. Hulu

2. Identify each company's e-business model and revenue-generation methods.

3 | Evaluating ASP Time and Billing Software

You own a Web design and consulting business that is growing rapidly. Now you need to automate your project management administration by using a time/billing/ expense application. One of your designers suggests that you rent the software from an ASP and access it over the Internet. You think that is a good idea, but need to know more about which ASPs provide project time/billing/expense software. (You may assume any other facts not stated here.)

1. Using the search engine of your choice, identify at least two ASPs that rent time and billing software.

2. Compare the products and services offered by the selected ASPs.

3. Choose an ASP for your project time and billing needs, and list the reasons for your choice.

4 | Evaluating Affiliate Marketing Programs

1. Visit the Discovering the Internet, Fourth Edition Chapter 7 Exercises Web page at **www.cengagebrain.com** and click the links below Exercise 4 to review the affiliate marketing programs offered by the following e-businesses:

   a. 1-800-FLOWERS.COM

   b. SuzySaid

   c. Facebook

   d. eBags

2. Write a brief description of each affiliate marketing program and how it works.

3. Which of these affiliate marketing programs might be a good match for an e-business that sells gift baskets? Why?

5 | Identifying B2B Exchanges by Industry

1. Use the search engine of your choice to identify at least one B2B exchange for each of the following industries:

   a. Photographic supplies

   b. Dental equipment

   c. Information technology

   d. Energy

2. Write a brief description of each B2B exchange you select. Identify the services provided to buyers and sellers and, if possible, how each exchange generates revenue.

6 | Evaluating Web Hosting Services

You and your business partner operate a boutique that specializes in monogrammed items, and you now want to open an online store. You have selected an installed storefront software package and a payment gateway service, and your company already has a merchant account. You do not want to manage your own Web server; therefore, you and your business partner now want to choose a Web hosting company and determine whether a shared hosting or dedicated hosting arrangement is best. (You may assume any other facts not stated here.)

1. Use the search engine of your choice to identify two Web hosting companies that offer shared and dedicated hosting arrangements.

2. Summarize the Web hosting companies' shared hosting and dedicated hosting services and fees. Then choose one of the hosting companies to host your online store and list the reasons for your choice.

7 | Reviewing Online Payment Methods

1. Using the search engine of your choice, research the following online payment methods:

   a. Store gift cards

   b. Smart cards

   c. Electronic cash

   d. Prepaid cards

e. Micropayments

f. Third-party or person-to-person (P2P) payments

2. Write a brief description of each payment method and discuss the role that each currently plays in e-business.

8 | Exploring Personalization and Customization

1. Visit the Discovering the Internet, Fourth Edition Chapter 7 Exercises Web page at **www.cengagebrain.com** and click the links below Exercise 8 to review the following Web sites:

a. Amazon.com

b. Netflix

c. Lands' End

d. My Yahoo!

2. Describe how each site uses personalization and customization.

9 | Redefining Markets

1. Visit the Discovering the Internet, Fourth Edition Chapter 7 Exercises Web page at **www.cengagebrain.com** and click the links below Exercise 9 to review the following Web sites:

a. Enterprise Rent-A-Car

b. Autoweb.com

c. Hotels.com

d. American Airlines

e. Hilton

2. Write a brief paragraph about each Web site, discussing whether the sponsoring business is involved in e-business disintermediation or e-business reintermediation. Give the rationale for your answer.

10 | Exploring an Online Auction

1. Visit the Discovering the Internet, Fourth Edition Chapter 7 Exercises Web page at **www.cengagebrain.com** and click the links below Exercise 10 to search each auction Web site for a Dunder Mifflin t-shirt, Tom Brady bobblehead, or other collectible item of your choice.

2. Select one of the collectible items, review the details about the item, and answer the following questions:

a. What is the item's description? What, if any, are the item's distinguishing features?

b. What are the starting and ending dates and times for the auction?

c. What is the starting bid?

d. What is the current bid?

e. How many bids have been placed?

f. Who is the seller? What is the seller's rating, if rated? Where is the seller located?

g. What is the payment method?

h. Who pays for shipping costs?

A | Exploring Other Browsers

Introduction

According to a market share report published by Net Applications, the Microsoft Internet Explorer browser versions have slightly more than 54 percent of the Windows operating system Web browser market. Competing Web browsers include the Firefox, Google Chrome, Safari (for Windows), and Opera browsers. Of these competing browsers, Firefox has approximately 22 percent market share, Google Chrome has about 13 percent market share, Safari has about 7 percent market share, and all other Windows operating system browsers combined constitute about 4 percent market share.

This appendix focuses on Firefox, Google Chrome, Opera, and Safari, which are available for free by downloading them from their vendors' Web sites. Each of these four browsers has features similar to those of the Internet Explorer 9 browser used in this text, such as menu commands, customizable toolbars, customizable search tools, tabbed browsing, RSS integration, and security features, including cookie management and phishing protection. Additionally, each browser has features that set it apart from the others.

Although Firefox, Google Chrome, Safari, and Opera share features with Internet Explorer 9 and with each other, the features might be named differently in each browser. For example, saved URLs are called favorites in the Internet Explorer 9 browser, but are called bookmarks in the Safari, Google Chrome, Firefox, and Opera browsers. The bar that contains the text box in which URLs are entered is called the Address bar in the Internet Explorer 9, Google Chrome, and Opera browse rs; it is called the Location bar in the Firefox browser. Additionally, window elements similar to the Internet Explorer 9 window elements with which you are now familiar might be located in a different place in other browser windows. For example, the Safari and Google Chrome browsers position page tabs at the top of the screen in the title bar area. You can use keyboard shortcuts in all the browsers, and some standard Windows keyboard shortcuts, such as CTRL+P to print or F1 to get help, are available in each of the browsers.

Despite similarities between browsers, it is a good idea to carefully review a browser's window elements and Help pages to familiarize yourself with the browser's features, keyboard shortcuts, user tips, and special terminology before you begin using a browser.

The Firefox Browser

Firefox v. 6.0, which is shown in Figures A-1 and A-2, is developed and made available as part of the Mozilla Foundation's Mozilla open source software project and managed by Mozilla Corporation. The Mozilla open source software project is a community of software developers and software testers who create open source software. Unlike proprietary software developed by companies such as Microsoft, open source software programming code is available to software users who can then, within licensing restrictions, modify the code. The Firefox open source browser has a reputation for a high level of security for conducting online banking or shopping transactions and for protection against hackers. Like Internet Explorer 9, the Firefox browser uses tabbed browsing, a separate pane for viewing bookmarks or history, and a customizable Search bar.

Additionally, the Firefox community of software developers has created a number of downloadable add-ons for Firefox, such as colorful Personas, or "skins," that change the browser's look.

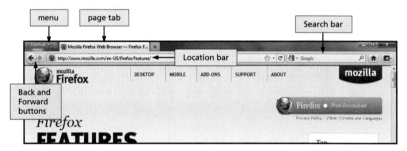

Figure A-1   The Firefox browser with the default Persona or skin.

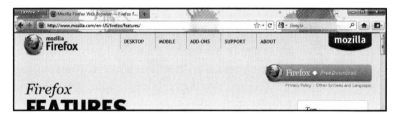

Figure A-2   The Firefox browser with the Paint Splat Persona.

The Google Chrome Browser

Developed by Google, Google Chrome v. 13.0, which is illustrated in Figures A-3 and A-4, also presents a streamlined interface with page tabs on the title bar. The Google Chrome Address bar is used both to enter URLs and to act as the search text box for the default Google search engine. For example, you can type a search query including Boolean operators in the Address bar, or you can drag text from a Web page into the Address bar to create a search query. When you create a new page tab, the new page shows thumbnails of the most visited Web pages, a link to History, the Google search engine Search box, and a list of recent bookmarks.

Similar to the Internet Explorer 9 InPrivate Browsing feature you learned about in Chapter 2, the Google Chrome browser offers a stealth mode in which you can open an Incognito window and then browse the Web from the window without updating the browsing history. When the Incognito window closes, cookies added during the browsing session are automatically deleted.

Figure A-3   The Google Chrome browser offers a streamlined way to quickly search the Web, and then select and view Web pages from the search results list.

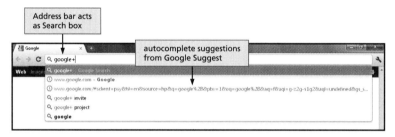

Figure A-4   The Google Chrome Address bar also acts as the Search box for the default Google search engine.

The Opera Browser

Opera v. 11.5, which is shown in Figures A-5 and A-6 on the next page, is a free Web browser developed by Opera Software. The Opera browser is another highly secure browser with features to protect against spyware and viruses that might infect your computer as you browse the Web. Opera was one of the first browsers to offer tabbed browsing, built-in RSS integration, pop-up blocking, multiple customizable toolbars, and an easy-to-use customizable search field with different search tool options.

Opera supports voice commands, making it a great tool for users who have trouble using a keyboard and mouse. Opera also offers a built-in e-mail client and newsreader, a chat client, and additional customizable features, such as different themes (skins) or color schemes.

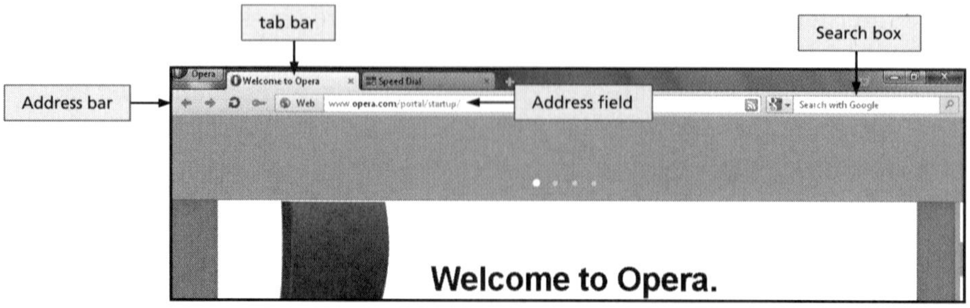

Figure A-5   The Opera browser is a highly secure browser with features to protect against spyware and viruses.

Figure A-6   The Opera browser has a Speed Dial tab that enables you to jump to a suggested or previously viewed Web site.

The Safari Browser

Safari v. 5.1 (for Windows), which is illustrated in Figures A-7 and A-8, is developed by Apple Inc. for the Windows operating system environment. Known for fast Web page download times and adherence to programming standards, the Safari browser devotes more screen space to Web page views by placing its page tabs at the top of the screen in the title bar area, and by keeping toolbars, buttons, and so forth to a minimum. The dynamic Top Sites feature, which "learns" a user's browsing habits, presents clickable thumbnail images of a user's most-visited Web pages on a new page tab. The Safari browser also uses Apple's Cover Flow file navigation technology to present history and bookmarked Web pages visually as thumbnail page images.

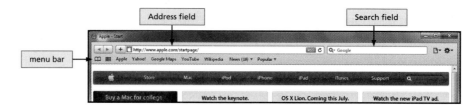

Figure A-7   The Safari browser is known for fast Web page downloads and adherence to programming standards.

Figure A-8   The Safari browser presents Top Sites, bookmarks, and history links visually.

Mobile Web Browsers

PDAs and smartphones, with their limited screen size and low memory capabilities, have led to the creation of the mobile Web browser market. Mobile Web browsers are also called microbrowsers, minibrowsers, or wireless Internet browsers (WIBs). Smartphone manufacturers, such as Android (Figure A-9) and BlackBerry, have created their own mobile Web browsers to work on their respective devices. In addition, mobile Web browser versions of Internet Explorer, Firefox (Figure A-10), Opera, and Google exist. Mobile browsers share many of the same features, including the ability to zoom in and out on a Web page and use touch technology.

Figure A-9   Mobile Web browser for Android smartphones.

Figure A-10   Firefox mobile Web browser.

EXERCISES

Use the Exercises to gain hands-on experience working with the Internet and the Web.

1 | Learning More About the Mozilla Foundation, the Mozilla Project, and the Firefox Browser

1. Using the search engine of your choice, search for information about the Mozilla project and the Mozilla Foundation. Then answer the following questions:

   a. What is the mission of the Mozilla project?

   b. Who launched the Mozilla project, and when? What is the relationship between the Mozilla project and Netscape?

   c. Who participates in the Mozilla project?

   d. What are the primary contributions of the Mozilla project to date?

   e. What is the Mozilla Foundation, and how does it support the Mozilla project?

2. Using the search engine of your choice, search for information about the latest Firefox browser features. Then answer the following questions:

   a. How is the Firefox browser similar to the Internet Explorer 9 browser? How is it different?

   b. What special features of the Firefox browser would you find most useful? What features would be least useful? Why?

2 | Comparing and Contrasting User Features of Popular Web Browsers

1. Using the search engine of your choice, search for articles, reviews, and reports that compare and contrast the user features of these popular Web browsers: Internet Explorer 9, Firefox, Opera, Safari (for Windows), and Google Chrome. Pay special attention to articles that discuss each browser's strengths and weaknesses.

2. Using your research, create a table that compares the primary user features of these five Web browsers. Follow the table with one or two brief paragraphs that describe the strengths and weaknesses of each browser. Indicate which of these five browsers (that you are not currently using) you would most like to download and explore in more detail, and explain why.

3. With your instructor's permission, download your preferred browser, test its features, and then write a brief summary of how well the browser performed against your expectations.

3 | Investigating Web Browser Security Features

1. Using the search engine of your choice, search for information about the built-in security features of the Firefox, Opera, Safari (for Windows), and Google Chrome browsers.

2. Using your research, write a one-page paper that describes the security features of each browser.

4 | Exploring Mobile Web Browsers

1. Using the search engine of your choice, search for information about mobile versions of the Firefox, Opera, Safari, Internet Explorer, and Google Chrome browsers, as well as the mobile Web browsers for Android and BlackBerry.

2. Choose four common capabilities of these browsers, and then make a table listing each mobile Web browser and whether it shares the capability as well as any additional information. If you have experience using mobile Web browsers, write a paragraph about your experience.

Index

phishing: Spam messages or malicious Web pages that attempt to collect personally identifiable information, credit card numbers, bank account numbers, and so forth. 208

phone numbers, searching for, 150–151

photo messages, composing with attachments, 194–195

physical topology: The layout in which its computers, printers, and other devices are arranged. 334–335

pictures. *See* images

pinning Web sites to taskbar, 79–80

plagiarism, 158, 159

planning, disaster recovery, 366–368

Polly, Jean Armour, 6

POP (Post Office Protocol): An e-mail protocol that stores and downloads messages to a client. 172

pop-up blockers, 50, 51

port: An opening in a device that is used to connect it to another device. 341

portal: Web portal; a Web site that offers a doorway to a vast range of content and services. 39

blog, 230–231

FindLaw legal resource, 157

types of, 258–265

posting: Sending messages to a list. 210

previewing

e-mail messages, 178

Web pages, 127

Web pages before printing, 81

primary source: Any document, item, or other source that provides firsthand information about a particular topic. 117

Print Preview, 81

printing

e-mail messages, 188–189, 222

Web pages, 81

prioritizing e-mail messages, 201

privacy

information, 96–99

InPrivate Browsing, InPrivate Filtering features, 100

opting out instructions, 100

search engine, 149

and social networking, 229

privacy statement: Terms of a privacy policy are made available to customers. 97, 98

Privacy Tab, Internet Options dialog box, 98–99

private key: A key known only to the organization and is used to decrypt the incoming data in a public key infrastructure. 374

private peering: An arrangement between NSPs and ISPs to set up dedicated connections to each other's networks. 346

protecting

computers from hackers, viruses, 91–92

against cyber bullying, 188

against e-mail viruses, worms, 183, 207

information privacy, 96–100

against malicious Web sites, 96

against spam, 214, 225

against unsafe social networking, 229

protocol: Standard or set of rules that computer network devices follow when transmitting and receiving data. 2

TCP/IP subprotocols (table), 346

proxy server: A server that hides an internal IP address from the outside world by substituting its own IP address for a source computer's IP address before sending outgoing e-mail or Web page requests. 372

public domain images, saving, 84

public key: Used by others in a public key infrastructure to encrypt data being sent to an organization; a public key is posted by the CA to a publicly accessible directory. 374

public key encryption, 374–375

public key infrastructure: The combination of organizations or individuals sending and receiving encrypted data, their public and private keys, and the CAs that issue the keys and digital certificates. 374

published: Information that is uploaded to a Web page. 5

pure-play e-retailers: Online only retailers. 402–403

Q

quality of search results, 117

Queen Elizabeth II, 7

queries, formulating search, 113–115

Quick Access Toolbar, 177, 181

QuickPick menu

adding search engines to, 144–146

removing search suggestions from, 146–147

searches, 142–144

R

Rackspace Managed Hosting, 420–421

radio, streaming, 272

radio frequency (RF) transmission: Wireless transmissions that use broadcast radio waves to transmit data over short distances, such as between two handheld computers or between a notebook computer and a printer. 337

real time: Online communications that take place simultaneously. 22

receiving

e-mail messages, 172–173, 179–181

e-mail using Windows Live Mail, 176

Web-based e-mail messages, 217–221

Recording Industry Association of America (RIAA), 316

Refdesk link, 282

reference desks, online, 282–285

reference tools, 275–287

Refresh button, Internet Explorer, 54, 55

Register.com, 352–353

registration, DNS, 352–355

reintermediation: The introduction of a new type of intermediary into a market. 397–398

remote computing

early history of, 12

overview of, 9–10

repeaters: Transceivers that relay data from the user to the service provider. 21

Reply (to message) button, Windows Live Mail, 177

replying to e-mail, 177, 181–183, 221–222

research

alternatives to search engines, 156–158

citing Web sources, 158

and plagiarism, 158, 159

Research button, Internet Explorer, 87

research tools, 275–287

reserve price: Lowest price at which a seller is obligated or willing to sell an item. 308

resolving: The process of translating a domain name into its IP address. 349

Respond group, Mail Home tab, Windows Live Mail, 177

restoring data, 366

revenues

B2C advertising, 403–405

e-commerce, 401

reverse auction: An auction in which a buyer names his or her own price for specific goods or services to competing sellers. 410

Rhapsody, 9

RIAA (Recording Industry Association of America), 316

Ribbon, 181

ring topology, 335

risks, transactional, 373–375

Roberts, Lawrence, 13

rogue WLAN: A WLAN created with a wireless router that uses network resources and exposes the network to security threats. 365

root name servers: The DNS servers at the top of the hierarchy that publish a directory of the next level of DNS servers, called the root zone file. 349